Haruki Murakami and the Search for Self-Therapy

SOAS Studies in Modern and Contemporary Japan

SERIES EDITOR

Christopher Gerteis (SOAS, University of London, UK)

EDITORIAL BOARD

Stephen Dodd (SOAS, University of London, UK)
Andrew Gerstle (SOAS, University of London, UK)
Janet Hunter (London School of Economics, UK)
Barak Kushner (University of Cambridge, UK)
Helen Macnaughtan (SOAS, University of London, UK)
Aaron W. Moore (University of Edinburgh, UK)
Timon Screech (SOAS, University of London, UK)
Naoko Shimazu (NUS-Yale College, Singapore)

Published in association with the Japan Research Centre at the School of Oriental and African Studies, University of London, UK.

SOAS Studies in Modern and Contemporary Japan features scholarly books on modern and contemporary Japan, showcasing new research monographs as well as translations of scholarship not previously available in English. Its goal is to ensure that current, high-quality research on Japan, its history, politics, and culture, is made available to an English-speaking audience.

Published

Women and Democracy in Cold War Japan, Jan Bardsley
Christianity and Imperialism in Modern Japan, Emily Anderson
The China Problem in Postwar Japan, Robert Hoppens
Media, Propaganda and Politics in 20th Century Japan, The Asahi Shimbun Company (translated by Barak Kushner)
Contemporary Sino-Japanese Relations on Screen, Griseldis Kirsch
Debating Otaku in Contemporary Japan, edited by Patrick W. Galbraith, Thiam Huat Kam and Björn-Ole Kamm
Politics and Power in 20th-Century Japan, Mikuriya Takashi and Nakamura Takafusa (translated by Timothy S. George)
Japanese Taiwan, edited by Andrew Morris

Japan's Postwar Military and Civil Society, Tomoyuki Sasaki
The History of Japanese Psychology, Brian J. McVeigh
Postwar Emigration to South America from Japan and the Ryukyu Islands, Pedro Iacobelli
The Uses of Literature in Modern Japan, Sari Kawana
Post-Fascist Japan, Laura Hein
Mass Media, Consumerism and National Identity in Postwar Japan, Martyn David Smith
Japan's Occupation of Java in the Second World War, Ethan Mark
Gathering for Tea in Modern Japan, Taka Oshikiri
Engineering Asia, Hiromi Mizuno, Aaron S. Moore and John DiMoia
Automobility and the City in Japan and Britain, c. 1955–1990, Simon Gunn and Susan Townsend
The Origins of Modern Japanese Bureaucracy, Yuichiro Shimizu (translated by Amin Ghadimi)
Kenkoku University and the Experience of Pan-Asianism, Yuka Hiruma Kishida
Overcoming Empire in Post-Imperial East Asia, Barak Kushner and Sherzod Muminov
Imperial Japan and Defeat in the Second World War, Peter Wetzler
Gender, Culture, and Disaster in Post-3.11 Japan, Mire Koikari
Empire and Constitution in Modern Japan, Junji Banno (translated by Arthur Stockwin)
A History of Economic Thought in Japan, Hiroshi Kawaguchi and Sumiyo Ishii (translated by Ayuko Tanaka and Tadashi Anno)
Haruki Murakami and the Search for Self-Therapy, Jonathan Dil

Haruki Murakami and the Search for Self-Therapy

Stories from the Second Basement

Jonathan Dil

BLOOMSBURY ACADEMIC
LONDON · NEW YORK · OXFORD · NEW DELHI · SYDNEY

BLOOMSBURY ACADEMIC
Bloomsbury Publishing Plc
50 Bedford Square, London, WC1B 3DP, UK
1385 Broadway, New York, NY 10018, USA
29 Earlsfort Terrace, Dublin 2, Ireland

BLOOMSBURY, BLOOMSBURY ACADEMIC and the Diana logo are trademarks
of Bloomsbury Publishing Plc

First published in Great Britain 2022
This paperback edition published in 2023

Copyright © Jonathan Dil, 2022

Jonathan Dil has asserted their right under the Copyright, Designs and Patents Act, 1988, to be identified as Author and Translator of this work.

Cover image: Hayley Atkins

All rights reserved. No part of this publication may be reproduced or transmitted in any form or by any means, electronic or mechanical, including photocopying, recording, or any information storage or retrieval system, without prior permission in writing from the publishers.

Bloomsbury Publishing Plc does not have any control over, or responsibility for, any third-party websites referred to or in this book. All internet addresses given in this book were correct at the time of going to press. The author and publisher regret any inconvenience caused if addresses have changed or sites have ceased to exist, but can accept no responsibility for any such changes.

Every effort has been made to trace the copyright holders and obtain permission to reproduce the copyright material. Please do get in touch with any enquiries or any information relating to such material or the rights holder. We would be pleased to rectify any omissions in subsequent editions of this publication should they be drawn to our attention.

A catalogue record for this book is available from the British Library.

Library of Congress Cataloging-in-Publication Data
Names: Dil, Jonathan, author.
Title: Haruki Murakami and the search for self-therapy : stories from the second basement / Jonathan Dil.
Description: London; New York: Bloomsbury Academic, 2022. |
Series: SOAS studies in modern and contemporary Japan |
Includes bibliographical references and index.
Identifiers: LCCN 2021036281 (print) | LCCN 2021036282 (ebook) |
ISBN 9781350270541 (hardback) | ISBN 9781350270558 (pdf) |
ISBN 9781350270565 (ebook)
Subjects: LCSH: Murakami, Haruki, 1949–Criticism and interpretation. |
Psychotherapy and literature.
Classification: LCC PL856.U673 Z57 2022 (print) | LCC PL856.U673 (ebook) |
DDC 895.63/5–dc23
LC record available at https://lccn.loc.gov/2021036281
LC ebook record available at https://lccn.loc.gov/2021036282

ISBN: HB: 978-1-3502-7054-1
PB: 978-1-3502-7058-9
ePDF: 978-1-3502-7055-8
eBook: 978-1-3502-7056-5

Typeset by Deanta Global Publishing Services, Chennai, India

To find out more about our authors and books visit www.bloomsbury.com and sign up for our newsletters.

Contents

Acknowledgments	ix
A Note on the Text	xi

	Introduction	1
	Diagnosis: What Is Murakami Seeking Self-Therapy For?	3
	Cure: Writing as Self-Therapy	18
	Four Therapeutic Threads in Murakami's Fiction	25
1	The Long Goodbyes	31
	Introduction	31
	Hearing the Unconscious in *Hear the Wind Sing*	32
	This Is No Place for Me: From Fitzgerald to Chandler to Murakami	39
	Mourning and Melancholia in *Pinball, 1973*	49
	The Last Goodbye: *A Wild Sheep Chase*	56
2	Self-Therapy and Society	67
	Introduction	67
	Hitting a Wall in *Hard-Boiled Wonderland and the End of the World*	68
	The Anatomy of Dependence in *Norwegian Wood*	78
	Passing through the Wall in *Dance Dance Dance*	91
3	The Return of the Real	103
	Introduction	103
	Welcome to the Desert of the Real: *South of the Border, West of the Sun*	104
	Blocks and Flows in *The Wind-Up Bird Chronicle*	116
4	Absent Mothers, Abusive Fathers, Heroic Children	131
	Introduction	131
	It's All Greek to Me: The Apollonian and the Dionysian in *Sputnik Sweetheart*	132
	The First and Second Half of Life in *Kafka on the Shore*	138
	Is There Hope *After Dark*?	152

5	Individuation, Alchemy, and the Death of the Father	159
	Introduction	159
	Crime without Punishment in *1Q84*	160
	The Alchemy of Recovery in *Colorless Tsukuru Tazaki and His Years of Pilgrimage*	176
	Meeting Mercurius in *Killing Commendatore*	188

Conclusion: Self-Therapy and Salvation   207

Notes   215
Bibliography   244
Index   254

Acknowledgments

This book has taken many years to write, and I have been supported along the way by numerous people, many of whom it is my pleasure to thank here. First on the list is Dr. Kenneth Henshall, who was my primary supervisor when I wrote my PhD thesis at the University of Canterbury, New Zealand, entitled *Haruki Murakami and the Search for Self-therapy* (2008). I spent part of my time working on that thesis in Japan on a Monbukagakushō scholarship and meeting regularly with Dr. Matthew Strecher, who was based at Tōyō University at the time. Ken and Matthew are my earliest academic mentors and I'm grateful to them both for the many hours they spent talking to me and reading my earliest drafts as I struggled to work out the ideas that would eventually make it into my thesis, in essence, the first draft of this book.

In 2018 I was granted a sabbatical from my present position at Keio University, and I decided that I would use the time to significantly rethink and update my thesis and get it published as a book. With an introduction from my colleague, Dr. Imoto Yuki, I approached Dr. Linda Flores of Oxford University's Oriental Institute, who kindly agreed to support my application to be a visiting scholar at the Institute for a year. I spent much of that year working on the first and second floors of the Bodleian Library and Radcliffe Camera, with regular journeys into the first and second basements of the Gladstone Link to look up different references. As readers of this book will come to realize, the architecture of these iconic buildings was a fitting space to be working on this project. I was also grateful to have a chance to share my research at Oxford's Nissan Institute of Japanese Studies and to engage with other scholars there.

One thing I realized during my time at Oxford, was that to truly understand what Murakami means when he says that he started writing fiction as a means of self-therapy (a central question in this book), I needed to find out more about his life, and I decided that when I got back to Japan, I would try to do this. Encouraged in large part by my mother, Tina Dil, who spent her early working life as a journalist, I made a trip to Kobe and started talking to several people who had known Murakami before he became a world-famous writer. An important person in this quest was Nagata Minoru, who sadly has since passed away from illness. Nagata-san is one of the unsung heroes of Murakami studies, someone who was determined to protect the history of Kobe High School and to never throw anything away (even when it sometimes got him into hot water). At the end of several hours with Nagata-san, he handed me a copy of an article with some valuable information in it. He never told me explicitly what this information was, but it proved to be an important clue in my own wild Murakami chase. I wish I could have sent a copy of this book to Nagata-san with my thanks to add to his collection.

Nagata-san's information eventually led me to several people who had known a former Kobe High School girl Murakami is sometimes connected with. It has been suggested that this girl played a role in shaping Murakami's early fiction. The information these people shared with me provided some valuable insights into how true this might be. As will become clear in this book, this is a delicate topic within Murakami studies and one that Murakami has so far refused to comment on. I am grateful to those who were willing to talk with me, and I hope that this book rewards the trust they showed in me.

I'm also grateful to Murakami, who agreed to be interviewed twice during different stages of this project—once when I was working on my PhD, and once when I was nearing the completion of this book. While I feel like I probably aged a lot during the interim period between the two interviews, he appeared rather timeless, and I hope he will be running and writing for many years to come.

The team I have worked with at Bloomsbury Academic, involved in the SOAS Studies in Modern and Contemporary Japan series, has been nothing but professional and encouraging in the process of bringing this project to publication. I am especially grateful for the space they provided to publish a book of this length, which takes a comprehensive look at each of Murakami's fourteen novels to date. I'm also grateful to the three anonymous reviewers of the book who gave useful feedback about how to make its argument clearer for readers. Dr. Kojima Motohiro read through an early draft of this book and gave me some valuable feedback and encouragement. My mother, Tina Dil, also read through the book, catching a number of errors and helping me to improve general readability, while my father, Lindsay Dil, offered excellent technical support.

Since writing my thesis, I have published several academic essays on Murakami and have benefited from the feedback of anonymous reviewers and conscientious editors. While most of this work has been substantially revised before appearing in this book, one book chapter and one essay appear in a form close to their original, and I am grateful to these publishers for their permission to reuse this material. The section on *Norwegian Wood* in Chapter 2 of this book first appeared in *Haruki Murakami: Challenging Authors*, published in 2016 by Sense Publishers and edited by Matthew Strecher and Paul Thomas. The section on *Colorless Tsukuru Tazaki and His Years of Pilgrimage* in Chapter 5 first appeared in the inaugural edition of the online journal *Murakami Review*, published in 2018 by the Murakami Forum.

Finally, I am grateful to my wife, Anne Kahurangi, who has been supportive of this project and up for the adventure every step of the way. If we are remembered fondly in any of the cities this project has taken us, it is usually because of her. I am also grateful to my children Jacob, Aiden, and Lindsay, each of whom has done their best to slow down the publication of this book in some way. Lindsay did this most dramatically by being born on the dining room floor of our Oxford apartment, followed by a flurry of midwives and ambulance workers. While all three of you are growing up to speak better Japanese than me, I will try not to hold it against you.

A Note on the Text

This book includes discussions of each of Murakami Haruki's fourteen novels to date, from *Hear the Wind Sing* (1979) to *Killing Commendatore* (2017). Each of these novels has been translated into English, and the full English titles are used in this book, except for any chapter where a book is part of the main focus of discussion, when an abbreviated title is sometimes introduced in the interest of brevity. The first time one of Murakami's novels is introduced in the main text, the romanized Japanese title and the original Japanese publication date are also provided.

Japanese names are presented in the common Japanese order, with the family name followed by the given name. An exception was made for the title of this book in the interest of readers unfamiliar with this convention. An exception is also made for authors with Japanese names writing in English.

Macrons are used to indicate long vowels in Japanese. An exception is made for Japanese words commonly found in English (i.e., Tokyo rather than Tōkyō). Italics are used to indicate Japanese words not commonly used in English (e.g., *Boku*).

Introduction

Murakami Haruki (b. 1949) started writing fiction as a means of self-therapy. He just did not know this at the time. Instead, the story he normally tells to explain his debut as a writer puts it all down to inspiration rather than introspection, a bolt from the blue that even he did not understand. In the spring of 1978, Murakami was twenty-nine years old, and with his wife of six and a half years, Yōko, he was the owner-operator of a jazz café-by-day, bar-by-night establishment called Peter Cat in Sendagaya, Tokyo. Within walking distance of Peter Cat was Jingū Stadium, owned by Meiji Jingū Shrine and home to the Yakult Swallows, the professional baseball team Murakami had come to support following his move to Tokyo from his hometown of Ashiya (near Kobe). While today filled in with permanent seating, in 1978 the area just beyond the stadium's outfield was a simple grass bank, and it was here, at the season opener—the Swallows versus the Hiroshima Carp—that Murakami had his moment. Stretched out with a beer in hand, he watched as David Hilton, a recently arrived import from the United States who was playing for the Swallows, stepped up to bat and hit a double. "In that instant," Murakami recalls, "for no reason and based on no grounds whatsoever, it suddenly struck me: I think I can write a novel."[1]

Murakami wasted little time turning inspiration into action. Immediately following the game, he went to Shinjuku to buy a fountain pen and writing paper and was soon working on what would become his debut novel. Peter Cat still needed to be run, of course, so the time he could dedicate to writing was limited. Murakami would first have to close and clean the bar each night before returning home to spend a few precious moments—short bursts of between thirty minutes to an hour—writing at the kitchen table.[2] That season the Swallows went on to win the Central League and then the Japan Series, a result few had anticipated at the start of the season, while Murakami's novel, later to be called *Hear the Wind Sing (Kaze no uta o kike*, 1979), would go on to win the Gunzō Prize for new writers. A couple of years later Murakami would let go of Peter Cat to write full-time and over the next several decades would establish himself as one of the dominant literary voices in not only Japan but the world, arguably becoming Japan's first truly global novelist.

"Yes, it is strange, isn't it," Murakami acknowledged in 1996 in an interview with Ian Buruma for *The New Yorker*. "Baseball is an American game. Hilton was an American batter. The kind of revelation I experienced that day was not very Japanese. Revelation is not really a Japanese concept."[3] Years later, he would add that revelation is probably not the right word here, offering epiphany as a better alternative, a distinction likely intended to emphasize the psychological rather than the supernatural nature of his experience.[4] This was not a message from the gods but from his own unconscious. The question is, what was his mind trying to tell him? With hindsight, Murakami has provided his own answer to this question. Speaking in 1995 with the Jungian psychologist Kawai Hayao, he put it this way: "Why did I start writing novels, even I do not really know, I just suddenly wanted to start writing one day. Thinking about it now though, I think it was some kind of step toward self-therapy."[5]

Murakami's insight here is the starting point for this book, which in five chapters will look at each of his fourteen novels to date and how they might be read as part of an ongoing therapeutic project on the part of their author. This does not mean that the aim of this book is to read everything in Murakami's fiction biographically (which would be impossible to do anyway). While biography will provide part of the story, the other part of the story will be the novels themselves, the therapeutic themes they introduce and develop, and how these themes might be illuminated by an eclectic mix of psychological theories. What I will try to explain in the process is how Murakami transformed his underlying therapeutic motive for writing into a literary career capable of capturing the hearts of millions. Many people write as a means of self-therapy, but not many of them become world-famous novelists. The question is why was Murakami able to do so?

Freud once explained how the unfiltered fantasies of other people tend to "repel us or at least leave us cold," which is why a writer, in seeking to overcome this resistance, "softens the character of his egoistic day-dreams by altering and disguising it, and he bribes us by the purely formal—that is, aesthetic—yield of pleasure which he offers us in the presentation of his phantasies."[6] This is analogous, I will argue, to what Murakami has done in his forty-plus-years writing career in regards to his traumas. While Murakami started writing fiction as a means of self-therapy, and while there are specific things he was seeking self-therapy for, he has not written about these things directly in his fiction (and he has only recently begun writing about some of them in his nonfiction).[7] Instead, what Murakami has done is to alter and disguise his traumas, while also bribing us with his own brand of literary pleasure (what Freud calls an "incentive bonus" or "fore-pleasure" which makes "possible the release of still greater pleasure arising from deeper psychical sources").[8] The first aim of this book is to recover as much of this altered and disguised biographical core to Murakami's writing as possible, a core he has often claimed is not there to find, and to understand how he fashioned it into compelling fiction through the influence of some important literary models.

The second aim of this book, as already touched on, is to then explore how Murakami went on to transform this therapeutic motive for writing into a literary career of global acclaim. This second aim is less worried about where Murakami's need to write came from, and more about where it has taken him. Here the analogy I will use compares Murakami's fiction to the rise of Nietzschean philosophy and Jungian psychology (both, as will be discussed later, direct influences on Murakami's fiction). What Murakami shares with Nietzsche and Jung is an engagement with the chaotic forces of the unconscious, a process which often starts as a response to personal struggles, but which at times evolves into something of greater cultural significance. In the end, I will argue that what self-therapy ultimately means for Murakami has similarities with what Nietzsche and Jung offered before him (arguably closer to the latter than the former) and that this is central to his message as a writer.

The next two sections of this introduction deal with two basic questions that arise out of Murakami's claim to be writing as a means of self-therapy: first, what did he need self-therapy for, and second, why did he think that writing fiction would be a good way to start the healing process? As will be seen, while critics have offered various historical and sociological causes for understanding Murakami's therapeutic fiction, there are also two biographical causes essential for understanding why he writes. What we will also see is that Murakami has very particular ideas about what writing as self-therapy means and that these ideas do not include writing directly about traumatic experiences for the cathartic relief this can bring. Instead, Murakami claims to not really know from where his stories come, except to say that they come from a place deep inside him which he sometimes describes as a hidden second basement. Understanding Murakami's metaphor of this second basement is essential for understanding what he thinks stories are, where they come from, and why they have the power to heal.

The final section of this introduction will offer a first look at the remaining five chapters of this book. In short, what this book argues is that there are four prominent therapeutic threads woven through Murakami's fiction that can be connected to his biography but which have also transcended this starting point as they have been transformed into works of literary fiction. The first thread, grounded in Freudian psychoanalysis, is focused on the need to break out of melancholia and into mourning so that healing can occur. The second thread, grounded in trauma studies, focuses on the theme of intergenerational trauma and the attempt to heal it through symbolic acts of self-sacrifice. The third thread, grounded in attachment theory, looks at how characters with avoidant attachment styles strive to achieve earned attachment, which is simply the ability to love and be loved in return. The fourth thread, grounded in Jungian psychoanalysis, examines the most sustained therapeutic theme in Murakami's fiction: the drive for individuation as a response to nihilism.

Diagnosis: What Is Murakami Seeking Self-Therapy For?

Murakami believes that there are "three types of emotional wounds":

> those that heal quickly, those that take a long time to heal, and those that remain with you until you die. I think one of the major roles of fiction is to explore as deeply and in as much detail as possible the wounds that remain. Because those are the scars that, for better or for worse, define and shape a person's life. And stories— effective stories, that is—can pinpoint where a wound lies, define its boundaries (often, the wounded person isn't aware that it exists), and work to heal it.[9]

So what are Murakami's wounds that remain? What are the scars that, for better or worse, have defined and shaped his life? The answer is not immediately obvious. As Jay Rubin, one of Murakami's English translators and still one of the best sources we have on Murakami's personal life, writes, "he had none of the early life-warping experiences that seem to propel certain sensitive souls towards writing as a form of therapy for themselves or their generation."[10] This is why so many critics turn not to Murakami's personal life but, rather, to the historical and social milieu which shaped him when trying to make sense of his underlying motives for writing. The most common approach sees Murakami as a spokesperson for the generation that came of age during the late 1960s, a time in Japan filled with political idealism, but which was followed by defeat and disillusionment (at least for those on the political left).

This, for example, is Matthew Strecher's starting point for understanding Murakami's fiction, and he goes on to note the deep sense of loss this defeat left for many in Murakami's generation. While not explicitly framing Murakami's literary project as a therapeutic one, Strecher emphasizes the constant quest for identity in Murakami's fiction outside of the prescribed avenues of state and economy. In particular, he sees Murakami's protagonists searching for their identity in two areas: in the unconscious and in their relationships with other people. Strecher writes, "Murakami's implicit question is, always, how can the first-person protagonist forge connections with an Other (conscious or unconscious) and thereby identify himself, prove to himself that he exists."[11] Murakami's search for self-therapy could easily be framed in this same way, with the desire to forge connections with the unconscious marking the first stage of recovery and the desire to forge connections with others marking the second.

Japan's postwar economic and social development is likewise behind two different approaches to Murakami's fiction offered by Paul Roquet and John Whittier Treat, both of whom emphasize the country's growing embrace of neoliberal economic policies. Building on arguments from Nakamata Akio, who has positioned Murakami as a practitioner in an emerging genre he calls the *iyashi-kei shōsetsu* (healing-type novel), Roquet sees Murakami as a pioneer in the field of "ambient literature," a genre offering "an aesthetic response to the demand for transposable calm" and which "rethinks the novel as a mood-regulating device."[12] Life in societies driven by neoliberal economic policies is uncertain and stressful for many people, and ambient literature, together with other forms of ambient media, is the balm consumerism manufactures to keep them going. This genre of ambient literature, Roquet writes, has two chief aims: "to generate calming moods and to provide a space to reflect back on therapy culture as a whole."[13]

While not a point I will focus on too much in this book, I agree with Roquet that Murakami's fiction has the power to "generate calming moods." Rubin writes of the many examples in Murakami's fiction of protagonists who perform "some mindless physical task—ironing a shirt, cooking pasta, mowing lawns—with meticulous attention to detail as an exercise in healing a wounded psyche—rather like Zen and the art of motorcycle maintenance."[14] Matt Alt argues that it is these Zen-like aspects in Murakami's writing which have made him popular in America, suggesting that it was the Buddhist scholar and popularizer of Zen philosophy in the West, D. T. Suzuki, who prepared the way. Alt goes so far as to compare Murakami to another successful Japanese export of recent years, Marie Kondo, the domestic organizational guru who in her books and Netflix series tells us to only keep things in our homes which "spark joy." Alt writes:

> It may seem churlish to speak of Murakami, literary titan, in the same breath as tidying-up guru Marie Kondo. Surely nobody reads Kondo for her prose; they turn

to her for advice to escape the tsunami of material goods inundating their lives. Yet the way we refer to Murakami's and Kondo's outputs is telling: One writes in a style often described as "magical realism"; the other dispenses texts brimming with "life-changing magic."[15]

Another way to say all of this is that Murakami's fiction offers readers an education in mindfulness, another buzzword of our times with cultural roots in Zen Buddhism. Though Murakami's characters are often thrown into bizarre situations, they manage to keep their cool and restore their equilibrium by returning to the present and by performing simple daily tasks with a sense of personal integrity and attention to detail. Such scenes can be soothing for readers and may even encourage them to begin integrating similar practices into their own lives (after reading a Murakami novel you may never cook a pot of pasta the same way again). The concept of mindfulness also has a strong following in contemporary therapeutic circles, a recognition of the way a practice of inner, detached watchfulness can help traumatized patients who are dealing with and processing potentially overwhelming experiences from their past.[16]

The only risk I see in this approach of Roquet and others to Murakami's fiction is that mood regulation may come to be seen as its defining characteristic. While Roquet's overall discussion of ambient media aims to consider "both sides" of the issue—"both the real mobility and healing on offer and the potentially dubious aspects of mediated mood regulation and therapy culture"—his specific discussion on Murakami is brief and goes little beyond suggesting that he is a pioneer in the field of "healing-style fiction."[17] At its most flippant, this approach might seem to relegate Murakami's fiction to the level of bubble baths and cat videos, things offered to help people reduce stress and feel better while simultaneously ignoring the underlying causes of their suffering. Mood regulation, I will argue, while a part of Murakami's fiction, barely scratches the surface of what it offers therapeutically. While Roquet's work can thus sensitize us to the issue of mood regulation and the wider therapeutic culture in contemporary Japan, ultimately it fails to consider any of the deeper threads of Murakami's therapeutic discourse.

John Whittier Treat likewise sees the rise of neoliberal economic policies as a vital backdrop for understanding Murakami's fiction, though he is less interested in its calming qualities. Instead, he builds on ideas from Saitō Tamaki, among others, to describe Murakami as "a novelist who has earned global acclaim for his best-selling stories foregrounding the dissociative tenor of daily life in Japan."[18] Dissociation, a condition which will be discussed in more detail later, is basically a psychological response to trauma or prolonged stress in which a person disconnects from their normal sense of self or reality (or both). Saitō has gone so far as to call Japan a *kairikei shakai* (dissociative-type society) and Treat sees Murakami's fiction as particularly ripe for exploring this psychological and cultural phenomenon. Thinking about the historical and material causes behind this shift in Japanese society, Treat observes, "We can interpret them as clinical and amenable to therapy long before we understand feelings as the poorly articulated expressions of a new social order accompanying neoliberal economics circling the globe."[19] For Treat, Murakami's fiction is more interesting for the ways it mirrors these dissociative tendencies in society than for any remedies it offers. If dissociation is the diagnosis, then at least part of the remedy is going to require reassociation: a reintegration of dissociated elements. This is a theme I will return to several times in this book.

A different sociological approach to Murakami's therapeutic fiction is offered by Carl Cassegård, who starts with the question, "What is the defining formative experience of modernity?"[20] His answer, provided to him by Walter Benjamin, is shock. Modernity, with its rapid changes and constant disruptions, is defined by the experience of shock, but Cassegård notes that with time a process of naturalization follows—we get used to the shocks of modernity and acclimatize ourselves to our new lived reality, even if we do not become well adjusted to it. Instead, naturalization in Cassegård's writing feels more like a post-traumatic state—we end up more dead than alive, more numb than feeling. Murakami's early fiction, Cassegård argues, is naturalized in this sense; his protagonists, who are dead within, are left with nothing else to do but to wait for change from without.

Cassegård divides Murakami's fiction into two main periods. In the early period, Murakami portrays protagonists "who accept loneliness as their sad but also sentimentally sweet fate."[21] This does not mean they are satisfied with this situation, however. Cassegård writes, "loneliness and longing for contact is one of the most clear and obvious instances in which Murakami manifests his discomfort in naturalized modernity."[22] In later fiction, this begins to shift, and detachment gives way to commitment. These later works, Cassegård explains,

> depict protagonists who attempt to combat the trend towards privatization by more or less forcefully committing themselves to other human beings. By their struggle, however, they find themselves having to deny naturalization as well, at least to a certain extent. Shock returns to their world, and even where mutual communication is achieved it tends to be painful, casting doubt on the success of their struggle.[23]

Cassegård sees more evidence of therapeutic growth in Murakami's fiction than either Roquet or Treat. Murakami's protagonists are doing more than simply modeling mood regulation or being overwhelmed by dissociative experiences. Admittedly, at times, Cassegård suggests, all they seem to be doing is sitting around and waiting for something to happen, but eventually, when the time is right, they make their move, committing themselves to others, even when this opens them up to the potential for shock again. It is a reading of Murakami's fiction that fits well with many of the arguments I will make in this book.

As useful as these historical and sociological approaches are for framing Murakami's therapeutic fiction in the broadest possible context, however, it would be a mistake to skip over the personal aspects of his search for self-therapy too quickly. Indeed, a closer look at Murakami's life reveals that there are, in fact, experiences from his late teens to early twenties that are essential for understanding why he writes. He is not only responding to the political disappointments of the late 1960s, the disruptions caused by neoliberal economic policies, or to the naturalization process which followed the shock of modernity, but to some very specific personal losses as well (though, of course, these personal losses all occurred within this broader historical and sociological context).

In particular, it is difficult to ignore two events that might be described as Murakami's wounds that remain: his falling out with his parents (particularly his father) and the complicated relationship he shared with a young woman from his hometown. I will start with the former.

Murakami's father, Chiaki, was a full-time schoolteacher and a part-time Buddhist priest (a tradition he carried on from his father, Benshiki, who was a full-time Buddhist priest), while his mother, Miyuki, was also a schoolteacher until the birth of her son and later ran a cram school called Murakami *Juku*.[24] Both taught Japanese language and literature, and both spent countless hours educating their only child, ensuring that he was deeply familiar with the Japanese classics, an effort Murakami's fiction shows was not entirely done in vain (even if it was not fully appreciated at the time). In a conversation with the writer Murakami Ryū early in his career, Murakami claimed to be so familiar with such classic works of Japanese literature as *Heike Monogatari* (*The Tale of Heike*), *Tsurezuregusa* (*Essays in Idleness*), and *Makura no sōshi* (*The Pillow Book*), that he could recite much of them by heart, while a common topic of conversation at the family breakfast table was Japan's oldest existing poetry collection, *Manyōshū*. Murakami was born in the ancient capital of Kyoto, but not long after his birth his father accepted a teaching position at Kōyōgakuin, a private institution in Hyōgo Prefecture's Nishinomiya City which covers middle and high school, so the family moved, first to Shukugawa, and then, coinciding with Murakami's graduation from elementary school, to Ashiya, suburban areas close to the port city of Kobe (where Murakami would later attend high school). Ashiya and Kobe more broadly are the backdrop to his debut novel, *Hear the Wind Sing*.[25]

Even Murakami acknowledges that, given his comfortable upbringing, there are few obvious reasons why he should have suddenly felt the need to start writing as a means of self-therapy. In a long interview for the magazine *Kangaeru hito* (Thinking Person) in 2010, he explained something of his upbringing and the way he felt drawn to the idea of writing as a means of self-therapy, despite his happy, problem-free childhood. He begins,

> I have no memory of ever being hurt in childhood or youth. I was raised in the peaceful suburbs of Shukugawa and Ashiya, a child of the so-called middle-class, and as an only child, I experienced no conflict and no problems in the home. Sure, my school grades weren't the greatest, but they were average, and I lived my life pleasantly, doing things I enjoy—reading books, listening to music, playing with our cats. I went to an ordinary public school, had enough friends, went on dates with my girlfriend, and played outside. It was a safe, peaceful time. To make a long story short, there is nothing about it that you might put into a novel.[26]

Murakami goes on to explain that while he loved reading growing up, he never felt the desire to write himself, suggesting that, unlike earlier generations who had experienced things like war and poverty, he simply felt he had nothing significant to write about.

As time went on, though, and particularly as Murakami left home and started to make his way in the world, he came to realize that despite his peaceful childhood, there were things he had lost and things he had been hurt by as he made the transition into adulthood. Twice in this part of the interview, Murakami emphasizes that he does not blame his parents for this situation, stating that they did the best they could raising him, offering him what they believed was the necessary know-how to live in society. At the same time, he acknowledges that their lifestyle and way of thinking are completely different from his own and that from this gap with his parents, "from this pain and feeling of separation, came stories from deep inside me."[27]

In his conversation with Murakami Ryū, Haruki explained something of the nature of his home environment, explaining to Ryū that, even as a young boy, he was given a sense by his father that you were supposed to abandon your personal desires in life, Murakami seeing this as a product of his father's Buddhist beliefs.[28] What he seems to be hinting at here is a subtle message he received about setting aside personal ambition in favor of the status quo, or as Murakami puts it in his conversation with Ryū, suppressing hunger for something more.[29] If Buddhism provides one possible explanation for where this philosophy came from, Sukegawa Kōichirō offers another, pointing to what might be described as Chiaki's survivor's guilt complex.[30] Chiaki was a war veteran and his experiences in China became wounds that remained with him until the end of his life, his trauma, in turn, being passed onto his son in subtle ways.

Murakami Chiaki was born on December 1, 1917, the second son of a family of six boys, their father the head priest at Anyōji Temple in Kyoto. His first significant emotional trauma in life came when he was sent out as a young man to live at a temple in Nara, probably with the intention of being formally adopted out, a not uncommon practice at the time. This arrangement did not last long, however, and Chiaki was soon back at Anyōji Temple with his immediate family, never speaking of this experience with his son (Haruki later heard the story from a cousin). Murakami writes, "I feel like this experience from his youth left a relatively deep scar on my father's heart."[31] He continues, "these kinds of memories become invisible scars, and while their shape and depth change over time, they stay with you until you die."[32] Generalizing further, he concludes, "People, to a greater or lesser degree, have heavy experiences that they can't forget or put into words. They live without fully expressing them, and then they die."[33]

Unfortunately for Chiaki, this experience was not to remain his deepest emotional scar in life. During the Second World War he was conscripted into the Japanese Imperial Army three times, and while he had some lucky breaks along the way, the experience left him deeply traumatized. Chiaki's first wartime expedition was in a transportation unit sent to China. Though the normal period of military service at the time was two years, this first assignment lasted only one, following which he was allowed to return to Japan.

The second time Chiaki was called up to duty, his appointment ended after only two months, the story Haruki was always told being that this was due to the generosity of a senior officer who believed Chiaki could serve the nation better through his studies. Murakami's later investigations into this story cast doubt upon it, records showing that his father did not enter university until roughly three years after his release from military duty. He also notes that the idea of his father being dismissed early from military service to study Japanese poetry, his academic specialty, is suspect from the beginning. Reading between the lines, one wonders whether this second reprieve from military duty was not, instead, related to an emotional or mental breakdown. Whatever the real reason for this early release, it turned out to be particularly fortuitous in that most of the soldiers assigned to Chiaki's regiment never returned to Japan alive. It was also timely, coming just a few days before Japan's attack on Pearl Harbor. It is unlikely that Chiaki would have been released from military service after this event, whatever the real reason was.

Chiaki's third call to duty saw him based domestically in Japan, but this also ended after only a few months, this time due to the end of the war. In relative terms then, Chiaki had a fortunate path through the war and avoided some potentially life-threatening situations (the man Murakami's mother had originally planned to marry was not so lucky, being killed in the war). None of this means, however, that Chiaki left the war behind psychologically unscathed.

Murakami vividly remembers as a child his father telling him stories about the war. In an interview with John Wesley Harding for the publication BOMB, for example, he recalls:

> [My father] told me a lot of stories about the war in China, so I'm interested. It might even be a kind of obsession. Sometimes the stories he told me were a little too bloody for a kid. I don't think my father intended to scare me. It was 1955 or '56, just after the war, and those memories were still vivid around then. To kill and to be killed. Anyway, I cannot eat Chinese food at all. I don't know exactly why not, but I cannot.[34]

In 2019, Murakami would finally share one of these wartime stories—an account of his father's regiment's beheading of a Chinese prisoner of war—in a personal essay.[35] His father never made clear to him whether this was an act he performed himself or whether it was something he merely witnessed, but Murakami is in no doubt that the experience stayed with his father for the rest of his life. He notes that such acts, while going against international law, were relatively common in the Japanese military of the time, prisoner executions seen by military officials as an effective way to initiate inexperienced soldiers into the horrors of war. It is also clear that in telling such stories to his son, Chiaki was in turn passing on something of his trauma to him. Recalling this particular story, Murakami reflects, "[T]he thing that had been weighing so heavily on my father's heart for such a long time—in contemporary language his trauma—was likely in part passed onto me, his son. This is what it means for hearts to be connected. This is also what history is."[36]

Murakami, in other words, experienced what today is called intergenerational trauma. Schwab explains the basic assumption behind this theory, referencing work by Abraham and Torok:

> [U]nless trauma is worked through and integrated, it will be passed on to the next generation. If this happens, the next generation will inherit the psychic substance of the previous generation and display symptoms that do not emerge from their own individual experience but from a parent's, relative's, or community's psychic conflicts, traumata, or secrets. This process is experienced as if an individual were haunted by the ghosts, that is, the unfinished business, of a previous generation.[37]

Understanding the sense of "unfinished business" Murakami carries on from his father is essential for understanding his fiction. As will become clear, there are numerous examples in his novels of characters who take up the unfinished business of an earlier generation and bring it to symbolic completion (or partial completion), and in the process heal not only themselves but also a member of this older generation. In this way, Murakami remains a postwar writer, someone who still writes in the shadow of the war, even though technically he is a member of the postwar baby boom generation. He explains, "I was born after the war, in 1949. Some people say, 'we have no responsibility, we were born after the war,' but I am not one of them. Why? Because history is a collective memory. We have responsibility for our fathers' generation. We have responsibility for the things our fathers did during the war."[38]

Storytelling was likely not the only (or even the primary) way Chiaki's trauma was passed onto his son. In reality, there was much more left unsaid than was ever said between them. Ian Buruma once asked Murakami whether he desired to talk with his father further about his experiences in China, to which Murakami answered in the negative: "It must be a trauma for him. So it's a trauma for me as well."[39] Murakami acknowledged to Buruma his difficulties in adulthood getting along with his father and speculates that this may even be related to why he and his wife never had children themselves (though interviews from earlier in Murakami's career reveal there was a time when they were thinking seriously about having children).[40] He goes on: "I think I inherited his experience in my blood. I believe in that kind of transmission."[41]

Whether intergenerational trauma is inherited directly through the blood or not, Murakami clearly picked up on what today we would call Chiaki's post-traumatic stress disorder and lingering sense of survivor's guilt. At times, Murakami recalls, his father could be difficult at home and showed signs of depression, his mother often complaining of her husband's drinking. While a popular teacher, Chiaki was not unknown to hit his students, though Murakami claims to have never seen this side of his father at home. Unlike today, physical punishment was more widely accepted in Japanese schools at the time and by all accounts, Chiaki was an effective and well-liked teacher, his funeral well attended by his former students. Murakami points out that his father mellowed with age, and he also emphasizes his many positive attributes—his reliability and sense of humor, as well as his ability to speak confidently in front of others. He was apparently quite the storyteller in the classroom, which suggests at least one source where Murakami's own storytelling abilities may have come from.[42] Though he had a naturally nervous temperament, Chiaki was extremely studious and exhibited what Murakami calls a "natural faith."[43] Nevertheless, it is clear that from Murakami's perspective, his father was too narrow in his thinking at times, and that for this reason, they were always on a collision course.

If Murakami had lived the life his parents wanted him to, it would have gone something like this: He would have attended a national university like they had (ideally Kyoto University), married a nice local girl, had some grandchildren, and gone on to do something professionally they considered respectable, ideally becoming a scholar.[44] His life decisions—to study at Waseda, a private university in Tokyo; to marry Yōko, a Tokyoite; and then to start a jazz bar with her, a job they considered on the edges of respectable society—thus placed a strain on the relationship that eventually turned into a long-term fissure. While Murakami's father appears to have been quietly proud of his son's literary career, this was seldom, if ever, expressed overtly, and both father and son kept their distance from each other for decades. Stubbornness, it would seem, is a trait that runs in the family.[45]

As well as the direct trauma of the war itself, Chiaki was also frustrated by the career compromises the war had forced upon him. Murakami describes this as part of his father's "chronic dissatisfaction."[46] As a young man, Chiaki had gone from studying at a small Buddhist school to one of Japan's premier universities, Kyoto Imperial University (today's Kyoto University), an impressive leap which demonstrates both his scholastic ability and strong work ethic. Murakami explains that for his father, study, "was like his reason for living."[47] He had wanted to go on to complete his postgraduate studies and become a university professor, but the interruptions of the war and the need to provide for his young family altered his plans, so in the end, he compromised and became a schoolteacher. What Chiaki wanted was for his son to take up the things he had not been able to do himself, but Haruki never showed any strong interest in academics. Chiaki was frustrated by a son who was growing up in a peaceful and increasingly prosperous postwar Japan who would not take his academic opportunities seriously. Murakami, for his part, describes the lingering sense of guilt he felt at not being able to live up to his father's expectations.[48]

The strain these differences of opinion put on Murakami and his wife early in their marriage is illustrated in an anecdote they shared with Rubin. Visiting Murakami's family home in Ashiya, Yōko awoke one night paralyzed from head to toe, a case of *kanashibari*, a medical/psychological condition known in Japan when people are under considerable stress. She had to wait until the paralysis abided so that she could find her husband, who was sleeping in another room. Clearly, the parents' disapproval of their marriage and lifestyle had made their visit a tense one, and so it is little wonder that Murakami and his wife began to see his parents less often.[49] While Murakami's estrangement from his parents was in part to protect himself, it was also necessary to protect his wife. He had to choose between filial piety and prioritizing the well-being of Yōko. He chose the latter and spent decades having little to no contact with his father (his relationship with his mother over the same period is unclear).[50] Near the end of his father's life, he made contact again and spoke with him face to face at a hospital, a moment in which he says he experienced "something like reconciliation."[51] For most of his adult life though, Murakami simply pursued his own goals with little to no contact with his parents.

Something of the pain this estrangement caused on Murakami's father's side is captured by Nishida Mototsugu, who had a long association with Chiaki both as a student and, later, in the poetry group they both participated in. He explains that over the years Chiaki seldom talked about his increasingly famous son, while those around him, sensing it was a sensitive topic, refrained from talking about him, also. Nishida does recall one occasion, though, when Chiaki uncharacteristically expressed his feelings about Haruki, lamenting, "More than being famous, I'd prefer he returned home with some grandchildren."[52] Such words may sound cold, but they also clearly come from a place of deep hurt. One senses in them both stinging criticism and a longing for reconciliation (though still clearly on his own terms).

Given this background, it is not surprising that father figures and families more generally are largely absent from Murakami's early fiction. Talking to Buruma, Murakami explained, "I can't express roots, and I don't want to write about families. I don't like families." Instead, he told Buruma that to find stories, "I must go into myself."[53] Yet, even with a physical and emotional gulf separating them over the years, the ongoing influence of Murakami's father on his fiction is not hard to see. Speaking in 2009 at his acceptance speech for the Jerusalem Prize, Murakami made one of his most public statements ever about his father, noting his background as a teacher and priest, and reflecting on what his life had meant to him (Murakami's father had died the previous year, aged ninety):

> As a child born after the war, I used to see him every morning before breakfast offering up long, deeply-felt prayers at the Buddhist altar in our house. One time I asked him why he did this, and he told me he was praying for the people who had died in the battlefield. He was praying for all the people who died, he said, both ally and enemy alike. Staring at his back as he knelt at the altar, I seemed to feel the shadow of death hovering around him.
>
> My father died, and with him he took his memories, memories that I can never know. But the presence of death that lurked about him remains in my own memory. It is one of the few things I carry on from him, and one of the most important.[54]

While Murakami does not hold the same Buddhist beliefs as his father, his fiction might be read as part of his own offering to those who died during the war, his own way of taking up the "unfinished business" of his father and those of his generation.

Needless to say, Murakami's strained relationship with his father does not need to explain every problem with father or authority figures found in his fiction, examples of which can be found aplenty. Some of these undoubtedly relate to his father, but certainly not all of them do, at least not directly. Speaking to me in 2005, Murakami put it this way:

> My father was not so authoritarian. I have no personal prejudice against him . . . at least not now. But father-like figures in this society, Japanese society—meaning the System—I despise those figures very strongly. Too strongly, I guess. I think that is why I couldn't get along in the literary world. If I see somebody who is strong and who gives orders, sometimes I get mad; that's my nature. Basically, I'm gentle, and I'm not a violent person . . . but if somebody in a high position orders me to do something, I get mad. . . . I hate those people and I hate their position. I think that feeling is unusually strong in me. . . . When I write something about those figures my writing might change somehow.[55]

Jay Rubin expresses a similar sentiment when he writes that Murakami's therapeutic tendencies may in part come from his "stubborn individualism," his tendency to avoid groups in a group-orientated society.[56] In other words, it was not just his father that Murakami needed to break away from, but Japanese society more generally, something that would explain the years he spent abroad early in his career, first in Greece and Italy, and later in the United States, and also his tendency in his early fiction, in particular, to reject Japanese literary models in favor of primarily American ones.[57]

The second possibility to explore when searching for biographical clues to Murakami's therapeutic fiction is the relationship he shared with a young woman in high school and beyond. Those who read Murakami's fiction cannot help but notice the reoccurrence of two dominant female character types, with Midori and Naoko in *Norwegian Wood (Noruwei no mori*, 1987) the prototypical examples. John Wray, interviewing Murakami for *The Paris Review*, usefully describes these types as follows:

> There seem to be two distinct types of women in your novels: those with whom the protagonist has a fundamentally serious relationship—often this is the woman who disappears, and whose memory haunts him—and the other kind of woman, who comes later and helps him in his search, or to do the opposite: to forget. The second type of woman tends to be outspoken, eccentric, and sexually frank, and the protagonist deals with her in a much warmer and more humorous way than he had with the missing woman, with whom he never quite connected.[58]

In this interview, Murakami explains that these common female types come from the position of his male protagonists, who are always caught between two worlds: the real world and a spiritual one. What some readers want to know is whether there are also real-world models behind them. Though Murakami usually denies it, the answer, I believe, is yes.

Murakami discourages readers from looking too deeply into his life for clues about his fiction, though the strength of these warnings can vary. At times he has said that he never writes stories based on his own life, while at other times he has softened this claim, stating that around 90 percent of it is not based on his rather boring life.[59] Perhaps a more balanced answer to the question of biographical influence in his fiction is found in an interview Murakami did for a Taiwanese publication where he explains:

> It's a question I get a lot. The answer is yes and no. I sometimes put something of myself in a novel and sometimes something of someone close to me. Sometimes I write myself straight, sometimes I write an idealized version of myself, and sometimes I write myself the way "I might have turned out." Sometimes I write something completely made up. Sometimes I combine things and create a composite. Sometimes I start writing with somebody in mind, but in the end, the character comes out completely different. Therefore, it is hard to determine what is based on a model and what is made up. But the most important thing is how realistic the final character feels and how powerfully they can call up the sympathies of the reader.[60]

Sticking with *Norwegian Wood*, some readers have noticed similarities between Midori and Murakami's wife, Yōko. Rubin, for example (who translated the novel into English and who knows Murakami and his wife on a personal level), notes their similar backgrounds in coming from merchant-class families from Tokyo and in their having attended socially upper-class high schools where at times they felt out of place. He even suggests there are similarities in their speech patterns.[61] Buruma also notices this connection, writing, "Yōko is the woman in his novels who redeems her man from the underworld. She is like Midori in *Norwegian Wood*."[62] Needless to say, neither Rubin nor Buruma is saying that Yōko is Midori; she is, however, clearly one of the models Murakami drew on in creating her. When it comes to Naoko, the other female character who dominates *Norwegian Wood*, Murakami is more emphatic, insisting that she is not modeled on anyone.[63] A closer look at Murakami's life reveals this may not be the case.

The existence of a real-world model for Naoko was first suggested over twenty years ago by Urazumi Akira in his book *Murakami Haruki o Aruku* (Walking Murakami Haruki), though it is a claim based on second-hand information and in the years since no further information has come to light. In his book, Urazumi recounts a trip he made to Murakami's alma mater, Kobe High School, and the discussion he had there with Nagata Sensei, a former teacher at the school who was also a student there the same time as Murakami and who in his retirement went on to become the school's historian. Urazumi records:

> According to Nagata Sensei, it appears that Murakami's high school girlfriend casts a large shadow over his later fiction. At the same time Murakami was in the newspaper club, there was a girl he was particularly close to. This girl, it is said, is the model for the girl who commits suicide in Murakami's early works and for Naoko in *Norwegian Wood*. This girl, K, was close to Murakami and it is rumored that they went out. As a couple, they shared a dark image. After K graduated from Kobe High School she went straight to International Christian University (ICU) [a school in Western Tokyo]. Murakami failed his first attempt at the university entrance exams and had to study for another year before entering Waseda University [also in Tokyo]. ICU, which K entered, is the location in which the protagonist from *A Wild Sheep Chase*, Boku, takes walks with "the woman who would sleep with anyone."[64]

My investigation into the K backstory confirms Nagata Sensei's basic account, though I can also understand why Murakami would claim not to be using a model for the dead girlfriends who appear frequently in his early fiction. While there is much about Murakami's former girlfriends, K and another girlfriend I will mention later, that remains unknown (Murakami has said in recent years that he is striving to be a gentleman, an ideal which explicitly prohibits talking about ex-girlfriends), I was able to find two people who knew K personally and were willing to share some of their memories with me.[65] One friend knew K primarily in high school, though she continued to keep in touch after this. The other friend knew K in the final months of her life, including right up to her death. I also asked Murakami directly about K, and while he did not deny her existence (including when I showed him a photo of her), he was not willing to go on the record about her, simply pointing out that it was too personal and sensitive a topic and emphasizing that what he writes is fiction not fact: "It's a story, not a statement. That's all I can say."[66]

Murakami's philosophy about the differences between stories and statements will come up again later, but for now, I would like to focus on what statements can be made about K, a former girlfriend who I believe did play a role in shaping Murakami's early fiction in particular. First, I should note that my two sources, who both knew K well and were with her daily for certain periods of her life, have no memory of ever meeting Murakami and did not know K was going out with him or had been out with him at the time they knew her. They have both heard since through acquaintances that this was the case. In other words, whatever the nature of the relationship between Murakami and K, it was not particularly public or well known at the time, even by those close to her, though the fact that they did have a relationship seems common knowledge today among those who knew her.

Both of my sources agreed that K was an extremely kind and generous person. They both had stories to share about acts of kindness she had done for them, even at times when they knew she was struggling with things herself. While she could be shy at first, she was a funny, intelligent, and philosophical person who spoke excellent English (her mother ran an English school). While Murakami and K may have shared a "dark image" at times as suggested by Nagata-Sensei previously, those who knew her well remember her more for her humor and depth.

At the same time, K was a very sensitive person, perhaps overly sensitive. Things could hurt her deeply and she made several attempts on her own life. In thinking about possible causes for K's ultimate suicide, it is important to note that nobody I talked to ever mentioned Murakami as a contributing factor. Instead, one friend catching up with her at university simply remembers her struggling with the "typical college angst," while the other friend wonders if the burden of having to live up to her father's high expectations was not a contributing factor. K's father was a graduate of the prestigious Tokyo University who had gone on to become the president of a bank branch. In other words, he had achieved a degree of worldly success and expected similar high standards of his children. Three of his children were able to live up to these expectations to some degree, while two of them struggled, K and one brother who had his own struggles as a young man (though, unlike K, he survived into old age).

Much like Murakami's father, I should note that K's father had an excellent reputation in the community as a hardworking and honorable man. Both people I talked to knew K's father well and spoke highly of him, explaining that he was nothing but kind and generous to them. In one sense, Murakami and K's fathers were simply products of their time. In his book *Shutting Out the Sun*, which looks at the cultural phenomenon of *hikikomori* (social recluses) in contemporary Japan, Michael Zielenziger interviews the child psychologist Watanabe Hisako, who explained to him the way intergenerational trauma continues to manifest in postwar Japanese society. Watanabe describes the psychological shock Japan's defeat brought to the nation and the way returning soldiers attempted to offset their sense of loss in the way they raised their children, particularly those who might be considered the elite of society. Watanabe explains:

> This process created very good, maybe "perfect" children, but at the cost of their own individuality.... They were not allowed to explore, to try or to fail, to have the experience of trial and error. They became good children, the sort of child of whom the traumatized parent could say, "Oh look, I succeeded. I made a new version of success to mitigate my traumatic experience."[67]

K's father does not appear to have been a war veteran (both people I talked to were unclear on this point, but he was considerably older than Murakami's father and was already a bank manager in the early 1930s). Whether or not he fought directly in the war, however, he belonged to the generation of Japanese men who were determined to restore Japan's honor and place in the world after the war through their own industry and in how they raised their families. For the children of these men, who had no direct memory of the war itself, this parenting style could at times feel cold, distant, and unloving, and they responded in different ways, either working hard to meet expectations, rebelling against them (Murakami's case), or buckling under the pressure (K's case). Neither Murakami's nor K's father deserve to be painted as monsters—they were both hardworking and responsible men—the kind of men who helped to produce Japan's postwar economic miracle. And yet from the perspectives of their children, there was at times something missing in their experience being raised by them—something perhaps best captured by the expression "unconditional love."

The exact timeline of Murakami's relationship with K is unclear. Several people have suggested that they were a couple at some point during high school, and Murakami's movements once he moved to Tokyo suggest that they reconnected again at some point while they were there. Murakami's general movements after he first moved to Tokyo can be traced through a series of essays he wrote early on in his career about the theme of moving house. Murakami started his university years in Tokyo in a dormitory called *Wakeijuku*, the model for the dormitory in *Norwegian Wood*.[68] Yet, similar to Watanabe Tōru, the main protagonist of *Norwegian Wood*, Murakami left the dormitory to live alone, opting for the cheapest place he could find at the student affairs office, a small apartment in Nerima Ward, Tokyo.[69] Murakami notes that he and his girlfriend at the time were not getting along, so the Nerima months of his life were a dark period.[70] Whether this girlfriend was K or not is unknown, but it is a possibility.

Murakami left Nerima after half a year in the spring of 1969, starting his second year of university living in Western Tokyo in a slightly more expensive apartment in Mitaka. In explaining this move to Mitaka (which is considerably further away from Waseda) in his essay series, Murakami emphasizes the extra space the new apartment provided and its proximity to nature. He makes no mention of the possibility that he moved there to be close to a woman, though this was likely the case, Mitaka also being the home of ICU. Many people see the vicinity of ICU (in particular the golf course it once owned) as the setting for Murakami's second novel, *Pinball, 1973* (*1973 nen no pinbōru*, 1980), which deals prominently with the theme of mourning the suicide of a former girlfriend.[71] When I asked Murakami whether he lived right next to the ICU golf course in Mitaka like people speculate, he replied, "Probably . . . possibly," which is as close to a yes as we are likely to get from him. Murakami would live in Mitaka for about two and a half years before moving to Bunkyō Ward, Tokyo, in 1971, the home of his new father-in-law. Murakami, aged twenty-two, married Yōko that year.

Clearly then, the years from 1969, when Murakami first moved to Mitaka, until 1971, when he moved away to live with his new wife, were an important period in Murakami's life in terms of his personal relationships. Murakami met his future wife, Yōko, at his very first class at Waseda University in April of 1968, though they did not go out straightaway, Murakami explaining that he was already going out with somebody at the time, so at first, they were just friends.[72] The only other girlfriend Murakami has ever mentioned besides his wife (leaving aside K) is someone he briefly refers to in an email exchange with a reader.[73] This girlfriend was a student at Kansai Gakuin University, a school in Hyōgo Prefecture's Nishinomiya city, which suggests that she was likely a girl from Murakami's hometown, perhaps someone he went out with after K left for Tokyo. It is possible that this girlfriend also plays a role in understanding the biographical background to Murakami's fiction, a hypothesis I will briefly consider in my later discussion of *South of the Border, West of the Sun* (*Kokkyō no minami, taiyō no nishi*, 1992). In terms of Murakami's early fiction, however, the question is to what degree K might have been a model for the Naoko found in *Norwegian Wood* and for the earlier Naoko in his first three novels—both of whom commit suicide. This is a complicated question and one that so far Murakami has refused to comment on.

There are enough differences between K and Naoko that, even if one chooses to see parallels, the heavy fictionalization of the underlying subject matter is clear. One of K's friends whom I talked to and who has read *Norwegian Wood* told me that, honestly, she does not see much of K in Naoko. Neither friend remembers K, like Naoko, studying French, for example, though, as already mentioned, she did love English. They also do not remember her being a fan of The Beatles. The friend who knew her in high school recalls her love for Audrey Hepburn and musicals at the time.

Perhaps the most important detail in terms of the question of biographical influence is the timing of K's suicide. In Murakami's first three novels we learn that Naoko hanged herself in a grove of trees near a tennis court during spring vacation at university. The Naoko in *Norwegian Wood* also hangs herself in some woods, this time near a sanatorium in Kyoto where she is taking a break from university. The two friends I talked to could not remember if K officially graduated from ICU or not. They both thought she might have, but they could not say for sure. They recalled that she did take some time off from school at one point. She also traveled to the United States for a brief period but returned home early. At the end of her life, K was working at the local city office building and living again in the family home in Kobe. In the end, she took her life in early January of 1972, my understanding being that she hanged herself in the family home.

In *Norwegian Wood*, the narrator, Watanabe Tōru, cannot ultimately decide between the two women in his life: Naoko and Midori. While he is attracted to Midori, he still feels a strong sense of responsibility toward Naoko. Naoko's death thus comes as a deep shock that at the same time frees him from his responsibility and ultimately allows him to reach out to Midori at the end of the novel. In Murakami's case, he made his choice sometime before K took her life. While K died in January of 1972 (sometime around Murakami's twenty-third birthday), he married his wife Yōko and moved away from ICU and Mitaka in October of 1971. Whatever support he had offered to K at earlier times then, it would seem unlikely that he was a big part of her life at the very end. Clearly then, as Murakami insists, there are major differences between his life and fiction. At the same time, I don't believe it is insignificant to know that there was a woman like K in Murakami's life. While Murakami may sincerely believe that she is not the model for Naoko (neither the first Naoko nor the second one), it is hard to know

K's story and not see some connection. K, I believe, is one of Murakami's wounds that remain.

Of course, as with the point made earlier about Murakami's father, not every dark and mysterious woman in Murakami's fiction necessarily needs to be traced back to K. Talking about the sense of loss that pervades his fiction and the real-world examples it is based on, Murakami has stated, "I had some friends who actually killed themselves, and I was missing them when I started to write, but at the same time, it's a kind of metaphor. I have lost many things: my values, my idealism."[74] Loss is a central theme in Murakami's fiction and a deep part of his appeal to millions of readers around the world. And yet I suspect that of all the people and things Murakami has lost along the way, few compare with the shock and hurt of losing K to suicide. In this way, Murakami's long silence—his refusal to go on the record about K—speaks volumes.

Putting these two events together—Murakami's falling out with his parents (particularly his father) and the suicide of K—we start to get a sense of what likely inspired his baseball epiphany. Though Murakami's childhood had been a happy one, his late adolescence and early adulthood were marked by some important losses, including increasing tension with his parents and the death of a former girlfriend. Marrying young, he did not have much time to process all of this, instead working long hours with his new wife to pay off their loans and to simply survive. Yet, as he reached the final year of his twenties, a period in which his financial situation was beginning to improve and where he was finally able to breathe a little, his epiphany came. It was time to start exploring these traumas, to begin a process of writing as a means of self-therapy.[75]

Cure: Writing as Self-Therapy

The notion of self-therapy implies that there is such a thing as a self to begin with and that this self has within it the means for self-healing. So what model of the self is Murakami working with? Interestingly, he sides with those who are skeptical of the concept of the self altogether, explaining that looking for a self is like peeling an onion—"a coherent self is nowhere to be found"[76]—a statement that at first glance might seem to reflect his father's Buddhist beliefs. While Murakami has sympathy for the "atmosphere of Buddhism," however, he is not religious himself, and his understanding of the self (or non-self) is not, strictly speaking, a Buddhist one.[77] Instead, while holding out little hope for the discovery of a self, he insists that we have little need for such a concept when in its place we have the *monogatari*.

Monogatari could be translated into English as story, tale, or narrative, but in Murakami's usage, it is a word that also carries psychological (and perhaps even spiritual) connotations. Though the word itself has been in the Japanese lexicon for centuries, its more contemporary, psychological definition owes much to the work of Kawai Hayao (1928–2007), the driving force behind the introduction of Jungian thought in Japan. Kawai spent his career reexamining many of Japan's great *monogatari*, from classic works such as *Genji Monogatari* (*The Tale of Genji*) to folk and fairy tales, through a Jungian lens, while also feeling free to adjust this lens to the Japanese cultural milieu as he saw fit. It is hard to underestimate the importance of Kawai's work for understanding contemporary Japanese discourse on the *monogatari*, which is what makes it so interesting when Murakami claims to have read little of Kawai's work and even less of Kawai's intellectual mentor, Carl Jung. Murakami speaks as if his ideas about *monogatari* came to him largely unmediated, while acknowledging that Kawai was the one person who understood these ideas better than anyone. It is interesting to ask where this ambivalence about Kawai's work and Jungian psychology more broadly comes from.

Murakami limits his public appearances in Japan, so it was with some excitement in 2013 that news spread of his scheduled attendance at the inaugural award ceremony for the Kawai Hayao *Monogatari-shō* and *Gakugei-shō* (The Kawai Hayao Story Prize and Arts Prize) held at Kyoto University. In the speech he gave for the occasion, *Tamashii no ichiban fukai tokoro* (The Deepest Part of the Soul), Murakami spoke of the deep connection he felt with Kawai Sensei, acknowledging in his speech that Kawai is the only person to whom he has ever felt compelled to attach the honorific title of Sensei. Seeking to explain where this sense of deference came from, Murakami noted that, more than the specific content of their many conversations, it was their shared experience of *monogatarisei* (or "storiness") which left him with the deepest impression:

> A *monogatari* is basically what is in the deepest part of a person's soul. . . . It's because it's there in the soul's depths that people can become linked together at the root. . . . The only person I've ever been able to feel that deep sense of connection with was Kawai Sensei. . . . In recent years, you often hear the word *monogatari*. For me, the only person who was really able to get what I mean when I use that word, to get the real meaning, accurately and completely, was Kawai Sensei.[78]

For Murakami, it is the universal power of *monogatari* which explains his global appeal as a writer.[79] He believes that despite differences in language and culture, our shared history as human beings means that we share important psychic depths and that *monogatari*—stories that come from a place deep within us—are the best tool we have for connecting with each other. Murakami's assertion here can be understood through a different metaphor for the self (or non-self) he has talked about on several occasions: the self as a four-level house.[80]

Murakami explains that above ground level in this metaphorical house are two floors, the first one a social space where people "get together, watch television, and talk," and the second a space dedicated to more private activities. In short, he is describing a public and private version of the self. Below these first two floors of the house is a basement, a space used less often, but one sometimes useful for zoning out. Though not Murakami's own language, I believe this first basement overlaps in part with Freud's notion of a personal unconscious. In Murakami's house metaphor, though, there is a second basement below this first one, though this is a room most people never discover: "This place has such a special door and is so difficult to find that usually you cannot enter. . . . If by some chance you do suddenly enter, what you find is darkness."[81] It is here, in this second basement, Matthew Strecher explains, that

Murakami discovered the *monogatari*: "What, then, is the basement level beneath the first basement? This, I think, is where the [*monogatari*] of which Murakami speaks is kept, and he is quite correct in saying that we do not normally enter this room—at least, not by our own will or volition."[82]

Murakami's idea here of a second basement resonates deeply with Jungian thought. Indeed, Jung had his own house metaphor to describe the expanded notion of Self he believed in, his inspiration coming from a dream, as he explains in his autobiography (more than likely the inspiration for Murakami's aforementioned house analogy).[83] Jung's dream likewise started with a two-storied house. Descending from the second floor to the ground floor and driven by a desire to explore "the whole house," Jung discovered a heavy door leading down into a cellar. This cellar felt very old to Jung, yet upon examining the stone slabs of its floor, he discovered one with a ring attached to it which he began to pull, revealing a hidden stairway to an even older cave below. In this cave he discovered "scattered bones and broken pottery, like remains of a primitive culture." This dream proved to be an important catalyst in his creation of depth psychology and his consequent break from Freud. Jung explains:

> It was plain to me that the house represented a kind of image of the psyche—that is to say, of my then state of consciousness, with hitherto unconscious additions. . . . The deeper I went, the more alien and the darker the scene became. In the cave, I discovered remains of a primitive culture, that is, the world of the primitive man within myself—a world which can scarcely be reached or illuminated by consciousness. The primitive psyche of man borders on the life of the animal soul, just as the caves of prehistoric times were usually inhabited by animals before men laid claim to them.[84]

The parallels here between Murakami's second basement and Jung's cave are obvious, so again, why is Murakami so reluctant to fully embrace the Jungian roots of his thinking on *monogatari*? In his Kyoto speech for the Kawai Prizes mentioned earlier, for example, he used the occasion to once again state for the record his general ignorance of Jung and even of the writings of his friend, Kawai Sensei, stating, "I've hardly read Kawai Sensei's books; I've only read the biography he wrote on Jung and his short autobiography, *mirai e no kioku* (Memories for the Future), published by Iwanami Shinsho. By the way, I haven't read any of Jung's works completely."[85]

Murakami went on, in his speech, to explain his reason for keeping a "respectful distance" from these figures, noting that his job as an author is to present readers with a well-written story, but also one that, from a psychological perspective, is unprocessed rather than filtered through the ideas or theories of somebody else.[86] Murakami expressed a similar idea to me when I asked him directly about the influence of Jung on his writing:

> I think the most important thing for my writing is to be unconscious. Once I get conscious about what I'm doing, I'm going to think, what's the meaning of this? I don't want to do that. I just want to write a good story. So that is my only interest. I don't want to read [Jung's] work because it could be dangerous for me as a writer.[87]

The same goes for other psychoanalytic theories too, starting with the father of psychoanalysis: Sigmund Freud. Murakami explained to Murakami Ryū early on in his career that he likes neither Freud nor psychoanalysis more generally.[88] Of course, someone like Murakami who has dived so deeply into Western literature and film is not going to be able to avoid exposure to psychoanalytic ideas completely, and he likely knows more about the theories of Freud, Jung, and others, than he likes to let on (there are numerous references to both Freud and Jung in his fiction). But as much as humanly possible, Murakami is determined to stay away from the direct influence of psychoanalytical thought, to not let somebody else's ideas influence what he finds in his second basement. Consequently, he does not define himself as a Jungian (or as the follower of any other psychoanalytic school).

This does not mean that Murakami is completely oblivious to the similarities between his and Jung's approach to questions of the self and unconscious. Speaking to Laura Miller, for example, he explained, "[T]he subconscious is very important to me as a writer. I don't read much Jung, but what he writes has some similarity with my writing. To me the subconscious is terra incognita."[89] There are also more indirect routes through which Murakami's loose Jungian influence has come. Murakami's wife, for example, who is the first reader of his fiction and whose feedback he greatly values (Murakami, in a reference to one of his favorite authors, F. Scott Fitzgerald, has called her his Zelda), is a dedicated reader of both Jung and Kawai, and so living with and discussing his fiction with her has naturally shaped his ideas to some degree.[90] In addition, Murakami is happy to acknowledge his respect for the Jungian-influenced writings of Joseph Campbell, such as his classic work *The Hero with a Thousand Faces*. Speaking to Matt Thompson of *The Guardian*, Murakami explains, "I'm looking for my own story in myself. That's also the experience of my protagonist: looking for something that is lost. When I'm writing I experience supernatural feelings. That's why I like Joseph Campbell. People are looking for their tales inside themselves. Without tales people can't live their lives."[91] Like Campbell, Murakami believes that our most powerful stories, the ones that come from and speak most powerfully to our second basements, are myths. He explains, "The more a *monogatari* fulfils its original function as a *monogatari*, the closer it gets to myth."[92]

Murakami thus believes in a self (or non-self) with hidden psychic depths, and he also believes that the healing power of a *monogatari* derives from this depth and the ways it speaks to this same depth within others. Self-therapy, in other words, is not about consciously working through problems in thought or behaviour—what today are called cognitive or behavioral approaches to therapy—but about reconnecting with an inner source of compensatory wisdom, an approach that has clear parallels with Jungian thought. While Murakami claims to not be a serious student of Jung, he is not unaware of their similarities, and his approach to questions of the self and therapy might usefully be described as Jungianism-light. He shares many of Jung's basic convictions about how the mind works without wanting to get too caught up in the specifics of Jung's concepts or terminology.

Two other labels Murakami avoids when describing his *monogatari* are postmodernist and magic realist, despite the prominent place they hold in Western approaches to his fiction. Instead, he believes the kinds of *monogatari* he writes point back to something premodern, as exhibited in the works of an author like Ueda Akinari (1734–1809), an Edo period writer Murakami enjoys who is most famous for his work *Ugetsu Monogatari* (*Tales of Moonlight and Rain*), a collection of tales with prominent (at least from our modern perspective) supernatural themes. Murakami notes that in Western culture and literature there is often a clear dividing line between this world and the other, the natural and the supernatural, and that as a result, the journey to the "other side" is usually presented as difficult and fraught. In Japanese culture, on the other hand, he sees the line dividing these two worlds as more porous and thus easier to slip over, which is why it is less surprising in Japanese stories when this happens, a tendency he also sees in other Asian cultures.[93] He observes that his East Asian readers seem less interested in defining his stories as magic realist or postmodernist, but, instead, tend to simply accept them as *monogatari*.[94]

One consequence of all this in terms of reading Murakami's fiction is that we constantly find ourselves shifting between psychological and supernatural interpretations of what is going on, and often even entertaining two or more competing interpretations at the same time. Strecher makes this point well, noting, "[T]here [is] always a tension between the metaphysical—indeed, the magical—and the psychological in his work. Put another way, one [is] constantly in doubt as to whether Murakami's characters [live] in a magical world or [are] simply out of their minds."[95] Strecher has done more than anyone to explain this tension in terms of the genre of magic realism, and, of course, he is entitled to do so; the point here is simply that this is not the way Murakami chooses to define his work.[96] He would prefer to be lumped in with a premodern writer like Akinari as simply a producer of *monogatari*. Whether or not this is possible is a question I will return to several times in this book.

While Murakami downplays the influence of psychoanalytic thought on his writing, it is important to note that one does not need to have studied Freud or Jung closely to have been influenced by their ideas, and this holds true for a writer who grew up in the cultural milieu of postwar Japan (Jungian thought was just entering the peak of its influence in Japan when Murakami debuted).[97] The Lacanian-influenced critic Slavoj Žižek has gone so far as to argue that in the postmodern West, "one is quite justified in saying that we have not only Jungian, Kleinian, Lacanian . . . interpretations of the symptoms, but symptoms which are themselves Jungian, Kleinian, Lacanian . . . that is, whose reality involves implicit reference to some psychoanalytic theory."[98] Psychoanalytic thought, in other words, shapes all of us today, whether we like it or not.

This book, of course, is not the first attempt to try and read Murakami's fiction through the lens of psychological theory. As Strecher observes, "Those who have spent a little time pondering Murakami Haruki's fiction will recognise the pressing need for some psychological grounding to his work," and many scholars have offered their arguments for what this grounding should be, with the classical psychoanalytic theories of Freud, Jung, and Lacan as the three main candidates.[99] There are also those, like Chikako Nihei, who see Western scholars in particular as moving in the wrong direction when they rely too heavily on "psychoanalytical theories to discuss [Murakami's] characters' internal [journeys] and end up writing a kind of introduction to psychology."[100] Nihei argues that we will read Murakami better when we move away from such Western theories (she includes postmodern theory in this category, too) and, instead, learn to read his fiction as *monogatari*.

I agree with Nihei that Murakami's *monogatari* paradigm is a useful framework for understanding his fiction which has some advantages over competing Western theories, especially if we want to understand his literary project on his own terms. I would simply add that this paradigm is already deeply influenced by psychoanalytic thought, particularly its Jungian strain. Murakami's thoughts on the *monogatari* are thus best seen as a hybrid phenomenon that blends (often unacknowledged) ideas from twentieth-century psychoanalytic thought and the traditions of Japanese storytelling, particularly a strain of that tradition which deals with what today we would call supernatural themes in a Japanese way. Kawai Hayao was the pioneer in developing this blend of Western and Japanese thought, and Murakami is its most important contemporary advocate, despite his general appeals to ignorance about this tradition. Murakami's views about the self, the second basement, and the power of *monogatari* also have important consequences for how he writes, which is the next focus of this section.

The therapeutic value of writing is well supported. James Pennebaker, an expert on the topic, summarizes the results of the many studies which have been done: "While the effects are often modest, the mere act of translating emotional upheaval into words is consistently associated with improvements in physical and mental health."[101] When it comes to the degree of these improvements, however, not all writing is created equal. Pennebaker points out the characteristics of the most therapeutically effective writing: it accentuates the positive while still acknowledging the negative, constructs a coherent story over time, and explores problems from multiple perspectives.[102] Researchers have proposed different theories for where these therapeutic benefits come from. Perhaps writing about negative experiences from the past allows us to lessen their impact over time, to break the cycle of rumination that leaves us feeling stuck, or symbolically allows us to work through unfinished business (this last point is particularly relevant to Murakami's fiction).[103] At any rate, the results are clear—writing as a means of self-therapy works—though some types of writing are more effective than others and individual differences do exist.

Murakami, however, is not necessarily using writing as self-therapy in this way.[104] He claims to write less to express a hidden message or to get something off his chest than to discover something unknown about himself. He explains:

> I think that writing novels ... is in many ways an act of self-therapy. Undoubtedly, there are those who have some kind of message and write it in a novel, but in my case at least, that is not how it works. Rather, I feel like I write novels in order to find out what kind of message is in me to begin with. In the process of writing a story, these kinds of messages just suddenly float up from the darkness—of course, most of the time, they are written in incomprehensible code.[105]

This is why Murakami values spontaneity in his writing process above all else: "[T]he story has to develop spontaneously. As far as I'm concerned, there's no point in plotting it out consciously from the beginning."[106] He describes the experience as like playing a video game with yourself:

At the same time you are creating the programme, you are also the player. And what's more, when playing the game, you completely lose all memory of having programmed it. The left hand doesn't know what the right hand is doing; the right hand doesn't know what the left hand is doing. To me this is the ultimate game, and it is also self-therapy.[107]

The process he describes sounds like what Jung meant by active imagination: "a sequence of fantasies produced by deliberate concentration."[108] Murakami has described it as like "dreaming while you're awake" or as a type of "mesmerism."[109]

This does not mean Murakami never thinks consciously about what he will write. Another analogy he likes compares his mind to a large cabinet of drawers, with each drawer containing a memory: a person, a conversation, or something he has read, for example.[110] This is the raw material he will use in the writing process, which involves opening the right drawer at the right time, and so keeping these drawers stocked up with useful material is an important part of the writing process. Here again, though, spontaneity is key. Murakami explains, "At the same time you know where everything is, it's vital that at unexpected times, unexpected drawers open. Without the unexpected, you won't end up with a good novel. You might say that writing a novel is a continuous accident."[111]

This is why Murakami places great emphasis on timing. He will sometimes write something—an opening scene or a piece of dialogue, for example—and then put it away in a (literal) drawer (or these days save it on his computer) for a period, not pulling it out again until the time is right. In the interlude what he has been doing is filling his (metaphorical) drawers with the necessary raw material. "It sounds paradoxical," Murakami observes, "but in writing a novel, the time not writing is important."[112] This is also why he never writes to a deadline—this is not a process he feels can be rushed—and it is also why he claims to have never suffered from writer's block; he simply does not write anything until the timing is right.[113]

This emphasis on spontaneity does not mean he believes everything will come out right first time. While the power of a *monogatari* depends on a spontaneous creative process that taps into the mysteries of the second basement, the first outpouring of a story will always be followed by a long, intensive period of revision. Even here, though, there is a strong sense in which the unconscious controls how far this process should (or even can) go. Murakami explains that in his revision process he is much like one of his readers who reread his novels many times over trying to close in on the mysteries they find: "In the same way that readers reread my work, I rewrite them many times from the first draft, and as I rewrite them, the mystery inside me contracts. I get closer to the heart of the matter."[114] Even so, the mystery never contracts completely—the heart of the matter always remains just out of reach—and then, at some point, he finds that he can go no further. He describes this final impasse he reaches as a basement, a symbol of a mystery in the darkness, or simply as a black box.[115] This is his sign that it is time to stop, at least for now. Of course, in time, this process begins again in a new writing project, something that makes reading his fiction as an evolving therapeutic project a worthwhile exercise. As Murakami puts it, "the works I've written so far are all separate and independent texts, but the sequence—or the flow—of one text to another is rather meaningful."[116] One purpose of this book is to tease out the meaning of this sequence or flow.

Murakami's emphasis on unsolvable mysteries is one of the issues that separates his fans and critics most fiercely. Where some have seen in his career a slow dive into mystery and depth, others have seen a superficial skirting along the surface or a confusing descent into obfuscation. Early on in Murakami's career, for example, Masao Miyoshi warned readers about playing his "symbol-deciphering game[s]," suggesting that they would soon reach their limits.[117] For Murakami, though, the increasing complexity and mysterious nature of his writing is less a cynical ploy than a necessity. Talking to the author Kawakami Mieko, he explains, "A *monogatari* is a *monogatari* because you cannot interpret it. . . . I think it is because the author does not know what is going on that meaning is free to grow within each individual reader."[118] This is also why Murakami tries not to interpret his own writing, especially immediately following its publication. It is for the reader to decide what a work of fiction means, which is why he believes that "a writer should not really talk about their own work."[119] Sales figures alone would suggest that Murakami is onto something here, that his quest to approach his inner "black box" equally resonates with something deep within his readers, connecting them at the root, as he likes to put it. While he acknowledges that in English we might call such stories myths, or in Jungian psychology, expressions of the collective unconscious, his preferred term is *monogatari*: stories which arise spontaneously from the second basement.[120]

Four Therapeutic Threads in Murakami's Fiction

This then is Murakami's working paradigm, the way he sees the process of writing as a means of self-therapy unfolding. So how does all of this fit together? In other words, in what ways are the biographical drivers of Murakami's search for self-therapy (his estrangement from his parents and the shock of K's death) expressed and worked out in his fiction (*monogatari*, he claims, which arise spontaneously from his second basement)? And how has this personal motivation for writing in turn been transformed into a literary project of global acclaim? Murakami, it should be clear by now, would resist such a rapprochement. We should not be looking for explanations in the rest of the house, he would say, for what comes out of his second basement. Or, in other words, do not try to understand my fiction by learning more about me. Instead, he would say, we should simply read *monogatari* as *monogatari*, letting them do their work in our own second basement.

Perhaps Murakami is right that this is the best way to read his fiction, but as an approach to literary criticism, it is a nonstarter. In what follows, I will, instead, be making a case for how I believe the different levels of Murakami's "house" might be linked together—to understand the ways his biography informs his fiction. But this approach also has its limits, and the risk I will be taking at times is in committing the biographical fallacy—the mistake of believing that everything in a work of fiction can be explained by a direct appeal to its author's life. Admitting such a limit, of course, is not the same thing as saying that biographical approaches to fiction have nothing to offer, and, indeed, I think that in Murakami's case we have not come close to exhausting this limit. A short justification for this approach is offered in what follows.

Biographical approaches to fiction go in and out of fashion, and for some Western critics today authors are dead, and readers are everything. While the same is not necessarily true in Japan, in terms of Murakami studies, biographical studies are still rare, likely because of a lack of compelling and readily available biographical material.[121] Murakami has been skilled at misdirecting our attention away from himself and protecting his privacy, although there are signs that this is starting to change.[122] Of course, author-centered approaches to fiction can be taken too far, and we should not see authors as the sole or final arbiters of literary meaning, but neither do we have to ignore their role in producing the texts we later come to interpret. Like an antagonist in a Murakami novel, the proclaimed death of the author has often turned out to be premature, and at least some critics and many general readers continue to be interested in the authors who produce the books they love. This book is one example of this continued trend.

Furthermore, in Murakami's specific case, I believe that we have allowed him to control the narrative a little too much in terms of how much (or how little) biographical material we should expect to find in his fiction. Part of this can likely be explained by the shift Murakami represents in contemporary Japanese literature in terms of a move away from heavily biographically influenced fiction. Many Japanese writers of the modern period have deliberately blurred the line between biography and fiction, while Murakami is often celebrated as a writer who broke the literary mold by writing purely inventive stories. For the most part, we have taken him at his word when he has said that there is not much of a biographical core to find in his writing. To be honest, we were probably relieved to finally have a modern Japanese writer who did not feel the need to constantly fictionalize the minutiae of their life, but who could simply write entertaining stories inspired by the messages bubbling up from their unconscious. And yet, what does it mean when this same writer also claims to be writing as a means of self-therapy? Can we really make sense of this claim without at least some understanding of the life behind the works? This book attempts to bring biography back into the mix of Murakami studies, not to elevate it above other approaches or to give it the final word on what the fiction should mean, but, instead, to allow it to play its contributing role in telling the larger story of what Murakami's fiction means.

As already mentioned, this book argues that there are four prominent therapeutic threads woven through Murakami's fourteen novels to date that have waxed and waned in prominence, and which can help to make sense of his novels' underlying therapeutic themes. These four threads again are (1) the journey from melancholia to mourning (which biographically can be connected to the loss of K), (2) the symbolic healing of intergenerational trauma (which can be connected to Murakami's relationship with his father), (3) the journey from avoidance to earned attachment (which can also be connected to Murakami's complicated relationship with his parents), and (4) the drive for individuation as a response to nihilism (which is connected to broader existential and cultural concerns). Each of these four threads is visible in Murakami's fiction from early on, and each has eventually led to a breakthrough in a particular novel, though this does not mean it has then disappeared from his fiction altogether. Instead, once a breakthrough occurs, the prominence of that thread tends to decline in Murakami's fiction, while another thread (or threads) comes to the forefront. The first thread, melancholia to mourning, finds its "resolution" in *Dance Dance Dance* (*Dansu dansu dansu*, 1988); the second, intergenerational trauma, in *The Wind-Up Bird Chronicle* (*Nejimaki-dori kuronikuru*, 1994–5); the third, avoidance to earned attachment, in *1Q84* (2009–10); and the fourth, individuation, in *Killing Commendatore* (*Kishidanchō-goroshi*, 2017). These four novels are thus important milestones within Murakami's ongoing therapeutic project.

Chapter 1 starts with the first thread—the journey from melancholia to mourning—and follows the journey of a single protagonist over three novels (the so-called Rat trilogy) as he struggles with (among other things) the death of a former girlfriend. This character often seems unaware of the therapeutic journey he is on, but a supporting cast of characters conveniently enters his life at opportune times and gently leads him along the way. At the same time, these supporting characters are connected at some level with the protagonist himself, and so there is much about the nature and purpose of his quest which resonates with the Jungian quest for individuation (thread four), which advocates for a dialogic exchange between our conscious self and the personified complexes which emerge from our unconscious. For Jung, individuation is a quest to discover "our innermost, last, and incomparable uniqueness," a journey of "coming to selfhood" or "self-realization."[123] It is a process whereby we gradually incorporate more of the unconscious into our conscious lives.

Both of these therapeutic threads (the journey from melancholia to mourning and the quest for individuation) continue in Murakami's next three novels explored in Chapter 2, *Hard-Boiled Wonderland and the End of the World* (*Sekai no owari to hādoboirudo wandārando*, 1985), *Norwegian Wood*, and *Dance Dance Dance*. These are stories where the loss of a past girlfriend is still an ongoing (though sometimes better camouflaged) theme and where the pull of melancholia remains strong. *Hard-Boiled Wonderland and the End of the World* and *Dance Dance Dance* also begin to introduce complications to the quest for individuation that come from conditions in late-capitalist Japan. More specifically, what one sees are forces of dissociation which act in direct opposition to the drive for individuation. The first major therapeutic breakthrough in Murakami's fiction occurs at the end of *Dance Dance Dance* when the same narrator first seen in the Rat trilogy is finally ready to break through a symbolic wall and connect with another human being. The solipsistic nature of Murakami's early melancholic fiction begins to break down and a desire for interpersonal connection emerges (a development also related to thread three: the journey from avoidance to earned attachment).

One consequence of breaking through melancholia and moving back into mourning is the return of what Jacques Lacan called the Real, or what Cassegård earlier described as shock. Chapter 3 shows protagonists dealing with this shock, but also ready to accept it (at least in the end) as a means of letting go of past illusions and accepting "reality." This begins in *South of the Border, West of the Sun* and reaches its climax in *The Wind-Up Bird Chronicle*, a novel that also deals directly with therapeutic thread two (the need to resolve intergenerational trauma). This second thread first emerges in *A Wild Sheep Chase* (*Hitsuji o meguru bōken*, 1982) but finds its most dramatic expression in *The Wind-Up Bird Chronicle*, arguably the most powerful of Murakami's therapeutic breakthroughs so far.

By 1995 then, the two therapeutic threads in Murakami's fiction most directly connected to his biographical losses had found their at least partial resolutions in fictional form: the need to overcome his melancholic response to the death of K and the need to resolve his intergenerational trauma with his father. So what has this meant for Murakami's fiction beyond this point? 1995 was also the year two traumatic events hit Japan, the Kobe earthquake in January and the Aum Shinrikyō sarin gas attack on the Tokyo subway system in March, both of which Murakami has responded to directly in his fiction and nonfiction. A Jungian might see synchronicity in the fact that just when Murakami had worked through his two most personal traumas in fictional form, Japan was rocked by two events which would require the services of a writer skilled in the art of therapeutic fiction. The way Murakami has responded to these two events has not been straightforward or uncontroversial, however, a topic I explore in Chapters 4 and 5.

In Chapter 4, I argue that Murakami's first three novels which followed the events of 1995, *Sputnik Sweetheart* (*Supūtoniku no koibito*, 1999), *Kafka on the Shore* (*Umibe no Kafuka*, 2002), and *After Dark* (*Afutā dāku*, 2004), show him moving in two different directions at the same time. First, what one sees is a conscious attempt on Murakami's part to pass on the therapeutic lessons of his own life to the next generation, to write stories about young people who are struggling with their own (often oedipal) challenges and trying to find a way through the darkness. At the same time, the way these lessons are presented is greatly complicated, I believe, by their older author, who is still developing therapeutic threads of his own, particularly the last two unresolved threads: the journey from avoidance to earned attachment and the desire for individuation. What this often involves is a kind of reversal of the Oedipus complex, a killing of a symbolic father figure which opens a protagonist again to radical questions about morality. In my discussion of *Kafka on the Shore*, in particular, I argue that behind the oedipal struggle of the young fifteen-year-old protagonist can be seen the struggle of the novel's much older author, who is simultaneously wrestling with the question of individuation in the second half of life. This adds a complicated duality to some of Murakami's fiction from this period.

Chapter 5 explores the way the last two therapeutic threads in Murakami's fiction have found their "resolutions." *1Q84* focuses on the theme of childhood deprivation and the ways it can arrest personal development, but also on the way love can overcome these limitations to help people achieve what is called earned attachment. The last two novels I examine, *Colorless Tsukuru Tazaki and His Years of Pilgrimage* (*Shikisai o motanai Tazaki Tsukuru to, kare no junrei no toshi*, 2013) and *Killing Commendatore*, take up subtle alchemical themes which can be interpreted through the Jungian lens of individuation. The link between alchemy and individuation is one of the more esoteric aspects of Jung's work, and the emergence of these motifs in Murakami's fiction is the strongest evidence yet of just how deeply the influence of Jung runs in his work. This process of individuation becomes increasingly necessary in a world where symbolic fathers are repeatedly killed and reborn and where the individual must learn to stand on their own.

At this point of the discussion, I wish to make two points about this fourth therapeutic thread in Murakami's fiction—the desire for individuation as a response to nihilism—which is the most sustained of the four threads. The first point is that this thread is deeply connected to the first three, indeed, that it has grown out of them. Peter Homans, who has looked closely at the way psychoanalysis as a field arose out of experiences of cultural loss related to forces of modernity and secularization, has identified three common stages many early psychoanalytical thinkers went through in the creation of their psychological systems involving mourning, individuation, and the creation of meaning. Homans writes:

> [I]ndividuation . . . is the fruit of mourning. Somehow, in a way that is not really understood, the experience of loss can stimulate the desire "to become who one is." That in turn can throw into motion a third process, what should be called "the creation of meaning." This action is at once a work of personal growth and a work of culture. In it, the self both appropriates from the past what has been lost and at the same time actually creates for itself in a fresh way these meanings.[124]

Murakami's therapeutic fiction follows a similar path, though before Murakami could enter the mourning stage, he first had to break out of his melancholia. Just like Homans observes in the case of psychoanalysis, individuation for Murakami is very much "the fruit of mourning," something which grew out of the losses which had marked his late adolescence and early adulthood.

The second point I wish to make is also related to Homans' previous quote. Homans sees the psychoanalytic movement as progressing from loss to individuation and then to the creation of meaning, something which is both "a work of personal growth and a work of culture". Murakami's therapeutic fiction is likewise a project which started from personal losses, but which has since gone on to deal with larger questions of meaning. What is meant by "the creation of meaning" here, I would argue, might usefully be understood through Nietzsche's advocation for a transvaluation (or reevaluation) of values.[125] For Nietzsche, "[m]an is a rope stretched between the animal and the Superman—a rope over an abyss."[126] This abyss is nihilism, and Nietzsche believed that certain elite members of society are tasked with the heroic job of crossing it, creating in the process the new values which can drive civilization forward. In doing so, these cultural elites would first have to leave behind the received wisdom and morality of the masses, boldly stepping into the unknown to create something new.

Murakami has been interested in the ideas of Nietzsche since at least middle school, and, I would argue, is both fascinated and repulsed by them, a dynamic which is seen in the growing conflicts between his protagonists, figures undergoing a Jungian-like process of individuation, and their antagonists, warped Nietzschean Supermen who believe it is their inherent right to rule over the masses. These warped Supermen are willing to transgress traditional moral standards of good and evil to achieve their aims, and Murakami's protagonists, in trying to oppose them, soon learn that they must come to do likewise. The question then is, what if anything separates them? In the discussion which follows, the differences between Nietzsche and Jung will become just as important as their similarities, and in general, I will argue that Murakami has more sympathy for Jung than for Nietzsche (again, despite his general denials of direct Jungian influence in his work). By the time I get to my discussion of *Killing Commendatore*, however, I will argue that this line has become so thin that, in the end, it is essentially meaningless. The "antagonist," it turns out, is none other than the unconscious of the protagonist himself, and it is by dealing with this dark side of the personality in a productive way that the quest for individuation can finally reach an important breakthrough, a moment which can be expressed through the language of alchemy.

While Murakami's writing career thus started as an unconscious response to personal loss (triggered by his baseball epiphany), it has since evolved into something with broader cultural significance. His search for self-therapy has, at the same time, prepared him to become one of the most prominent responders to the traumas of his age. He follows in the footsteps of Nietzsche and Jung before him, intrepid explorers of the unconscious mind who came to radically question the ways we think about ourselves and the moral systems which sustain us. Like these two predecessors, what Murakami ultimately battles is the abyss of nihilism, and what he offers as his antidote is the compensatory power of a deep unconscious from which mysterious messages emerge (much like Jung), while in his later fiction he adds to this the ideal of love as a saving force (what I will later describe as an appeal to Dostoevsky without God). While Murakami prefers, as much as possible, to leave the messages that float up from his second basement uninterpreted, to simply offer them to the world as carefully edited but at some level still unfiltered *monogatari*, this book, as a work of literary criticism, will seek to go beyond this, offering a picture of four therapeutic threads woven throughout Murakami's fiction which are worked through and "resolved" in different ways. This begins in the next chapter with an examination of Murakami's first three novels.

1

The Long Goodbyes

Introduction

The first thing one notices when looking for therapeutic themes in Murakami's fiction is just how gently it all begins. The narrator of Murakami's first three novels (technically two novellas and a novel), *Boku* (a first-person informal pronoun in Japanese commonly used by males; the narrator never tells us his name), is hardly aware of his need for self-therapy in the first novella, *Hear the Wind Sing* (hereafter in this chapter, simply *Wind*). However, as his story continues over the next two works, *Pinball, 1973* (1973-nen no pinbōru, 1980; hereafter *Pinball*) and *A Wild Sheep Chase* (hereafter *Sheep Chase*), we start to see that there are, in fact, things from his past that he is trying to work through. First, there is the death of his ex-girlfriend, Naoko, where the therapeutic goal can be described as moving from melancholia into mourning (therapeutic thread one). Then there is his relationship with Rat, an alter ego character who, among other things, represents the political disillusionment of the late 1960s. What one sees as *Boku* makes his journey back to Rat in *Sheep Chase* is the way Rat's story begins to link up with the story of postwar Japan itself—the ideological fever which gripped the nation during the wartime years and the way these ideological forces have continued to reinvent themselves in the postwar period. Breaking this cycle of ideological possession requires an act of self-sacrifice, a first attempt in Murakami's fiction at facilitating intergenerational healing (therapeutic thread two).

At the same time, there is a sense in these first three works that what *Boku* is really in dialogue with is himself, and that the characters he meets along the way are all in part expressions of his unconscious. From his alter ego Rat to the different women who appear and disappear at opportune times, there is much about *Boku*'s journey which resonates with the Jungian notion of individuation (therapeutic thread four), which describes a similar process of a conscious self dialoguing with its personified complexes. Furthermore, in the background to all this is *Boku*'s relationship with his hometown. In *Wind*, *Boku* is visiting this hometown for a short period during his summer vacation from university, but as the novels proceed, he does everything in his power to put distance between himself and this town. The conclusion of *Sheep Chase* sees *Boku* returning to his hometown one last time to shed tears for everything he has lost.

A final point this chapter makes is about the literary models Murakami was building on when he first started creating his brand of therapeutic fiction, an important part of understanding how he transformed his therapeutic motive for writing into successful literary fiction. While Murakami often mentions the names of Kurt Vonnegut and Richard Brautigan as important early literary influences, this chapter argues that in terms of his therapeutic themes, the examples of F. Scott Fitzgerald and Raymond Chandler were even more important. What both writers modeled for Murakami (both in their lives and in their fiction) was the power of reinvention: the way an individual from a relatively small town can move to a big city and reinvent themself, even becoming a literary symbol of that city, but also how the ghosts from their past may continue to haunt them in unexpected ways. Both Fitzgerald and Chandler created distinctive first-person narrators who find themselves pulled into the world of a colorful alter ego (or egos), with their implicit therapeutic quest being to dialogue with and connect with these alter egos in a largely unconscious attempt to reconnect with something lost within themselves. Neither Fitzgerald nor Chandler brings this therapeutic potential in their fiction to a satisfying conclusion, demonstrating, among other things, that therapeutically satisfying endings are not a prerequisite for successful literary fiction. I will argue that Murakami sensed this therapeutic potential in their work and borrowed from it when creating his brand of fiction.

Hearing the Unconscious in *Hear the Wind Sing*

Murakami has said that he wrote everything he wanted to in *Wind* in the first chapter; after that, he simply kept going because "of course, Chapter One alone doesn't make a novel."[1] The rest of the book he describes as "mostly stuff that came out unconsciously . . . almost like automatic writing."[2] This is what makes Chapter One of *Wind* such an interesting place to start when trying to understand Murakami's career. What was it that he wanted to say in his first novella before he simply ran out of ideas and let his unconscious take over?

One of the thoughts his first-person narrator offers in Chapter One is about the value of writing as a means of self-therapy, a topic he has mixed feelings about. He explains, "When you get right down to it, writing is not a method of self-therapy. It's just the slightest attempt at a move in the direction of self-therapy. . . . And yet I find myself thinking that if everything goes well, sometime way ahead, years, maybe decades from now, I might discover myself saved."[3] Writing here is little more than a starting point for the therapeutic process, but there is also hope that the broader process it leads to will have a significant payoff. But what exactly does *Boku* need to be saved from? What problem (or problems) is he dealing with?

One clear problem *Boku* has (and which he is striving to overcome through writing) is difficulty communicating, something he has struggled with from a young age. In Chapter Seven, he tells us that he was "a very quiet child. So quiet, in fact, that my worried parents took me to see a friend of theirs who was a psychiatrist."[4] Every Sunday, for about a year, he would make the journey to see this psychiatrist where he would be told stories, presented object lessons, and given treats. Though much of the meaning of these exchanges was lost on the young *Boku*, eventually the message got through: "Civilization is communication. . . . That which is not expressed doesn't exist."[5] For *Boku* the discovery was like a dam bursting. He talked nonstop for the next three months until he broke out in a fever. Once this fever subsided, he found that he was "no longer a chatterbox" but also no longer "tongue-tied." Instead, he had become an "ordinary kid."[6]

Unfortunately for *Boku* this lesson did not stick and years later he again found himself struggling with the same problem. In Chapter Thirty, he informs us that there was a time during high school when it was cool to say only half of what you were thinking. The problem, he realized years later, was that he soon became the kind of person who can only ever say half of what they think. By the time he realized this was a mistake, it was too late, and what is more, he no longer had any idea how it related to being cool. So is *Boku*'s inability to fully express himself still his problem at the beginning of *Wind*?

Boku does a lot in Chapter One to manage our expectations about what we are about to read. He begins by telling us, "There's no such thing as a perfect piece of writing. Just as there's no such thing as perfect despair."[7] This is advice he once heard from a writer, and he has taken it to heart as he begins to write himself, though despair is never too far away, with his problem being the limited scope of what he can write about. "I could write something about an elephant," he offers as an example, "but when it came to the elephant's keeper, I might draw a blank."[8] *Boku* senses that improving this situation is going to be vital for him as a writer (and person) and may even be connected to his ultimate salvation. What he must learn to do is to "tell the story of the world in words far more beautiful than these."[9] He assures us that he is trying to be honest in his account, though he admits this is difficult: "The more I try to be honest, the farther my words sink into darkness."[10] He ends the chapter by telling us that what we are about to read is not literature or art; it is more like a notebook with a line drawn down the middle, a simple method, it is implied, for tallying the losses and gains of his life so far.

There is a strong sense in *Wind* that *Boku*'s narrative is limited, that it has important omissions. When he writes, "I've told my story as best I can right now. There's nothing to add," the "right now" qualifier is essential.[11] Clearly, there is much more that he needs to add to his story; this is simply the best he can do for now. He is like a patient in their first therapy session, hesitant from years of silence and not sure about where to begin, but hopeful that this is the first step in a long and painful, but ultimately rewarding process. So what is it that *Boku* really needs to write about?

Kojima Motohiro usefully suggests that the answer to this question is found in this passage from Chapter Nineteen of the novel:

> The third girl I slept with was a French literature major I met in the school library, but the following spring vacation she hanged herself in the shabby grove of trees by the tennis courts. Her body wasn't discovered until vacation ended and the new school year began—she had been swinging in the wind for two whole weeks. Even today no one goes near that grove after the sun goes down.[12]

Kojima sees in this passage not just the central loss *Boku* is facing in this work but a foreshadowing of the central theme of Murakami's next five novels.[13] Thus, when *Boku* says that he must "tell the story of the world in words far more beautiful than these," what he is really saying is that he must tell the story of this dead girlfriend in a more powerful and redemptive way.

Another critic who sees *Wind* foreshadowing therapeutic themes found throughout Murakami's oeuvre is the clinical psychologist Muramoto Kuniko. In psychoanalysis, she explains, patients often have what is called an initial dream, which comes to foreshadow the major themes of their analysis, much like the trailer of a movie foreshadows the major themes of a movie. Muramoto describes *Wind* as Murakami's "initial novel," and sees it as establishing themes of dissociation and healing which have sustained his career now for over forty years.[14] What Muramoto notices about *Wind*, first and foremost, is the fragmented nature of *Boku*'s narrative, a characteristic that reminds her of the storytelling she often hears in her office from dissociated patients, often victims of violence and intergenerational trauma. While she describes *Boku*'s dissociation as still at healthy levels, basically meaning that he can function in society, she views the main symptoms of his dissociation as his emotional distance from his family and others and sees him starting a quest which is about pulling together fragmented memories from his past so that he can begin to heal himself and connect with people.[15]

Storytelling can be the start of healing. It is a way of bringing fragmented memories of the past back together again so that a fuller story can be told. In *Wind*, however, *Boku* is still in the early stages of this process. While his narrative touches on his trauma—the suicide of the third girl he slept with—it is not his primary focus. Instead, what he spends most of his time describing in *Wind* is a short trip he made back to his hometown several months after her death and the seemingly random things which happened to him there. She died in late March, it is suggested, and the story is set in August 1970. Absent from *Boku*'s narrative is the deep sense of loss and mourning we might expect if this novel were primarily about her. If *Boku* is seeking self-therapy through writing then, he is not doing it actively. Instead, he is sitting back and waiting for therapy to come to him. The interesting thing is that it does.

"It might be said that the only 'personality' in most of Murakami's *Boku*-narrated works," Rubin observes, "is that of *Boku* himself, whose perceptions never cease to fascinate. The other characters are functions of his psyche."[16] The question is what functions these other characters are fulfilling. The short answer is that they are there to take *Boku* from melancholia to mourning (therapeutic thread one), and at the same time they are offering him early hints of a Jungian-like quest for individuation he is just embarking on (therapeutic thread four). Given that this Jungian-like journey of individuation continues through all of Murakami's *Boku*-narrated novels (the Rat trilogy and the later novel *Dance Dance Dance*) and right up into Murakami's more recent fiction, it is worth taking a moment here to examine what it entails.

A central tenet of Jungian thought is that "the unconscious processes stand in a compensatory relation to the conscious mind."[17] What this means is that self-therapy, from a Jungian perspective, is an entirely feasible undertaking; all that it requires (though this is easier said than done) is receptivity to the messages coming from one's unconscious. For Freud, the unconscious was a site of repression, a place for things to go which the ego, watched over by the morals of society (as represented by the superego), could not bear to face. For Jung, while the unconscious includes these anti-social aspects, it is equally a source of wisdom and growth, with the art of self-therapy (or individuation) being about allowing the conscious mind to open itself up to this unconscious potential and become more whole.

The way one attends to the unconscious in Jungian psychology is by noticing the complexes working in one's life. A complex represents the way archetypal content manifests itself in the life of an individual with their particular personality, life experiences, and cultural background. The complexes primarily do their work in what Jung terms the personal unconscious, though they also have an archetypal core connected to what he called the collective unconscious. This collective unconscious is not some kind of mystical group mind, but, rather, those parts of our psychic life common to us all due to our shared evolutionary history. In Murakami's language, we might say that complexes belong more to the first basement, and archetypes more to the second. Archetypes are deemed as unknowable in themselves, but they can be hypothesized through the common tropes found in human storytelling across time (particularly in mythology). Jung believed that complexes usually appear in dreams, daydreams, and directed fantasies as actual personalities with whom one can converse and interact.

The "personified" nature of complexes offers a useful way to understand the compensatory nature of the secondary characters that appear in Murakami's *Boku*-narrated works. Jung notes, "Complexes do indeed behave like secondary or partial personalities possessing a mental life of their own."[18] Demaris Wehr explains how these secondary personalities function in the process of individuation: "Individuation consists in coming to know the multiple personalities, the 'little people' who dwell within one's breast. One needs to 'befriend' them at the same time as one distinguishes one's own voice from theirs. . . . Gradually the self displaces the ego as the center of consciousness."[19] Reading Murakami's fiction through a Jungian lens, who are the "secondary or partial personalities" that *Boku* must "befriend" in *Wind*?

The first important friend *Boku* meets on his therapeutic journey is *Nezumi* (or Rat), whom he first gets to know shortly after arriving at university. He cannot remember how they first met, but he remembers the event which ultimately bound them together—their crashing of Rat's shiny black Fiat 600 through a park fence in the early hours of the morning, all while under the influence of alcohol. Rat is less interested in the damage done to his car than in their good fortune in not being injured (it turns out he is rich), and he soon suggests that they "team up."[20] Their first item of business is to drink more beer together following which they both fall asleep on the beach. Given this chain of events, we might have expected them to wake up the next morning with sore bodies and hangovers, but, in fact, the opposite occurs. *Boku* describes:

> When I woke I was filled with an intense sense of being alive. It was weird—I had never felt that kind of energy before.
> "Man, I feel like I could run sixty miles!" I told the Rat.
> "Me too," he said.[21]

What is being suggested here is that there is something significant about this new "team"; *Boku* and Rat belong together.

Asked how he got the name *Nezumi*, Rat does not have a good reply: "Don't remember. Happened a long time ago" (*Wasureta ne. Zuibun mukashi no koto sa*).[22] This sense of *mukashi* (a long time ago) is another clue that Rat is a character with both personal and potentially archetypal undertones for *Boku*. Rubin reflects, "It is a nickname so old—so embedded in the psychic primordial slime of once-upon a time (*mukashi*)—that he has 'forgotten' how he came by it."[23] In terms of the Jungian complexes, he is a clear candidate for *Boku*'s shadow.

The shadow is the first complex Jung saw people encountering in their quest for individuation, and this is because the shadow, more than any other complex, is seen as having a strong connection to the personal unconscious. He explains, "To become conscious of it involves recognising the dark aspects of the personality as present and real."[24] This is naturally a disturbing process; the shadow represents those parts of ourself that are least socially acceptable, those parts we try to keep out of the public eye. It partly has its origins in our earliest years of socialization as we learn to create a persona or social mask that will allow us to function in society. Jung believed that the shadow is usually experienced in dreams and fantasies as someone of the same sex.

One of the easiest ways to recognize our shadow, Jung suggests, is to become conscious of the ways we project it onto others. Murakami offers an example of how this works in his nonfiction book *Underground* (in Japanese originally two books, *Andāguraundo* (1997) and *Yakusokusareta basho de* (1998)). These books examined, from the perspectives of the victims and members and former members of Aum, respectively, the 1995 Aum Shinrikyō cult sarin gas attack directed at commuters on the Tokyo subway system. Murakami recalls how he had earlier felt a deep sense of disgust when he observed members of this cult campaigning for the election of the Lower House of the Japanese Diet in 1990. In Jungian terms, the extremity of this reaction suggests he was in the grip of a complex, in this case, the shadow. Murakami writes, "I felt an unnameable dread, a disgust beyond my understanding." He goes on to note, "Psychologically speaking . . . encounters that call up strong physical disgust or revulsion are often, in fact, projections of our own faults and weaknesses. . . . These subconscious shadows are an 'underground' that we carry around within us."[25]

Rat, admittedly, comes nowhere close to inspiring this level of disgust or revulsion. Though he is at times moody, he is not an unlikeable character, and he invites feelings closer to pathos than repulsion. He is neither sinister nor evil but is someone facing deep disappointments (both personal and political) and is being left behind by the times. He could thus more accurately be described as *Boku*'s alter ego than his shadow, a part of himself that he is leaving behind in his hometown as he tries to build a new life in Tokyo. Does this then mean that Jungian readings of *Wind* are misplaced? Not necessarily, I would suggest.

First, as I will argue later, Rat can be seen as an important precursor to the kinds of antagonists (truly shadow-like characters) that do later appear in Murakami's fiction. In short, there is a line from Rat to later characters like Gotanda and Wataya Noboru (both discussed in later chapters), so that even though Rat is not a fully developed shadow-like character himself, he is worth exploring in this light. At this early stage in Murakami's career, the archetypal component of the complex is being downplayed and the personal component emphasized. Rat represents a part of *Boku* (and arguably also of Murakami at the time) that is still psychologically trapped in his hometown, still caught up in complicated family and personal relationships and unable to escape. In Murakami's later fiction, the darker side of these male characters, figures who at first befriend but later come to confront and challenge the central male protagonist, becomes increasingly emphasized. We start to see their true archetypal potential, the way they represent the shadow side of both self and society. That this full archetypal potential is not yet on display in Murakami's debut novel is not a problem from a Jungian perspective; indeed, it is entirely expected.

Second, placing Rat in this Jungian framework is useful for highlighting his compensatory role, for understanding the way he carries an important unconscious message *Boku* must receive (if not now, then later). The shadow is formed in part through a process of dissociation, a process of splitting off parts of the self connected with negative experiences of loss, trauma, or shame that then take on the form of another personality hidden within the self (a complex). Individuation is about bringing these different parts of the self back together again and becoming more whole. Rat is one example of how this process can be seen in *Wind*. The woman with only four fingers on her left hand is another.

Near the start of *Wind*, *Boku* wakes up in the apartment of a woman who is naked and fast asleep. Offering a brief description of her appearance, he finishes with the fact that she has only four fingers on her left hand. This becomes the central way she is identified in the novel, her name never revealed. The meeting between *Boku* and this woman highlights the two forces which are constantly working in *Wind* to bring *Boku* into contact with his significant others: J and his bar, and telephones. The night before meeting the woman, *Boku* had visited J's Bar, the hangout where he and Rat spend much of their time in the novel, only to find that Rat was not there. He thus decided to phone him. Calling Rat's number, though, *Boku* is startled to hear the voice of a woman at the other end. He assures us that Rat never lets anyone else answer his phone, and he cannot help feeling annoyed. Here we have our first indication that wires are beginning to cross, and that along with his alter ego or emerging shadow, Rat, *Boku* is now going to have to start dealing with a new presence in his life: the female other. *Boku* pretends to have dialed a wrong number and returns to his drinking. Yet just as he is about to return home, the Chinese bartender J suggests he go and wash his face in the bathroom. It is here that he finds the woman with the missing finger, drunk and lying on the floor. Consulting with J about what to do, he decides that it is best to take her home, and then he stays over just in case she has alcohol poisoning.

For males, the encounter with the shadow is followed in Jungian psychology by an encounter with the anima (in females, a corresponding complex is known as the animus). Jung writes, "The persona, the ideal picture of a man as he should be, is inwardly compensated by feminine weakness."[26] This meeting with the anima, Jung argues, always follows the meeting with the shadow: "[T]he integration of the shadow, or the realization of the personal unconscious, marks the first stage . . . without it a recognition of anima and animus is impossible."[27] This idea of a feminine complex within each male is one Murakami is open to, as he explained in an interview with Kawakami Mieko: "There is a female factor in myself. I think any male has that."[28] Wehr explains what the typical role of the anima entails: "'She' compels [her male counterpart] to enter the unconscious. 'She' also leads him into unexplored depths of feeling, relationship, and sensitivity."[29]

In the same way that Rat is not yet a full-blown "shadow" character, it is difficult to see the woman with the missing finger as a full-blown "anima" character, but, as with Rat, she is a precursor to the clear anima-like characters that do later appear in Murakami's fiction. Similar to Rat, there is a strong suggestion that there may be something both personal and archetypal about her. *Boku* explains at one point that there was something annoying about her voice, something nostalgic, something ancient (*furui mukashi no nanika da*; i.e., they are both connected by this sense of something *mukashi* or ancient about them).[30] A clue as to why she has suddenly appeared in *Boku*'s life is arguably provided by the woman herself when, suffering from a hangover, she says, "I feel half dead right now."[31] This could be just a figure of speech, of course, but it is likely also an indication of the role she is playing in trying to help connect *Boku* back to his memories of his dead girlfriend. The fact that she, like this former girlfriend, studies French is another indication of this role.

The connecting role played by telephones and J and his bar continues throughout the novel. After he first meets the woman, it at first seems unlikely they will meet again (she mistakenly believes he took advantage of her), but a telephone call from a radio DJ nudges them to connect again. The DJ is calling because a girl from *Boku*'s old high school has dedicated a song to him, The Beach Boys' "California Girls," a song from a record he once borrowed from her but failed to return. In an (ultimately futile) attempt to make amends, he later visits a record store near the harbor to buy a replacement copy, and it just so happens that the woman with the missing finger is working there.[32] Again, her reception is icy, but later she calls *Boku* on the telephone to invite him over for dinner, explaining that she got his number by visiting J's Bar and talking to Rat.

J plays an important role in the novel trying to help *Boku* connect with Rat. "I bet he wants to talk to you about whatever it is," J says on one occasion when Rat is particularly low.[33] *Boku* wonders why Rat would not simply come and talk to him then, allowing J to offer him some potentially useful feedback: "He's afraid. That you'll make fun of him."[34] *Boku* counters that he would never do such a thing, but J gently lets him know that this is not always how he is perceived: "You're a sweet kid, but part of you seems—how should I put this?—Above it all, like a Zen monk or something."[35] As *Boku* leaves for Tokyo again at the end of the story, it is J again who is most aware of the significance of what is happening. Speaking in the past tense he tells *Boku*, "You and the Rat made quite a team."[36] Perhaps they did, but from now on, J is suggesting, they will be going it alone.

So in the end, how therapeutic has *Boku*'s journey to his hometown been? What therapeutic value has there been in telling his story? On the surface at least, the answer is "not very much." Talking to the woman with the missing finger, *Boku* does open up a little about things from his past, particularly the violence he experienced during the student protests in Tokyo. Yet he concludes that ultimately the whole experience was meaningless.[37] He never moves from the topic of this political disillusionment to the personal loss which seems to be at the heart of his ennui. Perhaps *Boku* just needed more time with her, but this was not to be. In his Epilogue, he informs us that, once he left for the summer, he never saw her again.

The anticipated heart-to-heart with Rat, when it finally happens, is also anticlimactic. Neither *Boku* nor Rat seems to get what the other is saying. Rat, for example, opens with the burden of being rich and his desire to escape, and he asks *Boku* if he knows the feeling. "How the hell would I?" is *Boku*'s cold response.[38] Rat then talks a little about why he left university, the violence he experienced, and the feeling that he is being left behind in a game of musical chairs. The main thing he needs to talk about though, the problems he is having with a girl, he remains silent on: "To be frank, I decided not to share that with you. It's just a load of crap."[39] *Boku* does not probe, but simply offers him a general theory about how, despite our differences, we are all basically the same. After they finish talking and *Boku* drops Rat back at his home, he heads over to J's Bar. "Were you able to talk to him?" J asks. "Yeah, I talked to him," *Boku* replies.[40] This, of course, is true only in the most superficial sense. In terms of the things *Boku* and Rat really need to talk about, they have barely scratched the surface.

This novel is only the first in what would eventually become four *Boku*-narrated novels, and so the therapeutic themes examined here continue to play out in later works. *Boku* will have more chances to begin mourning the loss of his girlfriend and to talk to Rat. He will also have more opportunities to continue the journey of individuation he has just barely begun. While *Wind* thus has faint hints of an emerging Jungian struggle for individuation (suggestive of Žižek's claim mentioned earlier that today many of our "symptoms" already come prepackaged in some particular psychoanalytic form), in the end, it finishes before anything really gets started. What ultimately carries the novel is less its underlying therapeutic tensions or breakthroughs than the voice of *Boku* himself who is narrating the events of his summer in a cool, detached (perhaps even dissociated) way that hardly seems to register the deeper unconscious forces which are just emerging in his life.

Before examining how *Boku*'s therapeutic journey plays out in the next two novels of the Rat trilogy, in the next section I wish to dig a little deeper into the literary precedents for *Boku* and Rat, the ways they are modeled on characters found in F. Scott Fitzgerald's *The Great Gatsby* and Raymond Chandler's *The Long Goodbye*, and the ways these novels provided Murakami with a model for how therapeutic fiction might work.

This Is No Place for Me: From Fitzgerald to Chandler to Murakami

Murakami has said that his favorite three novels of all time are Fitzgerald's *The Great Gatsby*, Chandler's *The Long Goodbye*, and Fyodor Dostoevsky's *The Brothers Karamazov*, with *The Great Gatsby* in the number one spot.[41] While we do not yet have a Murakami translation in Japanese of *The Brothers Karamazov*, we do have translations of the other two novels in Murakami's list, an indication of the importance they hold for him. What Murakami also admits, moreover, is that for him personally, these two novels are not entirely separate works, but can be read together. This possibility is based on his view that Chandler's novel is a direct response to Fitzgerald's.

Murakami explains that Chandler was a hero of his in the 1960s and that he read *The Long Goodbye* at least a dozen times.[42] In his afterword to his translation of *The Long Goodbye*, he also discusses in detail the connection he sees between *The Great Gatsby* and *The Long Goodbye*, explaining, "From some point, I began to suspect that *The Long Goodbye* was modeled on Scott Fitzgerald's *The Great Gatsby*. Or if that's putting it too strongly, you might say that, personally at least, I began to read these two novels as one overlapping story."[43] Murakami is not surprised by this connection. One of the characters in *The Long Goodbye*, an alcoholic writer by the name of Roger Wade, who is partially modeled on Chandler himself, declares himself a fan of Fitzgerald, a feeling shared by Chandler who started work on a film script for *The Great Gatsby*, which was never produced for reasons beyond his control. Murakami also notes the biographical similarities between Fitzgerald and Chandler: their Irish roots, their problems with alcohol, and the way they survived financially through writing for Hollywood. More than this, though, he is interested in their similarities as writers: their instinctual need to write (expressed, for example, in the numerous letters they left behind); their reputations as stylists; and most of all, their sentimental and romantic tendencies.[44]

There are interesting parallels in the way that Fitzgerald became the representative writer of New York City during the booming interwar years; Chandler, the representative writer of Los Angeles in the booming postwar years; and Murakami, the representative writer of Tokyo in the booming bubble-economy years and beyond. None of these writers was born in the city they would later come to represent in the world of fiction, but each of them would create memorable first-person narrators who, through their observations, encounters, and adventures in their respective cities, would come to represent that city in the literary imagination. Early in his career, Murakami was often described by Japanese critics as a writer of city novels (*toshi shōsetsu*). What they meant by this, is that he writes stories reflecting the lives of young city dwellers and the isolation and atomization of the modern urban experience. The narrator of Murakami's first published short story, "A Slow Boat to China," would declare of Tokyo, "This is no place for me."[45] This is also a sentiment Murakami attributes to Fitzgerald and Chandler in relation to their chosen cities. He explains, "What connects the authors Fitzgerald and Chandler is the love-hate relationship they had with their respective cities—New York and Los Angeles—from start to finish. Even though they wrote many works set in these cities, in their real lives, they never once felt these were places for them."[46] What Murakami sees as true for Fitzgerald and Chandler in respect to New York and Los Angeles is arguably also true of his relationship with Tokyo.

Murakami's love of Fitzgerald is also well documented. He has described Fitzgerald as "a writer for me," as nothing less than "my teacher, my university, my literary companion."[47] He cannot remember the title of the first Fitzgerald story he read when he was sixteen, but he does remember reading *The Great Gatsby* two years later. In his first book of Fitzgerald translations, *Mai rosuto shitii* (My Lost City), Murakami dates the beginning of his infatuation with Fitzgerald to when he was nineteen, explaining that it began with a reading of *Tender Is the Night*. As with earlier experiences reading Fitzgerald, he explains that his first impression of the novel was not particularly strong, but that several months later he found himself drawn to it again, this time devouring it quickly and with renewed interest. He was finally hooked. Murakami would quickly work his way through the rest of Fitzgerald's novels and then through the short stories. He claims to have read the short stories "Winter Dreams" and "Babylon Revisited" at least twenty times each, analyzing them in great detail to understand where their deep appeal for him came from.[48] Murakami believes there are some writers whose greatness grabs us from the first line we read, while others take more time for us to appreciate.[49] For Murakami, Fitzgerald was an author of the second variety, though once his greatness finally registered, it never left him.

Yet despite Murakami's deep regard for Fitzgerald, when it comes to the question of direct literary influence, he remains guarded. For him, the answer as to whether Fitzgerald has influenced his fiction is yes and no: "In terms of style, theme, structure, and storytelling, I feel like the influence is close to zero. If he's given me anything, it's something bigger and vaguer. You might say it's the stance that someone should take towards the novel (whether as a writer or a reader). It's an awareness that in the end, the novel is life itself."[50] I will return later to the question of how Fitzgerald's philosophy of the novel has influenced Murakami. First, however, I would like to explore Murakami's first claim about the lack of direct literary influence from Fitzgerald. As I will argue in what follows, this is clearly an overstatement.

The dominant paradigm in Murakami studies for understanding his evolution as a writer was first introduced into the field by Murakami himself, who has divided the stages of his career in this way: "First there was the detached and aphoristic quality, then the telling of a story, and eventually I realized that that wasn't enough either. I haven't fully worked it out in my mind, but I think that's probably when I began to realize the importance of commitment. Commitment, I think, is all about relationships between people."[51]

Critics argue over whether Murakami has found the commitment he is looking for, but the basic trajectory is generally accepted, with 1995 seen as the major turning point. Here, though, I would like to focus on an underappreciated aspect of Murakami's aforementioned formulation—his emphasis on his early fiction as aphoristic—a trait which connects his fiction with Fitzgerald's. Finding such aphorisms in these early works is not difficult to do; indeed, as already pointed out, his debut novel opens with one about how neither perfect writing nor perfect despair exists. As explained, *Boku* finds consolation in this idea, but not a perfect escape from despair, with his ability to express himself simply being too limited. Fortunately, he soon finds another aphorism that helps him through this: "If one operates on the principle that everything can be a learning experience, then of course aging needn't be so painful."[52] *Boku* has survived so far by taking this advice to heart, though things have not always been easy. He has been "cheated and misunderstood, used and abused, time and again."[53] Now he has come to the final year of his twenties, and he is ready to tell his story. Aphorisms, it would seem, have helped him get to where he is today; writing, it is hoped, will help him to get to where he needs to be tomorrow.

The opening of *Wind* has similarities with the opening of Fitzgerald's *The Great Gatsby*, which has its own aphoristic quality. Nick Carraway, the narrator of Fitzgerald's novel, likewise opens his narrative with an aphorism: "Whenever you feel like criticizing anyone . . . just remember that all the people in this world haven't had the advantages that you've had." This is advice Nick received, not from a writer, but from his father, and it is something he has tried to live by, resulting in a tendency to "reserve all judgements."[54] Yet, with time, as with *Boku*, he has come to see the limits of this aphorism as a formula for living: "And, after boasting this way of my tolerance, I come to the admission that it has its limit. Conduct may be founded on the hard rock or the wet marshes, but after a certain point I don't care what it's founded on."[55] For a young person, the right aphorism can seem to promise the secret to life, the winning formula by which all life's victories might be won. *Boku* and Nick have both reached a stage where the vicissitudes of life have shown them that, in the end, no single aphorism is ever up to the job. Real life is simply messier than that.

This realization is what lies behind Fitzgerald's famous definition of intelligence: "[T]he test of a first-rate intelligence is the ability to hold two opposed ideas in the mind at the same time, and still retain the ability to function."[56] Life is full of contradictions and paradoxes, and so no single aphorism ever works all the time. Instead, one must learn to sometimes hold competing ideas together simultaneously. Fitzgerald's famous quote appears in *Wind*, in a scene where *Boku* is talking to Rat at J's Bar.[57] Rat has recently developed literary ambitions, and as he sits at the bar with *Boku*, he is running through a list of famous quotations. He offers the aforementioned Fitzgerald quote about intelligence, but he cannot remember who said it or where it comes from, and neither can *Boku*. The answer to Rat's question is that the quote comes from the first essay in the collection of essays Fitzgerald originally wrote for *Esquire* magazine entitled "The Crack-Up."

Murakami is a fan of "The Crack-Up" essays, explaining their background to Japanese readers in an essay. He notes how 1935 was a "sterile season" for Fitzgerald, who produced little work and faced many personal problems, but that even so, this sterile season brought literary fruit in the series of essays that appeared the following year. Murakami senses in them an indication of Fitzgerald's underlying resilience:

> [T]he essays move us greatly. We can sense a sympathy-evoking sound there, as if in writing them he was carving them from his own flesh. Moreover, the style is firmly noble and each word that he picked is filled with a fine sadness. There is no longer the unmanly sound of a drunkard's self-pity there, nor is there any dramatic, immature philosophy. What is there are the pathetic, earnest eyes of a man who takes seriously the essential sadness and sorrow that the act of living involves and tries to live rightly with a positive view of life.[58]

Murakami is clearly moved by the essays and particularly by this last idea of living "rightly with a positive view of life" despite its "essential sadness and sorrow." This is perhaps why the influence of the essay shows up so clearly in *Wind*.

"The Crack-Up" opens with this line: "Of course all life is a process of breaking down."[59] Fitzgerald then goes on to explain how increasingly serious cracks have begun appearing in his life of late, noting that it has taken him some time to recognize their true severity. As with his quotation about "a first-rate intelligence," he has found that the answer has come in learning how to live with competing ideas: "I must hold in balance the sense of the futility of effort and the sense of the necessity to struggle; the conviction of the inevitability of failure and still the determination to succeed."[60] Yet, over time, this has become increasingly difficult to do. He continues:

For seventeen years, with a year of deliberate loafing and resting out in the center—things went on like that, with a new chore only a nice prospect for a new day. I was living hard, too, but: "Up to forty-nine it'll be alright," I said. "I can count on that. For a man who's lived as long as I have, that's all you could ask."

. . . And then, ten years this side of forty-nine, I suddenly realized that I had prematurely cracked.[61]

This reminds us of *Boku*, who has struggled, not for seventeen years, but for fifteen, and who has reached, not the final year of his thirties, but the final year of his twenties.[62] Perhaps *Boku* has not yet cracked, but something in him has given. Like Fitzgerald, his aphorisms for living are no longer up to the job.

There are other similarities between *Boku* and the Fitzgerald of "The Crack-Up" essays. At times, they both briefly entertain strategies for dealing with their losses that end up being less than satisfactory. Fitzgerald, for example, tells of a woman who came to him, offering him a way out of his malaise:

Listen! The world only exists in your eyes—your conception of it. You can make it as big or as small as you want it. And you're trying to be a little puny individual. By God, if I ever cracked, I'd try and make the world crack with me. Listen! The world only exists through your apprehension of it, and so it's much better to say that it's not you that's cracked—it's the Grand Canyon.[63]

Murakami's narrator puts a similar sentiment this way:

Ascribing meaning to life is a piece of cake compared to actually living it.

I was in my teens, I think, when I discovered this, and it so completely blew my mind that I couldn't talk for a week. If I could just keep my wits about me, I felt, I could force the world to conform to my will, overturning whole systems of values, and altering the flow of time.

Sadly for me, it took ages to see that this was a trap.[64]

There are also places later in *Wind* where the influence of "The Crack-Up" essay again shows through. The chapter in which *Boku* and *Rat* finally have their heart-to-heart, for example, includes Rat quoting this passage from the New Testament: "Ye are the salt of the earth. But if the salt has lost its savor, wherewith shall it be salted?"[65] This feels like a random cultural reference for two drinking buddies in 1970s Japan to be sharing, but it is not so strange if we realize that the reference is probably not so much to the Bible itself as to Fitzgerald's essays, the first of which ends with this same New Testament passage.[66]

Murakami published his translation of "The Crack-Up" in 2019. In his brief introduction to the translation, he notes his affection for the essays, explaining that "from a long time ago, I have read them many times over." He had long had the ambition to translate the essays, but much like his translation of *The Great Gatsby*, he felt that he should wait until he was older and had a little more experience before attempting the project. He then goes on to admit the very specific influence the essays have had on his writing, noting:

Of course, I love Fitzgerald's novels, but if you ask whether I have taken any specific technical influence from them, the answer is not really—even if the same cannot be said for their psychological influence. In terms of the essays, however, I may have received some specific influence. When I'm writing a long essay, I always keep "The Crack-Up" essays and "My Lost City" in the back of my mind.[67]

The influence of "The Crack-Up" essays, as I have been arguing here, is not limited to Murakami's essays, but is found directly in his debut novel. Though Murakami's first collection of Fitzgerald short stories (indeed, his first-ever published translation; the collection also including the essay "My Lost City," mentioned by Murakami earlier) postdates the publication of *Wind*, he actually started translating Fitzgerald as a hobby well before he ever published his first novel.[68] It is thus possible that he tried translating "The Crack-Up" essays into Japanese much earlier and liked what he saw so much that he used it for inspiration in writing the opening chapter of *Wind*. Whether this is exactly how things went or not, the influence of the essays in *Wind* is clear.

Returning to the opening of *Wind* and its echo with *The Great Gatsby*, it is interesting to note that Murakami substitutes the setup of Nick receiving advice from his "father" with *Boku* receiving advice from "a writer," a change which feels significant. At a time of life when Murakami had lost the influence of his father, he was turning to authors, Fitzgerald chief among them, as new guiding lights. Indeed, Murakami refers to the authors he translates as his "teachers and advisors."[69] It is interesting to note in this regard, the context in which Murakami first spoke to Murakami Ryū about his father's philosophy of suppressing hunger (or ambition), a conversation I referenced in the introduction to this book. The segue into this part of their conversation came from Ryū's praise for a recent newspaper article Haruki had written on Fitzgerald for the Asahi Newspaper, where Murakami had described himself as a young boy who grew up never knowing hunger. In the article, Murakami describes first reading Fitzgerald at sixteen, but returning to him again when he was twenty-two (the same age he got married, but different from the age he gives in his first published translation of Murakami stories mentioned earlier, which was nineteen) with renewed focus and interest. For the next seven years (i.e., right up until he debuted as a writer), he found himself hungrily devouring Fitzgerald, explaining that at the time what he was doing was reconstructing his values and morality from zero. At the end of these seven years, Murakami found himself ready to write, describing the entire process as a kind of self-therapy or self-transformation.[70]

In this way, in his conversation with Ryū, Murakami explicitly juxtaposes Fitzgerald and his father, suggesting that the hunger his father tried to suppress in him was awakened by Fitzgerald. As with Murakami's father, Fitzgerald had his own lucky break with war, the First World War ending before he had a chance to fight, though he appears to have been disappointed by this timing. Rather than suffering from survivor's guilt though, Fitzgerald had the opposite reaction, recreating himself as a symbol of the exuberant jazz age. Part of Murakami's response to Fitzgerald might be explained by this very different reaction to the aftermath of war. While his father taught him to suppress ambition and to accept the status quo, Fitzgerald encouraged him to go out into the world and make his mark.

What Murakami also seems to have taken from Fitzgerald is a view of the novel and of writing as a life-sustaining force that can save one from forces of personal destruction. This is what he means when he says earlier that Fitzgerald taught him that the "novel is life itself." The critic Toshifumi Miyawaki, who has written extensively on the question of Fitzgerald's influence on Murakami, agrees with this point. Miyawaki explains, "To survive tragedy and adversity by writing was Fitzgerald's main occupation. The protagonists of Murakami's works also keep surviving despite whatever they have to face in the world around them."[71] In supporting this general argument, Miyawaki quotes Murakami, who writes:

> [Fitzgerald] always believed in writing no matter how deep his despair was, and it served as a talisman for him to the end of his life. He clung to the brilliance of the writing to the last moment of his life, no matter how unmanly he was said to be. He always believed that he could be redeemed someday as long as he kept writing. Hemingway, who looked like a winner, gave up his hope of ever writing again and killed himself after all. But Fitzgerald didn't.[72]

For Murakami, the stereotype of Fitzgerald as a self-destructive alcoholic belies a hidden inner strength. This is what he seems to mean when he says that Fitzgerald taught him that the "novel is life itself," and Miyawaki is undoubtedly right to suggest that this is probably the most important thing Murakami took from him. But I do not think we need to take Murakami at his word when he says that this is perhaps the only thing he took from him, that Fitzgerald had little influence on his "style, theme, structure, and storytelling." This is clearly an overstatement.

The most obvious place one sees Fitzgerald's influence on Murakami's writing is in the first-person narrative voice he favors, a point Murakami acknowledges:

> The main task of my protagonist is to observe the things happening around him. He sees what he must see, or he is supposed to see, in actual time. If I may say so, he resembles Nick Carraway in *The Great Gatsby*. He is neutral, and in order to maintain his neutrality, he must be free from any kinship, any connection to a vertical family system.[73]

Murakami has even said that his early novels might be thought of as a reimagining of Nick Carraway's life without Gatsby, but even this is not going far enough.[74] If Murakami's protagonists have Nick-like qualities, they also have their Gatsby-like counterparts. Male-male friendships, and eventually rivalries, are a central element of Murakami's fiction with deep Fitzgeraldian roots, and this starts with the relationship between *Boku* and Rat.

Boku, it should be noted, shows no awareness of any literary influence from Fitzgerald. Instead, he claims to have learned almost everything he knows about writing from one Derek Hartfield, a lesser-known contemporary of Fitzgerald and Hemingway who knew how to use "words as weapons," but whose writing and life ultimately turned out to be "sterile."[75] Hartfield ended his life in 1938 by jumping from the Empire State Building, a portrait of Hitler in his right hand and an open umbrella in his left. *Boku*'s own literary mentor, it would appear, was no Fitzgerald—he was not able to hold onto writing as a talisman until the end of his life. The conceit here, of course, is that no such writer ever existed; Murakami made him up.[76]

In the end, Hartfield is a red herring. He is the exact opposite of the kind of writers Murakami admires, those who, while they perhaps share Hartfield's self-destructive tendencies, are nevertheless able to continue using "words as weapons" until the end and whose lives and writing turn out to be far from "sterile." For Murakami, this is Fitzgerald first and foremost, but also Raymond Chandler, and it is here that the literary origins of *Boku* and Rat start to become clearer. If *Boku* is most clearly modeled on Fitzgerald's Nick Carraway (together with echoes of Fitzgerald in "The Crack-Up" essays), then Rat is most clearly modeled on Chandler's Terry Lennox, a character that Murakami believes, in turn, was modeled on Fitzgerald's Gatsby.

Murakami notes that while Hemingway is often said to have had the strongest influence on Chandler's style (something he agrees is plain to see), for him personally, looking at the question of influence more broadly and psychologically, it is Fitzgerald who had the deeper influence. What they share, he argues, is an unspoken, unseen awareness of what he describes as the "undertow of destruction."[77] In other words, they both shared self-destructive tendencies which they held at bay through writing. Looking at the characters they created, Murakami observes:

> If there is someone or something they are supposed to be fighting against, it is the weakness inside themselves, the limit which has been set for them. This fight on the whole is silent. The weapons they carry are their aesthetics, their standards, and their morality. In many cases, while they know the fight is one they will inevitably lose, they nevertheless straighten their backbone, avoid excuses, and offer no self-praise, but simply keep their mouths shut tight while passing through purgatory. In the end, the issue of winning or losing is of little importance.[78]

Murakami offers Roger Wade from *The Long Goodbye* as one example of a character who faces this self-destructive pull in Chandler's fiction, quoting a conversation he has with the private detective, Philip Marlowe: "Drunks don't educate, my friend. They disintegrate. And part of the process is a lot of fun.... And part of it is damned awful."[79] Murakami argues that Wade's notion of disintegration here is the same as Fitzgerald's idea of cracking up. Characters like Wade, he argues, are "floating along a river in a boat without oars, drifting towards a giant waterfall of destruction."[80] While they continue to fight the good fight, in many ways the morality that should sustain them has already been lost. What barely remains to keep them afloat are the traces of their own aesthetics and personal standards.[81]

Terry Lennox, also from *The Long Goodbye*, is one of the most important examples of such a character in Chandler's fiction. Marlowe finds himself getting involved in Lennox's life despite himself, explaining, "there was something about the guy that got to me."[82] Lennox, like Gatsby, is a man wrapped up in money, mystery, and criminal connections, yet Marlowe, like Nick, tries to remain a neutral observer: "I didn't judge him or analyze him."[83] Yet over time this becomes increasingly difficult to do, a dynamic

Murakami pays particular attention to and which is essential for understanding the way he has channeled Fitzgerald and Chandler into his work. Murakami explains:

> As most readers who have read both *The Long Goodbye* and *The Great Gatsby* will understand, in the same way that Nick Carraway slowly and intuitively begins to harbor complex thoughts of antagonism toward and even entrapment with Gatsby—feelings so deep that even he cannot fully fathom them—the same can be seen in the relationship between Marlowe and Terry Lennox, the slow and subtle emerging of which is the main point of the story. And in both cases, this is something that was not actively sought out. Without looking for it, the protagonists (narrators), through an accumulation of coincidences, are fatefully caught up in all of this regardless of how they feel. So why do they end up here? It goes without saying that they (the narrators) see in their counterpart (Gatsby and Terry Lennox) their alter ego. It is like they are looking at themselves in a slightly warped mirror. In it, they see a distorted identity, intense hatred, and irresistible yearning.[84]

Terry Lennox, like Rat, is a man who, while he inherited money, is highly critical of the rich. The source of his wealth is his marriage to Sylvia Potter, the daughter of Harlan Potter, a rich and powerful businessman. Terry is drunk when Marlowe first meets him, yet despite his better judgment, he helps him to get home. Later, Terry comes to him needing a favor. Marlowe helps him to escape to Mexico before learning that his wife Sylvia has been brutally murdered. Even after discovering this, though, Marlowe continues to protect Terry at great personal cost. The question is where this unearned loyalty comes from. What is Marlowe responding to in Lennox?

The key to understanding this question, according to Sarah Trott, is to note Terry's background as a war veteran, a fact that is repeatedly highlighted in the novel by the scars on his face and it is implied by his white hair (which it is suggested resulted from a traumatic wartime experience). Lennox is a war hero, having saved the lives of two other soldiers when a mortar shell was thrown into their foxhole, but this is also the main source of the scars he now carries, both physical and psychological. This, Trott argues, is an important part of why Marlowe responds to him; for while it is never explicitly stated in the text, she argues that, putting together several clues from Chandler's Marlowe works, it is possible to deduce that Marlowe is a war veteran too. In short, Trott argues, Marlowe copes with his wartime trauma by adopting the hard-boiled attitude he is famous for, but Terry offers him an opportunity to explore a dissociated part of himself: the traumatized war veteran. In other words, Marlowe, by trying to help Terry, is indirectly trying to help himself.

Chandler was a war veteran and, in fact, was the sole survivor of a German attack that seems to have left him struggling with his own form of post-traumatic stress disorder and survivor's guilt.[85] He is also known as a writer who would sometimes put parts of himself into his characters. Trott argues, for example, that Marlowe might be taken as a more idealized version of Chandler:

> Marlowe became everything Chandler would like to have been, but he instinctively retains the trauma that was imprinted onto him by his creator; the detective

embodies the thousands of men who went to war expecting to find glory, but instead returned frustrated and traumatized by their experiences. Marlowe became the prism through which we can view the trauma which tormented Chandler.[86]

Chandler's good friend, Natasha Spender, noted the way Chandler wrote himself into *The Long Goodbye*, noting that, "All three characters were drinkers, like Raymond himself, two of them disintegrating and despairing.... As with aspects of Raymond's own character, their dominance veered with his mood. Roger Wade his 'bad self,' Philip Marlowe his 'good self' and Terry Lennox his anxious one."[87] Consequently, *The Long Goodbye* might be described as a therapeutic novel. Trott argues that it can be read as "Chandler's attempt to rid himself of the psychological symptoms of his own combat stress."[88]

Could this explain why Murakami was so attracted to *The Long Goodbye* and why he felt the need to rewrite the Marlowe/Lennox relationship in a new form? Could his sensitivity to the issues of post-traumatic stress disorder, survivor's guilt, and alcoholism observed in his father, together with his own sense of survivor's guilt from the 1960s and early 1970s, have alerted him to the therapeutic motifs hiding in Chandler's novel and inspired him to write something similar? I believe this is the case, the nods Murakami is making to Chandler in his early novels being quite clear. J's Bar, for example, can be seen as a substitute for Victor's, the bar Marlowe and Lennox often drink at near the start of *The Long Goodbye*. Their drink of choice, gimlets, shows up in *Wind* in a scene where *Boku* meets a divorcee at J's Bar, which is likely a nod to a scene in *The Long Goodbye* where Linda Loring, Sylvia's sister, shows up at Victor's and drinks gimlets with Marlowe. Rat and Lennox's similar response to their unearned wealth has already been mentioned, but even more essential is the narrative structure Murakami is borrowing—the initial meeting between Marlowe and Lennox (involving intoxication), their long separation, and their final reunion. If *Wind* represents the first part of this three-part structure, the remaining two novels of the Rat trilogy are there to complete it. Even the original title of Murakami's debut novel when it was submitted for the Gunzō Prize, *Happy Birthday and White Christmas* (an English title which still appears on the cover of some Japanese versions of the book) likely owes something to *The Long Goodbye*. In *Wind*, this is an expression Rat always writes on the first page of the novels he later sends to *Boku* each year, *Boku*'s birthday falling on December 24. In *A Wild Sheep Chase*, there is also a scene where he encloses a check for 100,000 yen in a letter to *Boku*, intended to pay the expenses for a job he has asked him to do.[89] In *The Long Goodbye*, Lennox writes a note to Marlowe early on after he helps him out, and sends it together with a cashier's check for one hundred dollars: "He thanked me, wished me a Merry Christmas and all kinds of luck and said he hoped to see me again soon."[90] Following such hints, it is not hard to see how the relationship between *Boku* and Rat is indebted to the relationship between Marlowe and Lennox, which, in turn, is indebted to the relationship between Carraway and Gatsby.

Thus, in the same way that Nick Carraway and Jay Gatsby might be seen as reflecting two different sides of Fitzgerald, and Philip Marlowe and Terry Lennox two different sides of Chandler, *Boku* and Rat might be seen as reflecting two different sides of Murakami, a split that occurred as he tried to leave behind the traumas of his past and make a new life for himself in Tokyo. Part of what writing as self-therapy means in this case is trying to put these two "selves" back together again in some way. As he put it in one interview, Murakami feels like he has another self within him, and he suggests that he writes to reveal the relationship between these two selves.[91] This other self, it should be clear by now, is connected to his past and his hometown and the things he lost in the transition from childhood to adulthood. This was the part of himself he had to leave behind in Ashiya to make it in Tokyo (and eventually on the world stage).

Of course, just because Murakami had this personal motive for starting to write, it does not mean that the fiction itself was guaranteed to be any good. In this regard, the models of Fitzgerald and Chandler were important in showing him how to transform his therapeutic motive into compelling literary fiction. What Fitzgerald and Chandler modeled for him was how to diffuse psychological tensions into different characters, how to create compelling first-person narrators who can carry the story with their unique observations and wit, and how these stories can be given greater psychological depth by including a mysterious and significant alter ego (or egos) who in some sense carries a part of the protagonist's shadow. This becomes even clearer in *Sheep Chase*, the final novel of the Rat trilogy. Before looking at this novel, however, I will first look at how themes of mourning and melancholia begin to take prominence in *Pinball*.

Mourning and Melancholia in *Pinball, 1973*

To this point, I have been writing about the first therapeutic thread (the journey from melancholia to mourning) in Murakami's fiction in general terms, and I have assumed that most readers will have an intuitive sense of what it means. In this section, I will first expand on the differences between melancholia and mourning as defined by Sigmund Freud in his 1917 paper, "Mourning and Melancholia." The ideas in this paper, I will argue, offer a useful framework for understanding what *Boku* appears to be going through in *Pinball*, and, indeed, what many of Murakami's early narrators seem to be experiencing. A basic starting point here is to understand that mourning is described by Freud as a more conscious process, and melancholia as a more unconscious one.

"Mourning," Freud writes, "is regularly the reaction to the loss of a loved person, or to the loss of some abstraction which has taken the place of one, such as one's country, liberty, an ideal, and so on."[92] When someone or something close to you dies, Freud describes a tug-of-war that goes on between your heart and mind. What he calls "reality-testing" confirms to you time and again that the person or thing you loved is now gone, but another part of you remains determined to hold on, or as Freud puts it, "people never willingly abandon a libidinal position."[93] Mourning is the long and painful process of withdrawing libidinal attachments from one lost object to eventually reinvest in someone or something new. At the end of this, the ego becomes "free and uninhibited again."[94]

There are cases, Freud argues, however, where "the patient cannot consciously perceive what [they have] lost."[95] Yes, they know the person or thing they loved is now gone, but in some deeper sense, they do not yet know what this means for them. As

Freud puts it, the melancholic "knows *whom* he has lost but not *what* he has lost in him."[96] He concludes that "melancholia is in some way related to an object-loss which is withdrawn from consciousness."[97] While a less intuitive concept than Freud's notion of mourning, this is a good description of what *Boku* seems to be going through in *Pinball*. As Freud suggests, he knows *whom* he has lost—his French-studying university girlfriend who committed suicide—and in *Pinball* he even tells us her name: Naoko. What he does not yet seem to understand is *what* her death means for him. He spends much of his time in the novel in what might be described as a melancholic state, though not before making one last attempt at mourning.

Early in the novel, *Boku* recounts a trip he made to the train station close to where Naoko used to live, a pilgrimage orchestrated to try and bring about a sense of closure. He recalls Naoko's detailed description of the place and holds onto one detail in particular, her recollection of a dog that would constantly walk from one end of the train platform to the other. He is thus disappointed when he arrives at the station and the dog is not there. Without this dog, his pilgrimage feels incomplete, and so he waits to see what will happen. Eventually, a random dog shows up and *Boku* entices it onto the train platform with a stick of chewing gum to play its assigned role. He describes his internal monologue on the way home as follows: "It's all over, I kept telling myself on the train. You can forget her now. That's why you made this trip. But I couldn't forget. That I loved Naoko. That she was dead and gone. That not a single damn thing was over and done with."[98]

Boku has consciously tried to facilitate his mourning for Naoko, but in the end, he realizes it is still incomplete. Nothing is over. And yet life goes on, and so, too, must he. *Wind* was set from August 8 to August 26, 1970. *Pinball* is set from September to November 1973. In *Wind*, *Boku* was a biology major returning home for the summer vacation, but by the time we meet him again in *Pinball*, he has become a professional translator. Animals often represent a connection to the unconscious in Murakami's fiction, so his new career suggests a distancing from these forces, something which has been necessary for a time. His lunchtime visits to the local pet store to play with cats, though, suggest that he is still longing for something deeper.

If melancholia, as Freud suggests, is an unconscious condition, then its solutions must also derive from the unconscious, and this is exactly the case in *Pinball*. Similar to *Wind*, there is a sense that *Boku* is not actively seeking out therapy but waiting for it to come to him. He describes himself as often feeling "out of whack," something he describes as like trying to put together two different jigsaw puzzles at the same time.[99] His solution is normally to drink and go to bed, though he finds that in the morning things are only ever worse. On one of these occasions, though, he awakens to find twin girls in his bed. He does not seem particularly curious about where they came from, but simply welcomes them into his life.

The role of the twins is to gently lead *Boku* out of melancholia and into mourning again. They do this initially by encouraging him to hold a funeral for a telephone switch panel left behind by a repairman. As seen in *Wind*, phones are often a symbol in Murakami's fiction for connections with the unconscious, and so a funeral for a discarded switch panel—which the repairman describes as a mother dog connected to lots of little puppies—can be seen as an attempt to mourn a dead (i.e., melancholic) connection. The repairman's metaphor of the dog reminds us of the dog from Naoko's story, further strengthening the message that, in the end, this is all about her.

Before we get to the switch panel funeral scene, though, *Boku* offers us a recollection of the dormitory he once lived in and its single telephone: "Telephone switch panels were the last thing on our mind."[100] He describes the messages that would come to them, both through the telephone and through other mediums, too, like telegrams: "We were prone to so many disasters—lives lost to suicide, minds wrecked, hearts marooned in the backwaters of time, bodies burning with pointless obsessions."[101] Thinking back on this time in his life, *Boku* recalls:

> The phone calls made me think. Someone was trying to get through to someone else. Yet almost no one ever called me. Not a single person was trying to reach me, and even if they had been, they wouldn't have said what I wanted to hear. Each of us had, to a greater or lesser degree, resolved to live according to his or her own system. If another person's way of thinking was too different from mine, it made me mad; too close, and I got sad. That's all there was to it.[102]

Here is an expression of *Boku*'s famous detachment, his determination not to get too close to other people. And yet one also senses in this passage his desire for connection, a hope that someday, somebody, somewhere will call him and tell him what he needs to hear.

Traveling to a reservoir with the twins, *Boku* holds his funeral for the switch panel, offering these words from Kant as part of his eulogy: "The obligation of philosophy is to dispel all illusions borne of misunderstanding."[103] He then throws the switch panel into the water. Looking out over the reservoir, one of the twins asks, "How deep is it?" *Boku*'s answer is "Really, really deep."[104] For *Boku*, of course, this is not the end. There are still illusions in his life that need to be dispelled, still depths that need to be explored. Being the melancholic that he is, *Boku* does not even seem to realize what is about to come—a call from the unconscious. This time it will take the form of a pinball machine.

At first glance, the twins are suggestive of the woman with the missing finger from *Wind*, who at one point tells *Boku* that she has a younger twin sister who lives 30,000 light-years away. This woman disappeared from *Boku*'s life, and the twins are the new replacement, the new anima-guides that will continue directing him in his search for self-therapy. Yet, as the narrative unfolds, they also begin to offer reminders of Rat. Making suggestions for names they might be called, the twins put forward such opposites as right and left, vertical and horizontal, up and down, front and back, and east and west. *Boku* adds his own suggestion: entrance and exit. This supposedly random contribution releases this chain of thought: "Where there is an entrance, there is usually an exit. That's the way things are made. Mailboxes, vacuum cleaners, zoos, salt shakers. Of course there are exceptions. Mousetraps for instance."[105]

Nezumi in Japanese can mean either rat or mouse, so a mousetrap (*nezumitori*) clearly has associations with Rat, whose own story is alternating with *Boku*'s in *Pinball*. Like the allusion here suggests, there is a strong feeling in the novel that Rat is trapped, looking for an exit that may not exist. He is still in *Boku*'s hometown with the Chinese bartender J, but life is not moving forward for him: "It appeared as though time had stopped for the Rat, as if all of a sudden its flow had been severed."[106] In a clear nod to Gatsby, Rat spends much of his time staring out at an "unmanned beacon" that "sat alone at the end of a long, meandering pier."[107] A woman he is involved with lives near this pier, the flashing orange light of the beacon compared to a beating heart.[108] He is like Gatsby staring out at the green light, except that, unlike Gatsby, he will eventually give up on the woman he loves and leave town.

Boku is clear to point out that the story he is telling is just as much Rat's as it is his own.[109] And yet they never interact in the novel, since they are now living miles apart. In what sense, then, does this story belong to them both? Returning to Freud's ideas about melancholia, we find him explaining another key difference he sees with mourning: a deep self-hatred that arises in the melancholic that can potentially lead to suicide. Freud writes:

> The melancholic displays something else besides which is lacking in mourning—an extraordinary diminution in his self-regard, an impoverishment of his ego on a grand scale.... This picture of a delusion of (mainly moral) inferiority is completed by sleeplessness and refusal to take nourishment, and—what is psychologically very remarkable—by an overcoming of the instinct which compels every living thing to cling to life.[110]

This, admittedly, does not sound much like *Boku*, whose own melancholia, while perhaps inhibiting his happiness, does not feel self-destructive. So perhaps he is not a Freudian melancholic after all. Or is there another explanation?

"American modernism," Seth Moglen writes, "is famously a literature of loss.... By 1926, Gertrude Stein could tell Ernest Hemingway 'you are all a lost generation'—and he could, with a peculiar pride, attach it as an epigraph to his first major novel."[111] While acknowledging that the First World War was partly responsible for this sense of loss, Moglen believes that rapid economic transformation was the main culprit and that from the burden this socioeconomic shift produced arose a distinct form of American melancholic modernism in literature. Citing Freud, Moglen notes examples of the kind of melancholic self-hatred this situation produced in some writers, offering Hemingway as a prominent example. Fitzgerald, on the other hand, Moglen sees employing "strategies of splitting and displacement" as ways of minimizing this self-destructive impulse.[112]

"Strategies of splitting and displacement," of course, are also at the heart of Murakami's melancholic response to 1960s Japan and this explains his characters' Fitzgeraldian-like immunity to self-destructive impulses. In particular, it is the split between *Boku* and Rat that allows *Boku* to keep moving forward, to remain engaged in his therapeutic journey without "cracking up." This is why, while *Pinball* is a story about his life in Tokyo, it is also a story about Rat's life in (we might assume) Ashiya. It is only because *Boku* has placed this distance between himself and his old "friend" that he is able to carry on.

This split may reflect something Murakami discovered in the early stages of his writing process. Murakami has said that he started writing his debut novel in a realistic style but was dissatisfied with the result. He had an idea of what a literary novel should look like, but when he tried to write one, he did not like it.[113] To develop a new style, he then went back and wrote the first twenty to thirty pages of his novel again in English on a typewriter and then rewrote this English text back into Japanese.[114] Murakami suggests that "transplant" is a better word than "translate" for what he did, for he was not literally translating every English word back into Japanese.[115] Instead, while keeping the same basic meaning of the text, he took the simple, less ornate style his English version had necessitated and turned it into something with a similar feel in Japanese. Murakami notes how some people say his work has the feel of a translation in Japanese and he admits that there may be a kernel of truth to this. The payoff for this process was that he could create a literary rhythm and style distinctly his own.

There is a suggestion in this account that for Murakami to write something he was satisfied with, he first had to kill off another version of his writerly self. *Wind* has two writers—*Boku*, who is telling the story, and Rat, who is sending *Boku* a novel each year—and so it is interesting to consider whether Rat might in some way represent this other writerly self that eventually had to be killed off. This is an idea Shimizu Yoshinori has pursued. Like me, he sees Rat as a shadow-like character who is still underdeveloped in the true Jungian sense.[116] He also sees him as a part of *Boku* that was "abandoned because of despair, even 'another writer' in himself that had to be killed off."[117]

Returning to *Pinball*, we can see that *Boku*'s growing separation from Rat has been important for him to move forward. With his split from his alter ego or shadow to protect him, *Boku* is now free to answer the call of his unconscious, to begin moving from melancholia back into mourning, without the self-destructive tendencies that Freudian melancholia entails. He describes the way this call comes as follows:

> On any given day, something can come along and steal our hearts. It may be any old thing: a rosebud, a lost cap, a favorite sweater from childhood, an old Gene Pitney record. A miscellany of trivia with no home to call their own. Lingering for two or three days, that something soon disappears, returning to the darkness. There are wells, deep wells, dug in our hearts. Birds fly over them.
>
> —What grabbed me that Sunday evening in October was pinball.[118]

The reference to pinball here first reminds us of Rat. In *Wind*, there is a pinball machine at J's Bar that *Boku* and Rat play, *Boku* describing it as "a piece of junk that offers dead time in return for small change."[119] In *Pinball* though, the call of the pinball machine is connected to Naoko and the climax of the novel comes in a scene where *Boku* enters an old chicken warehouse that now stores old pinball machines, and through one machine in particular, converses with (we assume) her. This is the most therapeutic moment in Murakami's fiction to this point. *Boku* has finally broken through his melancholia to reconnect with the object of his loss once more.

So what is this cold world of the chicken warehouse *Boku* enters? Is this a supernatural or psychological space? In other words, at the end of *Pinball*, has *Boku* entered the realm of the dead to talk to his long-lost girlfriend, or is he simply talking to himself? This is the first example of a question that runs throughout Murakami's fiction, and the answer is probably a little of both, Murakami's stretchy concept of the *monogatari* allowing him to get away with this. As this is a problem that will come up repeatedly in Murakami's fiction, it is useful to quote Matthew Strecher at length here, who does a good job of delineating the different things that Murakami's "other worlds" can be.

> I have generally preferred terms such as metaphysical realm and other world, but many Japanese critics opt for the even less specific achiragawa, or "over there." Part of our challenge lies in the fact that this achiragawa is many things at once: a metaphysical zone, freed from the constraints of time and space; a wormhole, or conduit into other physical worlds; an unconscious shared space, similar to Jung's collective unconscious; a repository for memories, dreams, and visions; the land of the dead; the "world soul" of mysticism; heaven or hell; eternity. With respect to Murakami's fictional landscape, it is most effective to imagine this realm alternately as psychological or spiritual, though at times these clearly overlap. This is because the characteristics that mark the unconscious as envisioned by psychoanalysis, for instance, are frequently similar or identical to those that mark traditional visions of the underworld, of the mystical "world soul," and the spirit world. As we shall see, most of Murakami's stories shift back and forth between these two conceptualizations of "over there."[120]

Given my focus in this study, I tend to emphasize the psychological implications of these encounters with the world "over there," but it is important to note that in terms of the stories themselves, this is usually not an either/or choice. Instead, the stories offer us what might be thought of as metaphysical, supernatural, or magic realist events, which at the same time are clearly intended as psychological metaphors (sometimes explicitly so).

Boku's therapeutic relationship with the three-flipper Spaceship, the pinball machine that calls to him in the novel, goes back to 1970 and the immediate aftermath of the death of Naoko, a time in his life that felt like "living at the bottom of a dark hole."[121] One thing that helped him during this time was "conversing" with this pinball machine, "her" central message to him one of forgiveness: "It's not your fault, she said to me. . . . Not your fault at all. You did what you could."[122] Her final message is the same one he tries to offer himself when returning from his pilgrimage to Naoko's train station: "It is over . . . [o]ver and done with."[123]

This earlier conversation between *Boku* and the pinball machine feels more psychological than supernatural; it seems clear that he is talking to himself through the pinball machine, telling himself that he did all he could. His final conversation with the three-flipper Spaceship at the end of the novel, on the other hand, feels different. "Why did you come?" the pinball machine asks him. "I heard you call" is *Boku*'s simple response.[124] In this final meeting, it is less anything the three-flipper Spaceship says to *Boku* that seems to matter than the memories that spontaneously arise in her presence (memories which *Boku* never shares with the reader). This, the text implies, is a private moment between them that we, in part, are being excluded from. In a motif that will carry on throughout Murakami's fiction, *Boku* describes these memories as warm, a light he will carry with him until his death. It is hard not to hear Murakami speaking of K here, the scene perhaps an indication that he has reached the limit of what he will publicly share (even camouflaged in the form of fiction).

While this is a work about mourning the loss of a particular woman, and thus might be read in light of the loss of K, particularly when one realizes that the setting is likely modeled on the home next to ICU's old golf course that Murakami probably lived in, at the same time, Naoko seems to represent something larger. In one sense, she is a symbol of postwar Japan itself, a chance for *Boku* to explore the Freudian question of not only *whom* he has lost but *what* he has lost in himself. As Rubin explains, though Murakami is often dismissed as an apolitical and a-historical writer, most of his works "are set in carefully defined periods and, taken in aggregate, can be read as a psychological history of post-post-war Japan."[125] This rings true for *Pinball*. The age of innocence in Murakami's early novels is most commonly associated with the year 1963. Significant here is the 1964 Tokyo Olympics, which came to symbolize Japan's growing economic confidence and triumphant reentry onto the world stage following the postwar period of rebuilding. There are also several American references in the novella that reinforce this notion of 1963 as a special time. As Katō Norihiro points out, The Beach Boys' "California Girls" and the numerous references made to American President John F. Kennedy in *Wind* all point back to 1963. Kennedy's words are quoted; Rat wears a Kennedy pendant around his neck; and the woman with the missing finger speaks Kennedy's name in her sleep (though, of course, the assassination of Kennedy in 1963 also bookends this year as the end of such innocence).[126] Even more than these American references, though, it is the connection with Naoko that really marks 1963 as such a special time. *Boku* explains:

> It's hard enough to talk about the dead under normal circumstances, but it's even harder to talk about girls who have died young: by dying, they stay young forever.
> We, on the other hand, advance in age every year, every month, every day . . .
> I have just one photograph of her. Someone jotted the date on the back—August 1963. The same year Kennedy took a bullet in the head . . .
> She was fourteen then, and it was the most beautiful moment in her twenty-one years on this planet.[127]

Boku remembers Naoko talking about the community her family moved to in 1961 when she was twelve. The scene she describes is pastoral and idyllic: a peaceful green valley inhabited by a community of artists and eccentrics. Around the time of the Tokyo Olympics, however, development from the city reached their community. Finally, in 1966, when Naoko was seventeen years old, the well-digger who had provided the town with its delicious drinking water, was struck by a train and killed. From this point on, Naoko's fortunes seem to have literally dried up and a few years later she was dead. *Boku's* narrative is an attempt to understand not only her death, but also, to some degree, the innocence and lost innocence she represents.

Pinball is not the end of *Boku's* therapeutic quest. Most importantly, we still have the question of Rat, who at the end of the novel finally decides to leave his hometown and the woman he has been seeing there. *Boku* warns us that we should not expect the kind of denouement found in stories like Arthur and his Knights of the Round Table.

He has by no means found his holy grail. He has, however, moved ever so slightly forward in his quest for mourning and individuation. At the end of the novel, the twins disappear, going back to wherever it is they came from, though *Boku* does not seem concerned. As we should realize by now, when the time is right a new anima-guide will magically appear in his life, offering him the next step forward in his therapeutic journey. He just needs to keep his ears open.[128]

The Last Goodbye: *A Wild Sheep Chase*

Though Murakami's fiction is generally characterized as moving from detachment to commitment, if we look again at his quote on the topic, we can see that between the "detached and aphoristic" stage and the "commitment" stage, is a middle stage which he describes as focused on "the telling of a story."[129] This stage, according to Murakami, starts with *Sheep Chase*, and it is clear that for him this is where his career as a storyteller really started.[130] His confidence as a writer was growing, grounded in his emerging understanding of the power of *monogatari*.

Murakami talked about this growing sense of confidence in a lecture he gave at the University of California, Berkeley, quoted by Rubin. He notes his belief that "a story, a *monogatari*, is not something you create. It is something that you pull out of yourself," emphasizing again that it is spontaneity that makes this possible. He explains that at the start of writing *Sheep Chase* he had no idea what he would write, and that he "wrote the opening chapter almost at random." This might scare some writers, but Murakami claims to have felt no anxiety: "I was like a dowser searching for water with his divining rod. I knew—I felt—that the water was there and so I started to dig." He concludes, "The most important thing is confidence. You have to believe you have the ability to tell the story, to strike the vein of water, to make the pieces of the puzzle fit together. Without that confidence, you can't go anywhere."[131]

This confidence, in one sense, was a necessity. After the relative success of his first two novels, Murakami decided to sell Peter Cat so that he could write full-time. He was going all in, but he also had confidence that things would work out. This was not because he thought he was smarter or more talented than others. Instead, he was supported by his growing awareness of the second basement and his ability to dig down deep and find his stories there. There is a physicality to Murakami's description of the writing process which appears to be more than metaphorical. One gets a clear sense that when he writes he engages his whole body. He always insists that the physical work he did at Peter Cat prepared him to write, and it was while he was writing *Sheep Chase* that he quit smoking and started running, lifestyle changes that were about more than just physical health. Murakami is a strong believer in the body-mind connection and in the need for physical exercise as a counterbalance to the unhealthy forces which emerge during the writing process.

Becoming a full-time writer enabled Murakami to engage in a more ambitious project. Inspired in part by Murakami Ryū's *Coin Locker Babies* (1980), he knew that he wanted to write something longer and more sustained than either *Wind* or *Pinball*. The initial inspiration for the story, Rubin explains, came from a review of *Pinball* in which Takahashi Takako had "taken [him] to task for describing some bushes as looking like 'grazing sheep,'" Takahashi insisting that this was an inappropriate simile for a Japanese author given Japan's lack of sheep.[132] Murakami took exception to this comment and began researching the topic, actually traveling to Hokkaido to see with his own eyes the role sheep still play in Japanese society. Learning about the way sheep had been introduced and then largely abandoned as an economic commodity during the Meiji Period, Murakami began to see them as "a symbol of the reckless speed with which the Japanese state pursued a course of modernization."[133] His decision to take a sheep and make it a central symbol of his new novel can thus be seen as a conscious decision on his part to inject a larger historical consciousness into his writing, though, as will be seen, this is not unrelated to his search for self-therapy.

One way of understanding what Murakami means by his emphasis on the "telling of a story" in *Sheep Chase* is through Joseph Campbell's theory of the monomyth or hero's journey. For Campbell, the monomyth—a kind of meta-story that has continued to be retold in different forms down the generations—relates to the basic elements of a rite of passage, involving a separation, an initiation, and a return. He writes, "A hero ventures forth from the world of common day into a region of supernatural wonder: fabulous forces are there encountered and a decisive victory is won: the hero comes back from this mysterious adventure with the power to bestow boons on his fellow man."[134] What is interesting about this quest is the way it connects the personal quest with a collective benefit: the hero embarks on their adventure alone, but at the same time they are engaged in a battle for something with the power to renew their entire community.

Murakami, as mentioned, is a fan of Campbell's work, so *Sheep Chase* could represent a conscious borrowing from this "hero's journey" framework, but not necessarily so. Campbell's theory has influenced modern storytelling to such a degree, that one does not necessarily need to have even read his work to be influenced by it.[135] The most famous example of Campbell's influence in popular culture is the *Star Wars* franchise, George Lucas drawing deeply on Campbell's ideas when he was first structuring Luke Skywalker's saga. For Ōtsuka Eiji, the two figures who have done the most to bring these monomythic elements into contemporary Japanese storytelling are Murakami and the animator Miyazaki Hayao, Ōtsuka describing this as part of the "Star Warsification" of Japanese *monogatari*.[136]

In terms of the source material Murakami actually talks about for *Sheep Chase*, the main name he mentions is Raymond Chandler. He explains:

> The structure of *A Wild Sheep Chase* was deeply influenced by the detective novels of Raymond Chandler. I am an avid reader of his books and have read some of them many times. I wanted to use his plot structure in my new novel. This meant, first of all, that the protagonist would be a lonely city dweller. He would be searching for something. In the course of his search, he would become entangled in various kinds of complicated situations. And when he finally found what he was looking for, it would already have been ruined or lost.[137]

As I have already argued, the influence of Chandler goes back much further in Murakami's fiction than his third novel, which is really just a continuation of themes found in his first two works. Here, in this third novel, is simply the conclusion to *Boku*'s "long goodbye" to Rat. If hard-boiled detective elements are more pronounced in *Sheep Chase* than in Murakami's first two works, it may simply be because he was gradually becoming more aware himself of what he was doing—rewriting for himself a version of Chandler's *The Long Goodbye*.

The first step in the hero's journey is what Campbell labels the "call to adventure." He explains, "The hero can go forth of his own volition . . . or he may be carried or sent abroad by some benign or malignant agent." Campbell continues, "Refusal of the summons converts the adventure into its negative. Walled in boredom, hard work, or 'culture,' the subject loses the power of significant affirmative action and becomes a victim to be saved."[138] This is *Boku* at the start of *Sheep Chase*. Speaking to the woman who will soon save him, he summarizes his life to this point as follows: "It's been boring so far. It'll probably be the same from here on. Not that that bothers me. I mean, I take what I get."[139] This woman goes on to explain that when she meets someone new, she first has them talk about themselves for ten minutes and then concludes that they are the complete opposite of whatever they have just said. She concludes that *Boku* is not as boring as he thinks.

In *Boku*'s case, it is not entirely clear whether the call to adventure has come from a "benign or malignant agent." The initial impetus for his wild sheep chase comes from a strange request Rat makes out of the blue, to place a picture he has sent of some sheep someplace people will see it. Though *Boku* has no idea what is behind this request, he complies, placing it in an advertisement which, in turn, attracts the attention of a powerful right-wing organization. This organization, clearly an example of what Campbell would describe as a malignant agent, approaches *Boku* and offers him both carrots (money) and sticks (threats of financial ruin) to find a particular sheep in the picture with a star-shaped birthmark on its back. *Boku*, who does not appreciate being threatened and who feels like he has little to lose anyway, initially thinks about refusing this call to adventure, though eventually he succumbs. Important in his decision is the role of his new girlfriend.

The hero of a monomythic journey, Campbell explains, is always accompanied by a "supernatural aid" or "protective figure."[140] Campbell notes, "What such a figure represents is the benign, protecting power of destiny."[141] In *Sheep Chase*, the clear candidate for this role is *Boku*'s girlfriend, who always seems to know one step ahead of him what he should do next. On their first meeting she tells *Boku*, "for the time being—say, the next few months—don't leave my side."[142] Next, she tells him to expect a phone call regarding sheep. She gently coaxes him along when he is trying to decide whether to go on his wild sheep chase, and when they do finally make it to Hokkaido, she tells him the exact hotel he must stay in to meet the Sheep Professor, an important figure on his quest. Then, right when she has guided *Boku* to what Campbell calls "the first threshold" at the entry to the "belly of the whale," a stage that for *Boku* coincides with his final meeting with Rat, she disappears from his life without a trace, scared off, it is later revealed, by a figure known as the Sheep Man.

The other clear role this girlfriend has is to help bring *Boku* back to life. Early on she tells him, "you're only half-living. . . . The other half is still untapped somewhere."[143] Later, when they are making love, she tells *Boku* how alive she is feeling and asks if he

The Long Goodbyes

feels the same. "I'm right with you," *Boku* replies, "Truly alive."[144] "It seems like we're having a picnic, it's so lovely," the woman then adds—a comment *Boku* finds strange. This picnic reference reminds us of the opening chapter of the novel where *Boku* talks about the "Wednesday afternoon picnics" he used to take with the "girl who would sleep with anyone." *Boku*'s recollections of this girl are prompted by her death, but the important thing about this opening is how it takes us back to an earlier period in *Boku*'s life, 1970. The personal significance of this opening scene for Murakami is suggested by the location of these Wednesday afternoon picnics: the campus of ICU (i.e., the home of K).

Since we last saw *Boku* in *Pinball*, he has been married and divorced from a woman he worked with at the translation company. *Boku* had not particularly wanted a divorce, even after learning of her infidelity, but neither could he arouse himself enough to fight for their marriage. "I'm going nowhere staying with you," is his wife's simple conclusion.[145] The only thing they can agree on is that in the end, it was probably for the best that they never had children. *Boku* has failed in his first attempt to create a new family in Tokyo, and his distance from the family he left behind in his hometown has only widened. When he returned home around the time of his marriage to take care of some paperwork for the family registry, his main reaction was one of relief: "From that point on there was no hometown for me. Nowhere to return to. What a relief! No one to want me, no one to want anything from me."[146] Later, when he returns home to take care of some business for Rat, he does not even go home, choosing, instead, to stay in a hotel. J, when he learns this, is astonished: "You've got a home, haven't you? Why not stay there?" *Boku*'s reply: "It's not my home anymore."[147]

When we finally meet *Boku* again at the start of *Sheep Chase* then, he is finally alone in the world, not connected to anybody or anything. He is trapped in boredom and not looking for things to change, instead, embracing boredom as the defining quality of his life. His new girlfriend then appears and begins to magically take him from boredom into adventure, using as her primary weapon her "unblocked ears." Indeed, *Boku* first meets this woman through her ears, which appear in some photos he has been given for an advertising job (*Boku*'s translation company has gradually moved into advertising, which is connected to his growing disillusionment. "[W]here does anyone," he asks his business partner at one point, "deal in words with substance?").[148] Mesmerized by the ear shots, *Boku* organizes to meet the woman they belong to, who, it turns out, along with being an ear model, also works as a proofreader and high-class call girl. This woman, *Boku* soon learns, can keep her ears in two states: blocked and unblocked. When her ears are blocked, she is just an ordinary woman with nothing special about her. When her ears are unblocked, she sends *Boku* off into states of rapture, the likes of which he has never known. This is clearly an erotic experience for *Boku*, who informs us that she reveals her ears to him "mostly on sexual occasions."[149] There are many types of sex, *Boku* informs us early on in *Sheep Chase*. Sex with his new girlfriend in her unblocked-ear state seems to be a case of what he describes as "sex as self-therapy."[150]

When it is time for *Boku* and his girlfriend to find a hotel in Hokkaido, she tells him, "I've already got an image of a place."[151] She then has *Boku* read off a list of hotel names from the yellow pages until she tells him to stop. When they arrive at the selected location, The Dolphin Hotel, and *Boku* sees how rundown it is, he suggests they go someplace else. He has been given more than enough money by the organization to pay for somewhere better, but his girlfriend is adamant: "It's not a question of money. Our sheep hunt begins here."[152] They use the hotel as a base to start their search for the sheep, but with little to show for it initially. Then one day they learn why it had to be this hotel. The owner of the hotel informs them that the Dolphin Hotel was formerly the Hokkaido Ovine Hall, and even now the entire second floor is dedicated to sheep research—its curator, the owner's father, the ever-grumpy Sheep Professor.

The Sheep Professor provides an important link for explaining how the sheep with the star-shaped birthmark got from China to Japan. A student at Tokyo Imperial University, he had once written a thesis on the topic of a "unified scheme of large-scale agriculturalization for Japan, Korea, and Taiwan."[153] His talent for thinking about agriculture eventually gained the attention of the military, and he was recruited to set up a program to ensure Japanese self-sufficiency in sheep-raising (their wool, in particular, useful in the production of warm military uniforms). The Sheep Professor took up this challenge until one day, while out on an observational tour, the sheep with the star-shaped birthmark entered his body. He had become the temporary host of a parasitical sheep that seeks nothing but total power.

More than any specific ideology, the central sheep in *Sheep Chase* is best seen as a symbol of something like the Nietzschean will to power.[154] It uses whatever means are available to it in the search for total domination, the wartime ideology of Pan-Asianism represented by the Sheep Professor just one example. Centuries earlier, this same sheep was said to have entered Genghis Khan, while following its time with the Sheep Professor, it found a new host in the shady right-wing figure who now runs the organization which dominates postwar Japan and which has recruited *Boku*. This man is now dying, and so it is time for the sheep to find a new host, which is why the organization is so interested in finding it. Those who host the sheep feel incredible power while the sheep is within them. Once the sheep leaves, though, they become "sheepless," a state the Sheep Professor describes as hell.[155] He explains, "Ever since the sheep departed, I can't tell how much is really me and how much the shadow of the sheep."[156]

This Nietzschean will to power is a theme that runs through much of Murakami's fiction, so it is worthwhile exploring it in more depth. As mentioned, Murakami first read Nietzsche in middle school, and he is clearly conversant with the basic concepts of Nietzschean philosophy, but it is also worth considering how this influence may have also come to him through Fitzgerald, who was also deeply influenced by Nietzschean thought.[157] The value of this connection will become apparent later on when we see how frequently the antagonists in Murakami's fiction, figures driven by an unbridled Nietzschean will to power, take on Gatsby-like positions vis-à-vis their Nick Carraway-like narrator/protagonists.[158]

Fitzgerald's exposure to Nietzsche came primarily through the writings of H. L. Mencken, an American cultural critic and scholar who was the main popularizer of Nietzsche's ideas in America, particularly in his 1907 book *The Philosophy of Friedrich Nietzsche*. In 1922, Fitzgerald listed Mencken's book as number two on his list of top ten books and seems to have been drawn particularly to Mencken's ideas about a cultural aristocracy that could stand up against the increasingly dominant commercial interests controlling America.[159] Drawing on Nietzsche's philosophy, Mencken came to see society as a battlefield between three broad interest groups, only two of which are really in the fight. He saw the divisions as follows:

> In every healthy society there are three broad classes, each of which has its own morality, its own work, its own notion of perfection and its own sense of mastery. The first class comprises those who are obviously superior to the mass intellectually; the second includes those whose eminence is chiefly muscular, and the third is made up of the mediocre. The third class, very naturally, is the most numerous, but the first is the most powerful.[160]

Fitzgerald's fiction picks up on this formulation, while never quite getting on board with Mencken's last assertion that the intellectual class is the most powerful. Instead, he sees the tragedy of modern America in the way the muscular class has come to dominate, destroying anyone who stands in their way. This theme is directly explored in *The Great Gatsby*, where the ambition and intelligence of Gatsby are set up against the muscular and financial might of Tom Buchanan, with Gatsby seeking to position himself so that he can win back the affections of Tom's wife, Daisy. Nick Carraway is both a neighbor to Gatsby and a distant relative to Daisy, though his sympathies lie with Gatsby and the heroic way he tries to rise above his position in life to win the girl he loves (even if Daisy never seems entirely deserving of his affection). Ultimately, though, it is Tom who wins out, even though he has been cheating on Daisy with the working-class Myrtle. Myrtle is accidentally killed by Daisy in an automobile accident, and Gatsby is killed by Myrtle's husband, George, who mistakenly believes Gatsby did it. In the end, Tom and Daisy are described as "careless people" who "smashed up things and creatures and then retreated back into their money or their vast carelessness, or whatever it was that kept them together, and let other people clean up the mess they had made."[161]

Murakami, I would argue, takes this Fitzgeraldian dynamic and moves it in a slightly new direction. As with Mencken, society in Murakami's fiction is divided into three broad classes. First, there are those who, like the boss in *Sheep Chase*, are driven by an unbridled Nietzschean will to power, this drive being an end in itself. Their goal is simply to rise as high in life as possible, regardless of who they have to step over to get there, and the main people they step over are the next class: the general masses or simply the herd. To control the masses, these warped Nietzschean Supermen use whatever means are available to them: media, politics, even religion. It is only Murakami's protagonists, the third class, who slowly begin to work out what is going on, with slowly being the operative word here. It takes time for this to happen in Murakami's fiction, but slowly we see male protagonists moving from friendship to suspicion and finally to antagonism vis-à-vis their male counterparts.

So what is it that allows Murakami's protagonists to remove themselves from the herd to confront their Nietzschean-inspired nemesis? This, I would argue, is none other than the Jungian path of individuation I have been describing. Jung explains what this process means for an individual's relationship to the collective: "Every step towards fuller consciousness removes him from his original, purely animal participation mystique with the herd, from submersion in a common unconsciousness. Every step forward means tearing oneself loose from the maternal womb of unconsciousness in which the mass of men dwell."[162]

For *Boku*, this process of individuation begins with the process of moving from melancholia into mourning, but this is not the end. Slowly, he begins to incorporate the messages of his complexes, the shadow and the anima first of all, to transcend psychic splits within himself. Light and dark, male and female, even good and evil—his (perhaps impossible) quest is nothing less than to overcome all dichotomies and to become one.

Of course, it is overcoming these same dichotomies that motivates the Nietzschean Superman (or Übermensch), too. Lucy Huskinson writes, "The Übermensch is the symbol of human totality, the unification of opposite instincts in the pursuit of creation."[163] Or as Nietzsche puts it, "with every growth of man, his other side must grow too.... That man must grow better and more evil is my formula for this inevitability."[164] Both the individuated Self and the Nietzschean Superman are cultural elites, figures who have risen above the herd by confronting what is contrary in themselves. This is a dangerous process, though, for in transcending the herd they also leave behind its accepted values and morality, its commonsense positions on right and wrong. Is there then, that much separating them?

Jung, according to Huskinson's reading of his work, believed that there was, suggesting it was the Übermensch's tendency to take their gains as evidence of their inherent right to rule over the herd that separates them from the individuated Self. For Jung, such figures become "slaves of their own fiction" or victims of their "own inflated ego-consciousness."[165] In the end, the herd gets its shepherd, but at a cost. Jung explains, "The shepherd's staff soon become a rod of iron, and the shepherds turn into wolves."[166] These are ideas that resonate with *Sheep Chase*.

Boku in *Sheep Chase* is still in the early stages of the dynamic described here. He does not yet realize who or what it is he is up against, but simply takes the options that are offered to him. On his plane ride to Hokkaido, he reads *The Adventures of Sherlock Holmes,* but it is clear that *Boku* is no Sherlock himself; he misses the clues that are laid out before him about the connection of the right-wing boss and his friend Rat to the town of Junitaki where he ends up (the boss was born in this town and Rat's father owns a second home there which once belonged to the Sheep Professor). "How could I not have figured it out?" *Boku* later laments to himself.[167] But this, of course, is not the point. *Boku*'s real journey cannot be shortened through logical deductions. That would be like a therapist offering a brilliant analysis of a patient's condition and then saying, "so now I've told you what's wrong with you, get over it." Logical explanations are not what *Boku* needs, but the experience of discovering things for himself.

The grumpy Sheep Professor, I would suggest, has hints of Murakami's father in him, a connection that makes some of the hotel owner's comments about his father rather poignant. This son tells *Boku* and his girlfriend about the Sheep Professor, but he refuses to go with them to see him, explaining that his father dislikes him. This has not dampened the son's feelings for his father, though, who explains:

"Deep down in his heart he's kind. If you heard him play his violin, you'd know that. Sheep hurt my father, and through my father, sheep have also hurt me."

"You love your father, don't you?" said my girlfriend.

"Yes, that I do. I love him very much," said the Dolphin Hotel owner.[168]

The way the son sees it, his father is a victim. It is the state of being "sheepless," of living after war and ideological possession, which has made him who he is.

If the Sheep Professor reflects one part of Murakami's father, another part of him is arguably represented by the Sheep Man, a figure deeply traumatized by war. The Sheep Man is a curious figure who is only 140 centimeters in height. He looks like a human wearing a sheepskin costume but with horns that are real. He is hiding out in Junitaki, he says, because he does not want to go to war, though he never makes clear exactly which war this is.[169]

In terms of Campbell's monomyth, the Sheep Man also plays the role of a "threshold guardian." Campbell explains, "With the personifications of his destiny to guide and aid him, the hero goes forward in his adventure until he comes to the 'threshold guardian' at the entrance of the zone of magnified power."[170] This "zone of magnified power" in *Sheep Chase* is the house in Junitaki, owned previously by the Sheep Professor and now by Rat's father, the place where *Boku* and Rat will finally meet again. The caretaker of the house tries to call ahead for *Boku* and his girlfriend before they go there, but he cannot get through: "Not even a busy signal."[171] Even *Boku*'s girlfriend's ears go "out of commission" as they get closer.[172] On the way to the house they pass an ominous curve which even the sheep are afraid of, and once they get to the house, the girlfriend disappears, the Sheep Man later explaining that he chased her away, that she never should have come here, and that *Boku* will never see her again.

Finally, we are ready for the climax to *Boku*'s wild sheep chase (and, indeed, to the entire Rat trilogy), and the emotional payoff that will hopefully make his journey therapeutically worthwhile. What is interesting at first is the way *Boku* comes to realize that the Sheep Man he is talking to, this threshold guardian, is at the same time connected to Rat: "The more I thought about it, the more difficult I found it to escape the feeling that the Sheep Man's actions reflected the Rat's will."[173] The challenge *Boku* faces is how to get to Rat through the Sheep Man and have him come out of his hiding place, and the solution he finds is anger. *Boku* finally loses it, declaring to the Sheep Man, "Things have changed.... I'm very, very angry. Never in my entire life have I been angry like this."[174] He then picks up a guitar and smashes it against a fireplace.

Anger, of course, can play a useful role in therapeutic breakthroughs, and it does seem as if *Boku* is finally breaking through his detached cool in this scene, but only to a degree. He later admits to Rat that there was something calculated about his anger: "I was only trying to shake you up enough to show yourself."[175] Still, his plan works, and Rat finally makes his appearance, the house they are in suddenly becoming dark and cold. We know from the chicken warehouse scene in *Pinball* what this might mean. Indeed, it turns out that *Boku* has somehow passed over into the realm of the dead, Rat having hung himself from a beam in the kitchen a week before his arrival (the Sheep Man removed the body before *Boku* got there). The question is why Rat did this, and this is where Murakami is working himself up to the greatest therapeutic payoff of the trilogy.

Rat's answer, it should not surprise us by now, involves the sheep, which following its time with the right-wing boss, had selected Rat as its new host. This sheep, Rat explains, had wanted all of him—"[m]y body, my memory, my weakness, my contradictions'— and he had almost been willing to give it.[176] He explains the intoxicating power the sheep possessed, what I have been describing in terms of the Nietzschean will to power. "What it comes closest to," Rat explains, "is a dynamo manifesting the vital force at the root of all life in one solitary point of the universe."[177] Yet Rat, in the end, resisted this intoxicating power, his decision to kill himself an act of self-sacrifice. And he has taken the sheep down with him, something he was able to do for the following reason: "I guess I felt attached to my weakness. My pain and suffering too. Summer light, the smell of a breeze, the sound of cicadas."[178] Much like Fitzgerald and Chandler before him, Murakami has an image of where the battle is and how it might be won, with true strength residing in an acknowledgment of weakness. The only way to resist this Faustian-like bargain, paradoxically, is to fully embrace the weakest parts of yourself.

Here, I would argue, Murakami is taking up the "unfinished business" of his father (therapeutic thread two). He is seeking nothing less than redemption for the sins of the Second World War, that time in Japan's history where the power of the "sheep" ruled supreme. *Boku*'s alter ego Rat, by ending his own life, is doing what should have been done in an earlier generation. Rat, for his part, feels like the sacrifice was worth it. "And have you been saved?" *Boku* asks him after everything is over. "Yeah, I've been saved all right," is his quiet reply.[179] The Sheep Professor also seems to find a sense of salvation in what transpires. In his Epilogue, *Boku* describes the visit he made to the Sheep Professor to tell him the news. "It's all over," the Sheep Professor had cried, "all over. Over and done."[180] As *Boku* leaves the room, the Sheep Professor is face down, sobbing on his desk.

And then there is J, the Chinese bartender *Boku* and Rat left behind in their hometown. J is the closest thing to a father figure *Boku* and Rat have in the trilogy, but they have both left him behind in their hometown and made their ways separately to a small town in Hokkaido. So it is surprising when *Boku* finally makes it to the house where he will later meet Rat and offers these lines: "Now, if we could get J to come up here, I'm sure things would work out fine. Everything should revolve around him, with forgiveness, compassion, and acceptance at the center."[181] J is standing in here for China (and arguably all nations that suffered under Japan's imperial regime), with *Boku*'s message clear: Japan must seek forgiveness from its Asian neighbors. When he completes his job and receives the promised money from the boss's secretary, he takes it to J, asking that he and Rat be made co-partners in his bar—an offer, Rubin suggests, that almost comes across like paying war reparations.[182]

One of the central points of the monomythic journey, according to Campbell, is to make "atonement with the father." "One must have a faith," he argues, "that the father is merciful, and then a reliance on that mercy."[183] *Sheep Chase* does not mirror Campbell's monomythic structure perfectly (and neither does it have to), but on this point, Campbell does seem to capture what is at the heart of *Boku*'s therapeutic quest. He has been seeking a kinder, more merciful image of the father, and he has found it through healing the Sheep Professor, understanding the ways the Sheep Man is also connected to himself (through Rat), and finally reaching out symbolically for forgiveness from J. The hero's journey, again, is not just about healing oneself, but about bringing something back from the quest that can heal the community. In this case, it is a first attempt in Murakami's fiction at healing intergenerational trauma (therapeutic thread two).

Boku's final act in the novel is to walk from J's Bar to the beach, or at least what remains of it, in his hometown. Earlier in the novel, he has offered a detailed description of the price progress has inflicted on his hometown, including reducing its only remaining beach to a mere fifty yards (a description which is also true of the beach from Murakami's hometown he used to visit as a child). It is here, on what might be thought of as the last remaining patch of his childhood, that *Boku* finally breaks down and cries more than he has ever cried in his entire life. This is the final cathartic outpouring of the novel (and of the entire trilogy), an expression of grief for all that has been lost. So has *Boku* finally found self-therapy? Can he now be considered healed? Not entirely if the novel he next appears in, *Dance Dance Dance*, is anything to go by. Leaving aside the question of what *Boku* still has to accomplish, though, his gains have been significant. Aided by a cast of supporting actors, he has broken through his melancholia and found his way back to mourning again. He has finally been able to shed tears for all the things he has lost.

What we will see in Murakami's next three novels is a deeper reflection on what it might mean to seek self-therapy in the context of late-capitalist Japan. The broader interest in society at large seen in *Sheep Chase* continues, with the impediments that society can bring to the task of self-therapy explored more fully. While undoubtedly there is a solipsistic element to the therapeutic quest portrayed in the Rat trilogy, something which might be applied to Jungian psychology more broadly with its focus on a conscious mind dialoguing with its unconscious other, what one starts to see in Murakami's fiction is an interest in how these personal victories might enable someone to then connect with another person, though admittedly this only happens gradually over time. Indeed, the next novel we will look at, *Hard-Boiled Wonderland and the End of the World*, still clearly belongs to the more solipsistic stage of Murakami's career.

2

Self-Therapy and Society

Introduction

The three novels discussed in this chapter, *Hard-Boiled Wonderland and the End of the World* (hereafter *Hard-Boiled*), *Norwegian Wood*, and *Dance Dance Dance* (hereafter *Dance*), continue to develop, and finally to "resolve," therapeutic thread one (the journey from melancholia to mourning). In my discussion of *Hard-Boiled*, I will argue that the therapeutic subtext of this novel, arguably dealing with the death of a former girlfriend, while better camouflaged than in earlier works, is still there, and I will spend some time thinking about the ending of the novel, which might be described as a regression in terms of the therapeutic motifs found in Murakami's fiction. This ending, I will argue, says something interesting about where Murakami was at this stage of his evolving therapeutic/literary project. The next novel discussed, *Norwegian Wood*, is interesting for the way it more directly deals with content implicit in the Rat trilogy (a narrator's attempt to deal with the suicide of a former girlfriend), as if Murakami was finally ready to write the novel which Chapter One of *Hear the Wind Sing* had implicitly promised—a story about his dead girlfriend told in "words far more beautiful than these." In one sense, this was the novel Murakami had been trying to write from the beginning of his career, and its completion was arguably both a cathartic and anticlimactic moment for him (amplified, in turn, by its dramatic commercial success). *Dance* returns us to the story of *Boku* and brings us to a point where his inner solipsistic journey, at times explicitly portrayed through the language of Jungian individuation (therapeutic thread four), finally delivers him to a point where he is ready to connect to another human being. The reward of breaking out of melancholia here is interpersonal rather than just personal, and can be connected to thread three: the search for earned attachment.

What *Hard-Boiled* and *Dance* also add to the mix, as suggested at the end of the last chapter, are dynamics of dissociation caused by shifting conditions in late-capitalist Japan (*Norwegian Wood* is set in a different historical period—the late 1960s and early 1970s—and I examine it more in terms of dynamics of dependence, independence, and interdependence). *Dance*, in particular, might be read in light of Murakami's increased popularity after the publication of *Norwegian Wood* and the way he was struggling with his newfound notoriety. What *Hard-Boiled* and *Dance* also reveal, I suggest, are the struggles Murakami experienced in reconciling the therapeutic origins of his writing career with his increasing commercial success and growing status as a writer of literary fiction.

Hitting a Wall in *Hard-Boiled Wonderland and the End of the World*

In *Pinball, 1973* we saw a narrative strategy emerge in Murakami's fiction, whereby two complementary storylines (those of *Boku* and Rat) were alternated. In *Hard-Boiled* this strategy is taken up again, but in an even more complex and ambitious way, the novel alternating between *Watashi*'s (a more formal first-person pronoun than *Boku*) adventures in a futuristic "Hard-Boiled Wonderland" (the outer world of the novel), and *Boku*'s daily routines in a fantastic "End of the World" (the inner world of the novel). These two worlds, much like the two worlds of *Boku* and Rat, are connected in subtle ways and much of the fun of the novel is in trying to work out what that relationship might be.

In the outer world of a cyberpunk Tokyo, *Watashi* works as a *keisanshi* (translated by Alfred Birnbaum as a Calcutec), a human coding machine for classified data, computers being too easy to hack. In *A Wild Sheep Chase*, postwar Japan was controlled behind the scenes by a single organization run by a mysterious right-wing figure possessed by a sheep, but we were told that the death of the boss would likely bring about a "splintering of the organization."[1] This is the Japan we find in *Hard-Boiled*, where two organizations, the System and the Factory, are fighting for control, the battleground focused on information (though the possibility is left open that these two entities are still controlled behind the scenes by a single entity).[2] The System, we are told, "monopolizes everything under the info sun," doing everything in its power to protect its position, while the Factory "monopolizes everything in the shadows," doing everything in its power to infiltrate the System.[3] Even further in the shadows are the *Yamikuro* (creatively translated by Birnbaum as Inklings). These strange creatures live deep in the underground of Tokyo and "hate the world of light and all who live there," though they do cooperate with the Factory when it suits their purposes.[4]

In the inner world of the novel, a place known as the Town, *Boku* works as a Dreamreader, a job that involves reading old dreams stored in unicorn skulls. He is assisted in this work by a female librarian, whom he feels he may know from another world. When he is not working in the library, *Boku* lives with a retired Colonel and other ex-military men, all of whom seem to be suffering from a form of amnesia. The Town is surrounded by a wall, and those who enter it are required to surrender their shadow, an operation performed by the Gatekeeper.

While at first glance, *Hard-Boiled*, with its strange mix of science fiction and fantasy elements, looks like a novel that has moved beyond the overtly therapeutic themes of Murakami's early trilogy, a closer look reveals that it has simply become better at camouflaging them. This becomes clearer when you look at the work which preceded and inspired *Hard-Boiled*, a novella called *Machi, to sono futashika na kabe* (*The Town and Its Uncertain Wall*; hereafter *The Town*), published in the literary magazine *Bungakukai* in 1980. As anyone who reads *The Town* will quickly realize, this was Murakami's first (serious) attempt to write about the Town that later appears in *Hard-Boiled*.[5] Indeed, many sections from this earlier novella are simply cut and pasted into the later novel. At the same time, there are significant differences between the two works, which are useful for demonstrating how *Hard-Boiled* seeks to disguise its underlying therapeutic motif.

Shortly after Murakami published *The Town*, Murakami Ryū told him in a discussion that he thought he should write a sequel to it, something a little longer, suggesting (rather frankly) that, as it stands, the work is "a little weak." He also suggested that if Haruki is not careful, people will begin to "see through" what he is doing. Haruki acknowledged to Ryū that his guard may have been down a little when he wrote *The Town*, but he justified his decision by revealing how "relieved" (*sappari*) he felt after writing it.[6] In the discussion, Murakami seems to sense the truth of what Ryū is telling him, while also suggesting that it could not be helped. He simply had to write *The Town*—to get it out of his system—and after he did, he felt a whole lot better. In short, writing it was therapeutic.

Just because Murakami needed to write *The Town*, however, does not mean he had to publish it, and over time he has come to agree with Ryū's early assessment. "I'm not one to regret things I've done," Murakami writes in the notes that accompany *Hard-Boiled* in his collected works, "but in no small measure, I regret putting that novella [*The Town*] into print. I shouldn't have published it."[7] Murakami goes on to explain how he was asked by his editor to include *The Town* in his collected works, but that he refused. He acknowledges that while it went on to contribute positively to the way *Hard-Boiled* turned out, he still considers it a mistake (*shippaisaku*), and as such, he prefers to keep it out of the public eye as much as possible. This is why Murakami has never allowed *The Town* to be republished in Japanese nor to be translated, so those who want to read it must track down the relevant back number of *Bungakukai* (and, of course, read Japanese).

So what was it about publishing *The Town* that Murakami later came to regret? What is it about the novella that, in Murakami Ryū's words, might allow people to "see through" what Murakami is doing? On the surface at least, the story has the same feel as any Murakami story, its central themes of loss and memory staples of his writing. Indeed, I believe that if the story were to be made more widely available, fans would read it and enjoy it and that most would likely not see it as a mistake at all. There is a sense, though, in which *The Town* is perhaps a little too revealing; its meaning a little too clear; its ending a little too tidy. It is these features that make it something of an anomaly in Murakami's oeuvre, but this is also what makes it so useful for understanding what he is doing.

The Town starts much like *Hear the Wind Sing* does, with the narrator (another *Boku*) lamenting the limits of what he can talk about: "There are so many things I need to talk about, but so few I actually can. And to make matters worse, words die."[8] This idea of dying words is important in the story, the narrator wondering whether his words will ever live up to his subject matter: the death of his girlfriend. Chapter Two of the novella has the narrator directly addressing this (now dead) girlfriend, saying, "It was you who told me about the town."[9] The town this girlfriend had described was surrounded by a wall, and was difficult to enter. In it, she works as a librarian, while the "her" *Boku* knew in the outside world was merely her shadow. She once told *Boku* that she keeps a place in the library for him, where he can come and work as a prophet reading old dreams, though she also warns him that, should they ever meet there, she will not remember him. Then, just in case we are not sure what the narrator is suggesting here, he tells us, "You died in that imaginary town surrounded by a wall. It was six o'clock in the morning. . . . But what people buried was not you. It was your shadow. . . . You continue to work quietly in the back of that dim library."[10] *Boku* is being poetic here and his talk about different inner and outer shadows is confusing, but the general point is clear. His girlfriend is dead, though for him she still lives on in a town she once described to him where she works as a librarian. As soon becomes evident, his story is about going to visit her there.

The relative clarity of this setup, I would argue, was Murakami's first mistake. He never explains things this clearly, so in a sense, it does not feel very Murakamiesque. This is all toned down in *Hard-Boiled* where we still have a librarian working in a walled-off town, but where we have no idea who she might have been in another world, even though the narrator feels like he knew her someplace else. It is definitely never explicitly stated that she was his girlfriend or that she is now dead. Clearly, in hindsight, Murakami felt it was better to leave the "other world" identity of this librarian ambiguous, and so in *Hard-Boiled* this is what he does.

Following the imagined conversation between *Boku* and his girlfriend, *The Town* then moves into a description of the town itself, most of the details of which will be familiar to readers of *Hard-Boiled*. *Boku* starts to work at the library with the librarian (his dead girlfriend) reading old dreams. His shadow, much as he will do in *Hard-Boiled*, warns him about the dangers of the town and urges him to help plan their escape. But then in Chapter Twenty-three of the novella comes a scene unlike any found in *Hard-Boiled*. *Boku*, by this point, has decided to leave the town with his shadow, and so he is talking with his dead girlfriend for the last time. "I met your shadow when I was sixteen," he tells her, explaining that it was a "strange year."[11] They had met at a party, but he had been so shy that it had taken him months before he got the courage to call her up and ask her out. *Boku* describes the time they shared following this as like "living in a dream"—not an uncommon description of young love—but then clarifies that it was a "dark dream" or even what he suggests might be called a "dark heart."[12] Even so, *Boku* describes how he has not been able to let her go and suspects that he may now be too old to ever do so. Living this dark dream has been traumatic for him, but letting go of her would be like losing a part of himself. Being in this town with her again has been everything he could have ever wanted, but now it is time to say goodbye.

Publishing Chapter Twenty-three of *The Town*, I would argue, was Murakami's second mistake. Even more than the conversation between *Boku* and his pinball machine in *Pinball, 1973*, it is clear what Murakami is doing here. Though the framework is fictional, he is pouring out his heart to K, this woman he shared his own "dark dream" with, which is likely why Murakami Ryū offered his warning: people are going to see through this. Murakami's early narrators, while they are articulate, always seem to be holding something back. In this scene, however, the floodgates open. "I couldn't stop talking," *Boku* observes.[13] There are things he needs to say to this dead girlfriend and given that he is soon to leave the town, it is now or never. Chapter Twenty-three is one of the unguarded moments in the novella Murakami acknowledged to Ryū, and while writing this content down in such a direct and honest way was clearly cathartic, in hindsight he regretted his decision to put this in the public domain. *Boku* and his librarian friend in *Hard-Boiled* get nowhere close to this level of self-disclosure.

Another minor detail from *The Town* that is later not included in *Hard-Boiled*, but which highlights the theme of the novella well, is that along with the "real" wall of the town that *Boku* must confront, there is an imaginary wall that appears in his mind with which he sometimes converses. This imaginary wall is part of himself, and wrestling with its message reveals the internal struggle he is going through. Even after he determines to leave the town with his shadow, he remains uncertain about whether this is the right thing to do. "Where is the meaning in life?" his inner wall taunts him, "Where is the meaning in words?"[14] *Boku*'s retort is to ask, "Where is the meaning in this town? Where is the meaning of splitting life in two, of stuffing one's dark heart into the shelves of a library? What would be the meaning of an eternity of this?"[15] What *Boku* seems to be wrestling with is the choice between melancholia and mourning, the choice between staying in the town where he can be with his dead girlfriend forever, or the choice of returning to the world where the only compensation he has are words that die. In the end, *Boku* chooses the latter, more painful path. Near the very end of the novella, he declares, "I live on, and I continue to write. And what surrounds me, of course, is the smell of rotting flesh. I go to sleep with dark dreams and I arise with dark thoughts. The road I walk is dark, and only gets darker the further I go."[16]

For readers of *Hard-Boiled*, this is perhaps the most surprising part of *The Town*. *Boku* ultimately decides to leave the town with his shadow, to dive into the pool of water that promises his escape. Reading Murakami's fiction through a therapeutic lens, this feels like the right move, the one that promises the greatest therapeutic payoff. Much like Peter Pan's Neverland, the town is not a place one should stay in forever. J. M. Barrie's famous story presents Neverland as a place of childhood wonder, where pirates, Indians, and mermaids dwell, but it is also a place associated with death, inspired as it is in part by the death of Barrie's older brother, David, the day before he was to turn fourteen. To live in Neverland is to never grow old, to be locked away in a timeless eternity. Peter Pan, much like *Boku*, has difficulties holding onto his shadow, a symbol of the similar loss of identity he faces by remaining in this world. While the desire to reunite with the dead is understandable, one must return to the world of the living and live with the pain of loss. Which all makes Murakami's decision in *Hard-Boiled* to reverse this ending, to have *Boku* choose to stay in the Town, all the more interesting. It would seem that Murakami saw the tidy ending of this earlier novella as his final mistake, something he corrected when he later wrote *Hard-Boiled*. The question is, why?

Of course, one of the main things Murakami adds to *Hard-Boiled* to reposition the meaning of the Town is the "Hard-Boiled Wonderland" sections of the novel. From the perspective of *Watashi*, the outer protagonist, the Town is something buried deep within his unconscious mind, something he is unaware of until it is revealed to him one day by a scientist. From a therapeutic perspective, learning about this hidden inner world would seem to hold rich potential for *Watashi*. This is yet another example in Murakami's fiction of a buried, melancholic attachment that needs to be brought to the surface again so that a healthier process of mourning can begin. Yet, this possibility is greatly complicated in the story by the nature of the Town that is presented to him, a point that needs to be outlined in more detail.

Watashi's inner Town, at least originally, was his own unconscious creation. It is a place, we might say, created by his second basement. Unfortunately, his work as a Calcutec means that this Town and whatever personal meaning it has for him was hijacked by the System and a mad scientist for their own distorted purposes. This scientist calls the second basement many things in *Hard-Boiled*: a black box, an elephant graveyard, an elephant factory, or the core consciousness. His idea was to use this black box as a way of coding information so that it could not be hacked by the *kigōshi* (Birnbaum translates these rivals to the Calcutecs as Semiotics), figures who work for the Factory. Not even the individual in question understands the workings of their unconscious mind, so if data could be fed into and out of this system successfully, the scientist reasons, the code would be theoretically unbreakable. The problem he faced was the ever-shifting nature of the black box due to its ongoing responses to lived reality. You might feed data into the system at one point in time, but when you were ready to retrieve it, the system itself would have changed due to an accumulation of new experiences. The scientist's solution was to fix a person's black box at a certain point in time. This stable version of the black box could then be used for shuffling data.

This is the experiment the scientist carried out for the System. He describes the result as similar to having a stopped watch in one pocket and a ticking watch in the other. It is this stopped watch, this frozen version of the black box, which he could then use to shuffle data. This was all well and good in theory, but when the scientist tried his experiment out on living people, they all died, except one: *Watashi*. The scientist suspects that this was because of some innate talent *Watashi* possesses. Trying to work out what was going wrong, the scientist created computer simulations of the images coming from each Calcutec's black box, explaining that the "images were jumbled and fragmentary and didn't mean much in themselves."[17] He had to edit them, much like a film editor would do, turning them into a *monogatari*. In *Watashi*'s case, though, the *monogatari* which came from his black box was different: "Yours was the least random, most coherent. Well-plotted, even perfect. It could have passed for a novel or a movie.... It's as if you descended to the elephant factory floor beneath your consciousness and built an elephant with your own hands. Without you even knowin'!"[18]

The title the scientist gave to *Watashi*'s computer-simulated version of his black box was "End of the World" and then, driven by scientific curiosity, he went one step further, inserting this program back into *Watashi*'s mind. *Watashi* thus has three versions of his black box: the original one he unconsciously constructed for himself which continues to change over time, the frozen version set up for data shuffling purposes, and the computer-simulated version that the scientist decided to place within him. The problem is that a junction to this third version has been irreversibly set in motion by the scientist, so that *Watashi* is now a ticking time bomb. At some point, his mind will slip over to the third version of his black box and he will be lost to this world forever. In the outer world the lights will go out for *Watashi*, while in his inner world, *Boku* will live eternally in the scientist's simulated version of the Town.

This is all far-fetched, of course, even as far as science fiction goes, but this is hardly the point. But what then is the point? What is behind this admittedly convoluted plot device? At one level, of course, the science fiction elements of the plot here are a ruse. They are nothing more than a creative way of reexploring a familiar topic in Murakami's fiction: the way past trauma can split the mind in two (an unconscious part of the mind melancholically bound to the traumas of the past and a conscious part of the mind more adapted to the problems of living in the present—much like the Rat and *Boku* split previously explored). Consequently, the Town in *Hard-Boiled* might be seen as a new version of the town *Boku* left behind in the Rat trilogy, which, in turn, is just a fictional version of the real town Murakami left behind in Ashiya. What we have, in other words, is a fictional representation of Murakami's past traumas: the librarian (or dead girlfriend in the earlier novella) might be connected to K, the Colonel to Murakami's father. Self-therapy requires bringing these two worlds back together again or reincorporating dissociated memories from the past back into the present. Which is why, from a therapeutic perspective, *Boku*'s final decision in *Hard-Boiled* to stay in the Town feels wrong, even regressive. It is like he is choosing dissociation over association, melancholia over mourning, Neverland over reality. So what does this ending suggest about Murakami's evolving therapeutic project?

First, what it suggests is that the tidy ending Murakami offered in *The Town* was, from a therapeutic perspective, premature. In reality, Murakami was not yet ready to leave behind the Town, the melancholic attachments he felt to his past and particularly to K. In one sense, *Hard-Boiled* can be read as an elaborate allegory for how Murakami views the writing process. In the outer world, he is like a Calcutec, someone who is skilled at using different sides of their brain to achieve a particular purpose, but who is not necessarily aware of everything that is going on below the surface. At the start of the novel, *Watashi* finds himself in a slow-moving elevator on his way to see the scientist, so to pass the time he engages in one of his regular activities—counting the change in his left and right pockets simultaneously. This is a form of training, something useful in his job as a data shuffler where he must also relinquish conscious control so that different parts of his mind can operate independently. This is also how Murakami sees the writing process, noting, "I remember that in *Hard-Boiled Wonderland and the End of the World* the protagonist is a kind of specialist, a *keisanshi*, and I remember that scene: he can count with the right hand and the left hand separately the change in his pockets. I think that is what I have been doing, with the right and left hand doing different things. It's a kind of separation; it's a kind of split. The feeling of split is very important to me."[19]

In the inner world of his second basement, Murakami believes that what he is likely doing is something similar to *Boku*—unconsciously weaving together fragments of memory before they are lost forever. *Boku* spends his days as a Dreamreader, staring at unicorn skulls and trying to read the faint images that arise from them. Later, he learns that what he is actually doing is releasing the "last glimmers of mind into the air."[20] The role of the unicorns is to absorb the last remaining traces of mind from the people who enter the Town. This journey toward mindlessness starts when people first enter the Town and surrender their shadows, but the path to complete mindlessness takes more time. Each day the unicorns are led into the Town by the Gatekeeper where they collect remaining fragments of mind, and then each night they are returned back beyond the Town's wall where they release these fragments into the air. Yet even after the beasts die, faint traces of mind remain within them, and so the Gatekeeper burns their carcasses and removes their skulls, with the job of the Dreamreader being to release these final fragments of mind once and for all. The Town then is a place where minds (and memories) ultimately go to die. In the end, all that remains is mindless bliss.

For the longest time, *Boku* has no idea about what his job as a Dreamreader is all about; it is simply an exercise he is instructed to carry out. Then it finally dawns on him that what he has been doing is releasing the last fragments of the librarian's mind. Finally understanding the point of the exercise, he rushes back to the library with renewed purpose, exhausting himself in an all-night effort to try and pull the last remaining strands of her mind together: "Her mind is at my fingertips, moment by moment, in distinct increments of heat. It is not a question of quantity. Not number nor volume nor ratio. There is no reading everything of a mind."[21] Ultimately, though, *Boku*'s quest to reconstruct the librarian's mind is doomed to failure. The librarian's complete mind is irrecoverable. Even so, he now understands the personal significance of this place. His decision to stay in the Town at the end of the novel can thus be seen as a decision to keep sifting through the final strands of memory that remain, before they are lost forever.

The last place where memories seem to remain for *Boku* is in the Woods, a powerful space in the "End of the World" that he is often warned to stay away from. In *Hear the Wind Sing*, *Boku*'s girlfriend is described as dying in a "shabby grove of trees," her undiscovered body "swinging in the wind for two whole weeks."[22] The Woods in *Hard-Boiled* are a place for those with "undead shadows," those who still hold attachments to the outside world, and it is also a place deeply connected with wind.[23] In the presence of the librarian day after day, *Boku* finds his sorrow growing deeper and speculates, "I suppose these feelings are linked to forgotten memories."[24] In this state of mind he then travels through the Woods one day, barely making it to the library before losing consciousness. Two days later he awakens in his bed. "Did I not warn you about going into the Woods?" the Colonel reprimands him.[25] The Town runs on wind power, and when *Boku* later goes to meet the Caretaker who looks after the Town's power station, he again ventures into the Woods. The Caretaker admits that he hears voices coming from the Woods, and *Boku* cannot help but notice the wind rising while he is there. The reason he has gone to the Caretaker is to get a musical instrument, an accordion as it turns out, and it is later playing this wind instrument that he begins to spark connections with the outside world again. As he leaves the power station and the Woods, though, the first things he notices is the dying wind: "Gradually, the wail of the wind weakens as we walk farther from the power station. At the entrance to the Woods, we do not hear it at all."[26]

The Woods arguably hold the traumatic secret about the librarian that *Boku* must (re)discover. While this secret is never made clear in *Hard-Boiled*, read creatively in conjunction with Murakami's earlier fiction, it might be seen as this: In the outer world, *Watashi* had a girlfriend who hanged herself, her body blowing in the wind for two whole weeks before it was discovered. This was a deeply traumatic experience and so he buried its memory in his mind, telling his conscious self that it was not such a big deal and that he needed to move on. Over time, his memories of this girl have been slowly disappearing, but an inner part of himself, represented by *Boku*, is desperately trying to gather the last remaining fragments of memory and turn them into something that can help *Watashi* therapeutically, in short, a *monogatari*. This, of course, is a reading that goes beyond the information *Hard-Boiled* offers as a self-contained work, but it makes some sense when reading Murakami's fiction as an evolving therapeutic project. *Hard-Boiled* hides its therapeutic theme, I would argue, because Murakami had taken Murakami Ryū's advice to heart. At this point in his career, he still needed to keep writing about K; he just needed to do it in a less obvious way.

This then is the first justification that might be offered for the ending of *Hard-Boiled*. Yes, there are dangers that come with overstaying in Neverland, but there are also memories that *Boku* must rescue from there before they are gone forever. Self-therapy requires bringing dissociated memories and conscious narratives of self back together again, but timing is also important, and *Boku* still feels he needs more time to discover the personal significance of this Town for him. Read in the context of his evolving therapeutic project, what Murakami seems to be saying here is that, at this point of his career, there was still a wall he could not break through. He could not yet let go of his melancholic attachment to K.

A second possible justification for the ending of the novel is to recognize that the decision to stay in the "End of the World" is perhaps not really *Boku*'s to make. Nor does it seem to be *Watashi*'s. Instead, their fates have been sealed for them by an inhumane scientist who, in the past at least, was working for the System. In this way, *Boku*'s choice to remain in the Town is not a choice at all; instead, it is something forced upon him by others. Self-therapy is still desirable here; it is just no longer possible because of the ways the unconscious is being used and abused by the System. The ending of the novel, in other words, represents not a personal failing, but a systemic one. This, in turn, might be read as Murakami coming to terms with what it might mean to be writing therapeutic *monogatari* as an increasingly successful commercial product. In what ways is the (commercial) system colonizing his second basement for its own purposes and what does this mean about the authenticity of the therapeutic process he is engaged in?

Reading *Hard-Boiled* as this kind of meta-critique about the challenges of writing as self-therapy as a commercial enterprise is an interesting exercise, but it also paints the novel in an extremely pessimistic light. Characters are stripped of their agency, their fates entirely determined by external forces. But is this really the message the novel offers? Are there not also avenues of resistance and hope? There are some, I would argue, and it is noticing these that shows how the fates of *Watashi* and *Boku* are not as determined as they first appear.

Watashi's first reaction to the scientist's revelation about what he has done to him is not resignation but anger. He is furious:

> They had stolen my memories from me! Nobody had that right. Nobody! My memories belonged to me. Stealing memories was stealing time. I got so mad, I lost all fear. I didn't care what happened. I want to live! I told myself. I will live. I will get out of this insane netherworld and get my stolen memories back and live. Forget the end of the world, I was ready to reclaim my whole self.[27]

Part of this effort to reclaim his "whole self" involves *Watashi* making a dangerous underground journey with the scientist's granddaughter, another of Murakami's female-aid-figures who helps the central male protagonist on his quest. They are forced to go into the realm of the Inklings where they face a trial involving leeches and water. In terms of plot development, this journey helps them to reunite with the scientist, and for *Watashi* to learn more about what has happened to him, but as Susan Fisher notes, there is also a strong mythical aspect to this part of the novel which suggests there is more than just this involved. The novel explicitly mentions the Orpheus myth as one precedent for this underground journey (Orpheus descending into the underworld to retrieve his wife, Eurydice), but Fisher also notes the Izanagi and Izanami parallel (with Izanagi making a similar underworld journey for his wife, Izanami, the leeches in the story the clearest indication of this parallel).[28] But then who is *Watashi* going to rescue? In terms of the immediate storyline, he is going to rescue the scientist, but this hardly seems to merit the mythical proportions of this part of the story. Read another way, though, what we are seeing here is a foreshadowing of the final journey he will make. Like Orpheus and Izanagi before him, *Watashi* will be descending to the underworld to try and rescue the (now dead) woman he loves.

In the end, *Watashi* fails in this quest. Instead of saving the woman, he ends up stuck in "the end of the world" with her. In the language of Joseph Campbell, this is a failed monomythic journey because there is no return. In the language of Freud, it is a story about the dangerous pull of melancholia. But is all hope lost? Is there not still some possibility that in the future our hero will be able to return from the underworld (The End of the World)?

Rebecca Suter notes how the "rational, pseudo-scientific explanation" offered in the novel for why *Watashi*'s quest is destined to fail (the experiment carried out by the scientist) is potentially undermined at one point near the end of the novel, just before *Watashi* crosses over to The End of the World. The scene Suter has in mind is one where a model of a unicorn skull that has been presented to *Watashi* by the scientist magically begins to glow, much like the unicorn skulls *Boku* dreamreads in The End of the World. This is something also seen by the female librarian *Watashi* is with at the time (not to be confused with *Boku*'s librarian), and so we suspect that this is more than just a figment of *Watashi*'s imagination. Suter writes, "Unless it is a collective hallucination, then, the scene can only be read as an intrusion of the reality of The End of the World into that of the Hard-Boiled Wonderland, a bridge between these two realms that belongs to the ontological, not epistemological, level."[29] In short, what Suter sees here is the power that *Boku* holds to affect events in the outer world, something that cannot be entirely contained by the logic of the science fiction narrative.[30] For Suter, this episode "raises more riddles than it solves," but her general observation is an interesting one. The power of the System is strong, but *Watashi* and *Boku*'s ultimate fate may not be as determined as the scientist's story suggests.

In the Hard-Boiled Wonderland sections of the novel, the switchover to the third circuit, The End of the World, is described as irreversible, something that is pointless for *Watashi* to resist. Many characters also try to convince *Boku* of a similar futility in resistance. "[T]his Town is perfect," the Colonel says to *Boku* at one point, "And by perfect, I mean complete."[31] Talking about the Wall which surrounds the Town, the

Gatekeeper continues this theme of perfection: "The bricks fit perfect; not a hair-space between them. Nobody can put a dent in the Wall. And nobody can climb it. Because this Wall is perfect. So forget any ideas you have. Nobody leaves here."[32] It is *Boku*'s shadow who sees through this perfection, seeing it for what it really is and concluding that the "Town is perfectly wrong."[33] He is constantly examining his surroundings, looking for evidence that the Town is not as hermetically sealed as it first appears. He explains to *Boku*, "The Town seems to contain everything it needs to sustain itself in perpetual peace and security. The order of things remains perfectly constant, no matter what happens. But a world of perpetual motion is theoretically impossible. There has to be a trick. The system must take in and let out somewhere."[34] For many people, of course, melancholia or depression does feel like a hermetically sealed prison from which it is impossible to escape, but the reality is that many people do eventually find an exit. *Boku*'s shadow represents this part of the self that even in the darkest of circumstances still holds out hope for escape.

Boku's shadow is constantly searching for these points at which the system takes in and lets out. "Look at the sky," he says to *Boku* at one point. "Where do those birds go when they fly over the Wall? To another world. If there was nothing out there, why surround the place with a Wall? It has to let out somewhere."[35] He later hypothesizes that the Southern Pool, a body of water that *Boku* has been told has a dangerous undertow that sucks people away, leads to this outer world. He thus suggests that they dive into this Pool together as their escape plan. While the scientist's story suggests that there is no escaping the End of the World, this is not something *Boku*'s shadow can accept, and the evidence he sees of imperfections in the system, places where connections with the outside world remain possible, gives him cause for hope. And the glowing unicorn skull in the outer world suggests this may be more than just wishful thinking. So if we accept that the choice to remain in the Town is not as forced as it might first appear, then we return to the point of what to make of *Boku*'s decision to stay. What is the meaning of the Town for him?

Boku's shadow points out the problems of the Town, the way its lack of negative emotions such as disillusionment and depression are premised on its lack of opposite emotions such as joy and love.[36] *Boku* gets this, but he feels drawn to the Town regardless. He describes what he feels in different ways—an attachment, a responsibility, even love—and he says that he would regret leaving it.[37] What he hopes is that by staying in the Town he will slowly begin to recall things and that this might provide the key to his own creation. "No, I doubt it," is his shadow's astute reply, "Not as long as you are sealed inside yourself. Search as you might, you will never know the clarity of distance without me."[38] Who is right then, *Boku* or his shadow? Perhaps the answer is both. Clearly, remaining in the Town forever is not the answer, but then *Boku* may be right that the timing is not yet right to leave. Perhaps there is still something precious he needs to save from the Town before it is too late. In terms of therapeutic breakthroughs, timing is everything.

Murakami has said that writing about this Town was one of the hardest things he has ever done and that he rewrote the ending of *Hard-Boiled* six or seven times trying to get it right. In the end, though, he sticks by his final decision to have *Boku* stay.[39] This may reflect Murakami's growing understanding of the difficulties of seeking self-therapy in late-capitalist Japan, something that is suggested in the novel by the presence of the System and the scientist. More than this, though, I believe that it points to Murakami's growing understanding of what this Town meant to him and his desire to salvage what he could from it before it was too late. Memories, *Hard-Boiled* suggests, eventually die, but transformed into something else—a *monogatari*—they have the power to sustain us and to carry us forward into the future. Of course, there are dangers that come with remaining in the Town too long, the possible Peter Pan syndrome of losing yourself to Neverland and never growing up or facing the future. But there are also risks that come with leaving too early, of not truly saying your last goodbyes. *Hard-Boiled* is a novel that walks this fine line between possible psychological regression and meaningful last goodbyes.

Murakami's next novel, *Norwegian Wood*, walks this same fine line. Sitting on the threshold where his memories of an earlier time are just beginning to fade, a thirty-seven-year-old narrator begins to narrate the traumatic story of his past, telling of two women he was once involved with, one who would eventually take her own life. This woman had faced her own traumas through the suicides of others, and in the end, the temptation of Neverland—of wanting to reunite with the dead—was just too strong for her. But what then is the path out of this temptation? How can one face the challenge of growing up?

The Anatomy of Dependence in *Norwegian Wood*

Norwegian Wood was initially marketed as a "100% love novel," yet whether love is involved in any of the complicated relationships which make up this novel is itself a complicated question.[40] In terms of understanding Murakami's fiction through the "detachment to commitment" framework already discussed, this is a novel which sits somewhere between these competing poles, a novel which, while it fails to establish what commitment might look like, at least is thinking about what it might mean, provided one understands what Murakami means by commitment. What many critics mean when they use this framework are political detachment and political commitment, and so the debate focuses on whether Murakami has found a model of political engagement. If one looks again at Murakami's quotation about the shift from detachment and aphorisms, to the story element, and finally to commitment, however, they will see that Murakami is not really talking about politics here at all. Instead, he says, "[c]ommitment . . . is all about relationships between people." Of course, thinking about relationships between people might lead to questions about politics, but this does not seem to be what Murakami primarily has in mind. Instead, it would be more useful to classify his fiction as evolving from detachment to attachment (or what I have been describing as therapeutic thread three: the journey from avoidance to earned attachment).

Murakami's first four novels can all be classified as solipsistic works. A nameless narrator (or narrators) engages in a quest that in the end is all about him (even if it potentially has larger cultural, historical, or political ramifications). The other characters in the novels are often nameless, identified more by the role they play in helping the main protagonist to learn something about himself (or not to learn it, as the case may be). This starts to change with *Norwegian Wood*, where the majority of characters are given real names and where they seem to exist in their own right with their own subjective viewpoints and problems. Now the question of self-therapy becomes not just about how a self can heal itself, but also about how it might begin to connect with other human beings. While this quest for connection is one each of the characters in *Norwegian Wood* ultimately fails, their attempts at least allow us to see where the problem lies.

Given what I am suggesting here is the emerging focus on attachment in Murakami's fiction, it is useful to provide a brief introduction to the field of attachment studies and what it might predict about the journey from detachment to attachment. For attachment theorists, attachment relationships begin in childhood, particularly in the mother-child bond (or whatever relationship or relationships substitute for it), and this primary attachment experience then has profound implications for later relationships, including romantic ones. Ideally, this primary attachment relationship provides what is called a secure base, and if this is the case, a secure attachment style results. In less than ideal situations, however, other attachment styles may emerge—avoidant, ambivalent, and disorganized, the three commonly discussed.[41] Most relevant to Murakami's fiction, I would argue, is the avoidant attachment style in which the human need for intimacy is often downplayed in favor of self-reliance. A child may learn that appeals for intimacy are ignored or downplayed by caregivers, and so over time, they stop making attempts. In adulthood, avoidant people will often talk positively about their home life, describing their parents as good or normal, but there will often be a surprising lack of detail when they try to explain exactly what was good. Instead, they will often claim to not recall much of their childhood, to not see it as very important, or to not say much about it at all.[42]

One area of life an avoidant attachment style might express itself is in attitudes toward sexual intimacy, a topic relevant to *Norwegian Wood*. "[A]voidant individuals," Mikulincer and Shaver explain, "are vulnerable to melancholic sexuality," or what they describe, quoting research from others, as "an arctic wasteland, cold and devoid of relationships."[43] The physical and emotional aspects of sex are separated, with emotional intimacy downplayed or even avoided. Looking at the research, Mikulincer and Shaver describe how "several studies have found that avoidant attachment is associated with more positive attitudes toward casual sex, such as acceptance of loveless sex and acceptance of uncommitted sex."[44] As will be seen later, this is an attitude mostly strongly seen in *Norwegian Wood* in a character called Nagasawa, though it also has some application to the main protagonist, Watanabe Tōru.

While attachment styles are rooted in childhood experiences, they are not necessarily set in stone. Researchers note cases where avoidant, ambivalent, or disorganized attachment styles become secure later in life, a phenomenon known as "earned attachment." Daniel Siegel explains, "These are adults who appear to have had difficult childhoods, but have come to create a coherent narrative: They have made sense of their lives. The children attached to these adults have secure attachments and do well!"[45] This possibility is important in Murakami's fiction and finds its clearest expression in *1Q84*, which can be seen as the breakthrough work for this particular therapeutic thread.

Thinking about the question of attachment in Japanese society, one famous theory that deserves attention is that presented by the psychologist Doi Takeo in his 1971 book *Amae no Kōzō* (*The Anatomy of Dependence*). While not without its critics, Doi's theory has remained influential and argues for the prominent place that issues of dependence occupy in Japanese interpersonal relationships. His study is primarily a linguistic one, with the noun *amae* at its center, a word, he writes, that denotes "an affirmative attitude" toward the spirit of dependence.[46] Doi's argument is not that such an attitude is unique to Japan; indeed, he acknowledges that it is a human universal, biologically grounded in the parent-child relationship.[47] Rather, he claims that many Japanese have a heightened awareness of issues related to dependence, evident linguistically in the many words the Japanese language has to account for it and its related concepts, and a propensity to carry positive associations with dependence into adulthood. What Doi's theory might sensitize us to is the way a secure attachment style in Japan might include a wider tolerance for dependence than a Western model, which favors individualism coupled with healthy interdependence.

The character in *Norwegian Wood* who is most open about her need for *amae* is Midori, one of the two main women in the novel that Watanabe drifts between (the other being Naoko). From the moment she invites herself into Watanabe's life, it is evident that what Midori seeks from him is unquestioning acceptance, something she feels has been missing from her life to this point. Midori lost her mother to a brain tumor two years before meeting Watanabe, and her father is dying from the same disease, though she does not reveal these facts to Watanabe initially. This alone might seem to explain her deep need for *amae*, but she makes it clear that her dissatisfaction with her parents originates long before their illnesses. She confesses to Watanabe, for example, that she found it difficult to feel sadness when her mother died, an emotional coldness she attributes to the lack of love she received as a child:

> It's true I have a cold streak. I recognize that. But if they—my father and mother—had loved me a little more, I would have been able to feel more—to feel real sadness for example.... I was always hungry for love. Just once, I wanted to know what it was like to get my fill of it—to be fed so much love I couldn't take any more. Just once. But they never gave that to me. Never, not once. If I tried to cuddle up and beg for something, they'd just shove me the other way and yell at me.[48]

The expression in the final sentence here, "to cuddle up and beg for something," comes from the Japanese verb *amaeru* (from the same root as the noun *amae*) and is translated in one dictionary as "to behave like a spoilt child; to fawn on."[49] Midori's attempts to *amaeru* her parents, to depend on them completely and to have them respond to her emotional needs, were rejected, and she believes this has left her emotionally stunted.

Midori goes on to explain to Watanabe that what she is looking for in a relationship is "selfishness. Perfect selfishness."[50] She playfully narrates a scenario for Watanabe to clarify her meaning. Imagine, she begins, that I ask you (or some other man) to go and buy me strawberry shortbread. You leave immediately and buy it for me, but when you return I say I don't want it anymore and throw it out of the window. This, Midori explains, is what she is looking for. Watanabe is confused, responding, "I'm not sure that has anything to do with love."[51] Perhaps he is right, but for Midori at least, such a provocation is at least a possible precursor to love. She goes on to explain that what she wants from the man in her scenario is an apology: "Now I see, Midori. What a fool I've been. . . . To make it up to you, I'll go out and buy you something else. What would you like? Chocolate mousse? Cheesecake?"[52] Still confused, Watanabe asks Midori what would come next: "So then I'd give him all the love he deserves for what he's done . . . to me, that's what love is."[53]

Amae, as this passage suggests, is the experience of receiving unquestioning acceptance from another human being, even in the face of bad behavior, which, in turn, opens up the recipient to the possibility of love and ultimately to the ability to love in return. The act of throwing the shortbread out of the window in Midori's scenario is a test—a way of seeing whether she can be loved despite acting like a spoilt child. Simply telling her to grow up in such a scenario is not going to work. The prerequisite for maturity here is a stage of emotional dependency that Midori has yet to experience. It is only when one has passed through this stage that a more mature relationship based on reciprocity can develop. It is this belief in *amae* as a necessary developmental stage that distinguishes Midori's more positive feelings toward dependence from Naoko's more negative ones.

This deep need for *amae* can also help explain another facet of Midori's personality: her insatiable curiosity about sex and more particularly her lack of a social filter when discussing such matters with Watanabe. Examples in the text are not difficult to find. Midori, for example, asks Watanabe to try fantasizing about her when he masturbates and to report back on the results, asks probing questions about the masturbation practices of other boys in the dormitory where Watanabe lives, and asks to be taken to a porno flick: "a real S and M one, with whips."[54] Midori recognizes that she is pushing boundaries with Watanabe, but she puts it down to simple curiosity: "I don't want you to get the wrong impression—that I'm a nymphomaniac or frustrated or a tease or anything. I'm just interested in that stuff. I want to know about it."[55] Yet, her constant provocations go beyond normal boundaries; in short, she appears to be testing the limits of *amae* in her relationship with Watanabe. How much will he let her get away with? This deep need for *amae* also explains her ability to hold a grudge when Watanabe forgets her (usually because he is lost in his thoughts for Naoko) or when he fails to notice something like a new hairstyle. As Midori's sister explains over the phone on one occasion when Watanabe calls and tries to apologize, "[O]nce she gets mad, she stays that way. Like an animal."[56] This is the flipside to Midori's need for *amae*—reject her appeals and she may never forgive you.

This is not to say that Midori's need for *amae* marks her as a weak character in the novel. Rather, it is her willingness to *amaeru*, to indulge Watanabe's kindness at the risk of rejection, which ultimately gives her character vitality. She is hoping to move from dependence to interdependence, to first be unconditionally loved and then to love in return, and this, it should be noted, is not unconnected to her sexual curiosity. Sex is many things in *Norwegian Wood*: at times a form of exploitation, at other times an attempt at growing up, and at still other times, an attempt at healing (examples can be found in what follows). Midori's embrace of sexuality can be read as an embrace of life itself, an idea that will be explored more fully in the discussion later on Watanabe.

It is here again that she offers one of her strongest contrasts to Naoko, a character who retreats not only from sexuality but from life itself.

Watanabe's first flashback in the novel is to an autumn day in 1969. He is in a meadow with Naoko, and he remembers her talking about a fenceless well that was "deep beyond measuring, and crammed full of darkness."[57] Watanabe is unsure whether the well is real: "It might have been an image or a sign that existed only inside Naoko."[58] For Naoko, though, it is clearly a threat; she fears falling in, though she is positive that as long as she stays with Watanabe, this will never happen. Watanabe tries reassuring her by saying that the solution then is for her to always stay with him, an offer which Naoko rejects: "It would just be wrong—wrong for you, wrong for me. . . . Don't you see? It's just not possible for one person to watch over another person for ever and ever. . . . What kind of equality would there be in that?"[59] At the heart of the issue for Naoko is fairness.[60] She doesn't believe it is right for one person to do all the giving and another to do all the taking. As she later explains, "The one thing I don't want to be is a burden to anyone."[61]

The well, of course, is naturally interpreted as a symbol of Naoko's psychological state. In its mysterious depth and darkness, it might easily be taken as a symbol for death, and, indeed, Naoko takes her own life near the end of the novel, suggesting that she has finally stumbled in. The Japanese word for well, *ido*, is also a homophone in Japanese for the Freudian id, and so the well might also be taken as a symbol of Naoko's fear of Eros; indeed, her inability to perform sexually is deeply connected to her psychological decline in the novel. The only time Naoko experiences coitus is with Watanabe on her twentieth birthday, the traditional coming-of-age birthday in Japan, but, rather than using this as an occasion to pass over the threshold from adolescence into adulthood, she retreats again, back into adolescent ambivalence. The approach of her twentieth birthday, she explains, felt unnatural, "Like somebody's pushing me from behind."[62] This unease is shared by Watanabe, who confesses: "There was something strange about Naoko's becoming twenty. I felt as if the only thing that made sense, whether for Naoko or for me, was to keep going back and forth between eighteen and nineteen. After eighteen would come nineteen, and after nineteen, eighteen. Of course. But she turned twenty."[63]

This idea of sex as a rite of passage on the pathway to adulthood runs throughout *Norwegian Wood* and relates to an earlier relationship between Naoko and Kizuki, Watanabe's best friend growing up. As teenagers, Naoko, Watanabe, and Kizuki had spent much of their free time together, though only Naoko and Kizuki had been romantically involved, an arrangement that had lasted until Kizuki took his own life at seventeen. While Watanabe had always assumed that Naoko and Kizuki were sexually active, on the night he and Naoko have sex, he learns this was not the case, that although they had experimented sexually and felt very open and natural together, Naoko's inability to achieve genital stimulation had meant that they had failed to experience coitus.

Looking back, Naoko sees the problem as one of failing to pay their debts to society—in short, of failing to grow up. She speculates to Watanabe that had Kizuki lived, they most likely would have stayed together, growing increasingly unhappy. Watanabe wonders if this had to be the case, but Naoko is convinced, her reasoning being as follows:

Because we would have had to pay the world back what we owed it. . . . The pain of growing up. We didn't pay when we should have, so now the bills are due. . . . We were like kids who grew up naked on a desert island. If we got hungry, we'd just pick a banana; if we got lonely, we'd go to sleep in each other's arms. But that kind of thing doesn't last forever.[64]

The opposite of the individuating hero in Jungian psychology is the *puer aeternus* or eternal child. It is a kind of Peter Pan syndrome where the temptation of staying in childhood replaces the need for individuation and adult responsibility. Opting for this deceptively risk-free existence, however, entails its own risks. Robert Segal explains, "To live as a *puer* . . . is to live as a psychological infant and, ultimately, as a foetus. The life of a *puer* in myth invariably ends in premature death, which psychologically means the death of the ego and a return to the womb-like unconscious."[65]

Naoko first faces the premature death of her elder sister and then of her boyfriend Kizuki. The question she faces is whether she will face the same fate or not. Her struggle in some ways mirrors that of Holden Caulfield from J. D. Salinger's *The Catcher in the Rye* (a novel Murakami has translated into Japanese), which is referenced in *Norwegian Wood*. At one point, for example, Reiko, Naoko's roommate, accuses Watanabe of deliberately speaking like Salinger's Holden: "Don't tell me you're trying to imitate that boy in *Catcher in the Rye*?"[66] Midori's criticism of the political radicals around her as "a bunch of phonies" also has echoes of Holden.[67]

Both *The Catcher in the Rye* and *Norwegian Wood* take their titles from cultural references that are used less for their original meanings than for what they reveal about a central character's state of mind. In Holden's case, he famously misremembers the words of a Robert Burns poem, turning a reference about "meeting" in the rye that hints at the theme of sexual promiscuity into one that deals with his desire to "catch" or protect children so that they will never have to face the pains of the adult world. The title of *Norwegian Wood* comes from the famous Beatles' song of the same title which is mentioned numerous times in the novel, but the imagery and feelings Naoko derives from it relate just as much to the way its title was translated into Japanese as something like *The Woods of Norway*. The original reference in the Beatles' song is not to woods as such, but to the material used to decorate a woman's home ("She showed me her room, isn't it good, Norwegian wood") and so it could be said that the title and theme of Murakami's novel were found in mistranslation. Murakami, of course, is a translator himself and a musical connoisseur, and has indicated he is aware of the original meaning of the reference, though this is hardly the point. Rather, like Holden, Naoko is using the song to tell us not something about the original cultural reference, but about herself. She explains, "That song can make me feel so sad. . . . I don't know, I guess I imagine myself wandering in a deep wood. I'm all alone and it's cold and dark, and nobody comes to save me."[68]

The more substantial comparison between *Norwegian Wood* and *The Catcher in the Rye*, however, is with Naoko and Holden, and the way ambiguity about sex prevents them from growing up. As readers of Salinger's novel will know, there are strong parallels here with Holden who, while deeply interested in sexual matters, ultimately remains ambivalent about, and sabotages, opportunities for sex. Like Naoko, Holden ends up in some kind of institution, and while there are clearly differences between them, it is fair to say that they both struggle with issues of psychosexual development.

In terms of Naoko's relationship with Kizuki, it might be said that in one sense they had perfect *amae*, an ability to ask anything of the other and to get it, but this was possible only because they had cut themselves off from society. In this way, their deep sense of interdependence and connection could not survive the transition into adulthood, symbolized in the story by their inability to experience coitus, the one thing they could not give each other. Kizuki's solution was to take his own life, and while Naoko struggles on for a while longer, she eventually follows Kizuki into death. What their journey suggests is that while the experience of *amae* is an important landmark on the path to adulthood, it cannot be its end point; there must be a more painful experience beyond this where one differentiates oneself from others and engages with society more broadly.

Naoko's sexual closure in the novel is mirrored by her linguistic closure. Shimizu Yoshinori points out that the only name offered in *Norwegian Wood* for Naoko's condition is *kotoba sagashibyō*, a neologism that might be translated as "word-seeking disease" or perhaps "not-having-the-right-words-to-say disease."[69] The one night she opens up sexually to Watanabe is also the one night she most fully opens up to him verbally—"Naoko was unusually talkative that night"—but she soon closes up again.[70] The first stage of her verbal closure began with her sister's suicide. Naoko had discovered her sister's dead body, and for a time following this, had found it difficult to communicate with others. Beyond this early loss of language through shock, there seems to be a deeper, ongoing struggle with language that plagues her throughout the novel. "I can never say what I want to say," she complains at one point, "It's like I'm split in two."[71] Following her sexual encounter with Watanabe, she retreats from Tokyo into the relative peace of Ami Hostel, a sanatorium in the hills of Kyoto where people work the land, embrace each other's weaknesses, and try hard to practice a policy of complete honesty. Watanabe visits Naoko there, and they also communicate frequently through letters, but even here Naoko's problems with language continue. "Writing is a painful process for me," she explains in one of these letters.[72] With hindsight, her roommate at Ami Hostel, Reiko, comes to see Naoko's inability to write as the first sign of her final mental and emotional breakdown.[73] Losing language is the first step in her losing her life.

Naoko has a deep sense of her own flaws and is reluctant to remain in a relationship where she will remain forever dependent. She asks to be remembered by Watanabe (which is partly why he is writing his narrative), but she is reluctant to ask for much more than this. She is struggling to grow up and become an adult, but an extended adolescence is not sustainable in the long run, and so ultimately, she chooses a premature death. This might seem to suggest that a more tough-minded independence is the only way forward, yet the example of her sister contradicts this. On the surface, this sister had appeared confident and competent, and while not without her dark moments, had seemed self-sufficient in the way she had dealt with things: "She was the kind of person who took care of things by herself. She'd never ask anybody for advice or help."[74] In the end, this sister's suicide comes to personify the pain of trying to go it alone—the way that disconnecting from others is not ultimately a solution to the pain that human relationships can bring. Another character in the novel that personifies this downside of independence is Nagasawa.

Watanabe and Nagasawa's friendship starts from a literary connection. When Nagasawa first meets him, Watanabe is reading Fitzgerald's *The Great Gatsby*, and when questioned about it, he explains that he is reading it for the third time. This is enough for Nagasawa, who declares, "Well, any friend of Gatsby is a friend of mine."[75] What Nagasawa is impressed by is Watanabe's independence, his ability to stand above the herd and have his own personal tastes (Fitzgerald not being a popular writer at the time). Nagasawa expounds, "If you only read the books that everyone else is reading, you can only think what everyone else is thinking."[76]

In Chapter 1, I described the male–male dynamic in Murakami's fiction between an individuating protagonist and his Nietzschean rival, while also arguing for the importance of Fitzgerald's fiction as an important early model for this dynamic. The relationship between Watanabe and Nagasawa is an important milestone in this development, the nod to Fitzgerald clear throughout, though Nagasawa is still a friend rather than an antagonist to Watanabe. Nagasawa studies law at Tokyo University and is destined for the Foreign Ministry. He is also, despite his loyal girlfriend, a womanizer, and though Watanabe questions his lifestyle, he soon starts accompanying him on his sexual exploits. In terms of attachment theory, Nagasawa is clearly an avoidant type, his celebration of commitment-free sex a perfect description of melancholic sexuality.

Like any good burgeoning Nietzschean Superman, Nagasawa lives above the common values and morality of the herd, forging ahead on his own terms, seeking to test the limits of his capabilities. His primary motivation in life, he claims, is less power and money than a desire to test himself in the biggest field possible: the nation. "Sounds like a game," Watanabe suggests, to which Nagasawa promptly agrees.[77] Nagasawa believes in working hard, but he also holds in contempt those whose hard work amounts to little: "That's not hard work. It's just manual labor. . . . The 'hard work' I'm talking about is more self-directed and purposeful."[78] In his conception of himself as a self-made man, there are parallels with some of Fitzgerald's charismatic but famously flawed characters, including, of course, Gatsby. As with his literary predecessors, there is also a sense that behind Nagasawa's polished exterior is a deeply troubled soul.

We never find out what happens to Nagasawa beyond joining the Foreign Ministry and moving to Germany.[79] We do know what happens to his girlfriend though, the long-suffering Hatsumi: two years after he leaves for Germany, she marries someone else, and two years after that, she kills herself. Cause and effect here are unclear, Hatsumi killing herself long after she separated from Nagasawa, but her downward spiral arguably starts with her relationship with him. Their relationship feels doomed from the start, with his need for independence and hers for dependence in clear competition.

At the dinner where Nagasawa, Hatsumi, and Watanabe celebrate Nagasawa's passing of the exam for the Foreign Ministry (incidentally, one of the most emotionally charged scenes in Tran Ang Hung's film adaptation of the novel), Hatsumi starts to challenge the two boys on their promiscuous ways, and one incident in particular where they swapped sexual partners. Defending his actions, Nagasawa retorts, "You can't even call what I do fooling around. It's just a game. Nobody gets hurt."[80] Hatsumi is outraged and uncharacteristically lets her frustrations show. She admits that she is hurt, but Nagasawa is deaf to her complaint, justifying his actions with the simple assertion, "[t]hat's the kind of man I am."[81] Nagasawa is an extreme individualist, an unapologetic avoidant type who rejects any form of *amae*. His final words of advice to Watanabe are, "Don't feel sorry for yourself. . . . Only assholes do that."[82]

While dependence causes problems for many characters in the novel, Nagasawa's hard-headed independence is far from being its antidote. Early on, for example, Watanabe describes Nagasawa as a man who "lived in his own special hell."[83] This hell comes from deep paradoxes that leave him outwardly successful but inwardly suffering:

> There were sides to Nagasawa's personality that conflicted in the extreme. Even I would be moved by his kindness at times, but he could, just as easily, be malicious and cruel. He was both a spirit of amazing loftiness and an irredeemable man of the gutter. He could charge forward, the optimistic leader, even as his heart writhed in a swamp of loneliness.[84]

This, of course, is who the Nietzschean Superman must be, embracing such opposites and eventually transcending them in search of the next stage of human development.

If characters like Naoko and Hatsumi need others too much, and if someone like Nagasawa needs them too little, then where does this leave us? Is Watanabe, the central protagonist of the novel, the one who is supposed to show us where the happy medium might lie? It might be nice if he did, but like many things in Murakami's fiction, it is not this tidy. Watanabe is not unlike Nagasawa in some ways with an avoidant attachment style that keeps him disconnected from others, but unlike Nagasawa, he is not convinced that this is a good thing. Instead, he is trying to break through avoidance to find earned attachment, to put himself in a position where he could truly love another human being.

Nagasawa believes that he and Watanabe are "a lot alike," that "[n]either of us is interested, essentially, in anything but ourselves . . . neither of us is able to feel any interest in anything other than what we ourselves think or feel or do."[85] Speaking to Hatsumi, he explains, "[Watanabe] may be a nice guy, but deep down in his heart he's incapable of loving anybody. There's always some part of him somewhere that's wide awake and detached."[86] He observes, "Where Watanabe and I are alike is, we don't give a damn if nobody understands us."[87] Watanabe objects to this last claim, arguing that he does care if people understand him—at least some people (assumedly Naoko and Midori).[88] And yet, even he has to admit that there is something awry in his relationships with others. As he explains to Naoko, "[S]ometimes I think I've got this hard kernel in my heart, and nothing much can get inside it. I doubt if I can really love anybody."[89] Later he confesses to Reiko, "Like Naoko, I'm not really sure what it means to love another person."[90]

Despite these reservations, Watanabe demonstrates deep commitment to Naoko, and though he falters along the way, he does stick with her to the end. The language he uses to justify this commitment is unrelated to love, however; rather, he employs a language of responsibility. As he puts it to Midori, "All I know is, I have a kind of responsibility in all this as a human being, and I can't just turn my back on it."[91] If it is not love which is motivating Watanabe, then perhaps it is codependency. From the beginning of his narrative, Watanabe confesses that "Naoko never loved me," and we've already established that he doubts his ability to love another person.[92] So what's in this relationship for him? Talking with Reiko, Watanabe explains that what he is looking for is nothing less than a form of salvation: "Naoko and I have to save each other. It's the only way for either of us to be saved."[93] This kind of language might seem to support a codependency diagnosis; Watanabe is identifying himself as a savior figure who will stick by Naoko regardless of the personal costs. Is this what keeps him going?

This theme of female victims and male healers runs throughout Murakami's fiction (*The Wind-Up Bird Chronicle* is another prominent example). Yet, I would argue that there is more to Watanabe's motivations than codependency alone can explain. An important point in all this is that Watanabe is seeking salvation not only for Naoko but also for himself. A truly codependent relationship would not seek this kind of development, the dark reward being the validation that comes through maintaining the martyr's role. If we take Watanabe's desire for mutual salvation at face value then, we have to acknowledge that he is seeking to move beyond this impasse, to break out of the avoidant attachment style he favors to find earned attachment. While this is not a goal he ultimately achieves in the novel, his ambition at least is clear.

The major discovery Watanabe claims to make in the novel is formulated in this way: "Death is not the opposite of life but an innate part of life."[94] This can be understood in several ways, not least of which is an acknowledgment on Watanabe's part of the important roles Kizuki and Naoko continue to play in his life, even after their deaths. More than this, though, what Watanabe seems to be seeking through this philosophy is a mythical solution to the dichotomy of life and death, archetypal forces that tear him in different directions. Indeed, the whole way his potential love interests develop between the opposing poles of Naoko and Midori seems designed to make just this point and gives the narrative (among other possible psychoanalytic readings of the text) a strong Freudian flavor.

For Sigmund Freud, the drive for sex is included in the life instincts, part of what he called Eros, a general catchphrase for the human drives related to survival and reproduction. In Freud's early writings, these life-sustaining drives were given the primary focus, together with an examination of the way their clashes with socially derived moralities cause psychological problems for individuals. Yet, Freud eventually had to acknowledge the human potential to subvert Eros, indeed, our ability to choose death over life, and it was this that caused him, late in his career, to propose the notion of a competing death drive (one of his followers would later propose calling this Thanatos, in contrast to Eros). *Norwegian Wood* provides examples of both poles, with Midori most clearly a symbol of Eros and Naoko a symbol of Thanatos. The question for Watanabe is: Which path will he follow?

This life/death dichotomy extends to the settings of the novel itself, with the life and energy of Tokyo most clearly associated with Midori and her sexual energy, and the quiet hills of Kyoto associated with, if not quite death itself, a liminal space approaching it. Ami Hostel is constantly described as a place cut off from the world: the journey there is long and arduous, and on one of his visits Watanabe even encounters Naoko in a perfect, perhaps even ghostly form that is not quite of this world (demonstrating that even in Murakami's most realistic novel, the fantastic is still never far away). Midori reinforces this sense, commenting to Watanabe on his return to Tokyo that, "[y]ou look like you've seen a ghost." Her suggested solution is to "go drinking with me and get a little life into you."[95]

This mythical undercurrent to the novel can help make sense of what to many readers is likely to be the most disturbing or perplexing part of the novel: Reiko's backstory and Watanabe's decision to sleep with her near the end of the novel. Reiko's story is revealed in long conversations with Watanabe, her psychological difficulties starting when the pressure of her dream to become a concert pianist became too much. A man she eventually married saved her from her first mental breakdown. Sticking with the theme of dependence in the novel, Reiko comments, "I figured that as long as I was with him, I would be all right."[96] For a time this proves true, but things fall apart when she is later seduced by one of her piano students, a thirteen-year-old pathological lesbian.

Reiko is surprised by the sexual desire this girl arouses in her, but eventually she comes to her senses and pushes her away. The girl is hurt by this rejection and takes her revenge by spreading rumors about Reiko in the local community. Socially ostracized, Reiko's emotional problems resurface, and it is here that her husband makes a crucial mistake; when things are at their worst and Reiko is pleading with him to get them away to make a fresh start somewhere, he asks her for one more month to get his business affairs in order. As Reiko later confesses, this was the moment everything ended.[97] She had felt she could depend on this man completely, so his delayed response, while reasonable in the context of his own life and career, to her was a fatal blow.

Following Naoko's death, Reiko decides to leave Ami Hostel in an attempt to rehabilitate herself in the world. On her way to Asahikawa in Hokkaido, she stops off to visit Watanabe in Tokyo, their reunion turning into an impromptu memorial of sorts for Naoko (primarily a sing-along with Naoko's favorite song, *Norwegian Wood*, playing a prominent role). Following this makeshift funeral, they then make love four times, a number Rubin suggests is significant because of its cultural weight in Japan as a homophone for death.[98] She then offers Watanabe some parting advice about growing up and becoming an adult, and suggests that he made his final decision to be with Midori a long time ago.[99]

We are far from the traditional formulas of the romance genre here, despite the way *Norwegian Wood* is sometimes marketed.[100] It is one thing to have Watanabe sleep with Naoko in the novel, but what can we make of his decision to sleep with Reiko, Naoko's older roommate, when it is clear he has already committed himself to Midori? One response is that Reiko is standing in for Naoko here, right down to wearing her clothes when she shows up at Watanabe's apartment. Their sexual act is presented as a ritual, a way of coming to terms with Naoko's death and a preparation for returning to the world of the living. Reiko, of course, has her own motivation; her original trauma was social and sexual in nature, so she is seeking sex as a form of healing. What Watanabe seeks, on the other hand, is nothing less than a way to bridge the gap between life and death.

When Naoko first retreats into Ami Hostel, the only means she and Watanabe have of communicating initially is through letters, a slow, ponderous form of communication suited to her position in a liminal space approaching death. The novel ends with a telephone call to Midori, a much more immediate form of communication that is suited to Midori's position in the land of the living. Watanabe is finally ready to express his commitment to her, but Midori responds by asking him where he is, a question he cannot answer. Watanabe's confusion here suggests that he is still lost between two worlds, though his reaching out to Midori through the telephone call at least indicates the direction he is heading.

Of course, it is worth remembering here that it is the thirty-seven-year-old Watanabe who is telling us this tale and finishing his story here. While we still have many questions, he is deliberately choosing not to fill us in. Watanabe has survived, but has he grown up? Did he eventually get together with Midori, and if so, are they still together now? It is impossible to know, but the opening of the novel and the way the story is told makes this feel unlikely.

Given what this book has been arguing about Murakami's fiction, one might suspect that writing *Norwegian Wood* would have been deeply therapeutic for him. In *Hear the Wind Sing*, the suicide of *Boku*'s girlfriend was a traumatic event from his past that he still did not have the words to write about, but here is a Murakami protagonist writing directly and honestly about death. It is as if Murakami was finally ready to write the novel he wanted to debut with. Rather than this bringing relief, though, the publication of *Norwegian Wood* seems to have paralyzed him for a time, Murakami explaining that he could not write anything for five or six months afterward.[101] Murakami explains this uncharacteristic lull in his writing as a consequence of the sudden fame *Norwegian Wood* brought him: "Before *Norwegian Wood*, my books sold nice, small figures. I lived a very quiet, happy life. But after *Norwegian Wood* I wasn't so happy anymore."[102] In short, Murakami's personality was not suited to the sudden rise to fame his success had brought. But I would argue that there was also likely a very personal reason for these post-publication blues. Murakami had finally spoken the unspeakable.

One of the consequences of the 1960s, Murakami has said, is that he lost his faith in words.[103] Explicitly, what Murakami is talking about here is political disillusionment, an acknowledgment of the way clever slogans failed to deliver on real change. When one reads his fiction, however, this loss of faith in words takes on a different, more personal meaning. First in *Hear the Wind Sing*, and then later in *The Town*, Murakami's narrators are constantly bemoaning the ineffectiveness of words to speak truth. "The more I try to be honest," *Boku* says in *Hear the Wind Sing*, "the farther my words sink into darkness."[104] "Words die," a different *Boku* despairs in *The Town*.[105] Talking with the librarian in *The Town*, *Boku* confesses, "I'm afraid to talk. If I put it into words, then everything is going to sound so ordinary." "Everything is ordinary," the librarian tries to comfort him, but clearly for *Boku* this is not enough.[106] He needs the story of this librarian, his dead girlfriend, to be more than ordinary. As *Boku* puts it in *Hear the Wind Sing*, he needs to "tell the story of the world in words far more beautiful than these."[107]

There is a sense, then, in which writing *Norwegian Wood* was both necessary and anticlimactic for Murakami. By finally putting this story into words, a story based in some part on the suicide of K, he was making it something ordinary. This is not a criticism of *Norwegian Wood* itself, which is well written, a breakout novel that would go on to create the Murakami phenomenon. It is simply an acknowledgment that words always have their limits. There is a part of Murakami that would have preferred to keep this story unwritten, to keep the promise of its beautiful telling always as an event for the future. But this could not be. At some point, the spell of Neverland had to be broken and Murakami had to come back to the world. He had to speak the unspeakable and turn it into something ordinary.

Hirano explains how the original Japanese version of *Norwegian Wood* came with an afterword that was removed from later versions. In it, Murakami dedicated the novel to certain unnamed individuals both living and dead and explained that it was a very personal novel for him to write, much like Fitzgerald's *The Great Gatsby* and *Tender Is the Night* are personal novels for him.[108] I have already written a lot about the influence of *The Great Gatsby* on Murakami's fiction, but it is useful here to also take a brief look at the influence of *Tender Is the Night*, a novel which is particularly important for understanding *Norwegian Wood*. *Tender Is the Night* is the story of a doctor, Dick Diver, who marries one of his patients, Nicole, in part out of deep feelings of responsibility for her, but who later becomes interested in a beautiful young actress, Rosemary, who shows some interest in him. Dick wrestles with what to do—his feelings of responsibility versus the desires of his heart—but ultimately, he ends up with neither woman. The dynamics of this love triangle are applicable to Watanabe (Dick), Naoko (Nicole), and Midori (Rosemary).[109]

As I mentioned in Chapter 1, *Tender Is the Night* is the novel which made Murakami fall in love with Fitzgerald. To refresh the story, he read this novel, did not think much of it at first, but then several months later found himself drawn to it again in a very powerful way. The question is why this novel should have captured him in this way. Undoubtedly there were many reasons, but one of them was likely the resonance the story must have had with his own complicated love triangle with K and his future wife Yōko. In the newspaper article on Fitzgerald I referenced in Chapter 1, Murakami says that his fascination with *Tender Is the Night* started when he was twenty-two, the age at which he got married and later learned about K's death. In the introduction to his first translation of Fitzgerald stories, he says that his fascination with *Tender Is the Night* came when he was nineteen, a time when he was likely involved with both women. Whatever the real age was, it is not difficult to imagine how this story about competing feelings of responsibility and sexual interest could have captured his attention around these years.

As Hirano describes, the publication of *Norwegian Wood* was not only painful for Murakami but also for his wife, Yōko. Of course, she may have been affected by the sudden rise to fame too, but this is less likely, given that she was in the background to begin with.[110] Instead, a more likely scenario is that the publication of *Norwegian Wood* was painful because it was so personal. It was making something private potentially public, even if this personal story had been carefully camouflaged. This is not to suggest that every detail in *Norwegian Wood* needs to or even can be traced back to real-world events; it is still a work of fiction. And yet, as Murakami confessed in his original afterword, it was also an extremely personal novel for him. Removing this afterword from later versions of *Norwegian Wood* was a small attempt to hide the personal nature of this novel, but it was already too late. To borrow a cliched expression that seems appropriate for Murakami's fiction, the cat had already been let out of the bag.

While the immediate aftermath of publishing *Norwegian Wood* was not pleasant for Murakami, in terms of his evolving therapeutic project, it was undoubtedly an important work to write. In *Hard-Boiled* we saw protagonists who had hit a wall, who seemed stuck in their therapeutic journeys, and who, as a result, were locked in their own personal Neverland, The End of the World. In *Norwegian Wood*, we see similar characters who face similar challenges, and, as a result, suffer premature deaths. Watanabe is torn about what to do, pulled between both Midori and Naoko, life and death, but his final decision to call Midori is a life-affirming one. In Murakami's next novel, *Dance Dance Dance*, he would return to the story of *Boku* from the Rat trilogy, this time offering an ending that suggests the possibility of emotional breakthroughs and connections with others, a resolution to the first therapeutic thread in Murakami's fiction.

Passing through the Wall in *Dance Dance Dance*

Dance Dance Dance is set in 1983, four and a half years after *Boku*'s last adventure in *A Wild Sheep Chase*. The period following this earlier adventure, it is revealed, was a difficult time for *Boku*, his main task being to recover his sense of equilibrium. The way he did this was by blocking his ears for a time to any potential calls from the unconscious: "I scarcely talked to the cat. The telephone rang. I let it ring. If someone knocked on the door, I wasn't there."[111] Once he regains his balance a little, though, the calls begin again, starting with a recurring dream about the Dolphin Hotel and someone who is crying for him there. This hotel in Hokkaido, which his girlfriend with the magical ears had led him to in *A Wild Sheep Chase* and which was the home of the Sheep Professor (but which has since been transformed into a 26-story, ultra-modern complex) comes to play a central role in *Dance*.

Dance makes it clear that the Dolphin Hotel, along with another building in Hawaii that *Boku* enters when he is there on vacation and in which he sees six skeletons, are places for *Boku*. The person who has been crying for him, he learns, is his girlfriend with the magical ears from *A Wild Sheep Chase*, her name finally revealed as Kiki. Kiki later tells him that what was really calling him back to the Dolphin Hotel, however, was himself: "It was you who called yourself. I'm merely a projection. You guided yourself, through me."[112] The six skeletons and the building in Hawaii are likewise something which has come from within him: "'They're you,' says Kiki. 'This is your room. Everything here is you. Yourself. Everything.'"[113]

In the Introduction, I mentioned Murakami's description of the writing process as something like playing a video game where he is both the (unconscious) designer and the (conscious) player of the game. This is similar to what *Boku* is doing here, playing a game that appears to have been designed for him by him. It is much like Jung's description of the dream-work, in which every detail is ultimately about the dreamer:

> The whole dream-work is essentially subjective, and a dream is a theatre in which the dreamer is himself the scene, the player, the prompter, the producer, the author, the public, and the critic.... This simple truth forms the basis of what I have called interpretation on the subjective level... all the figures in the dream are personified features of the dreamer's own personality.[114]

Boku recognizes his resistance to this game. Talking with the Sheep Man, the same mysterious figure from *A Wild Sheep Chase* who now lives deep within the new Dolphin Hotel, *Boku* declares, "I wanted a life completely dissociated from this place."[115] In other words, he would prefer to keep his impulse for individuation shut down. In the end, though, *Boku*'s conscious wishes are no match for his unconscious desire for growth. He explains, "I couldn't get this place out of my mind. I tried to forget things, but then something else would pop up. So it didn't matter whether I liked it or not, I sort of knew I belonged here."[116] This game of gradually reconnecting with his unconscious is being directed by the Sheep Man, who several times describes himself as a switchboard operator.[117] His job is to connect *Boku* with different parts of himself (much like J's role in *Hear the Wind Sing*), and to do this he only needs *Boku* to continue doing one thing: dance (i.e., keep moving forward in his therapeutic quest).

Another character who helps *Boku* in his therapeutic quest is Yuki, a young girl he meets at the hotel. She has several roles that make her an interesting addition to *Boku*'s supporting cast of characters. On the one hand, she has the role of connecting *Boku* back to his youth. When *Boku* first meets her, she is a troubled thirteen-year-old, but music acts as a bridge that slowly allows them to open up to each other. *Boku* first listens to Yuki's music, and then she starts listening to his, and this takes him back to an earlier time in his life. *Boku* describes how being with her "took me back years. Made me feel helpless, a teenage boy pining away again for a girl who could almost have been Yuki."[118] This aspect of the story can at times feel uncomfortable. Boku is thirty-four years old, Yuki thirteen, so many of the comments he makes to her—describing how beautiful she is, describing their outings as dates, etc.—almost sound like grooming. But this is not *Boku*'s intention. Instead, by being with her, he is remembering somebody else. While this other person is never mentioned in the novel, it is likely Naoko, who in *Hear the Wind Sing* was described as being at her most beautiful at age fourteen.

At other times, *Boku* takes on a pseudo-parenting role toward Yuki, filling in for the biological parents that continually let her down. Yuki's parents are divorced, and she lives with her mother, Ame, a brilliant photographer who often forgets her daughter when she enters one of her periods of creative frenzy. Her father, the author Hiraku Makimura, is less of a genius than Ame and thus less caught up in his work, but he is emotionally distant and unable to connect authentically with his daughter. His solution is to throw money at her and to hope that things work out for the best. Much like some of the characters in *Norwegian Wood*, *Boku* recognizes the need Yuki has to *amaeru*, to indulge completely in the love of another person—ideally one or both of her parents. As he puts it, "she needs a situation that accepts her one hundred percent."[119] He also recognizes that she is unlikely to get what she needs, and so his advice to her is to do the only thing she can: grow up.[120] One senses in this new role of *Boku* a shift in

Murakami himself, who never had children of his own. He seems to be consciously thinking about what he can offer his young readers to guide them through the often difficult journey of life. The fact that one of Yuki's incompetent parents is the author Makimura Hiraku, a play on Murakami's name, perhaps also suggests some underlying anxiety about taking on this role.

A final role Yuki plays is much like that of Kiki in *Sheep Chase*. She is a clairvoyant who guides *Boku* along in his therapeutic journey when he gets stuck. Indeed, she often gives him the answers to questions he has not even begun to ask himself, the central example being the news that his childhood classmate and recent friend, Gotanda, a movie star known for his wholesome roles, killed Kiki. But here is where *Dance* gets complicated, the question of whether Gotanda really killed Kiki, at least in this world, never definitively answered. Gotanda does remember killing Kiki, but it is an unreliable, dissociated, dream-like memory that is not supported by any physical evidence.

The relationship between *Boku* and Gotanda is central to the novel and so deserves further attention. First, it is possible to note the connections with Chandler's *The Long Goodbye*, a work that I have already suggested was central to the structure of the earlier Rat trilogy. In *Dance*, *Boku* is taken in by the police when a prostitute he slept with, Mei, is murdered. *Boku* had left his business card with her, and this is the only identifying information she is carrying at the time of her murder, making him a suspect. The police hold *Boku* overnight, first getting him to make a long statement, and then, just when he thinks he is finished, getting him to rewrite the whole thing out by hand before signing it. *Boku* fittingly references Kafka's *The Trial* to explain the absurdity of the situation he is in, but the scene also resonates with *The Long Goodbye*, where Marlowe is taken in by the police but avoids giving them what they want to protect his new friend, Terry Lennox. In *Dance*, *Boku* is protecting Gotanda, who bought the prostitute's services for him and who will lose his career if the media gets wind of what has happened. Like Marlowe, *Boku* proves himself a loyal friend, a man willing to challenge authority to protect someone he feels connected to, even if he does not really know why. While Rat was the Terry Lennox-like figure of the early trilogy, here the role is being taken up by Gotanda.

Gotanda's confusion about whether or not he killed Kiki also has a parallel in *The Long Goodbye*, but this time with a different character. Roger Wade, an alcoholic writer, comes to believe that he may have killed Lennox's wife, Sylvia, and that his heavy drinking is simply a way to prolong the dissociation keeping him from remembering this fact. As with Gotanda, his growing conviction that he is the murderer contributes to his suicidal thoughts (though in the end, it turns out he was not guilty. Instead, it was his wife, Eileen, who killed Sylvia, driven by jealousy—she was once married to Lennox). While Gotanda's guilt is never cleared in *Dance*, his growing sense of paranoia mirrors Wade's in many ways.

In Jungian terms, Gotanda's persona shines so bright that his shadow has taken on a dark life of its own, and so from time to time, he feels the need to release the pressure and restore equilibrium. In this respect, he is not dissimilar to the trader who appears in Murakami's earlier short story "Barn Burning" (1983), who likewise commits crimes to maintain a sense of equilibrium and who is explicitly compared to Gatsby.[121] "It's happened before," Gotanda explains to *Boku* at one point. "I get this gap between me

Gotanda and me the actor, and I stand back and actually observe myself doing shit. I'm on one side of this very deep, dark fault, and then unconsciously, on the other side, I have this urge to destroy something. Smash it to bits."[122] He gives several examples from his life of times when this urge has taken over: pushing a friend off a small bluff, setting fire to mailboxes, killing four cats, using a slingshot to shatter a neighbor's window. Now he believes he may have gone one step further and killed Kiki.

In the end, confronted by *Boku*, Gotanda admits that he did it: "Maybe I didn't do it wilfully. But I did. I strangled her."[123] This seems a clear admission of guilt, but then Gotanda immediately goes on to complicate matters:

> But I wasn't strangling her, I was strangling my shadow. I remember thinking, if only I could choke my shadow off, I'd get some health. Except it wasn't my shadow. It was Kiki. It all took place in that dark world. You know what I'm talking about? Not here in this one. And it was Kiki who led me there. Choke me, Kiki told me. Go ahead and kill me, it's okay. She invited me to, allowed me to. I swear, honestly, it happened like that. Without me knowing. Can that happen? It was like a dream. The more I think about it, the more it doesn't feel real. Why would Kiki ask me to kill her?[124]

Why indeed? And then just to complicate matters further, Kiki later appears to *Boku* in a dream and tells him that she is not dead after all:

> Maybe he did kill me. For him it's like that. In his mind, he killed me. That's what he needed. If he didn't kill me, he'd still be stuck. Poor man.... But I'm not dead. I just disappeared. I do that. I move into another world, a different world. Like boarding a train running parallel. That's what disappearing is. Don't you see?[125]

"No, I don't," is *Boku*'s honest reply, and it is probably the honest reply of most readers, too, who by this point have probably given up on trying to make sense of all this, even if they are still enjoying the ride. So what is going on here?

What *Dance* offers, in the end, are different interpretive possibilities, none of which alone is completely satisfactory. It is a literary technique Murakami has come to master over the years, often mixing different metaphysical, psychological, and allegorical possibilities into his stories but without enough explicit direction to say which possibility is "right." Readers are thus left to entertain different hypotheses and to come to their own conclusions or to no conclusion at all, as the case may be. This is the world of the *monogatari*, where dream-like metaphysical possibilities abound but where everything just may (or may not) in the end be an elaborate psychological allegory. In *Dance* we might frame some of these different interpretive possibilities in this way: Who is Kiki? Who killed her? And what does the word "killed" even mean in this situation?

One possible way to read *Dance* is through the dissociative category of identity alteration, or what used to be called multiple-personality disorder. We know that Gotanda feels like he killed Kiki, even though there is no physical evidence. For example, he emphasizes that he does not own a shovel. "If I found a shovel," he reasons,

"I'd know I did it."[126] *Boku*, on the other hand, clearly owns a shovel. We know this because he buys it to bury his dead cat near the start of the novel. Is it possible that *Boku* and Gotanda are the same person, and that what *Boku* remembers as the burying of his cat was, in fact, him burying Kiki in a dissociated state? *Boku* constantly describes his job as a writer of magazine articles as cultural snow shoveling, an interesting choice of words when considering the aforementioned theory. Are his constant references to shoveling a subconscious return to the dissociated burial scene?

Unlike the more widely known concept of repression, which is normally traced back to Freud, the idea of dissociation goes back to the work of Pierre Janet, who saw in his patients a common strategy of splitting off memories or even parts of the self in the face of debilitating trauma. Bessel Van der Kolk explains, "Dissociation is the essence of trauma. The overwhelming experience is split off and fragmented, so that the emotions, sounds, images, thoughts, and physical sensations related to the trauma take on a life of their own."[127] The (by no means easy) remedy to dissociation is thus the opposite of this process of splitting and fragmentation. Van der Kolk explains, "If the problem with PTSD [Post-traumatic Stress Disorder] is dissociation, the goal of treatment would be association: integrating the cut-off elements of the trauma into the ongoing narrative of life, so that the brain can recognize that 'that was then, and this is now.'"[128]

Dissociation is most often discussed in relation to victims of trauma, but it is not uncommon for perpetrators of violence to also commit their crimes in a dissociated state. Stenberg and Schnall explain how "Perpetrators of a crime can be as disconnected from what is happening in the present as their victims."[129] Gotanda's description of killing Kiki in a dream-like state resonates with this idea. In addition, Gotanda feels like the presence of *Boku* is important to him personally. Shortly after he shares his thoughts about the significance of the absence of a shovel, he says to *Boku*, "Whenever I'm with you, I feel so relaxed. I never feel the gap. You don't know how precious that is. I don't want to lose a friendship like ours."[130] The reason why he does not feel this gap with *Boku* may be because he and *Boku* are the same person.

While it is possible to read *Dance* in this way as a murder mystery in which the true identity of the murderer is masked by dissociation, however, it is impossible to know whether this is actually the case, given that the murderer is never unmasked. We have a murder without a body and only the dream-like confession of Gotanda to go by. What also makes the hypothesis difficult to accept is that this is not the first time we have met *Boku* (at least if we have been reading Murakami's fiction in chronological order). Are we really to believe that *Boku*, the seemingly ordinary, if somewhat melancholic, character we have been following since his first trip back to his hometown as a university student, has now suddenly become a murderer with multiple personalities? Instead, while recognizing that *Boku* and Gotanda are likely connected in some way, most readers will probably search for other hypotheses to explain what is going on.

Reading *Boku*'s psychological journey in light of the earlier Rat trilogy, one distinctive possibility which emerges is that this is a novel about working on, and arguably even resolving, Murakami's first therapeutic thread: the journey from melancholia to mourning. *Boku*'s movements in the novel bring him into contact with two prostitutes—Mei and June—the former paid for by Gotanda and the latter by Yuki's father, Makimura. These prostitutes, yet another example in the novel of the way expense accounts have come to substitute for personal relationships, are, at the same time, a mythical rite of passage for *Boku* on his road to recovery, a way for him to break out of his melancholia once and for all. The night Gotanda hires two prostitutes feels at first like a repeat of the kinds of sexual conquests of Nagasawa and Watanabe in *Norwegian Wood*. Before long, though, it becomes clear what the evening is about for *Boku*. Sitting around with his old classmate and the two women, *Boku* notes that "memories of high school came to mind" and that the whole thing was "like being at a class reunion."[131] *Boku* likes Gotanda, in part because he takes him back to an earlier, simpler time in his life.

June, the next prostitute, shows up at *Boku*'s hotel one night when he is staying in Hawaii. He wonders what to do, but finally decides to "let June in."[132] From a therapeutic perspective, the question then becomes why *Boku* needs to let Mei (May) and then June into his life. The answer to that question goes back to the most significant death in *Boku*'s life. *Boku* struggles throughout the novel to identify the six skeletons he sees in Hawaii. One clear candidate is Dick North, Ame's lover and personal assistant who dies in the novel when he is hit by a truck and who is easy to identify among the skeletons because of his missing arm. Rat must also be among the skeletons, *Boku* insists, given that he is such a significant person from his past. Then there is Mei, who ends up murdered after *Boku* sleeps with her. After Gotanda's confession, *Boku* concludes that Kiki must represent another of the skeletons, and after his suicide, Gotanda becomes the obvious candidate for the fifth. This leaves just one more skeleton to account for.

One possibility for skeleton number six is the Sheep Man who is gone when *Boku* makes his final journey into the darkness of the Dolphin Hotel. One would think, however, that his skeleton would have been easy to identify. Another more ominous possibility *Boku* considers is that the sixth skeleton is his own.[133] This possibility seems to be foreshadowed in an earlier scene where the clairvoyant Yuki talks to *Boku* in the past tense: "You were such a good guy . . . I never met anyone like you." "Why the past tense?" *Boku* wonders.[134] In the end, though, *Boku* does not die, and the question of the sixth skeleton remains unanswered. The obvious skeleton *Boku* is missing is Naoko's, and it is recovering from her death which explains the reason why he needed to "pass through" May and June. In *Hear the Wind Sing* we learn that Naoko hanged herself during spring vacation and that her body was not discovered for two weeks when school started again, which would place her death around mid-to-late March and the discovery of her body around late March to early April. The funeral would have been shortly after this, so we can assume that in some sense, *Boku*'s life froze in April of 1970 when he learned of Naoko's death. This is why *Boku*'s recovery, his journey from melancholia back into mourning, requires him to pass through May and June.

This, of course, does not answer the original question about how to interpret Kiki's murder, but this, I believe, is because this murder is related less to Murakami's first therapeutic thread—the journey from melancholia to mourning—than to his fourth: the drive for individuation, which grows out of the need to mourn. This fourth therapeutic thread, while evident in the early Rat trilogy, was still faint, but here in *Dance* it begins to become more prominent, and just at the moment when Murakami's first therapeutic thread finally finds its resolution (a point I will return to shortly).

In Chapter 1, I described the girl with the magical ears (Kiki) as an example of an anima-guide, someone who takes the male protagonist by the hand and leads him deeper into his unconscious. The death of Kiki thus represents the death of *Boku*'s anima (the anima is also sometimes translated as the soul). This death occurs (in some metaphysical space at least) at the hands of Gotanda, who from a Jungian perspective is the most recent manifestation of *Boku*'s shadow (though *Boku* is unable to fully grasp this fact). Kiki, as mentioned earlier, even describes herself as a projection, evidence of the way her murder is supposed to be read in psychological terms as a case of failed (or at least temporarily thwarted) individuation. What appears to be behind this failure is the spirit of the age, the exuberance and excess of late-capitalist Japan, represented first and foremost by Gotanda.

In the same way that Gatsby can be read as a symbol of the promise and perversion of the American Dream, Gotanda can be read as a symbol of Japan's shadow during the height of the bubble economy. This relates less to the period in which the novel is set (1983) than to when it was written and published, a point Shimada Hiromi explains:

> Undoubtedly, the bubble [economy] casts a shadow over Murakami's work, and in *Dance Dance Dance* this is particularly pronounced. From the outset of the story, the date of March 1983 is recorded, and that is when the story is set, but the story was written from December of 1987 to March of the following year, and the atmosphere of this period is reflected in the narrative.[135]

Examples of what Shimada is talking about here are not hard to find. Characters are constantly explaining how almost everything can be written off as a business expense and *Boku* is constantly noting how "[w]aste is the name of the game."[136] Gotanda personifies this excess, a man who sells his wholesome image for monetary gain and then uses it to buy expensive cars and prostitutes. The glittering surface of what the novel calls "advanced capitalist society" is hiding a dark shadow that is mirrored in the light and darkness of Gotanda himself.

Boku mirrors Nick Carraway in the way he holds off judging his new friend. After Gotanda's confession, his first reaction is to go easy on him, suggesting that they take a break together in Hawaii. Considering that there is no physical evidence, he believes Gotanda is being too hard on himself, and he seems to hold out hope that he is not the murderer after all. Even after Gotanda's suicide, which appears to be an admission of guilt, *Boku* is not so sure. "Who knows?" he says in response to Yuki's question about whether he thinks Gotanda did it, "Maybe he did and maybe he didn't."[137] What *Boku* does know is that he likes Gotanda, noting that, "Each time we met I liked him more. That doesn't happen very much, especially not at my age."[138]

While Rat was still a likable enough alter ego, Gotanda is a potentially darker shadow character, though *Boku* largely fails to appreciate how deep this darkness goes. In terms of the journey of individuation, then, this is still not a full confrontation with the shadow, which comes only later in Murakami's fiction. At the same time, *Boku*'s inability to appreciate the darkness of his own shadow is mirrored by his inability to appreciate the darker aspects of the economic system he is participating in, which he also tends to acknowledge but not confront. *Boku*'s critique of the economic system he is participating in is constant throughout the novel, but the fact remains that he continues to participate in it regardless. In the end, he takes a "love it or leave it" approach: "If I don't like it, I can move to Bangladesh or Sudan. I for one am not eager to live in Bangladesh or Sudan. So I kept working."[139]

For Slavoj Žižek, such logic is simply the way things work in our supposedly post-ideological age. For Marx, ideology was a form of "false consciousness," a distortion of reality that prevented people from grasping the true material conditions of their existence.[140] The antidote to such deception was consciousness-raising. For Žižek, however, in late-capitalist societies, people already know. The power of the system comes not from what it hides from us, but from how it gets us to continue doing despite our knowing; the system, in other words, takes our cynicism into account from the beginning. Žižek explains, "we know there is no truth in authority, yet we continue to play its game and to obey it in order not to disturb the usual run of things.... Truth is suspended in the name of efficiency: the ultimate legitimization of the system is that it works."[141]

This is *Boku*'s position in *Dance*. He does not believe the system will change, so his only choice is whether he will play the game or not. Žižek, in a quote that seems made for Murakami's fiction, explains such an attitude as follows: "[I]t seems easier to imagine 'the end of the world' than a far more modest change in the mode of production."[142] Murakami had an interest in Marxism growing up and his politics, in general, are left-leaning. This is perhaps evident in the early Rat trilogy, where the theme of class tension is lightly touched on (Rat's complaints about the rich, for example, or the woman with the missing finger complaining about the struggle of growing up poor). Rat's death, then, might also represent the death of a voice of class-consciousness in Murakami's fiction, and his replacement, Gotanda, is more intent on enjoying the excesses of late-capitalist Japan than critiquing it. While Gotanda's (and arguably Japan's) late-capitalist persona shines bright, however, it is hiding a soul-destroying, anima-murdering shadow that needs to be dealt with.

In conclusion, Kiki's murder might be read in at least two other ways besides the dissociation narrative examined earlier. First, it might be read as a message about failed individuation. *Boku*'s inability to recognize the depth of his own shadow (in the form of Gotanda) means that he has lost his soul (Kiki). In the world of the novel, this murder has taken place in some other metaphysical realm, freeing *Boku* and others from any legal ramifications for what has happened, but not from the psychological ramifications, which he needs to confront and incorporate into consciousness if he wants to achieve individuation. Second, this failure might be read as a larger political allegory, a kind of reworking of Fitzgerald's examination of the American dream for bubble economy Japan. In this allegorical reading, *Boku* (representing Japan) has failed to recognize his shadow (represented by Gotanda) leading to the premature death of his soul (Kiki). In either reading, *Dance* is a novel that ultimately ends in failure, *Boku* failing to grasp the true reason for Kiki's death.

That *Dance* so clearly wrestles with the problems of late-capitalist Japan, while offering little more in the end than resignation, supports those critics who see in

Murakami's fiction from this period little more than political detachment and failed political commitment. If commitment simply means breaking through detachment and reaching out to another human being, however (the definition of commitment Murakami actually offers), then *Dance* can be read as a novel in which a form of commitment finally emerges in Murakami's fiction, and where his first significant therapeutic breakthrough occurs. When *Boku* meets Yumiyoshi, a woman who works at the reception of the Dolphin Hotel, she at first appears as just one more example of someone that has been put there for him. When he first sees her, for example, he explains that there "was something about her expression I responded to, some embodiment of hotel spirit."[143] As the novel progresses, though, it becomes clear that Yumiyoshi is different from the other women in the story.

Near the end of the novel, in June, *Boku* returns to Hokkaido and the Dolphin Hotel one last time. His desire is to be with Yumiyoshi. "Yumiyoshi," *Boku* says, calling her on the phone from his hotel room, "I need you. I mean, I really need you. Like I've never needed anything before. Please don't disappear on me."[144] Much like Watanabe's call to Midori at the end of *Norwegian Wood*, this is *Boku*'s attempt to return to the world of the living, to connect with a real-life human being. "I've made it back to reality," he explains, "that's the important thing. I've come full circle. And I'm still on my feet, dancing."[145] When he finally gets with her at the end of the novel, he describes the experience in this way: "We touched. Her body and mine. Smooth, but with a certain gravity. Yes, this was real. Unlike with Mei. Mei had been a dream, fantasy, illusion.... But Yumiyoshi existed in the real world. Her warmth and weight and vitality were real."[146] Yumiyoshi thus represents someone outside of the solipsistic quest which has brought him to this point. The fruit of self-therapy here is the ability to now connect with another human being (an expression of therapeutic thread three).

Finally, together with Yumiyoshi in the Dolphin Hotel, *Boku* opens the door to his hotel room only to be confronted by the same darkness he has experienced on previous occasions. This darkness is *Dance*'s representation of the second basement. It is also, in some way, a return to the Town from *Hard-Boiled*. Suggestions of this connection can be found in the novel, such as when *Boku* expresses his predicament in this way:

> Perhaps the lines were crossed. I had to get clear what it was she [Kiki] wanted from me. Enlist the help of the Sheep Man and link things up one by one. No matter how out of focus the picture, I had to unravel each strand patiently. Unravel, then bind all together. I had to recover my world. But where to begin? Not a clue. I was flat against a high wall.[147]

This is the wall of melancholia which many of Murakami's protagonists have faced. It is a wall holding memories of a hometown and the people who once lived there. And here we find a Murakami protagonist finally ready to pass through this wall in an attempt to connect with a human being waiting on the other side. At the end of *Dance*, reunited with Yumiyoshi, *Boku* finally learns how to pass through this wall. This is something he has earlier seen Kiki do in the building in Hawaii, but it is not until the end of the novel that he is ready to do it himself. As he enters the darkness of the

Dolphin Hotel corridor, hand in hand with Yumiyoshi, though, *Boku* makes a serious mistake—he lets go of her hand as she passes through the wall. While Yumiyoshi calls for him to follow her, he is initially reluctant, not sure if he will ever make it back. Yet a decision has to be made, and *Boku* finally makes one, his motivation described as follows: "I loved her, I couldn't lose her. I followed her into the wall."[148]

Boku has been trapped in the Dolphin Hotel, a world just for him, and reconnecting with dissociated parts of himself has been an important part of his therapeutic journey. In the end, though, it is the desire to connect with another human being that frees him from himself. It turns out the final scene with the wall was just a dream, one from which *Boku* awakes in a panic. Is Yumiyoshi still there or has she disappeared? "Of course, I'm here," Yumiyoshi reassures him. "People don't disappear so easily."[149] *Boku*, it would seem, has passed the test. Motivated by his desire for another human being, he has finally found the strength to pass through the wall of melancholia and escape his own solipsism. This is a therapeutic breakthrough, a moment Murakami's fiction had been working up to for close to a decade.

The novel ends much like many of Murakami's earlier novels with a cathartic outpouring of tears, but this time with a twist. The novel began with someone crying for *Boku* because he was unable to cry for himself. Now, holding Yumiyoshi in his arms, he cries, but in a different way: "I cried inside. I cried for all that I'd lost and all that I'd lose."[150] This is an expression of grief, a return to mourning, but one different from the earlier examples. First, *Boku* is not alone, he is holding someone else; and second, his "tears" are somehow contained within himself. What has made this possible is sharing this experience with Yumiyoshi. In the end, it is her example (and the earlier example of Kiki, his anima) that has shown him what to do.

Murakami recognizes the breakthrough *Dance* represents, noting to John Harding in an interview the change he sees:

> [**Murakami**]: In *A Wild Sheep Chase* the protagonist is lonely and isolated. His wife walked away. She left him by himself. He doesn't look for anything, he's just lonely. But in *Dance Dance Dance* he's looking for connections—connections with everybody. The characters are getting more positive.
>
> [**Harding**]: Why do you think that is?
>
> [**Murakami**]: I think that is what I felt at that time. I'm writing the books to change myself, you know. Writing books is just an experience to me. So when I've finished writing a book, I have changed. I don't write books for bread and butter. I just write books because I want to be something new.[151]

Here Murakami is expressing the way his fiction is also part of a personal therapeutic quest and the way *Dance Dance Dance* was an important milestone on this journey. The first therapeutic thread in his fiction had finally found its resolution—the wall of melancholia had been breached.

What followed this breakthrough can be described as a return of the Real, a breakdown of past illusions and a return of shock and pain, a theme which is explored in Murakami's next two novels, *South of the Border, West of the Sun* and *The Wind-Up Bird Chronicle*. What one also sees is a much more dramatic emergence of the shadow.

While *Boku* in *Dance* still struggles to remain nonjudgmental vis-à-vis his shadow, Gotanda, in *The Wind-Up Bird Chronicle* we finally see an antagonist emerge in Murakami's fiction who is recognized as evil almost straightaway and who must be fought to death. If Murakami's characters really want to connect with their significant others, they are now going to have to start paying a price.

3

The Return of the Real

Introduction

Murakami has explained how *South of the Border, West of the Sun* (hereafter *South of the Border*) and *The Wind-Up Bird Chronicle* (hereafter *Wind-Up Bird*) started as the same writing project and only later split into two separate novels during the writing process.[1] *South of the Border* is a much lighter novel than *Wind-Up Bird* and lacks the same historical depth, but both novels in their own ways deal with the piercing of everyday illusions and with what Lacanian-influenced theorists, such as Slavoj Žižek, describe as the "return of the Real," or what in the introduction to this book was described as the return of shock. This return of the Real can be seen as a natural consequence of the breaking through of the melancholia described in the previous two chapters and thus reflects a new stage in Murakami's writing career. In the case of melancholia, the unconscious nature of the condition means that the pain of the original loss can be kept at bay and together with strategies of splitting (i.e., the introduction of an alter ego who carries the greater burden of this loss), the more destructive elements of the melancholic state can be minimized or even avoided. But this strategy is arguably not sustainable in the long term, and psychological health requires a return to mourning and a confrontation many times over with the sources of one's pain. This process, in turn, brings potential therapeutic risks and rewards.

In *South of the Border*, the narrator slowly begins to come to terms with events he felt he had left in his past, the reminder of which reappears in the form of a woman who may not be who she first appears. Following Katō Norihiro's lead, I will read this novel as a ghost story with a message, and I will also suggest that it signifies a shifting role in Murakami's fiction in what I have been describing as his anima figures. *Wind-Up Bird* takes this piercing of everyday illusions to even greater depths, starting with an illusion of marital contentment, and ending with the illusion of Japanese postwar peace and prosperity itself. The novel suggests that beneath the seemingly calm surface of postwar Japan are traumas seeking to tear the country and individuals apart, and it is only by attempting to confront and heal these traumas, which are intergenerational in nature, that hope for a healthier way forward can be found. *Wind-Up Bird* is one of Murakami's most important novels and offers a convincing and creative portrayal of the nature of intergenerational trauma in modern Japan and the need for its healing in symbolic form. In one sense, it might be read as the response to Murakami's baseball epiphany, and the works which follow it are thus best seen in a slightly different light.

Welcome to the Desert of the Real: *South of the Border, West of the Sun*

In a classic scene from the sci-fi action thriller *The Matrix*, the hero Neo awakens from his computer-simulated reality to discover the desolate, war-torn reality it has been hiding. "Welcome to the desert of the real," his guide Morpheus famously announces (his words playing off a quote from Jean Baudrillard's *Simulacra and Simulation* referenced in the film). Murakami's *South of the Border*, while not a story about computer-simulated realities, has its own Matrix-like moment—an experience where what the main protagonist, Hajime, took to be reality is suddenly and brutally pulled back to reveal his own "desert of the real." Instead of talking about this in terms of simulacra and simulation, however, I will use the more old-fashioned terms of illusion and disillusion, a nod to what I see as the Fitzgeraldian antecedent to this theme.

"The ultimate and defining moment of the twentieth century," Slavoj Žižek writes, "was the direct experience of the Real as opposed to everyday social reality—the Real in its extreme violence as the price to be paid for peeling off the deceptive layers of reality."[2] This is what Alan Badiou termed the "passion for the Real," or what Žižek calls the "return of the Real," and it is a useful way to think about what is going on in both *South of the Border* and *Wind-Up Bird*. What seems to have brought on this return of the Real in Murakami's fiction was his experience sitting in a library at Princeton University and reading accounts of Japan's wartime aggression in Mongolia and China, an experience that was both disturbing and deeply meaningful for him. The fictional payoff of this research is most evident in *Wind-Up Bird*, which deals directly with the theme of war, but considering that these two novels started as the same writing project, it is not surprising when we see the theme of an emerging passion for the Real first appear in *South of the Border* and then later amplified in the longer and more ambitious *Wind-Up Bird*.

South of the Border begins less with this passion for the Real, however, than with an example of what James Hillman calls the "anima child," a complex in Jungian thought said to awaken "nostalgic *pathos*, that yearning for intimacy with 'earlier' times and the first home."[3] In Murakami's novel, this anima child takes the form of Shimamoto, a young girl who, due to an early bout of polio, walks with a limp, and someone with whom the main protagonist Hajime shares a love of music, books, and cats.[4] Both Shimamoto and Hajime are only children, and this shared experience allows them to connect and become something like childhood soul mates. Whether or not Murakami ever knew a girl like Shimamoto, he is clearly drawing in part on his childhood memories in the way he portrays Hajime's early life. He explains, "Like Hajime, I was an only child. In the home I lived in with my parents, I had my own unique world. The three main components that made up that world were music, books, and cats."[5]

Hajime's friendship with Shimamoto includes the first nascent signs of his sexual awakening, yet the object of his desire is still so distant, so incomprehensible, that it remains abstract and safe. It is sexual desire which will later ignite Hajime's passion for the Real and which will lead him to the desert of the real, but early in his relationship with Shimamoto, this is still something far off in the future. With Shimamoto, his longing is for something which lies south of the border, a reference to a Nat King Cole song they both love and listen to on Shimamoto's father's record player.[6] At the time, Hajime had no idea the song was referring to Mexico. Instead, it conjured up images of a magical place intermixed with an increasingly powerful but confusing sexual awareness. Hajime explains, "I was convinced something utterly wonderful lay south of the border. When I opened my eyes, Shimamoto was still moving her fingers along her skirt. Somewhere deep inside my body I felt an exquisitely sweet ache."[7]

Hajime's early relationship with Shimamoto finished at the end of elementary school when he moved house (though only to a place two stations away on the local train line), and they both started attending separate junior high schools—not insurmountable obstacles but ones that were too difficult for young friends of the opposite sex to overcome.[8] Not fighting harder to maintain this relationship is something Hajime later comes to regret: "I should have stayed as close as I could to her. I needed her, and she needed me."[9] In the end though, regrets are powerless to change the past, a theme repeated several times in the novel. "Hajime," Shimamoto offers on one occasion when they meet again years later, "the sad truth is that certain types of things can't go backward. Once they start going forward, no matter what you do, they can't go back the way they were. If even one little thing goes awry, then that's how it will stay forever."[10] All that remains for Hajime is the Fitzgeraldian directive to keep moving forward, despite the constant pull of the past, a sentiment captured well in the final line of *The Great Gatsby*: "So we beat on, boats against the current, borne back ceaselessly into the past."[11]

The next important female Hajime meets after Shimamoto is Izumi, who becomes his high school girlfriend and with whom he shares his first sexual experiences, though not the experience of coitus—Hajime's impatience to go all the way constantly being offset by Izumi's desire to take it slowly. Instead, Hajime's first experience of coitus is with Izumi's older cousin, an eruption of the passion for the Real that has ramifications for the rest of his life. Izumi is described as an "honest, pleasant girl, someone people liked."[12] She comes across in the story as someone good, though not necessarily deep, Hajime well aware of her virtues, but still frustrated by the fact that he "could never discover within her something special that existed just for me."[13] Yet, none of this excuses what he does to her by cheating on her with her cousin. Hajime suddenly realizes that "I am a person who can do evil."[14] Yet, he also claims to have felt no guilt at the time it happened, simply describing it as a "physical force" that swept him and Izumi's cousin off their feet.[15] This physical force can be read as an expression of the passion for the Real.

In his earlier relationship with Shimamoto, Hajime had felt that in his imagined world south of the border, "something absolutely vital lay waiting for me."[16] In his relationship with Izumi's cousin, on the other hand, he is no longer satisfied with distant objects of longing. He explains, "What I sought was the sense of being tossed about by some raging, savage force, in the midst of which lay something absolutely crucial. I had no idea what that was. But I wanted to thrust my hand right inside her body and touch it, whatever it was."[17] It is this desire—to thrust his hand into her body and touch this crucial something—that demonstrates his passion for the Real. Hajime is no longer pining for a world south of the border; he is seeking for what might lie west of the sun.

Later in the novel this difference is explained to Hajime by Shimamoto. Like Hajime, Shimamoto confesses that she also used to wonder what lay south of the border, and when Hajime asks her what her image was, she replies, "I'm not sure. Something beautiful, big and soft."[18] Immediately, though, she contrasts this with another place that lies west of the sun. She explains this second location through a description of what she calls *hysteria siberiana*, an illness suffered by farmers in Siberia. Working in the open fields day after day, and surrounded by nothing but the horizon of the land in all directions, some farmers would eventually lose their minds and head off in desperation in the direction of the setting sun, eventually collapsing in exhaustion and dying. Hajime asks Shimamoto what might lie west of the sun, but she does not have a clear answer: "I don't know. Maybe nothing. Or maybe *something*. At any rate, it's different from south of the border."[19]

Writing about similar longings through the lens of Lacanian psychoanalysis, Žižek suggests that the question we are dealing with is how to relate to the "void of the Real." In heading off in the direction of the setting sun, what these farmers are searching for, from a Lacanian perspective, is "the impossible-real limit of the human experience that we can approach only indefinitely, the absolute Thing toward which we have to maintain a proper distance—if we get too close to it we get burned by the sun."[20] For the farmers intent on testing this limit, what they eventually discover is death, and this is the same for Hajime, whose own passion for the Real eventually leads him to a similar discovery. Before exploring this theme in more detail, though, I will first consider some possible biographical influences behind this novel.

Whatever biographical core exists in *South of the Border* may never be fully known, unless Murakami chooses to fill us in on the details. I asked him about these possible biographical influences directly, but he declined to comment, insisting that he could hardly remember what the novel was about. At a more general level, however, he has already admitted the personal nature of this work, explaining, "*Ressentiment* is kind of an old word, but I feel like there are scenes from my life that have stuck with me, some of them very vividly. I suspect that [*South of the Border*] is a novel which, while removing them from context, links a number of these scenes together and fictionalises them."[21] *Ressentiment*, the French equivalent of the English word resentment, has a long history in philosophical thought (including in the writings of Nietzsche), but for our discussion here, the English word resentment works just as well. What Murakami seems to be hinting at here is an experience (or perhaps experiences) he had being the object of someone else's resentment, most likely a female he hurt in his adolescence. This biographical core to the novel is suggested not only by Murakami's aforementioned comment but also by the literary influences the novel is building upon, stories which at one time or another captured Murakami's imagination.

We have already seen the way the early scenes with Shimamoto seem to capture something of Murakami's early life, and this continues in later scenes. Many people who have visited Murakami's old high school in Kobe, for example, see it as the model for the high school in *South of the Border*. Hajime explains, "Our school was on a hilltop, and we had an unbroken view of the town and the sea. Once, my friends and I filched some records from the Broadcast Club room and flung them off the roof—like Frisbees, they sailed away in a beautiful arc."[22] Visiting Kobe High School, Urazumi Akira went to the roof of the school and looked out at the view, describing it as a great fit with this passage in *South of the Border*.[23] The high school setting, at least then, suggests that Murakami is borrowing from personal experience.

What about Hajime's relationship with Izumi? Is this based on some real experience too? An interesting link between *Norwegian Wood* and *South of the Border* is the similarities of the scenes where the main protagonist is leaving his hometown for university in Tokyo. In both novels, this journey is accompanied by feelings of guilt related to a girl they are leaving behind. In *South of the Border*, Hajime offers this description of his train trip to Tokyo:

> On the bullet train to Tokyo, I gazed listlessly at the scenery outside and thought about myself—who I was. I looked down at my hands on my lap and at my face reflected in the window. Who the hell am I? I wondered. For the first time in my life, a fierce self-hatred welled up in me. How could I have done something like this?[24]

What Hajime has done, of course, is to hurt Izumi by sleeping with her cousin. While earlier he expressed a lack of guilt for what he did, here things are more complicated. For the first time in his life, Hajime despises himself. In *Norwegian Wood*, Watanabe has a girlfriend who does not want him to go to Tokyo, and whom he thus breaks up with. He describes his train trip to Tokyo as follows: "Thinking about all the things that made her so much nicer than the other girls at home, I sat on the bullet train to Tokyo feeling terrible about what I'd done, but there was no way to undo it. I would try to forget her."[25]

In both these novels, a male protagonist leaves behind in his hometown a nice girl whom he has hurt in some way, which leaves him feeling guilty as he travels to Tokyo to make a fresh start. At the same time, there is no question of him staying behind to be with this girl or of trying to patch things up. Something is calling him to Tokyo (or at least pushing him away from his hometown), and so he is determined to go, regardless of the personal cost. I asked Murakami whether he left a girlfriend behind in Kobe when he first moved to Tokyo, and whether this girlfriend might be the girlfriend from Kansai Gakuin he once mentioned in an email exchange with his readers, and he said, "maybe." So "maybe" these two accounts of a male protagonist leaving behind a girl in his hometown—scenes from Murakami's two most biographical novels—are based on a real experience (and "maybe" they're not). If there is a biographical precedent to the Izumi and Izumi's cousin storyline in *South of the Border*, however, it would explain Murakami's deep attraction to one of Fitzgerald's short stories, "Winter Dreams."

As I explained in Chapter 1, Murakami read "Winter Dreams" more than twenty times when he first discovered it, trying to understand where its deep appeal for him came from. I have already argued that Murakami's interest in Fitzgerald's *Tender Is the Night* came from parallels between the love-triangle story plot and his own life at the time, and the same may be true for "Winter Dreams." This is a story about Dexter Green, which in its basic elements mirrors the episode with Hajime, Izumi, and her cousin. Dexter Green is a boy who dreams of wealth in a way that can be connected with the passion for the Real. The narrator says, "He wanted not association with glittering things and glittering people—he wanted the glittering things themselves."[26] Early in life he becomes entranced by a girl named Judy Jones, and for a time she returns his attention; but Judy uses men as playthings and discards them when the next more interesting one comes along, so Dexter eventually forces himself to give up on her. He achieves his goal of becoming rich and becomes engaged to Irene Scheerer, who, like Izumi, is described as a good person, even if she is not as exciting as Judy. At the same time, though, Dexter joins two clubs in the city that he knows Judy frequents, and even after he becomes engaged, he continues to attend these clubs (Hajime is the owner of two jazz clubs that he moves between, and it is at one of these clubs that he later reunites with Shimamoto). One night, Judy shows up at one of the clubs and in short order asks Dexter if he has a car so that they might escape together (Hajime and Shimamoto later escape by car to Hajime's holiday home in Hakone). The narrator of "Winter Dreams" informs us:

> It was strange that neither when it was over nor a long time afterward did he regret that night. Looking at it from the perspective of ten years, the fact that Judy's flare for him endured just one month seemed of little importance. Nor did it matter that by his yielding he subjected himself to a deeper agony in the end and gave serious hurt to Irene Scheerer and to Irene's parents, who had befriended him.[27]

"Winter Dreams" is part of *The Great Gatsby* cluster stories—Fitzgerald often using his short stories to explore themes and techniques he would later rework into a novel. In other words, Dexter is a precursor to Gatsby, someone who dreams of riches as a way of getting the girl of his dreams. What *South of the Border* presents us with, then, is the first example in Murakami's fiction where he would take the perspective, not of a Nick Carraway-type narrator—the nonjudgmental observer—but of a Gatsby-like character—a figure who is willing to sacrifice lesser things for something more. As the narrator tells us in "Winter Dreams," "Dexter was at bottom hard-minded.... He was completely indifferent to popular opinion.... So he tasted the deep pain that is reserved only for the strong, just as he had tasted for a little while the deep happiness."[28] He shares with (the younger) Hajime little guilt for the pain his passion causes others.

Years later, Dexter is told by an acquaintance that Judy's physical beauty has faded, the result of a loveless marriage to a man who has not treated her well. The narrative then focuses on what this revelation does to Dexter, the narrator explaining, "The dream was gone. Something had been taken from him."[29] The novel ends with Dexter's own words: "Long ago ... long ago, there was something in me, but now that thing is gone. Now that thing is gone, that thing is gone. I cannot cry. I cannot care. That thing will come back no more."[30] This is Dexter's final moment of disillusionment, the point at which his winter dream finally melts away to reveal the desert of the real.

In *South of the Border*, this moment of disillusionment takes longer to arrive. Hajime describes the period following high school until he reaches thirty as "[y]ears of disappointment and loneliness. And silence. Frozen years, when my feelings were shut up inside me."[31] What brings on the first thawing of these frozen years is his marriage to a woman named Yukiko, whom he meets on a vacation. Yukiko, like Izumi before her, is a good person who deserves nothing but love and loyalty from Hajime, but history will repeat itself when Hajime is tempted into a relationship with another woman. This time it is not Izumi's cousin that will provide the temptation, but Shimamoto, who on a rainy night mysteriously reappears in Hajime's life.

If Murakami's childhood is loosely represented by Shimamoto, and his teenage years by Izumi and Izumi's cousin, then his adult years are represented by Hajime's marriage to Yukiko and his opening of a jazz club, which, of course, has similarities with Murakami's real life. In one sense, *South of the Border* reads like an alternative version of Murakami's life, a fantasy of what it might have looked like if he had not closed his jazz club to write fiction, but had, rather, continued to work and expand it, and maybe even had children. Hajime gets his start in the jazz club business through a loan from his new father-in-law. His father-in-law's response to his marriage to Yukiko—"You're not children anymore, so if you like each other it's up to you"—is much like the response Murakami received from Yōko's father in real life.[32] At the same time, Hajime's father-in-law quickly moves beyond any biographical starting point to become a symbol of the soul-destroying nature of late-capitalist Japan and the way this is creeping into Hajime's life. Much like *Dance Dance Dance*, *South of the Border* is a novel set in the historical period of Japan's bubble economy and offers a critique of the excesses of the age. Hajime explains, "I felt I was taking a dishonest shortcut, using unfair means to get to where I was. After all, I was part of the late-sixties–early-seventies generation that spawned the radical student movement. Our generation was the first to yell out a resounding 'No!' to the logic of late capitalism, which had devoured any remaining postwar ideals."[33]

What this leads to in Hajime's life is feelings of dissociation—a questioning of both himself (depersonalization) and the reality he is living in (derealization). Sitting in his BMW one day waiting for the lights to change, for example, these thoughts run through his head: "These hands clutching the steering wheel—what percentage of them could I really call my own? The scenery outside—how much of it was real? The more I thought about it, the less I seemed to understand."[34] Yet, even if his life is an illusion, Hajime is not yet ready to give it up, his distaste for his increasing entanglements in his father-in-law's dodgy financial dealings notwithstanding. Instead, what will finally undo him are the women from his past who slowly begin to reappear in his life.

One day, Hajime receives a postcard informing him that Izumi's cousin has died. He does not have to think twice about who sent it to him—Izumi—her act, as Hajime sees it, evidence of the resentment she still holds toward him. Later, he learns from an acquaintance who has seen Izumi that she is no longer beautiful, to the point where the children in her apartment building are afraid of her. His acquaintance quickly reassures Hajime, though, that he should feel no responsibility for this situation, stating:

> I have no idea what went on between you and her back then. But whatever it was, it wasn't your fault. To some degree or other, everyone has that kind of experience. Even me. No joke. I went through the same thing. But there's nothing you can do about it. Another person's life is that person's life. You can't take responsibility. It's like we're living in a desert.[35]

The desert reference here comes from the Disney film, *The Living Desert*, which is mentioned several times in the novel. For this friend, this film's depiction of a desert provides the perfect analogy for the ultimate meaninglessness of life:

> Our world's exactly the same. Rain falls and the flowers bloom. No rain, they wither up. Bugs are eaten by lizards, lizards are eaten by birds. But in the end, every one of them dies. They die and dry up. One generation dies, and the next one takes over. That's how it goes. Lots of different ways to live. And lots of different ways to die. But in the end that doesn't make a bit of difference. All that remains is a desert.[36]

It is amusing that one of the most nihilistic moments in Murakami's fiction comes from a reference to a Disney film, but given the reality this friend is presenting, it is perhaps not surprising that Hajime decides to live with his illusions a little while longer. He describes his club as an "imaginary place," or as a "castle in the sky," and it is here that he spends much of his time.[37] He then adds a second club and together they offer him an escape from the desert his friend has described. What breaks the spell in the end is the reappearance of Shimamoto, though his final disillusionment takes time to materialize. At first, she appears to be very much a part of his dream world and reconnects him to a more innocent and happier time in his life.

As mentioned already, Murakami tends to stay away from offering clear interpretations of his novels. In the case of *South of the Border*, though, he has expressed some mild frustration that readers have failed to understand how scary this story is supposed to be. What *South of the Border* is, Murakami explains, is a story about a revengeful ghost (an *onryō* in Japanese, or more specifically in this case, an *ikiryō* or living spirit), an idea taken from traditional Japanese literature and folklore, and which in this case is modeled on Ueda Akinari's *Ugetsu Monogatari* (*Tales of Moonlight and Rain*).[38] First, I will explain the model Murakami is borrowing from, and then how this plays out specifically in the case of *South of the Border*.

The idea of *ikiryō* or living spirits has come to play an important role in Murakami's fiction, with prominent examples found in *Kafka on the Shore*, *1Q84*, possibly in *Colorless Tsukuru Tazaki and His Years of Pilgrimage* and in *Killing Commendatore*. Perhaps the most famous example of a living spirit in Japanese literature is Lady Rokujō in *Genji Monogatari* (*The Tale of Genji*), one of Genji's lovers, who, driven by jealousy (but unknown to her "conscious self"), attacks and kills another of Genji's lovers and later his wife. *South of the Border* entertains similar ideas but is most explicitly modeled on "The Kibutsu Cauldron" in Ueda Akinari's *Tales of Moonlight and Rain*. In this story, a man named Shotaro marries a dutiful wife named Isora, a union arranged to help him settle down, and yet as the narrative informs us, even after he marries, "there was no getting around his willful, dissolute nature."[39] Driven by what might be described as his passion for the Real, Shotaro runs off with a prostitute, Sode, but she later dies, the suggestion being that she was attacked by Shotaro's dutiful wife, Isora, as a living spirit. Shotaro is distraught at Sode's death, the narrative explaining that he "longed for the Land of the Dead."[40] Deep in mourning, he later meets a woman who is visiting a grave with some flowers and water. He learns that this woman is visiting the grave of her master, whose house just happens to be close by and where his beautiful mourning mistress still lives.

Shotaro decides to visit this mistress, thinking that they may be able to share their grief. The mistress, when she meets Shotaro and hears his story, starts to push aside a folding screen that is between them and says, "So we meet again after all this time. . . . Let me show how I repay your cruelty."[41] Shotaro then realizes to whom he has been talking: the jealous living spirit of his scorned wife, Isora. The narrator tells us that "Her face was ghastly pale, the bleary eyes appalling."[42] Driven by resentment, she has first taken the life of Shotaro's mistress, Sode, and now it would seem she has come for Shotaro himself.

The fact that Shimamoto always shows up at Hajime's club on rainy nights is the first clue that she is some kind of ghost or living spirit. Anthony Chambers explains how the title *Ugetsu Monogatari* is a reference to the belief that came to Japan through China that, "mysterious beings appear on cloudy, rainy nights and in mornings with a lingering moon."[43] In the Introduction, I suggested that Murakami sees Ueda Akinari as a model for the kind of *monogatari* he is trying to produce—stories where the line separating this world and the other is thin. *South of the Border* thus offers a useful case study to explore how close Murakami has come to his desired model. *Ugetsu Monogatari*, Chambers explains, is often described as a collection of ghost stories, gothic tales or tales of the supernatural, though he objects to this last description, explaining, "'supernatural' is probably an inappropriate word, since what is considered to be supernatural in one time or culture is regarded as merely strange—but natural— in another."[44] He explains that Akinari shared the beliefs of his time, and so it is difficult to determine whether he is telling supernatural tales or natural ones that merely sound supernatural to us. Chambers also objects to calling these stories fantastic, quoting Tzvetan Todorov's assertion that "the basis of the fantastic is . . . the ambiguity as to whether the weird event is supernatural or not."[45] Todorov's definition here is a perfect explanation of Murakami's fiction, where such ambiguity is paramount, indicating that Murakami is a master of what Todorov calls the fantastic. As much as Murakami is modeling himself on a writer like Akinari then, we must admit that, in the end, it is impossible for modern readers to return entirely to a premodern mindset.

In Murakami's fiction, we have already seen countless examples of a lost, struggling male in whose life an intuitive female suddenly appears—what I have been calling, following Jung, Murakami's anima-guides—who then lead their male counterpart back into the heart of his therapeutic quest. From a different psychoanalytical perspective, these female helpers might be seen as examples of what Jacques Lacan, early in his career, meant when he said that "woman is a symptom of man." Žižek explains, "If we conceive the symptom as it was articulated by Lacan in the 1950s—namely as a *ciphered message*—then, of course, woman-symptom appears as the sign, the embodiment of man's fall, attesting to the fact that man 'gave way as to his desire.'"[46]

A useful example of what Žižek is talking about here can be seen in the classic film *Casablanca*, which is one of the cultural references *South of the Border* is playing with. Near the end of *South of the Border*, Hajime goes up to the pianist of the jazz trio who works for him and asks him not to play "Star-Crossed Lovers" anymore. "You've played it enough for me," he says, "It's about time to stop."[47] The pianist wants to know why, wondering if he does not like the way they play it, but Hajime explains that this is not the problem, admitting that it is the song itself which he no longer wishes to hear. "Sounds a little like Casablanca to me!" the pianist notes, a suggestion Hajime agrees with. After that, when the pianist would see him, he would break into a few bars of "As Time Goes By," the same song American expatriate Rick Blaine (played by Humphrey Bogart), the owner of a jazz club, does not want to hear from his pianist Sam (played by Dooley Wilson) because it reminds him of a past lover, Ilsa Lund (played by Ingrid Bergman) in *Casablanca*. When Ilsa, like Shimamoto, shows up at Rick's club years later, the first thing she does is ask Sam to play "As Time Goes By," which sends Rick back in time through his memories to the romance he shared with her in Paris years earlier.

Ilsa fulfills the role described by Žižek earlier, of embodying the fall of Rick and showing him how he has lost his way. Rick, we learn, used to be something of an idealist, running guns to Ethiopia during its war with Italy and fighting with the loyalists in the Spanish Civil War, but now he is a cynic, locked away in his bar in Casablanca, while the European powers surrounding him are embroiled in the Second World War. As a man with a mysterious past who throws the best parties in town, he is partly modeled on Gatsby, but the idealism or romanticism he once entertained is more political than Gatsby's ever was. At first Ilsa's appearance only deepens Rick's cynicism, and he is determined to remain neutral in the dramas that surround him. He is a symbol of America itself in the early years of the Second World War, determined to remain on the sidelines until something wakes him from his slumber. Rick is constantly declaring his neutrality in the film, his unwillingness to put his neck on the line for anyone or anything that does not serve his interests. Yet, over time the appearance of Ilsa softens him and reminds him of the ideals he once held. Once he learns the real reason for why she left him, he decides to help her and her politically minded husband to escape to America so that they can continue their resistance efforts.

Is Shimamoto Hajime's symptom in this Lacanian sense? Does she awaken him to some ideal he has let die? In a small way, she does. Hajime's father-in-law, who is involved in insider-trading, gives Hajime and Yukiko some information that can make them a lot of money, and initially, they take his investment advice. But Hajime eventually tells his wife to pull their money out, showing that he is no longer willing to be so tied up in his father in-law's dubious financial dealings. The reappearance of Shimamoto arguably plays a role in this decision. He has decided that he would rather live a less extravagant life on his own terms.

However, this is not really the ultimate message Hajime's reunion with Shimamoto brings. Instead, what she offers is something closer to what Žižek describes as Lacan's later conception of the "woman as symptom" formulation. Žižek explains:

> If, however, we conceive the symptom as it was articulated in Lacan's last writings and seminars . . . namely as a particular signifying formation which confers on the subject its very ontological consistency, enabling it to structure its basic, constitutive relationship to enjoyment (*jouissance*), then the entire relationship is reversed; if the symptom is dissolved, the subject itself loses the ground under his feet, disintegrates.[48]

In this latter case, the appearance of the woman does not return the man to a forgotten ideal; instead, she causes him to question his very ontological consistency—to basically fall apart. In Casablanca, Rick is living in the desert of Morocco, but he has created his own little oasis within his bar. Ilsa appears and tells him he needs to come back to the desert so to speak, to engage with the world at large. If Ilsa's role was closer to Lacan's second definition of the woman as symptom, she would have reappeared in Rick's life, consumed him in a return of the passion for the Real, and then finally abandoned him to the desert of the Real.

Lacanian psychoanalysis, of course, is not the only framework that might be used to explain this shifting role of the female characters in Murakami's fiction. Jung's concept of the anima is more than open to these more destructive elements. Writing about the role of the anima, Jung explains:

> She is the much needed compensation for the risks, struggles, sacrifices that all end in disappointment; she is the solace for all the bitterness of life. And, at the same time, she is the great illusionist, the seductress who draws him into life with her Maya—and not only into life's reasonable and useful aspects, but into its frightful paradoxes and ambivalences where good and evil, success and ruin, hope and despair, counterbalance one another.[49]

In short, anima figures in Jungian thought can both save and destroy their male counterparts, and in *South of the Border*, Hajime seems to encounter this more destructive side. Shimamoto, in her childhood form, was a compensatory figure for Hajime, someone who, due to her own situation, could understand his sense of isolation as an only child and connect with him. In her adult form, she at first seems to return to this role, but gradually we see that she is more dangerous. Not only is she no longer a compensatory figure but she also seems intent on destroying Hajime, on taking his life, if possible. If this seems like a strange turn of events, it may be because this older version of Shimamoto is not Shimamoto at all. Instead, she may be Izumi's living spirit, a figure who has come to take her revenge on Hajime in the form of Shimamoto. Katō Norihiro explains how the key to understanding this aspect of the novel is found in its color symbolism.

In *South of the Border*, Shimamoto is most often associated with the color blue, Izumi with red. Early in the novel, for example, we are offered this description of Shimamoto's clothing: "Shimamoto had on a blue sweater with a round neck. She owned a fair number of blue sweaters; blue must have been her favorite color. Or maybe she wore those sweaters because they went well with the navy-blue coat she always wore to school."[50] When she reappears in Hajime's life, Shimamoto is still wearing blue, a fact Hajime immediately notices: "You still like blue, I see," he says. Shimamoto is flattered he remembers.

In *The Great Gatsby*, blue is the color of illusion and fantasy. Gatsby's famous parties are held in what are called the "blue gardens" and in the famous scene where Gatsby organizes to be alone with Daisy and where it is raining, Nick describes how "a damp streak of hair lay like a dash of blue paint across her cheek."[51] In a similar fashion, blue is the color of illusion in *South of the Border*, and red the color of disillusionment. The association between Izumi and red starts after an incident where she and Hajime are experimenting sexually in his bedroom. Hajime's aunty shows up unannounced, and Hajime is forced to let her into the house. This aunty had heard from his parents that they would be away and so she has decided to drop by and cook him a meal. This leaves

Izumi trapped in his bedroom, and though he eventually manages to sneak her out of the house when his aunty goes to the bathroom, when they finally get to see each other again, she is clearly upset by what happened. Earlier, in his bedroom, she had stripped down to reveal "light-blue panties and a matching bra."[52] Now, talking to Hajime on a park bench, she is wearing a red sweater and beige coat.[53]

There are other examples in the novel, however, where this simple color code seems to break down. For example, Hajime recalls a strange incident as an adult in which he thought he saw Shimamoto walking in Shibuya. On this occasion, though, instead of wearing a blue coat, she had on a red coat and was also carrying a red department store shopping bag. Hajime trails her, trying to find out if it is really her, and eventually he follows her into a coffee shop. Unsure of her identity, he never says anything to her, but watches as she makes a telephone call and later disappears into a taxi. As he is watching her leave, a man then grasps him by the arm and gives him an envelope with some money inside. The message Hajime takes from this brief encounter is that the man wants him to leave the woman (whoever she is) alone.

Years later, when Hajime meets Shimamoto again, she confirms that it was her that day, which seems to support the idea that the color symbolism of Shimamoto as blue and Izumi as red is not that reliable. Near the end of the story, however, after Shimamoto has left Hajime again, he is driving down Gaien Higashi-dori in Tokyo when he thinks he sees Shimamoto, this time wearing blue pants and a beige raincoat. He parks his car as quickly as possible and jumps out to see her, but she is already gone. Slowly it dawns on him that the Shimamoto he thought he saw was dragging the wrong leg, and that at any rate, Shimamoto's leg had largely been fixed through an operation. Standing next to a crosswalk signal, he begins to get dizzy. "The signal," the English translation tells us, "turned from green to red, from red to green again," but this could just as well read from blue to red, from red to blue again (the "go" traffic light in Japan described as ao (blue)). Katō points out that this is the moment in the novel where things finally become clear. Years ago, Hajime had seen Shimamoto (in red) disappear into a taxi. Now, in the present, right in front of him, another taxi pulls up with Izumi inside. There is something strange about her, though, and Hajime wonders if she is even alive. He concludes that she is, though clearly the beauty and innocence she once possessed are now gone. This is Hajime's sign that the Shimamoto he has reconnected with in adulthood is not the same Shimamoto of his youth. Instead, it is the *ikiryō* or living spirit of his old girlfriend Izumi, who has come back to take her revenge.

What Hajime should have noticed all those years ago in Shibuya was not the woman he thought he saw (Shimamoto), but the color she was wearing (red). This was a sign that the woman he was looking at was not Shimamoto, but Izumi (or her living spirit in Shimamoto's form). Even the road Hajime had been driving down in his final sighting of Shimamoto, Katō points out, confirms this connection, Gaien Higashi-dori running between Akasaka (literally Red Hill) and Minami Aoyama (literally South Blue Mountain). To repeat then, on a road running between "red" and "blue," Hajime spots a woman he thinks is Shimamoto wearing red and blue, but then realizes it is not her. Distraught and standing by a traffic light which is flashing from red to blue, he sees a taxi then pulling up, with the woman sitting in the back of the taxi only feet away from him. This is a similar moment to the one Shotaro has at the end of "The Kibutsu Cauldron," where he sees the "ghastly pale" face. Hajime describes Izumi's face as "[l]ike a room from which every last stick of furniture had been taken."[54] Izumi (as a living spirit) has come back to take her revenge on him, to take his very life if possible, and here she has appeared at the end in her true form to let him know it was her all along.

Izumi's death wish for Hajime is clear in the scene where Hajime and Shimamoto make their final trip to Hakone together. On their way there, Shimamoto says, "When I look at you driving, sometimes I want to grab the steering wheel and give it a yank. It'd kill us, wouldn't it."[55] Hajime tries to laugh this off, but Shimamoto keeps offering him hints about what being with her would require: "Hajime," she begins, "this is very important, so listen carefully. As I told you before, there is no middle ground with me. You take either all of me or nothing. That's the way it works."[56] All or nothing, life or death, this is the option she represents. Being with Shimamoto again, Hajime recalls the earlier occasion when he had flown with her to scatter the ashes of her dead baby in a river. He recalls looking into her eyes afterward and the eerie feeling it had given him, but he only now realizes what he saw. He explains:

> It was the first time I'd been face-to-face with death. So I'd had no distinct image of what death really was. But there it was then, right before my eyes, spread out just inches from my face. So this is the face of death, I'd thought. And death spoke to me, saying that my time, too, would one day come.[57]

The novel makes clear then that what Shimamoto has come back for is Hajime's life, and if Katō's reading is right (which I believe it is), it is not Shimamoto who has come back, but Izumi in the shape of Shimamoto. She has taken the shape of Hajime's anima child to seduce him into death, the ultimate revenge for the hurt he caused her. Seeing her in the taxi with the lights flashing from blue to red, the horror story behind the love story is finally revealed. Welcome to the desert of the real.

Hajime does not die in the novel. Instead, when he wakes up in Hakone, Shimamoto is gone without a trace, and later he discovers that the envelope of money that was given to him by the mysterious man years earlier has also vanished from its secure location. Was all this just a dream then, a fantasy of a man who, having reached middle age and subconsciously driven by guilt over his past, drives to Hakone to kill himself, but who in the end does not go through with it? It is the ambiguity of these events that lets us know we are in the realm of the fantastic. As in earlier Murakami novels, there are several ways the story might be read. What is clear, though, is that Hajime's blue world is now gone forever. As he puts it, "I had no more illusions."[58] Finally, standing in the desert of the real, Hajime's conclusion is this:

> I don't know if I have the strength to care for Yukiko and the children, I thought. No more visions can help me, weaving special dreams just for me. As far as the eye can see, the void is simply that—a void. I've been in that void before and forced myself to adjust. And now, finally, I end up where I began, and I'd better get used to it. No one will weave dreams for me—it is my turn to weave dreams for others. That's what I have to do. Such dreams may have no power, but if my own life is to have any meaning at all, that is what I have to do. Probably.[59]

There is no salvation in the world of blue, except perhaps now as a tool to reach out and help others who must also survive the desert of the real. Much like "Winter Dreams," this is a story about romantic disillusionment, though told through the framework of a ghost story, much like "The Kibutsu Cauldron." Even though Hajime has survived for now, Izumi may still get her final revenge. What is most scary about this story, Murakami insists, is that Hajime does not know when Shimamoto might reappear again.[60] Even after seeing what is behind her in the vacant face of Izumi, it seems that Hajime may still be susceptible to Shimamoto's ghostly charms. Hajime's recommitment to his family at the end of the novel, then, is not necessarily based on solid ground, and could easily dissolve again. However, like other Murakami protagonists before him, he has tentatively decided to remain in the world of the living, at least for now.

Murakami's next novel, *Wind-Up Bird*, is a complicated story about the difficulty of understanding another person in a marriage, and the way the trauma of the Second World War still lives on in the psyches of Japanese people today, even for those who were not yet born during the war. It is interesting to remember that Hajime's story was originally part of this larger story, but that as the novel grew, Murakami's found it easier to pull these two strands apart. In *Wind-Up Bird*, we do not learn much about the main protagonist's childhood or youth, the people he loved or perhaps hurt along the way. This has all been removed to *South of the Border* so that we can focus, instead, on a man who is desperately searching for his missing wife in the present and who must dive not so much into his past as into the past of his nation. What we might keep in mind as readers is the way Hajime's initiation into the desert of the real might enable us to understand the even more violent and traumatic initiation awaiting the protagonist in *Wind-Up Bird*.

Blocks and Flows in *The Wind-Up Bird Chronicle*

When reading Murakami's fiction as an evolving therapeutic project, it is hard to overestimate the importance of *Wind-Up Bird*. Indeed, I would argue that it is nothing less than the conclusion to the first half of Murakami's therapeutic project, a psychological breakthrough that was the answer to his baseball epiphany. The novels which precede *Wind-Up Bird*, as we have seen, are primarily about Murakami's "long goodbye" to his adolescence and early adulthood and his coming to terms with the death of a former girlfriend (therapeutic thread one). The temptation his protagonists often faced was to follow different representations of this lost girl into a world of death, but through a gradual process of returning from melancholia to mourning and by learning how to "pass through the wall" and connect with others, they eventually found a way back to life. What has been less touched on so far (except in the discussion of *A Wild Sheep Chase*) is the theme of Murakami's inherited trauma from his father (therapeutic thread two), and his need to somehow make sense of (and perhaps even atone for) the violence of the Second World War. This theme is taken up directly in *Wind-Up Bird*, connecting it strongly with *A Wild Sheep Chase*, and making it Murakami's most violent novel to date.

Wind-Up Bird only introduces this broader historical focus slowly, however, starting, instead, with a domestic drama involving a man and his wife: Okada Tōru and his wife Kumiko. Tōru is unemployed, having recently quit his job as a legal aid, so he spends his days doing household chores and, more recently, looking for the family cat which has gone missing. This cat, which joined Tōru and Kumiko shortly after their marriage six years earlier, is an important symbol of the life they have built together, so its disappearance points to an impending crisis, something Tōru at first fails to see—just one example of the many blind spots that plague him in the novel.[61] Much like *South of the Border*, reality is a fragile thing in *Wind-Up Bird*, constantly threatened by a passion for the Real, a desire to test the limits of what reality is that takes both sexual and violent forms. The first indication of this in the novel is a phone call Tōru receives from a woman who seems to know him and who wants ten minutes of his time so that they can come to "understand each other."[62] Before long, this mysterious woman is offering sexually explicit descriptions of herself, forcing him to abruptly end the phone call before her requested time is up.

We have already seen in Murakami's fiction the ways telephone calls can act as a call from the unconscious, prompting the protagonist to engage in a therapeutic quest. What is different here, as becomes clearer later in the novel, is that this is not a call from Tōru's own unconscious, but from that of his wife, Kumiko. In short, the quest Tōru will undertake into the second basement (in this case a labyrinth-like hotel and particularly one of its rooms, 208) is into a world that is not just his own. It also belongs to Kumiko (indeed, it is primarily her world) and is also accessible to the novel's antagonist, Wataya Noboru (Kumiko's brother).

The opening chapter of *Wind-Up Bird*, taken from a 1986 short story Murakami wrote called "The Wind-Up Bird and Tuesday's Women," has all the elements we have come to expect from a Murakami story—references to music, food, cats, and mysterious women. As Jay McInerney once pointed out to Murakami, this opening also has similarities with Raymond Carver's short story "Put Yourself in My Shoes," which also begins with an unemployed male protagonist receiving a telephone call. Here is the opening line of *Wind-Up Bird*: "When the phone rang I was in the kitchen, boiling a potful of spaghetti and whistling along with an FM broadcast of the overture to Rossini's The Thieving Magpie, which has to be the perfect music for cooking pasta."[63] And here are the opening lines of "Put Yourself in My Shoes": "The telephone rang while he was running the vacuum cleaner. He had worked his way through the apartment and was doing the living room, using the nozzle attachment to get at the cat hairs between the cushions. He stopped and listened and then switched off the vacuum. He went to answer the telephone."[64]

When this similarity was pointed out to Murakami by McInerney, he quickly acknowledged it, later writing, "I was certainly not conscious of this when I wrote it, but it can definitely be said that the two beginnings are quite similar in atmosphere."[65] There is also a similarity between Murakami's opening and the opening of Carver's "Are You a Doctor?" which begins, "In slippers, pajamas, and robe, he hurried out of the study when the telephone began to ring. Since it was past ten, the call could be his wife."[66] This story has similarities to Murakami's novel, in that the call is from a mysterious woman whom the protagonist, against his better judgment, continues to talk to and later actually goes to meet, despite having scant information about her identity. In short, the opening of *Wind-Up Bird* feels particularly Carveresque.

In terms of understanding the deeper influence of Carver on *Wind-Up Bird*, however, we have to turn to the first Carver story Murakami ever read (around 1982 as he recalls) and still his favorite short story of all time, "So Much Water So Close to Home," the significance of which has been pointed out by Akashi Kayo.[67] Murakami was deeply impressed when he first read Carver's story in an anthology, describing it as like being struck by lightning.[68] There are different versions of "So Much Water So Close to Home" that for simplicity's sake can be divided into a short version and a long one. It was the long version Murakami first read, which he describes as the "more accomplished of the two," and which I will therefore stick to in the discussion which follows.[69] As Akashi explains, there are two main reasons why Murakami translates an author—because of the sympathy he feels when reading their work, and because of something he feels he can learn from them.[70] In the case of Carver, what Akashi argues Murakami had to learn was something about the perspective of women who are hurt by, and misunderstood by, men. She concludes that Carver's short story inspired the creation of Kumiko in *Wind-Up Bird*.

"So Much Water So Close to Home" is the story of a married couple, Stuart and Claire, told from the first-person perspective of Claire. Water imagery is central to the story and plays an important role in the main event which comes to deeply strain the relationship of the couple. Stuart had gone fishing with three friends when they discovered the naked body of a dead woman, an apparent rape and murder victim, in the river. It had taken the friends a long drive and hike to reach their camping spot, so after some discussion, they decided that, since the woman was not going anywhere, they would continue with their fishing trip as planned and report the body to the authorities when they returned to civilization. Later, they tie some nylon around her wrist and connect it to some tree roots so that she will not float away and cause them any problems. Then they fish and wash their dishes in the same river. Stuart believes they made a reasonable decision and later tries to defend it, but Claire is deeply disturbed by the choice they made.

Claire decides to attend the girl's funeral, but as she is driving there, a strange incident occurs when she pulls off the road at one point to take a break by a river. Before long she is startled by a man tapping on her window, asking her if she is okay. She recognizes this man as the driver of a green pickup truck that had been following her for much of her journey but who had recently overtaken her. Perhaps it is the color of the truck which puts her on edge (the murdered girl was last seen getting into a male's green car), but she refuses to wind down her window and talk to him. She senses him looking at her breasts and legs and feels threatened, even if, on the surface, he is just expressing concern for her welfare. The man eventually gives up trying to engage her and drives away.

There are numerous other examples in the story of male violence (or potential violence) against females, all of which seem to be pointing to undercurrents of violence in the relationship between Stuart and Claire. At one point in the story, they drive to a picnic area near a creek where people are fishing. "So much water so close to home," Claire thinks to herself, "why did he have to go miles away to fish?"[71] She stares into the water, and these thoughts eventually float to the surface of her mind: "Nothing will be any different. We will go on and on and on and on. We will go on even now, as if nothing had happened."[72] Claire is facing a crisis, but Stuart simply wants things to go back to normal, and it is this sense of male obliviousness to female pain that links the story closely with *Wind-Up Bird*, according to Akashi.[73] For Claire, the water the girl was lying in so far away feels deeply connected to the water she lives in daily: there is so much water—so much potential for male violence—so close to home.

Akashi convincingly argues that Murakami picks up Carver's water imagery connected to male violence against women and brings it into his own fiction, starting with two short stories he wrote with female narrators, "Sleep" and "Kanō Kureta" (the second a story which has not been translated into English yet, but whose narrator, Kanō Creta, is very similar to the Kanō Creta who appears in *Wind-Up Bird*). In "Sleep," the female narrator, like Claire, is a housewife with one son. One day, she stops sleeping altogether and begins to live a secret life at night free from family responsibilities. The first night this begins she awakens from a terrifying dream paralyzed, and next notices an old man standing at the end of her bed. The man then pulls out a pitcher of water and begins pouring it over her feet, the woman feeling as if they would simply melt away. She tries to scream but no sound comes out. Then the man disappears, and the woman can move again. Despite this ominous dream, however, the woman becomes determined to enjoy the extra time her sleeplessness provides her with, and she begins to do all the things at night her life as a housewife has taken from her. She also comes to resent her husband and son, who she feels will never understand her. The violence here is subtler than what is found in "So Much Water So Close to Home," but the imagery of the pouring water and the dissolving feet does have resonance with the imagery of Carver's story (this is perhaps even clearer in Murakami's translation of Carver's story which is titled "*Ashimoto ni nagareru fukai kawa*," which might be translated as "The Deep River Which Flows at our Feet"). "Sleep" ends with the woman driving her car to a park by the harbor (another body of water). Soon, she finds herself surrounded by shadowy men who are rocking her car and trying to tip it over (suggestive of the scene with the man tapping at Claire's window). The story ends before we find out what happens to her.

"Kanō Creta" is an even more disturbing story about male violence. Kanō, she informs us early in the story, has a problem. Whenever men see her, they want to rape her, and over her lifetime many of them have. Her sister, Malta, makes her living listening to water, having traveled to the island of Malta to study her strange craft, and she diagnoses Creta's problem as related to her inner water, encouraging her to learn how to listen to it. Creta begins working for Malta, helping her to look after the stored water samples she has collected from all over Japan. Hidden away from the world, for a time Creta's life becomes peaceful, though a random visit from a male police officer who immediately wants to rape Creta, upsets this equilibrium. The two sisters end up killing the police officer and burying his body, but his ghost continues to live with them. Even this, however, Creta adjusts to, and her life seems to be going so well that she decides it is time for her to leave her sanctuary and to follow her dream of becoming a designer of thermal power stations. She quickly succeeds in this career, having a natural gift for the task, and is finally able to live the life she has always dreamed of, until one day when a large man with burning green eyes, shows up and kills her. The narrative ends by informing us that at the moment of death, Creta finally heard the sound of the water inside herself.

Akashi links the man with the burning green eyes who kills Creta with the green car that picks up the young girl before her rape and murder, and the green pickup truck that follows Claire on the way to the funeral. She also notes the similarities in Japanese between the names Claire (Kurea) and Creta (Kureta).[74] In Akashi's reading, the water that flows through "So Much Water So Close to Home" continues to flow through "Sleep" and "Kanō Creta," and then on through *Wind-Up Bird*, opening Murakami's fiction up to a new perspective: that of the female hurt by male violence. While Akashi's reading is a valuable one, I also think it is important to recognize the way *Wind-Up Bird* seeks to move beyond this starting point, indeed, the way it is structured around the quest of a male protagonist to get beyond his ignorance of his wife's pain, which, in turn, has consequences for the way water imagery develops in the novel, too. This can also be connected to Carver's work, though this time to his poetry rather than to his prose, a point I will return to near the end of this chapter.

Wind-Up Bird is a novel filled with characters who are suffering from post-traumatic stress, both women who have been abused by men, and men who have experienced the savagery of war. As a result, these characters all struggle with different forms of dissociation—at a deep level they find it difficult to connect with both themselves and the world around them. Kumiko's first traumatic experience was in childhood. From the ages of three to six, she was sent to live with her grandmother in Niigata, an experience that was not unpleasant, but which turned ugly when the time came for her grandmother to return her to her parents. This grandmother, who wanted Kumiko to stay with her as a means of staying connected to her son, became increasingly erratic and began physically and verbally abusing her and hurting herself. Kumiko, who was still just a child, could not comprehend what was going on and found that her only solution was "to shut herself off from the outer world."[75] She retains no memory of what happened in the following months.

When Kumiko's memory picks up, she is living with her immediate family again but feeling disconnected from them. The only person who reaches out to her during this time is her older sister, but she dies a year after Kumiko returns from Niigata, the cause, everyone is told, being food poisoning. This sister's death is connected with Noboru, the oldest of the three siblings, who somehow defiled her and who later turns his attention to Kumiko. The exact nature of what Noboru does to his sisters remains unclear. Later, in a letter to Tōru, Kumiko writes, "Strictly speaking, he did not defile our bodies. What he did was even worse than that."[76] What he likely did is the same thing he did to Creta, who describes him inserting something hard into her from behind that was not his penis (she reports that Noboru was impotent). After a while, Creta felt herself splitting in two and then she reports that from her divided body crawled something she had never seen before, something that was as "wet and slippery as a newborn baby."[77] In the traumatic moment, Creta experienced what many victims of sexual trauma report, a kind of out of body experience, and a feeling that this was not actually happening to her. She was "like a dead person watching her own autopsy."[78] Things started gushing out of her and she was unable to stop the flow. She explains, "I knew that I should not let this happen, that I should not allow my very self to spill out this way and be lost forever, but there was nothing I could do to staunch the flow."[79]

A useful way to understand what is happening here is offered by Peter Levine, an expert on somatic approaches to treating trauma, who finds in shamanistic descriptions of spiritual disease a strong correlation with modern trauma patients. Levine writes:

> When people are overwhelmed, their "souls" may become separated from their bodies. According to Mircea Eliade (an important scholar of shamanistic practice), "rape of the soul" is by far the most widespread and damaging cause of illness cited by shamanic healers. Missing important parts of their souls, people become lost in states of spiritual suspension. From the shamanistic point of view, illness is a result of being stuck in "spiritual limbo."[80]

"Rape of the soul" is an expression which captures well what Noboru does to women in *Wind-Up Bird*. When Kumiko says he has done something worse to her than raping her body, this would seem to be what she is pointing at, an act that has left her stuck in "spiritual limbo." She has become separated from her own body (dissociated), and this is causing havoc in her life.

Kumiko's post-traumatic condition leaves her feeling split and questioning the nature of everyday reality (in other words, she is experiencing both depersonalization and derealization). As she tries to explain to Tōru before her disappearance, "Sometimes, though, I can't tell about things. I can't tell what's real and what's not real . . . what things really happened and what things didn't really happen. . . . Just sometimes, though."[81] Later, in a letter to Tōru where she is explaining why she had an affair with another man (later it turns out she had affairs with several men), she explains the sense of split she experienced, noting, "Half of me was here, and half there."[82] Early in the novel, Tōru is oblivious to all of this, unable to comprehend the inadequacy of his sense of their shared reality. In the original Japanese version of the novel, it is only at the end of Book Two, while floating in water, that his epiphany finally comes.[83] The sexually provocative woman who keeps calling him is Kumiko.

The men in the novel, too, former soldiers who returned home damaged from the war, bear their own signs of post-traumatic stress disorder. The most important example here is Lieutenant Mamiya, who witnesses one of the most traumatic scenes in the novel, the skinning alive of a man named Yamamoto. This skinning occurs under the direction of Boris the Manskinner, a figure Lieutenant Mamiya will meet again after the war when they are both forced to work in a Siberian coal mine. Murakami has explained how the battles that ensue in the novel between Lieutenant Mamiya and Boris the Manskinner and between Tōru and Noboru are connected, so that Tōru's job, in one sense, is to complete the things that Lieutenant Mamiya could not do for himself.[84] This should remind us of a point I made in the Introduction, where I argued that Murakami has a deep need to take up the "unfinished business" of his father.

After witnessing the human skinning, Lieutenant Mamiya is dropped into a desert well and left to die. As he lies at the bottom of the well and watches the movement of the sun across the sky each day, he begins to feel something he can only describe as "huge, cosmic love."[85] Later, in a letter to Tōru, he explains that he felt like he "was able to descend directly into a place that might be called the very core of my own consciousness" and that what the light was trying to show him was "something very much like heavenly grace."[86] But then the moment passed, and in the end, Lieutenant Mamiya feels like the true meaning of this revelation alluded him, something which leaves him feeling empty:

> What I suffered with most down there in the well was the torture of being unable to attain a clear view of that something in the light: the hunger of being unable to see what I needed to see, the thirst of being unable to know what I needed to know. Had I been able to see it clearly, I would not have minded dying right then and there. I truly felt that way. I would have sacrificed anything for a full view of its form.[87]

Lieutenant Mamiya is eventually rescued from the well, but his failure to see what he needed to see in that light continues to haunt him. He eventually returns to Japan and (like Murakami's own father) becomes a teacher, but he never truly feels alive or knows what it means to love another person.[88] He feels like his life is little more than a dream and that he is nothing more than an empty shell.[89] This, then, might be seen as the first item of unfinished business Tōru must take up. Like Lieutenant Mamiya, he will also descend into a well to try and glimpse something which might be described as the very core of his own consciousness. And in the darkness of the well, he will search for something like heavenly grace, something that can make sense out of the senselessness of human suffering.

The second item of unfinished business that Tōru must take up from Lieutenant Mamiya's life comes from his failure to kill Boris the Manskinner. This is something Lieutenant Mamiya had tried to do in the Siberian coal mine, waiting a long time for his chance, but in the final moment, and at close range, he had failed in his mission. Firstly, this was because the gun he opportunistically grabbed was not loaded, but even after Boris gives him two shells, he still could not do it, his shots missing their mark despite his being at close range and despite his being a competent marksman. Boris gloats that Lieutenant Mamiya is simply not qualified to kill him, and he leaves him with a curse: "Wherever you may be, you can never be happy. You will never love anyone or be loved by anyone."[90] Tōru cannot go back in time and kill Boris, but in some mysterious way he can take up Lieutenant Mamiya's unfinished business through his interactions with Noboru.

Gaber Maté, in his foreword to Peter Levine's book *In an Unspoken Voice*, usefully explains the way failed action in traumatic situations leaves people feeling permanently frozen in their lives:

> Potentially traumatic situations are ones that induce states of high physiological arousal but without the freedom for the affected person to express and get past these states: danger without the possibility of fight or flight and, afterward, without the opportunity to "shake it off," as a wild animal would following a frightful encounter with a predator. What ethologists call tonic immobility—the paralysis and physical/emotional shutdown that characterize the universal experience of

helplessness in the face of mortal danger—comes to dominate the person's life and functioning. We are "scared stiff." In human beings, unlike in animals, the state of temporary freezing becomes a long-term trait. The survivor, Peter Levine points out, may remain "stuck in a kind of limbo, not fully reengaging in life."[91]

Lieutenant Mamiya's recovery from the war would have been very different if in that final moment, facing Boris the Manskinner, he had been able to pull the trigger and successfully execute him, but this was not to be, and so his curse is to be stuck in limbo.

What is needed to get past such a traumatic experience is what Pierre Janet, the father of modern trauma studies, called "the pleasure of completed action."[92] Peter Levine explains, "Trauma represents a profound compression of 'survival' energy, energy that has not been able to complete its meaningful course of action."[93] Naturally, survivors of trauma cannot simply go back in time and complete what they ideally should have at the time. But in the present, in symbolic ways, they often can. The paralysis and fear they felt at the time of their trauma can be transformed into the powerful emotions of rage and anger. Action can replace inaction and the energy bound up in their nervous system can finally be discharged.

This idea has application not just to this novel, but to all of Murakami's early fiction, and particularly to the so-called detachment phase of his career, which is why the breakthrough, when it finally comes in *Wind-Up Bird*, is so significant. Right back in Murakami's debut novel, *Hear the Wind Sing*, *Boku* is talking with the woman with the missing finger about his experience during the student protests in Tokyo. He describes how a riot cop knocked out one of his teeth and the woman wants to know if he desires revenge. *Boku* is adamant that he does not. "So then there's no meaning, right? ... No meaning to having your tooth knocked out." "Nope," is *Boku*'s simple reply.[94] *Boku* wishes to dismiss the violence he experienced as something of no consequence, but the consequences for his life are clear. He has experienced none of what Janet calls "the pleasure of completed action," and the result, unsurprisingly, is that he remains frozen. Tōru will be the first Murakami protagonist to break through this frozen state and to do so will require him to confront his anger.

Tōru's personal trainer in this regard is Kasahara Mei, the young girl he meets at the end of the closed-off alley behind his home. She is a character consumed by what I have been calling the passion for the Real, the desire to understand what life is when pushed to its limits. The first time he meets Mei, the conversation quickly turns to death, and she offers her thoughts on the subject:

> I wish I had a scalpel. I'd cut it open and look inside. Not the corpse ... the lump of death. I'm sure there must be something like that. Something round and squishy, like a softball, with a hard little core of dead nerves. I want to take it out of a dead person and cut it open and look inside.[95]

This desire to see the "lump of death" is what caused her to cover her boyfriend's eyes while riding on the back of his motorcycle, killing him and injuring herself. "You've got to really push the limits if you're going to trick it into coming out," she explains to Tōru.[96] For her, this gooshy something inside people is the only real thing in the world.[97] At one point, she pulls Tōru's ladder up from the well, abandoning him down there and perhaps leaving him there to die. Someone else rescues Tōru before he has a chance to find out just how far she was willing to go.

This can all be seen as part of Tōru's preparation. He must slowly strip himself of everything inessential, everything connected with everyday reality. Entering the well, he senses this separation from the world above and the lives of ordinary people: "I am no longer one of them, however. They are up there, on the face of the earth; I am down here, in the bottom of a well."[98] Or as he puts it a few lines later, "The break between 'people' and me is now total."[99] This is the first step of what Campbell describes as the hero's journey, "detachment or withdrawal," the necessary transferring of "emphasis from the external to the internal world."[100] This is similar territory to what we have already seen in *A Wild Sheep Chase*, but here the hero's journey becomes more intentional. Tōru will make a conscious decision to commit to the quest and to follow it through to its end, even if it means death.

The main example Joseph Campbell offers of a hero who goes "forth of [their] own volition" is Theseus, who, when he learns of the half-bull, half-human Minotaur who is consuming human sacrifices in a labyrinth in Crete, immediately volunteers to kill the beast.[101] The Theseus story is one of the sources Murakami is borrowing from in *Wind-Up Bird*, even if Tōru takes a little longer than Theseus to make his decision.[102] There are numerous references to labyrinths in *Wind-Up Bird*, and when the character Ushikawa (Bull River) appears later in the story (or simply Bull as he is often called— "the more I hear that, the more I feel like a real bull," Ushikawa states), we know our hero is getting close to his final battle.[103] Ushikawa is not the Minotaur in the novel, however; he is simply its representative (Ushikawa works for Noboru, who is the real beast that must be confronted). The most important labyrinth in the novel is the hotel where Kumiko (or some part of her) lies. Each time Tōru manages to make his way to room 208, he is interrupted by a knock at the door and warned to leave, but in the end, he will need to stay and face whoever or whatever is waiting for him on the other side.

Before this climactic encounter, though, there is an earlier one where Tōru first experiences rage and violence: the scene where he spots the singer he happened to see perform on the night Kumiko had an abortion. Kumiko had become pregnant three years into their marriage, something they both felt they were not ready for (though Tōru, who had gotten a girl pregnant in college and who had helped her get an abortion, wanted to keep it). They had both anguished about what to do, but in the end, Kumiko had made the decision alone, having the abortion while Tōru was away on a business trip in Hokkaido. She tells him the news over the phone, following which Tōru goes to a bar, where he hears a singer perform. At the end of his performance, the singer gives a strange object lesson, a magic trick as it turns out, where he appears to burn the flesh of his hand over a candle. Later, he tells everyone in the audience that the anguish they felt during the trick was an example of the human power for empathy.

Years later, in a moment where Tōru's quest to find Kumiko has stagnated and where the only thing he can think to do is to go to Shinjuku each day and people-watch, he spots the same singer carrying his guitar case and he begins to follow him. Thoughts of the abortion return to him as he follows the man, and he realizes that this was an important turning point in his life with Kumiko. Thinking about this, he finds that "Gradually, I began to sense a quiet anger growing inside my body, an anger directed toward that something that remained invisible to me."[104] He follows the man into an apartment building and is met by a swinging baseball bat. A fight ensues, and Tōru eventually gets the upper hand, and he finds that as he does, "I found my terror turning to unmistakable anger."[105] Feeling "intense hatred," Tōru then smashes the man with the bat.[106]

Later that night, Tōru has a dream where the violent events of the day repeat themselves, but this time, at the end, the man takes a knife and begins to peel off his skin. The removed skin of this man then begins to crawl over the floor toward Tōru and eventually covers his own body like a new skin. He wakes up terrified, but at the same time, he now knows what he should do. He declares, "I could not—and should not—run away, not to Crete, not to anyplace. I had to get Kumiko back. With my own hands, I had to pull her back into this world. Because if I didn't, that would be the end of me. This person, this self that I thought of as 'me,' would be lost."[107] In the English version of the novel, this is the end of Book Two.

If Tōru is to save Kumiko and save himself, he must first embrace the anger and potential for violence he has discovered within himself. Unlike earlier Murakami protagonists, he can no longer simply shrug his shoulders and say this is the way things are. He must demand something more. In Jungian terms, Tōru has finally learned how to embrace his shadow—that part of himself that is most socially unacceptable, most dangerous, but also most powerful. By integrating the shadow, he is now ready to face his nemesis, Noboru (or at least some part of him), in room 208. In some sense, too, Tōru is now also no longer the one seeking healing but, instead, is ready to take on the role of healer, something that becomes increasingly apparent in Part Three of the novel. Tōru, in short, has experienced a therapeutic breakthrough, and this, I would argue, reflects a similar transformation that Murakami was likely going through at the time. Taking on the unfinished business of his father, he first had to learn about the potential for violence within himself. It was only by achieving this first victory that he could go on to experience the second, which, I believe, is the single most important psychological breakthrough in Murakami's fiction.

This second breakthrough comes in the final confrontation between Tōru and Noboru. Murakami has said that Noboru came to him out of his reading on the Nomonhan incident and Japan's war in China more generally, while visiting Princeton University.[108] Inspired undoubtedly by his father's stories, this part of the war had fascinated Murakami ever since he was a young boy. He recalls, as a child, finding a book on the Nomonhan incident at his school library and feeling like he was being sucked into the images he saw.[109] Sitting in the library at Princeton years later, he had the chance to think deeply about the significance of this war for him, concluding that, "the fascination for me is that the origin of this war was all too Japanese, all too representative of the Japanese people."[110] *Wind-Up Bird* is clearly a product of this research, and no character more so than Noboru.

Noboru's uncle, Wataya Yoshitaka, was sent to Manchukuo in 1932 to investigate conditions for raising sheep, their wool indispensable for the war uniforms that would be needed to fight the Soviets in the north, details suggestive of *A Wild Sheep Chase*. Yoshitaka then contacts Ishiwara Kanji (a real historical figure) just one year before the Manchurian Incident, connecting the Wataya family with some of the central historical figures and events of this period. At the end of the war, this uncle had initially been forced to lie low, but eventually found his way into politics, serving in the Japanese Diet. Noboru is being set up as his political successor, a progression that takes him from academic to media pundit and finally into the world of politics. Tōru watches all of this in disbelief, wondering how other people cannot see through Noboru.

We have seen in Murakami's fiction a slow evolution of the male counterparts to the central male protagonists, from an early character like Rat in the first three novels, to Nagasawa in *Norwegian Wood* and Gotanda in *Dance Dance Dance*. With Noboru, we finally have a true antagonist, an unambiguous embodiment of evil that Tōru reacts to immediately. In one part of the novel, Tōru describes his usual method for dealing with people he does not like—he simply assigns them to a realm having nothing to do with himself, and he finds that over time his negative feelings toward them dissipate. With Noboru though, this strategy does not work. He explains, "When it came to Noboru Wataya, though, my system refused to function. I was unable simply to shove Noboru Wataya into a domain having no connection with me. And that fact itself annoyed the hell out of me."[111] "OK, let's face it," he finally admits, "I hated the guy."[112]

This feeling is mutual, and Noboru, who at first seems to show only disinterest in Tōru (he is not even worthy, it would seem, of disdain), increasingly comes to see him as a worthy competitor and even as an existential threat. To return to the Nietzschean model examined earlier, Noboru is the warped Superman slowly learning how to exert his influence over the masses, while Tōru is the ordinary man who through a process of individuation, his embracing of the shadow as we have already seen, is learning how to stand against him. This is something Creta clearly understands, explaining to Tōru, "Noboru Wataya is a person who belongs to a world that is the exact opposite of yours.... In a world where you are losing everything, Mr. Okada, Noboru Wataya is gaining everything. In a world where you are rejected, he is accepted. And the opposite is just as true. Which is why he hates you so intensely."[113] She then goes on to describe the relationship in a way that resonates deeply with Jungian psychology, explaining, "Hatred is like a long, dark shadow. Not even the person it falls upon knows where it comes from, in most cases. It is like a two-edged sword. When you cut the other person, you cut yourself. The more violently you hack at the other person, the more violently you hack at yourself."[114]

In one sense then, Tōru's final battle with Noboru can be seen as a battle with himself. This is like reading Theseus' battle with the Minator as an allegory for what we all must do: defeat the beast within ourselves. This is a point Joseph Campbell also makes, arguing that

> The labyrinth is thoroughly known; we only have to follow the thread of the hero path. And where we had thought to find an abomination, we shall find a god; where we had thought to slay another, we shall slay ourselves; where we had thought to travel outward, we shall come to the center of our own existence; where we had thought to be alone, we shall be with all the world.[115]

In Tōru's case, this labyrinth leads him to room 208, where a scene repeats from earlier in the novel: Tōru talks with a woman in the dark when a knock comes at the door, but this time, instead of running away, he stands his ground. A man enters the room, and a fight ensues. This man has a knife and cuts Tōru to the bone. Tōru has a baseball bat and swings furiously in the dark, at first making no contact. Eventually, he connects with the man, and then a second and third time. Now all that remains is for Tōru to finish him off. He explains:

> I didn't want to do it, but I had no choice. I had to finish him off: not out of hatred or even out of fear, but as something I simply had to do. I heard something crack open in the darkness like a piece of fruit. Like a watermelon. I stood still, gripping the bat, holding it out in front of me.[116]

The scene resonates with an earlier one set during the war where a Chinese prisoner is killed by the same method, bashed to death with a baseball bat as punishment for the way he earlier killed a Japanese soldier. This climactic scene in *The Wind-Up Bird* is, thus, the moment where everything finally comes together—the past with the present. While most readers will likely pass over the lines which follow with little thought, they may be some of the most therapeutic in all of Murakami's fiction: "Then I realized I was trembling. All over. And there was no way I could stop it."[117]

This trembling is the reward of completed action. It is a physical, nonvoluntary act which finally sets free the trauma of the past. Levine gives us a good accounting of the importance of this trembling, explaining the way he has seen it time and again in the therapeutic process. He explains:

> These gyrations and undulations are ways that our nervous system "shakes off" the last rousing experience and "grounds" us in readiness for the next encounter with danger, lust and life. They are mechanisms that help restore our equilibrium after we have been threatened or highly aroused. They bring us back down to earth, so to speak. Indeed, such physiological reactions are at the core of self-regulation and resilience.[118]

When he comes back to his senses, Tōru is sitting back in his well, but now something is different. He soon realizes the well is filling with water and he becomes convinced that he will "die in its rebirth."[119] This kind of rebirth is something Campbell's monomyth predicts: "The effect of the successful adventure of the hero is the unlocking and release again of the flow of life into the body of the world."[120] Years earlier, Tōru had been told by Mr. Honda, another war veteran in the novel who works as a spiritualist, that he should be "careful of water" and here the warning seems to have been validated.[121] Murakami has said that he wrote *Wind-Up Bird* with the intention of having Tōru die at the end by drowning, a kind of atonement he felt was necessary to complete the work, an idea inspired in part by the ending of Jack London's *Martin Eden*.[122] When he got to the end of the novel, however, he simply could not go through with it, and so he changed his intended ending to have Tōru rescued by a character called Cinnamon (the son of another character called Nutmeg). This is not the ending Murakami may have been anticipating, but it does fit with Campbell's theory of the hero's journey, which states that, "The hero may have to be brought back from his supernatural adventure by assistance from without. That is to say, the world may have to come and get him."[123]

If *Wind-Up Bird* started as a short story channeling Carver's "So Much Water So Close to Home," it ends with new waters emerging from a well that have a very different meaning. These are not the waters of male violence but new waters offering renewed hope, a baptism that might wash away the sins of the past. Murakami, I have argued, inherited trauma from his father, and in his own way he tried to take on his father's "unfinished business." Part of his method for doing so was to turn to surrogate fathers, literary role models who could show him a new way forward. In the early works, I argued strongly for the influence of Fitzgerald and Chandler, both alcoholic writers who sought redemption through writing. With Carver, we can add a third alcoholic writer to the mix who perhaps even more than the first two was able to find a form of redemption in his life through fiction. Later in his life, Carver quit drinking and entered a peaceful and productive final period, with the poet Tess Gallagher, before his death from lung cancer at the age of fifty.

Near the end of his life, Gallagher recalls a trip she made with Carver to Morse Creek, a favorite spot of theirs. They drove out in their jeep and looked out together over the water. Then together, without speaking, they slowly walked to the river's mouth. This was a difficult journey. Carver had only part of his right lung remaining, but with some rests along the way, they made it to their destination. Gallagher writes, "We savored it, the river's freshwater outrush into saltwater, that quiet standing up to life together, for as long as it was going to last. 'When it hurts we return to the banks of certain rivers,' Czeslaw Milosz writes. For Ray, I think poems, like rivers, were places of recognition and healing."[124]

"I'm interested in poetry that talks about the larger issues," Carver explains in one interview, "life and death matters, yes, and the question of how to behave in this world, how to go on in the face of everything. Time is short and the water is rising."[125] The water is rising, indeed, and Murakami, I would suggest, shares Carver's sense of urgency—is just as interested in talking about the larger issues of life and death—and nowhere more so than in *Wind-Up Bird*. "The places where water comes together with other water," Carver writes in one of his most famous poems, "Those places stand out in my mind like holy places." This is very different water imagery to what we saw in Carver's earlier short story, but it is imagery which also shows up in Murakami's fiction, a point I will elaborate on more in the next chapter. In the same poem, Carver writes:

> I'm 45 years old today.
> Would anyone believe it if I said
> I was once 35?
> My heart empty and sere at 35!
> Five more years had to pass
> before it began to flow again.[126]

Murakami was in his mid-forties when he began writing *Wind-Up Bird*, and it was the work which allowed things to "flow again" for him. This might sound like a big claim, but it is one supported by comments Murakami has made about the novel. Writing *Wind-Up Bird*, he has said, "was an extremely important thing for me personally. I think it probably took me about three years to recover from the experience."[127] In an even stronger statement, he has said, "If this novel has no meaning, then perhaps my life has no meaning," something he makes clear he does not believe is the case.[128] Speaking with me about the novel, Murakami was clear about the therapeutic breakthrough it represents, stating, "I freely used my imagination. I lived in that world and I think I was cured. And I realised that I had to live my life."[129]

Murakami explains how after most of his early novels he had always felt like he could do better, that given more time he could have improved the work in some way (except for *Norwegian Wood*, which for him is a different kind of novel). With *Wind-Up Bird*, however, he did not have this feeling. Not that he believes it is a perfect novel. Rather, he is convinced it is the best work he could do at the time and he has no regrets spending what he recognizes is likely to have been the most important time of his career, the mid-forties when a writer often produces their most important and ambitious work, invested in this project.[130] At the end of writing *Wind-Up Bird*, he explains, "I honestly felt like I had got it all out. I was empty."[131]

Which might make us wonder what could follow. Was this the end of Murakami's search for self-therapy, and if so, what has writing fiction beyond this point meant for him? Murakami took a break from writing fiction after *Wind-Up Bird* to work on two nonfiction books that dealt with the Aum Shinrikyō attack. When he returned to writing fiction, one noticeable trend was a focus on the psychological battles of younger characters, a break from the general pattern in his novels where the age of his central protagonist tended to track closely to his own age. What Murakami seems to be consciously doing post-1995 is turning to his younger readers and offering them models for how they might begin to work on their own psychological problems, something he seems to have felt qualified to do after his breakthrough in *Wind-Up Bird*. But in other ways, one also sees Murakami's therapeutic project moving in new directions. It is these competing impulses, I would argue (offering therapeutic models to younger readers and continuing his own therapeutic project) that makes some of this later fiction so complex.

4

Absent Mothers, Abusive Fathers, Heroic Children

Introduction

In Chapters 1 and 2, I focused on the journey from melancholia to mourning in Murakami's early fiction and the symbolic breakthrough of *Dance Dance Dance*, while in Chapter 3, I argued that a consequence of this breakthrough was the return of the Real and the need to work through intergenerational trauma in symbolic form, which reached a climax in *The Wind-Up Bird Chronicle*. Connecting these two breakthroughs with Murakami's own claim to be writing as a means of self-therapy, we might argue that they reflect, in fictional form, the resolution of the two threads of his therapeutic fiction most directly connected to his personal losses (the loss of K through suicide and the intergenerational trauma he inherited from his father). What one sees in Murakami's next three novels, *Sputnik Sweetheart* (hereafter *Sputnik*), *Kafka on the Shore* (hereafter *Kafka*), and *After Dark*, are two competing directions in Murakami's post-1995 fiction.

First, all three of these novels tend to focus on younger protagonists, and might be seen as an attempt on Murakami's part to transfer some of the psychological insights from the first stage of his writing career into a form relevant to his younger readers. This can be seen most clearly in *Sputnik* and *After Dark*, which detail the journeys of such young people in relatively straightforward ways. At the same time, I would argue that Murakami is continuing to develop the remaining two therapeutic threads I have identified in his fiction, and in this chapter, I will argue particularly for the relevance of thread four: the drive for individuation as a response to nihilism. What makes this complicated is that the therapeutic goals many psychoanalysts see as defining the first half of life (often expressed through the oedipal struggle of breaking free of psychosexual dynamics grounded in the family and accepting society's established moral order) is the exact opposite of the goal they see as central to the second half of life (which involves an undoing of this earlier process: a symbolic killing of the father, representing the established moral order, and a wrestling with the questions this raises). This is a dynamic which first appears in *Kafka* and which continues in the novels discussed in the next chapter.

It's All Greek to Me: The Apollonian and the Dionysian in *Sputnik Sweetheart*

One way to read *Sputnik Sweetheart* is as a response to young people who are looking for something more in their lives and who, as a result, are tempted into groups like Aum Shinrikyō. Murakami spent time interviewing such young people for his book *Yakusoku sareta basho de* (The Place that was Promised, 1998). As a creator of *monogatari* himself, Murakami was personally challenged by the rise of Asahara Shōkō, the leader of Aum, who built a death cult around his own storytelling abilities. Murakami admits that what Asahara offered his followers was a "risible, slap-dash story," and something outsiders could easily dismiss as "regurgitated tripe."[1] Nevertheless, he recognizes the power this story had for Aum's followers, and acknowledges that "in a limited sense, Asahara was a master storyteller who proved capable of anticipating the mood of the times."[2] Before ridiculing Asahara's *monogatari*, Murakami believes we first need to think about what we can offer in return. As a novelist, he sees this as his "big task," something he has always tried to do in his writing, but also something he will "have to deal with much more seriously from here on."[3]

As Murakami's first post-Aum-attack novel, *Sputnik* came with high expectations—critics wondering how the events of 1995 might have shaped Murakami's fiction and his search for commitment. For many critics, the novel which materialized, with its focus on characters caught in the pain of unrequited love, felt less about the "big task" Murakami had set for himself than a return to the complicated love story genre already seen in *Norwegian Wood* and *South of the Border, West of the Sun*. Katō Norihiro makes the strongest case for how *Sputnik* does, in fact, engage with Murakami's desire to respond to Aum, suggesting that the two main stories of unrequited love—the love of the male narrator K for the aspiring writer, Sumire, and the love of Sumire for the Japanese-born Korean, Miu—model two different types of love: one grounded in this world (the desire of K for Sumire), and one aspiring for something beyond this world (the desire of Sumire for Miu).[4] In this reading, Sumire stands in for the young idealistic Aum follower, who is looking for something transcendent, but who is not sure how to get it or how to navigate the dangers this quest entails.

What such a person needs is a mentor, and Sumire has two: the male narrator K, who does his best to explain things to Sumire and talk her through her psychological blocks, and Miu, the older female who brings a needed discipline to Sumire's life, but who also entices her to make the journey to the other side. Though not a central part of his argument, Katō notes the possibility that Miu's role in the story may be intentional, that she may be deliberately guiding Sumire to a place where she can make her journey to the other side.[5] This may be the case, or perhaps her motivations are more unconscious, but either way, her role in the novel is clear. What Miu is primarily doing is initiating Sumire into the Apollonian side of human nature so that she might later have the strength to face an encounter with the Dionysian.

In the opening of *The Birth of Tragedy*, Friedrich Nietzsche writes:

We will have achieved much for the study of aesthetics when we come, not merely to a logical understanding, but also to the immediately certain apprehension of the fact that the further development of art is bound up with the duality of the Apollonian and the Dionysian, just as reproduction depends upon the duality of the sexes, their continuing strife and only periodically occurring reconciliation.[6]

The Apollonian, Nietzsche explains, relates to the visual arts and to dreams and is predicated on principles of self-knowledge and moderation. The Dionysian, on the other hand, is experienced in moments where the individual loses themselves in the collective, or where culture is again swallowed up by nature—an experience analogous to intoxication, which includes a loss of self and an abandonment of the moderation that keeps things like "exuberant sexual promiscuity" and "the wildest bestiality of nature" at bay.[7] Nietzsche suggests that art requires both Apollonian control and Dionysian abandonment, and this is a theme that runs through *Sputnik*, primarily in the influence of Miu on Sumire. Intuitively, Miu seems to recognize that Sumire is destined for an encounter with the Dionysian (something she herself experienced fourteen years earlier), and so initially her main objective is to strengthen the Apollonian side of Sumire's personality.[8]

When we first meet Sumire, she is a deeply creative but highly undisciplined individual, her hair always a mess and her fashion sense modeled on a character from a Jack Kerouac novel. She wakes each day around noon and slowly makes her way to a nearby park (or coffee house on rainy days) where she smokes and reads books. By eleven at night, she is finally ready to settle down and do some work, and when she does, the writing pours out of her. The problem is that she can never bring any of this work to completion. As K puts it, "Sumire wrote some works that had a beginning. And some that had an end. But never one that had both a beginning and an end."[9] What she lacks is not creative energy but the ability to give structure to what she creates. In other words, the Apollonian side of her personality is underdeveloped.

Shortly after she meets Miu at a wedding reception, Sumire begins to work for her, and her lifestyle and appearance change dramatically. Miu quickly becomes aware of how Sumire lives and the force it is going to take to instill discipline in her, and so she starts out gently, at first only asking her to come in to work three days a week between the hours of ten and four. Later, when Sumire adjusts to this schedule, she ups the ante and asks her to come in five days a week. Miu also does not allow smoking in her office, providing Sumire with an incentive to quit. Her life quickly becomes more disciplined and regulated (much like Murakami chose to regiment his own life shortly after he became a full-time writer). Along with this new routine, comes a new look, one that K notices straightaway:

Sumire arrived at my apartment a little before five. I didn't recognize her. She'd taken on a complete change of style. Her hair was cut stylishly short, her bangs still showing traces of the scissors' snips. She wore a light cardigan over a short-sleeve, navy-blue dress, and a pair of black enamel, medium-high heels. She even had on stockings. Stockings? Women's clothes weren't exactly my field of expertise, but it was clear that everything she had on was pretty expensive. Dressed like this,

> Sumire looked polished and lovely. It was quite becoming, to tell the truth. Though I preferred the old, outrageous Sumire. To each his own.[10]

Blue in *Sputnik* is the color of the Apollonian, and so the navy-blue dress Sumire is wearing here is significant. Miu drives a navy-blue Jaguar and often wears navy-blue clothes, and soon Sumire is modeling herself on her. Gradually, Sumire is led to embrace more Apollonian attributes. She starts to develop the inner discipline and strength she will later need to pass her test.

At the same time, this turn toward the Apollonian distances Sumire from her writing. The day after she first meets Miu, she sits down to write and finds that "not a single sentence came to her," something that for Sumire was "next to impossible."[11] Soon she is wondering whether her "novel-writing days are over," an idea she is uncomfortable with, wondering if what she is going through might be called a "defection."[12] Perhaps it could be seen this way if the only point of the exercise was to win Sumire over to the Apollonian side forever, stranding her from other important parts of herself, but this is clearly not the case. Miu, like K, believes in Sumire's potential as a writer; she simply believes that "now's not the time. The strength you need to open that door isn't quite there."[13] Developing the Apollonian side of her personality is a way to build up the strength required to open this door: the gateway to the Dionysian.

One of the key setbacks Sumire faced early in life was the death of her mother when she was just three years old. She knows only two things about this mother, that "she was good at remembering things" and that she "had nice handwriting."[14] Her mother's good memory is ironic in that Sumire now struggles to even remember her mother's face. Symbolically, Sumire's mother might be thought of as the Greek Goddess of memory, Mnemosyne, which would make her symbolic father Zeus. Early in the story, Sumire's father is described as "remarkably handsome," and as "an almost mythic figure to the women in Yokohama who needed dental care."[15] Mnemosyne and Zeus in Greek mythology are the parents of the muses, so when Miu (Sumire's muse) shows up in her life and she feels immediately attracted to her, she is clearly also feeling an unconscious connection to her mother (Miu is seventeen years older than Sumire). The muses are the goddesses of literature, art, and science and their role is to inspire writers, artists, and scientists in their work. Sumire is inspired by Miu, but in a way, initially, that turns her away from writing for a time.

Sumire diagnoses her problem as a writer as follows: "I'm not transported anywhere."[16] What she needs, K believes, is the right metaphor. Metaphors, by their very nature, are designed to transport us somewhere new, a fact suggested by the Greek etymology of the word.[17] The metaphor K offers to Sumire involves the ancient Chinese ritual of shedding the blood of dogs onto a gate containing the bones of dead soldiers, so that the souls of these soldiers can be revived and they can protect the city. This, K suggests, is an apt metaphor for what a novelist must do. He explains:

> Writing novels is much the same. You gather up bones and make your gate, but no matter how wonderful the gate might be, that alone doesn't make it a living, breathing novel. A story is not something of this world. A real story requires a kind of magical baptism to link the world on this side with the world on the other side.[18]

If the color of the Apollonian in *Sputnik* is blue, the colors of the Dionysian are white and red—the colors of bone and blood. "So what you're saying is that I go out on my own and find my own dog . . . [a]nd shed fresh blood?" Sumire asks. "It's a metaphor," K clarifies. "You don't have to actually kill anything."[19]

The meaning of Sputnik in Russian is traveling companion, and this is what Sumire and Miu become when they later travel to Europe together, and finally end up on an unnamed Greek island.[20] Sumire's nickname for Miu is Sputnik Sweetheart, something she came up with after their first meeting, due to Miu mistakenly labeling the author Jack Kerouac as a Sputnik, rather than a Beatnik writer. Despite the positive associations of this nickname, however, Sumire soon ends up feeling more like Laika, the dog who was sent off into space on Sputnik 2, never to return. In the final analysis, the novel suggests human beings are nothing more than "lonely lumps of metal in [our] own separate orbits."[21]

Which is why Sumire's quest is so important. What the novel suggests is that the desire to be saved from the outside is often destined to fail. Instead, we experience lives of loneliness and must find the strength to live (and create art) inside ourselves. While Miu's early role is to initiate Sumire into the world of the Apollonian, she is clearly also a representative of the Dionysian forces that Sumire must learn to deal with. Dionysus is the god of wine and music, which are both connected to Miu's job of importing wine and arranging the occasional concert. Music is the one topic of conversation Sumire and Miu never tire of talking about and wine is woven throughout their story. In one sense, Sumire has become intoxicated by Miu, wanting her in every sense of the word, but Miu cannot return her interest because of what happened to her fourteen years earlier. The first time Miu mentions this event, the scene starts by telling us that, "For a second, the light dyed [Miu's] eyes the crimson of the wine."[22]

What happened fourteen years ago is that Miu witnessed the Dionysian side of herself, but this was such a shocking and traumatic experience that to deal with it, she split in two, her sexual desire now existing in some other metaphysical realm. K reads this story after he finds a floppy disc inside a red suitcase Sumire has left behind, after she disappears on the Greek island. Fourteen years earlier, as a music student in Switzerland, Miu had entered a red gondola, guided by a man with white stubble and red cheeks, but after going around once, the Ferris wheel had failed to stop, eventually returning her to the top of the ride before completely shutting down. She was abandoned, and though she tried desperately to get someone's attention, it was to no avail, and so eventually she fell asleep. When she woke in the middle of the night, she used the binoculars she had with her to look out from the gondola, eventually finding her own apartment. Looking through her own window, she recognizes a man, Ferdinando—someone she knows from her stay in the town who has shown interest in her, but by whom she feels sexually threatened. He is naked, and soon she sees that he is with a woman she recognizes as herself. Ferdinando and Miu's doppelgänger then start having sex, Miu describing it as "meaningless and obscene, with only one goal in mind—to make me thoroughly polluted."[23] When she woke the next morning, she was covered in blood and her hair had turned white (much like the post-traumatic white hair of Lennox in *The Long Goodbye*). This is what makes her unable to respond to Sumire's desire, but it is also what enables her to understand what Sumire must go through when she herself finally crosses over to the other side.[24]

Miu reveals this story to Sumire, who records it on her computer, and it is this story, among other things, that pushes Sumire to make her own journey to the other side. I have already mentioned the way Miu might be connected to Sumire's mother, and so it is useful to note the way Ferdinando in her story overlaps in subtle ways with Sumire's father. This connection is made most strongly in the novel through descriptions of both men's handsome noses. Indeed, Miu notes that by the end of her experience in the Ferris wheel, the man did not even seem like Ferdinando at all, and that he may not have been Ferdinando from the beginning. What Miu presents to Sumire through her story, then, is what Freud calls the "primal scene": an image of her own parents engaged in sexual intercourse (Miu's doppelgänger representing her mother and Ferdinando her father).[25] Though this is not the way Sumire consciously interprets the story, unconsciously it touches something deep within her (related to fundamental questions she has about her own identity) and prompts her to make her journey to the "other side" in search of answers.

Throughout most of the novel the boundary between this side and the other side is represented by mirrors. In an early description of Sumire's apartment, one of the details K includes is the fact that she did not have "a decent mirror."[26] Later, when Miu first offers Sumire a job, Sumire looks into Miu's eyes and feels "her own soul being sucked into the other side of a mirror."[27] When Sumire moves into a new apartment to be closer to Miu and her new job, Miu sends her a full-length mirror as a housewarming gift. The lesson Miu takes from her Ferris wheel experience is that "Just a single mirror separates us from the other side."[28]

Despite all this foreshadowing, however, when the moment finally comes for Sumire to pass over to the other side, the most likely scenario is that she simply opens the door of their Greek cottage and leaves (perhaps, much like what happens later to K, she was enticed by music, the sounds of Dionysus, and walked to the top of the island's mountain and then simply vanished). The cottage they stay in has white walls, a red roof, and a green door. On the night Sumire disappears, she is initially wearing blue pajamas, but is later changed into pale-green ones by Miu, which suggests that she is now ready to pass through the green door. This is the conclusion K comes to, with his working supposition being that what separates this world and the other is "a kind of door."[29] In the end, whether this passageway is a mirror or a door is of little consequence; the end result is the same. As K concludes, "Sumire went over to the other side."[30]

K eventually returns to Japan without finding out where Sumire has disappeared to, his responsibilities as an elementary school teacher meaning he cannot stay away forever. Back in his apartment, he receives a phone call from a woman he sometimes sleeps with, the mother of one of his students. This woman asks him to come down to a supermarket where her son (nicknamed *Ninjin*, meaning Carrot, because of his long face and unkempt hair) has been caught shoplifting. It is an unexpected development in the novel, and it takes the story in an unexpected direction. Murakami explains, "[U]ltimately, the protagonist returns to Tokyo from Greece without having found Sumire. As for what would happen next, even I didn't know. Then Carrot appeared.

It was a kind of salvation."[31] Murakami, as mentioned, tries to write his stories in as spontaneous a way as possible. While writing *Sputnik*, however, he seems to have reached an impasse. The emergence of Carrot (who reminds us in part of "pre-Miu" Sumire with his unkempt appearance) was the breakthrough he was looking for.

K makes his way to the security office at the supermarket where Carrot is being held. Carrot, however, is largely unresponsive to what is going on around him and K is surprised to discover that this is not his first offense. While there had been no obvious signs of trouble in the classroom, inwardly Carrot has been struggling, and this has manifested as an involvement in petty crime. Following his questioning in the security office, K asks Carrot's mother if it would be all right to walk him home. She allows it, and as they walk together, K searches for the right words to say, searching for something that might break through the boy's emotional distance. While it seems counterintuitive, the solution he finds is to talk about loneliness:

> Being all alone is like the feeling you get when you stand at the mouth of a large river on a rainy evening and watch the water flow into the sea. . . . I can't really say why it's such a lonely feeling to watch all the river water mix together with the sea water. But it really is. You should try it sometime.[32]

This feels like another Carveresque moment in Murakami's fiction, another reference to the idea that "The places where water comes together with other water" are "holy places," with the negative emotion of loneliness transformed here into a poetic metaphor. This is not dissimilar to the scene in *South of the Border, West of the Sun* where Shimamoto asks Hajime if he knows "any good rivers? A pretty river in a valley, not too big, one that flows fairly swiftly right into the sea?"[33] Of course, given my earlier reading of this novel (informed by Katō), this may, in fact, be Izumi's living spirit, but regardless of who it is, her purpose in that moment is clear. She wants to release the ashes of her dead baby into this river, and what she wants to know is, "will the child's ashes flow to the sea, mix with the seawater, evaporate, form into clouds, and fall as rain?"[34] She is seeking an answer to her pain through the cycle of water. She is seeking her own holy place.

Though Carrot makes little response to K's monologue, by the time they get home his mother notices a slight change in him, an improvement from the boy in the security office who had been "off in another world."[35] Talking with K, it would seem, has allowed him in some small way to reconnect with this world again. Following this encounter, K decides to break things off with Carrot's mother. Perhaps, he reasons, Carrot has sensed something of what was going on between them and this has contributed to his confusion. At any rate, he is starting to feel a stronger sense of responsibility toward the young people he teaches, a desire to connect with them and to keep them from fading away to the other side. "I know you're going to be a wonderful teacher," Carrot's mother says near the end of their conversation. "You almost are."[36]

In the final chapter of the novel, Sumire returns to Tokyo. Or does she? She calls K in the early hours of the morning from a phone booth. Katō rightly questions whether this scene is best thought of as a dream or reality.[37] Sumire disappeared on the Greek island wearing nothing but pajamas and sandals. Somehow, months later, without money and without her passport, she has mysteriously reappeared in Tokyo. In the end, the unanswered questions this resolution leaves are perhaps less important than the mythical motifs on display. Talking about the journey she has taken to get back, Sumire explains, "It wasn't easy, but somehow I managed it. Like a fifty-word précis of Homer's Odyssey."[38]

What is new about this odyssey in the context of Murakami's fiction is that it is not the male narrator who has engaged in it. Instead, we are looking in on Sumire's odyssey from K's perspective. This point is emphasized in the story through its inversion of the famous phone conversation in *Norwegian Wood*.[39] In the last scene of that earlier novel, Watanabe calls from a phone booth to Midori. She asks him, "Where are you now?" He wonders, "Where was I now?" The novel ends with the line, "Again and again, I called out for Midori from the dead center of this place that was no place."[40] So is Watanabe back from the world of the dead or not? We cannot say for sure, and the same is true for Sumire in *Sputnik*. "Where are you now?" K asks her. "Where am I? Where do you think I am? In our good old faithful telephone booth," Sumire replies.[41] When K replies that he will come and get her, though, Sumire replies, "I'd like that. I'll find out where I am and call you back."[42] Why would Sumire need to find out where she is when she has just told him? This is because she may, like Watanabe, not yet be fully back in the land of the living. This ambiguous ending, as in *Norwegian Wood*, is clearly a part of the novel's design.

Murakami has explained how *Sputnik* was something of a transitional work for him, an opportunity to revisit his established style and technique as a writer one last time before moving on to new things.[43] For Murakami, style is synonymous first and foremost with Fitzgerald, and stylistically speaking, *Sputnik* may be the closest thing to *The Great Gatsby* he has ever written, for it is the first time his central male narrator is not the main actor in the story. As K puts it, "this story is about Sumire, not me."[44] Up to this point in Murakami's fiction, the male narrator has always been the one on the quest, the one seeking self-therapy, but here is a narrator who is not seeking his own salvation, but the salvation of a young person close to him. It is as if Murakami, having found healing in the writing of *The Wind-Up Bird Chronicle*, was now looking to his younger readers and the question of how he might offer something similar to them. This trend of focusing on younger protagonists continues in Murakami's next novel, *Kafka on the Shore*, where the main protagonist, Tamura Kafka, is just fifteen years old.

The First and Second Half of Life in *Kafka on the Shore*

Thematically, *Kafka* is one of Murakami's most overtly therapeutic novels, a fact not celebrated by all. Kuroko Kazuo, for example, who was an early supporter of Murakami's career, was disappointed by the therapeutic tone of *Kafka* and what it says about our times. Kuroko writes, "The reason so many readers received 'therapy' from this novel was undoubtedly its ability to suggest . . . in the most crucial part of the story, our ability to not face . . . the violence that symbolizes the reality we live in."[45] Similarly, Komori Yōichi questions *Kafka*'s wide international success, which he sees as less a cause for celebration than a dangerous sign of the times. Komori believes that *Kafka* has been largely "consumed as a commodity that brings 'salvation,' 'relief' and 'therapy,' and this in the face of a shared social pathology that has spread since 11 September 2001 (9/11). This cannot be taken as a good thing."[46] For both Kuroko and Komori, therapy is a poor substitute for politics—a way of trying to feel better without actually changing anything.

But is *Kafka* really as reassuring a novel as Kuroko and Komori suggest? Is it really a story about finding salvation, relief, and therapy despite the conditions of violence we live in? Perhaps this is one way of reading the novel, but the message of *Kafka* is not necessarily as straightforward as this verdict suggests. One of the great challenges in interpreting *Kafka*, I will argue, is that it is actually two things at once: a story about the psychological challenges faced in both the first and second halves of life. This dual nature exists, I believe, because Murakami is doing two things at the same time: both offering a model of therapy for his younger readers and continuing with his own therapeutic project. In the Introduction to this book I argued, adapting Peter Homans' insights into the birth of psychoanalysis, that Murakami's fiction moves through four identifiable stages: melancholia, mourning, individuation, and the creation of meaning—the last resonating with Nietzsche's idea of the need for a transvaluation (or reevaluation) of values. *Kafka* is a work where this last stage of Murakami's therapeutic project begins to come into focus.

"The first half of life—birth, childhood, adolescence, and young adulthood," Robert Segal writes, "involves the establishment of oneself as an independent person, one with a firm place in society."[47] The Oedipus complex and Freudian psychology more generally, Segal suggests, are focused on these early life tasks. Once these goals are achieved, however, new psychological tasks emerge, which for Segal are better captured by Jungian psychology. He writes, "The prime, if not sole, goal of the second half of life is likewise consciousness, but now consciousness of the unconscious rather than of the external world."[48]

So how is *Kafka* firstly a novel dealing with the tasks of the first half of life? How might it be read through a Freudian lens? This novel, I would argue, is Murakami's most Freudian to date, with its views on the unconscious as a site of repressed sexuality and violence being unmistakable. The main protagonist, fifteen-year-old Tamura Kafka, is presented by his father, the sculptor Tamura Kōichi, with a twist on the traditional oedipal prophesy: not only will he kill his father and sleep with his mother, but he will also sleep with his elder sister—the adopted sibling his mother chose to take with her when she left Kafka and his father years earlier. Kafka was just four when his mother and sister left, and as the novel begins, he is about to turn fifteen. This is the birthday he has decided he will run away from home. As his alter ego, the boy named Crow, informs him, though, this may not solve a thing. "I don't want to rain on your parade or anything," Crow offers, "but I wouldn't count on escaping this place if I were you. No matter how far you run. Distance might not solve anything."[49]

This is because the curse Kafka carries is buried within his DNA. Before leaving home, Kafka looks at himself in the mirror one last time and considers the question of his genetic inheritance: "I gaze carefully at my face in the mirror. Genes I'd gotten from my father and mother—not that I have any recollection of what she looked like—created this face."[50] He then thinks about what this might mean for the fate awaiting him: "I could probably kill him [his father] if I wanted to—I'm definitely strong enough—and I can erase my mother from my memory. But there's no way to erase the DNA they passed down to me. If I want to drive that away I'd have to get rid of *me*." Kafka continues, "There's an omen contained in that. A mechanism buried inside of me."[51]

Kafka's curse, in one sense, is simply the curse of human nature itself—the potential for violence and destructive sexuality we all carry within us. The question he wants to answer is how he can eliminate these destructive tendencies without at the same time destroying himself. The first possible answer the novel offers is through culture. Kafka runs away from Tokyo and ends up in Takamatsu, Shikoku, where he finds a home in the Komura Memorial Library. The first thing he does once he gets there is to start reading books, beginning with Burton's translation of *Arabian Nights*. Clearly, what Kafka is doing here is wrestling with the question of the dark side of human nature, or what might be thought of as the uncivilized drives of the Freudian id. Thinking about the stories he is reading, he notes, "They're full of obscene, violent, sexual, basically outrageous scenes. Like the genie in the bottle they have this sort of vital, living sense of play, of freedom, that common sense can't keep bottled up. I love it and can't let go."[52]

At the library Kafka also finds a mentor, Ōshima, who gives him mini-lessons on topics ranging from Greek tragedy to *Genji Monogatari*. Culture, and literature more specifically, are offered to Kafka as guides that a young person might consult on their life journey as they seek to understand the unconscious forces they are up against. Kafka also spends time building himself up physically, spending time at the gym and being mindful of what he eats. Much as with the case of Sumire in *Sputnik Sweetheart* (Sumire, like Kafka, was hurting because of the absence of her mother—both characters find it painful that they struggle to remember their own mother's face), there is a sense that for a young person destined for an encounter with the Dionysian, the first task is to build up the Apollonian aspects of the self. As the boy named Crow puts it, Kafka must become "the toughest fifteen-year-old on the planet."[53] The importance of the Apollonian virtues—self-discipline, the attainment of knowledge, moderation—might, thus, be taken as Murakami's first lesson to his young readers.

This message is reinforced with the introduction of Nakata, the old man whose story alternates with Kafka's in the novel, and who describes himself as like "a library without a single book."[54] Nakata came face to face with the Dionysian aspects of human nature as a young boy (a scene where he is hit by his school teacher, who just the night before had experienced an intensely erotic dream that left her feeling unsettled) and this left him traumatized, cut off from his memories and with a weak sense of self. Nakata cannot read and has become, instead, "the proverbial blank slate."[55] This lack of knowledge and culture has been compensated to a degree by Nakata's supernatural abilities: he can talk to cats and make objects fall from the sky. Unfortunately, his losses have also made him vulnerable to manipulation. This becomes clear when the mysterious Johnnie Walker appears in the story and has Nakata kill him. Nakata later explains, "Johnnie Walker went inside Nakata. He made me do things I didn't want to. Johnnie Walker used me, but I didn't have the strength to fight it. Because I don't have anything inside me."[56]

Kafka paints a picture of modern Japan where at certain moments an entranceway opens between this world and another, an uncorking of the genie bottle if you will, causing Dionysian forces of sexuality and violence to erupt again back into the world. Nakata is a victim of forces unleashed during the Second World War, and Saeki, a woman Kafka meets in the Komura Library, is a victim of forces unleashed in the late 1960s (her boyfriend was killed in the student protest movement, a case of mistaken identity). Now the entrance is to be opened again, and the question is, what will this mean for Kafka? Will he, like Nakata and Saeki before him, be traumatized by his encounter with the Dionysian, or will he somehow find a way through sexuality and violence toward healing? Just as with Sumire, his attention to the Apollonian is to prepare himself for a later encounter with the Dionysian.

The first message *Kafka* offers, then, is clear and uncontroversial: read books, learn things, exercise—find the knowledge and discipline you need to wrestle with the darker forces of human nature inside of you. What follows in *Kafka*, however, is much less clear and potentially more disturbing. Kafka begins to embrace his father's oedipal prophecy, to accept that he may have killed his father (even if the theory requires him to have separated from his body and flown from Shikoku to Tokyo to do it—a case of spirit projection), and to embrace the idea of sleeping with Saeki, a woman he comes to believe (or at least fantasizes) could be his mother. Later in a dream he also rapes Sakura, a girl he meets on his bus ride to Shikoku, who he comes to believe (or again fantasizes) could be his sister. After all of this, Kafka then finds himself ready to return to society, making the choice to return home to Tokyo. So what is this supposed to mean? Is Murakami really telling his young readers that the best way to overcome an Oedipus complex is to embrace it?

In what follows, I will explore three possible answers to this question. The first will take seriously an idea presented in the novel that "[e]verything's a metaphor."[57] It will suggest that the novel's answer to the above question is yes, but only as a metaphor for a process of psychological transformation. The second approach will examine a reading of the novel offered by Katō Norihiro, who has argued that not everything in *Kafka* should be read as a metaphor. Though Katō's reading is not without its problems, it does offer a radically different approach to how we might understand the aforementioned problem. Finally, I will offer a third approach that requires us to see *Kafka* not primarily as a story about the tasks of the first half of life, but, rather, about the tasks of the second half. This third approach will focus not on the message the novel seems to offer young readers, but, rather, on what it suggests about the next stage of Murakami's own evolving therapeutic project.

So first, how might *Kafka* be read as an elaborate psychological metaphor? This is a reading strategy the novel itself encourages, most overtly through Ōshima's explanations to Kafka about what he is going through and how this might be understood through the concept of irony. Ōshima explains:

> [I]rony deepens a person, helps them mature. It's the entrance to salvation on a higher plane, to a place where you can find a more universal kind of hope. That's why people enjoy reading Greek tragedies even now, why they're considered prototypical classics. I'm repeating myself, but everything in life is metaphor.

> People don't usually kill their father and sleep with their mother, right? In other words, we accept irony through a device called metaphor. And through that we grow and become deeper human beings.[58]

If we apply this advice to how we should read *Kafka*, the message seems to be something like this: Don't get caught up in the question of whether Kafka *really* killed his father and *really* slept with his mother and sister. Instead, accept that the novel is offering you metaphors and through irony find "salvation on a higher plane." This is an approach to the novel taken by Inez Martinez, who argues that the best way to read *Kafka* is as a "metaphorical experience of patricide and incest as a healing initiation through imagination."[59]

Of course, there are many things in life which are impossible or too risky to work through in reality, but which can still be worked out with the aid of metaphor and imagination. Psychomotor therapy offers one example of how this works, and it is a therapeutic model with interesting parallels to *Kafka*. Psychomoter therapy, as Van der Kolk describes, is most commonly a group-based form of therapy whereby a "protagonist" assisted by a "witness" recreates what are called "structures," metaphorical representations of relationships which enable the "protagonist" to relive and rewrite important events from their past. For example, Van Der Kolk describes a psychomotor therapy session he attended for a woman named Nancy (the protagonist) who was assisted by a therapist, a man called Albert Pesso (the witness). As Nancy told her story, Pesso would witness the changes he observed in her, making comments such as, "A witness can see how crestfallen you are when you talk about your father deserting the family."[60] As different characters entered Nancy's narrative, different members of the group were invited to sit at locations around the room determined by Nancy to play different roles. The job of these metaphorical stand-ins was not to adlib responses, but, rather, to represent spatially the relationships the protagonist was talking about, and to say the things the protagonist explicitly asked of them to say. At other times, different versions of the same character were represented, a good father to play off against the bad father, for example, enabling the protagonist to have conversations that would be impossible in real life. In this way, the protagonist was able to engage in a deeply imaginative and spatially represented reenactment of her past experiences and inner world, and through the aid of an experienced witnesser, begin to process traumatic events from her past. Van der Kolk explains, "Protagonists became the directors of their own plays, creating around them the past they never had, and they clearly experienced profound physical and mental relief after these imaginary scenarios."[61] He goes on to note, "It's as if you could go back into the movie of your life and rewrite the crucial scenes."[62]

This, in essence, is what Kafka (the protagonist) is doing, with the boy named Crow his witness and Sakura and Saeki the role players he has recruited to play the necessary parts in his therapeutic drama. He starts by saying things like how great it would be if Sakura were his sister and Saeki his mother, but later he begins to offer stronger versions of these fantasies, presenting them more as theories and possibilities than mere wishes, even holding onto their roles in the face of contradicting evidence. For example, Kafka is excited when Sakura says she has a brother his age, but he conveniently forgets that he has misrepresented his age to her to try and hide the fact that he is a runaway. As Kafka puts it to Miss Saeki, "metaphors help eliminate what separates you and me."[63] While the case against Sakura's biological connection to Kafka is stronger than the case for Saeki, in the end it matters little in either case. What Kafka needs most of all is the experience of confronting the mother who abandoned him, and Miss Saeki is the person who implicitly agrees to play this role.

The boy named Crow acts as the witness to Kafka's internal changes, like the role of the witness in psychomotor therapy, but also in a way that mirrors the role of the chorus in Greek tragedy. The novel informs us that Kafka in Czech (Franz Kafka's first language) means crow, but its Japanese rendering as *karasu*, as Shimizu Yoshinori points out, is also close to *korosu* in Japanese, the Japanese rendering of the Greek word "koros" (or chorus in English), the collective group of actors in ancient Greek theater who supplemented the action of the play by singing, dancing, and speaking in unison.[64] The chorus, Ōshima explains, "stands at the back of the stage and explains in unison the situation or what the characters are feeling deep down inside. Sometimes they even try to influence the characters. It's a very convenient device."[65]

In a similar way, the boy named Crow is a very convenient device in *Kafka*, allowing Murakami to externalize the therapeutic changes going on in Kafka. Like a good therapist, the boy named Crow prepares Kafka for the challenges ahead and helps him to clarify his main goal. "You have to forgive her [Kafka's mother]," he says to Kafka as he makes his final journey into a forest which is at the same time also a journey into himself. "That's the only way you can be saved. There's no other way!"[66] What this scene suggests is that the heart of Kafka's therapeutic quest is actually unrelated to his oedipal curse. Instead, what he needs more than anything is to recover from a bad attachment experience (in this case from the mother who abandoned him and the father who was at times both neglectful and abusive). This observation fits well with Murakami's own take on the novel, which downplays the importance of the Oedipus motif. He explains:

> The Oedipus myth is just one of several motifs and isn't necessarily the central element in the novel. From the start I planned to write about a fifteen-year-old boy who runs away from his sinister father and sets off on a journey in search of his mother. This naturally linked up with the Oedipus myth. But as I recall, I didn't have that myth in mind at the beginning. Myths are the prototype for all stories. When we write a story on our own it can't help but link up with all sorts of myths. Myths are like a reservoir containing every story there is.[67]

Saeki may not be Kafka's biological mother, but in the end, by playing her assigned role, she offers him a metaphorical way to heal the hurt little boy inside (and at the same time, Kafka plays the role of Saeki's boyfriend she lost years earlier, the transference, in this case, working in both directions). As Kafka makes his way deeper into the forest and discovers a town lost to time, he meets Saeki, who takes on her role of "mother" one last time and expresses regret for having abandoned her only son. She then asks the question, "Kafka—do you forgive me?"[68] "I do forgive you," Kafka replies, and then the boy named Crow, taking on the role of the chorus or witness, describes what is happening: "**Mother, you say. I forgive you. And with those words, audibly, the frozen part of your heart**

crumbles" (bold in original).⁶⁹ This is clearly the central therapeutic scene of the novel, a place where, instead of the confusion that has come to Kafka through embracing his oedipal curse, he now finds forgiveness and the courage necessary to return to the world.

This does not mean, however, that everything about Kafka's journey can be reduced to a metaphor. For example, Kafka's dream about raping Sakura might be forgiven on the grounds that, unlike an idea presented in the novel, responsibility does not actually begin in dreams but with what we choose to do in reality. Also, the killing of Kafka's father might be forgiven on the grounds that it is built on a supernatural premise which is beyond belief (i.e., he must not have actually killed his father; that is why he can return to society at the end of the story without the fear of being institutionalized). On the other hand, Kafka, as a minor, does actually sleep with Saeki, the first time while she is in some kind of dissociated state and thus not even aware of what is going on.⁷⁰ In psychomotor therapy, for example, while different people take on different symbolic roles for the benefit of the protagonist, there are clearly ethical lines that should not be crossed, and sex would be one of them. Obviously, *Kafka* is fiction, so even if a character like Kafka has crossed moral or ethical lines, as readers we can still distance ourselves from these transgressions and read them as psychological metaphors for ourselves. Admittedly, some readers will be more comfortable doing this than others.

This leads us to a second approach to the novel, which argues that there is much in it which should not be read metaphorically. This is a reading proposed by Katō Norihiro, who suggests that what the novel is about is a fifteen-year-old boy who has murdered his father, but who is unaware of this fact because he is struggling with dissociative identity disorder (i.e., he has multiple personalities). Katō acknowledges that the simplest approach to the question of who killed Kafka's father is the one suggested by the novel—Kafka killed his father as a "living spirit" on the night he woke up in the grounds of a Shinto shrine in Takamatsu covered in blood. This was the same night Nakata killed Johnnie Walker in Nakano, Tokyo, a scene where despite stabbing Johnnie Walker repeatedly with a knife, he later found no traces of blood on his hands or clothes. The supernatural explanation for what happened, the story suggests, is that Kafka became a living spirit, flew from Takamatsu to Tokyo, and, through Nakata perhaps, proceeded to kill his father before returning to his body in Shikoku. This is like what happens in *The Tale of Genji* when Lady Rokujō, driven by jealousy, becomes a living spirit and attacks and eventually kills the main wife of Prince Genji, Lady Aoi. Lady Rokujō has no memory of what happens at night but finds that when she awakes in the morning, her hair smells of smoke from the incense the priests have been burning to ward off evil spirits, much like Kafka wakes up in the Shinto shrine covered in blood but with no knowledge of how it came to be there.⁷¹

While admitting that this is probably the answer to the murder Murakami intended in *Kafka*, Katō wonders if this is a solution modern readers can accept and he concludes that, for most people, the answer is no.⁷² He thus goes on to look for a naturalistic solution to the murder, his conclusion being that Kafka has multiple personalities and that this is why he can be his father's murderer while retaining no memory of actually having done it. A key scene in his analysis is the opening one where Kafka and the boy named Crow are sitting in Tamura Kōichi's study and planning their escape. Katō notes how, despite their obvious fear of the father and the dangers of being in his study, Kafka and the boy named Crow seem to be taking their time, and he suggests that this is because the father is already dead. He also notes the time and attention Kafka takes cleaning himself before leaving the house, which suggests that what he is doing is cleaning away the evidence of his crime. He also notes the knife Kafka takes with him, which he suggests is the likely murder weapon.[73]

What the novel becomes then for Katō is a murder mystery, where the murderer turns out to be the narrator himself, but where this fact is hidden because of a split in his personality (much as the murder of Kiki might be read in *Dance Dance Dance*). Maria Flutch, for example, who follows Katō's general interpretation, summarizes the Kafka part of the story as follows:

> Kafka is a highly damaged, schizoid boy who, abandoned by his mother at the age of four and tormented by his violent, abusive father's Oedipal curse, murdered the father on his 15th birthday, a fact that is repressed deep in his unconscious. The boy lives in his self-created personality, naming himself Kafka. His alter-ego, named Crow (the translation of "Kafka"), speaks to him at important junctures, "translating" his feelings and ideas into words. His "abject" self, the murderer, is never named, and does not appear in the novel as a 15-year-old boy.[74]

In addition to the textual evidence he provides, Katō cites the importance of the shōnen A (boy A) legal case to the novel, a reference to the fourteen-year-old boy in Murakami's hometown of Kobe who committed a series of crimes in 1997. The boy, known by the pseudonym Sakakibara Seito, assaulted three children and killed two others before being caught. He had worked up to his crimes by first abusing animals, which links him thematically with the cat killer Johnnie Walker in *Kafka* who beheads cats so that he can build a flute. One of shōnen A's victims was beheaded and the head left on a school gate. Katō also notes the guardian figure shōnen A created for himself, a figure he called Bamoidooki, whom Katō compares functionally to the role played by the boy named Crow in *Kafka*. While acknowledging Murakami's disavowal of the connection of *Kafka* to the shōnen A case, Katō makes a convincing argument for its background influence, noting that what *Kafka* then becomes is a novel about the "recovery of a completely broken person."[75]

At the same time, Katō acknowledges the problems this strict psychological reading of the novel creates—the main one being the newspaper reports that clearly date the death of Tamura Kōichi to the evening of May 18, ten days after Kafka left Tokyo. This leads Katō to propose two murder dates: a first one on which Kafka killed his father; and a second one ten days later, involving Nakata and Johnnie Walker, which somehow allowed the first murder to appear in the world. Katō's theory is motivated by the unbelievability of the "living spirit" storyline, so it is ironic that he introduces his own plausibility-stretching explanation to make his hypothesis work. Katō openly admits that he may be engaging in a misreading; he simply believes it is justified given the nature of the novel itself.[76]

Katō's resistance to the novel's own explanation of living spirits, an aspect of the novel which can be read as part of Murakami's ongoing attempt to write a premodern *monogatari* for the modern world, is interesting. Speaking with Kawai Hayao several years before he wrote *Kafka*, Murakami asked Kawai (who has written about *The Tale of Genji*) whether the supernatural elements in the tale (such as living spirits) were "actually part of reality."[77] Kawai insisted that they were, and Murakami immediately restated his question just to make sure he was clear: "Rather than being a narrative device, they're part of reality?"[78] Kawai again insisted that this is the case, to which Murakami responded, "But contemporary writers would have no choice but to use them as a kind of narrative device."[79] Kawai agreed with this assessment, suggesting that this is what makes it hard to write a *monogatari* in the modern world. Murakami then went on to make a comment that seems particularly relevant to what he is trying to do in *Kafka*, noting, "I have a sense, though, that even if you started something like that as a device, at some point it would transcend that function."[80]

Murakami, as his conversation with Kawai suggests, was interested in inserting the literary device of living spirits into *Kafka*, in the hope that at some point it would transcend its function as a mere literary device and somehow initiate us into something like a premodern *monogatari*. In other words, he does not want us to read the idea of living spirits as a postmodern or magic realist literary technique, but as something real within the story itself, much like premodern readers would have read the account of Lady Rokujō in *The Tale of Genji*. Katō's reading of the novel shows that this is something many modern readers are reluctant or unable to do. Instead, Katō's approach is to dismiss the novel's own ideas about living spirits in favor of a psychological explanation (multiple personalities) which can be used to make sense of the novel, even if this creates other interpretive problems.

What links these two approaches so far is that they are both focused on a young man who is struggling with the challenges of the first half of life. The first approach sees Kafka more as an everyman—someone who is struggling with the universal challenges of human nature we all face (the Dionysian forces of sex and violence). The second approach sees him as a broken individual—someone who has committed a serious crime and who is dealing with it through dissociation. What these approaches agree on is that Kafka's abandonment by his mother is the root cause of his psychological difficulties and that learning to forgive her is at the heart of his therapeutic quest. What then of the criticisms from Kuroko and Komori which opened this section? In what ways does this therapeutic payoff come by ignoring larger questions about society and violence? In other words, while Kafka finds forgiveness for his mother, what about his relationship with his father? In the metaphorical reading, Kafka comes to accept that he has (metaphorically) killed his father, but at the same time, Johnnie Walker, who seems deeply connected to Tamura Kōichi, is planning his own return to the world as an even more powerful entity. In short, even as a metaphor, the only thing he may have achieved by killing his father is to make him stronger. In Katō's reading, while Kafka learns to forgive his mother, he still has not faced the secret some other part of him knows—that he committed patricide. His return to society at the end of the novel must thus be read as a delusional act. In either approach, the problem of society and the father remains.

The third approach I will look at offers a different view of Kafka's engagement with his mother and father, from the perspective of the psychological tasks of the second half of life. This approach will start with Joseph Campbell's ideas about the monomyth already examined in relation to *A Wild Sheep Chase* and *The Wind-Up Bird Chronicle*. *Kafka* also maps well onto the hero's journey template; in fact, it follows it more comprehensively than either of the two earlier works mentioned. To trace just some of these steps, Kafka's call to adventure comes when he decides to run away from home, and he finds his mentor in Ōshima, a biological woman who thinks, dresses, and behaves like a man. Ōshima takes Kafka to a cabin deep in a forest, and it is in this forest that he later meets two threshold guardians, soldiers who disappeared in this same forest decades earlier during a military exercise. They take Kafka even deeper into the forest to a town which has been lost to time.[81] What all of this is building up to is what Campbell calls the initiation stage of the hero's journey.

In the town, Kafka experiences what Campbell describes as "the meeting with the Goddess," who in Kafka's case is his mother substitute, Saeki. Campbell strongly connects this Goddess figure with a return to the mother, noting, "Whatever in the world has lured, whatever has seemed to promise joy, has been premonitory of her existence."[82] As mentioned already, meeting his mother again (or at least her substitute) and finding the power to forgive her provides the climax to Kafka's therapeutic journey. He then faces the next challenge Campbell identifies, the temptation of remaining with her, the monomyth requiring the hero to return to the world. Campbell explains, "The seeker of the life beyond life must press beyond her, surpass the temptations of her call, and soar to the immaculate ether beyond."[83] Urged on by Saeki, this is what Kafka does, leaving the town and working his way back through the forest in an example of what Campbell calls the magic flight.

I have already emphasized numerous times the way Kafka makes peace with his mother, so it is perhaps not surprising that he successfully completes this first step in the initiation stage of the hero's journey. What follows is where things become complicated, Campbell describing the next step as "atonement with the father." In the Freudian version of the first half of life, an important step in breaking through the Oedipus complex comes in accepting the authority of a new "father": the so-called superego. The child enters society and learns how to play by the rules of a larger game. This socialization process, in turn, helps to tame the impulses of the id. In other words, we become civilized. For Campbell, "atonement with the father" reflects a reversing of this earlier oedipal stage. What it involves is "the abandonment of that self-generated double monster—the dragon thought to be God (superego) and the dragon thought to be Sin (repressed id)."[84]

With the superego slain and the id unleashed again, the next stage Campbell identifies is apotheosis, the "divine state to which the human hero attains who has gone beyond the last terrors of ignorance."[85] Apotheosis means to make divine; the hero who has killed God is now ready to take His place. What then follows is the "ultimate boon," Campbell writing that the hero is now "a superior man, a born king."[86] What this part of the initiation requires, Campbell argues, is being "twice born" or becoming "the father."[87] It symbolizes a passing "from the infantile illusions of 'good' and 'evil' to an experience of the majesty of cosmic law, purged of hope and fear, and at peace in the understanding of the revelation of being."[88] "

This passing from "illusions of 'good' and 'evil'" to an "understanding of the revelation of being" is an expression of Campbell's final embrace of mysticism—an opening up to an experience of cosmic oneness he sees as the final reward of the hero's journey. Segal explains:

> Having interpreted hero myths psychologically, Campbell proceeds to interpret them metaphysically as well. The hero's journey, he says, takes him to not just a deeper human world but also a deeper cosmic one. He discovers an unknown part of not just himself but the cosmos itself. . . . The ultimate meaning of hero myths is that all is one. Psychologically, not only is there an unconscious realm beyond the conscious one, but the two realms are really one, and consciousness will eventually return to its unconscious origins.[89]

According to John Gentile, what Campbell ultimately offers is a "blending of Eastern pantheism and Western Gnosticism; it is a form of the perennial philosophy that argues that all the world's myths . . . are simply metaphors pointing to a sacred unity."[90] Is this also what Murakami has found through his therapeutic fiction, or is there another way of interpreting the monomythic elements found in his work? While there are moments in Murakami's fiction that make an appeal to mystical oneness (Lieutenant Mamiya's revelation in the well is one example), in general the oneness or wholeness his protagonists seek tends to be more psychological than cosmological. It might be understood through the Jungian notion of individuation, but also through the Nietzschean idea of the transvaluation of values, which offers a useful framework for understanding Kafka's journey.

The Nietzschean hero, like the monomythic one, must first come to a realization of the death of God and embrace their own God-like potential, overcome illusions of good and evil, and gain the boon that can only come to the "superior man." That Campbell is in part channeling Nietzsche in his description of the hero's journey is made clear in comments he made to Bill Moyer in *The Power of Myth*. There, he discusses the three transformations of spirit Nietzsche described in *Thus Spake Zarathustra*: those of the camel, the lion, and the child. The stage of the camel represents obedience and a willingness to carry the burden of tradition. Next comes the lion, the destroyer of tradition who rejects what has previously been loaded upon the beast of burden. Campbell writes, in a line that links well to his ideas about "atonement with the father," that "the task of the lion is to kill a dragon, and the name of the dragon is 'Thou shalt.'"[91] Finally, when the dragon (or superego) has been killed, the child emerges, a figure, Campbell writes, who has "[n]o more rules to obey."[92]

Kafka is a work wrestling with the question of the father and this struggle is clearly articulated in Nietzschean terms. Talking with Ōshima, Kafka explains how his father seemed "connected to something very unusual," and he asks Ōshima if he knows what he means. "Yeah, I think so," Ōshima replies, "Something beyond good and evil. The source of power, you might call it."[93] What Kafka seems to fear is his own connection to this same power, and he wonders if this is why his mother abandoned him.[94] By issuing his oedipal curse, Kafka also wonders if what his father really wanted was for him to "take over his will," something he resists but which the monomythic formula suggests might actually be necessary.[95] For Campbell, the hero must learn to see behind the menacing mask of the father to the more human face beneath.[96] He writes, "One must have a faith that the father is merciful, and then a reliance on that mercy."[97]

We never meet Tamura Kōichi in the novel, but he is clearly a menacing figure and the idea of Kafka relying on his mercy is never entertained. This is equally true of the other "father" figure in the novel, Johnnie Walker, who is clearly connected to Tamura Kōichi in some way (and may, in fact, be his father in a different metaphysical space). In a motif that will reappear in Murakami's later fiction, Johnnie Walker orchestrates his own death at the hands of Nakata so that he might transform himself into an even more powerful entity. What he demonstrates is how killing the father is never that easy. To put it in terms found later in *1Q84*, all that killing the father achieves is the creation of a temporary vacuum; someone new always comes to takes his place.

In *1Q84* this notion of the ruler who must be murdered for a new ruler to arise is explored explicitly through ideas found in James Frazer's *The Golden Bough*, a work which also influenced Freud. In *Totem and Taboo*, Freud described the act of killing the father not as a psychological wish buried deep within the son's psyche (as in the Oedipus complex), but as an event which has already occurred. Playing with an idea first put forward by Charles Darwin, he describes a primal scene in which an alpha male dominated access to a harem of females and banished other male competitors from the group. Eventually, the discarded sons banded together to kill the father whom they both respected and feared. The guilt that ensued after the murder was the bond upon which a new social order was founded, and the dead father returned in name to fulfill an important new symbolic function. This is not dissimilar to the scenario Johnnie Walker envisions. Killing him, he suggests, will only make him stronger.

As Žižek explains, this is one of the classic dilemmas of psychoanalysis:

> What characterizes the human universe is the complication in the relationship between the living and the dead: as Freud wrote apropos of the killing of the primordial father, the murdered father returns more powerful than ever in the guise of the "virtual" symbolic authority. . . . The double meaning of the term "spirit" (if we ignore the alcoholic association)—"pure" spirituality and ghosts—is thus structurally necessary. . . . The fundamental problem here is how to prevent the dead from returning, how to put them properly to rest.[98]

With Johnnie Walker, we do not even have to ignore the alcoholic association. He is spirit in all three senses of the word.[99] The question Kafka faces, though, is the same one Žižek presents here. How can his dead father properly be put to rest? This is a question the novel fails to answer but which continues to reappear in Murakami's fiction.

At first glance, *Kafka* seems a work repelled by the idea of "atonement with the father." The problem is not how to open up to the merciful side of the father, but, rather, how to kill him once and for all. At the end of the novel, Kafka makes a choice to return to the world, but so does Johnnie Walker, a fact which in large part undermines the happy ending of the therapeutic plot. If the end point of the monomythic quest is "becoming the father," then Kafka does not appear to be a monomythic hero. He has stumbled at one of the most important hurdles of his initiation.

Yet, while Kafka never comes to see his father in a positive light, in some ways he does become more like him. Just like his father, he learns to flaunt conventional concepts of right and wrong and he goes some way toward becoming what Leslie Paul Thiele describes as the Nietzschean hero, someone who, "like his classical counterpart, is a breaker of taboos and custom. Like the proud Oedipus, the hero kills his father and sleeps with his mother. He blasphemes, he violates, and he destroys. Out of the ashes emerges a new regime."[100] This, I would suggest, is why Kafka's journey is so confusing. While we assume that as a fifteen-year-old boy he should be engaged in the tasks of the first half of life, in many ways he is involved in the tasks of the second.

Kafka becomes more like his father not through a conscious choice, but through choosing to embrace his fate. "Sometimes fate is like a small sandstorm that keeps changing directions," the boy named Crow tells him at the start of the novel. "You change direction but the sandstorm chases you. You turn again, but the storm adjusts."[101] At the beginning of the novel, the boy named Crow encourages Kafka to embrace this sandstorm. "This storm is you," he explains. "Something inside of you. So all you can do is give in to it, step right inside the storm, closing your eyes and plugging up your ears so the sand doesn't get in, and walk through it, step by step."[102] This is something Kafka learns to do, going one step beyond merely giving in to his fate to truly embrace it. As the boy named Crow reports later in the novel, "If there's a curse in all this, you mean to grab it by the horns and fulfill the program that's been laid out for you."[103]

Later though, the boy named Crow also acts as the voice of conscience, as Kafka continues to embrace his fate and transgress moral boundaries. In his dream about raping Sakura, for example, she objects to what he is doing. "I want you to remember something," she says, "You're raping me. I like you, but this isn't how I want it to be."[104] Later, when thinking about the dream, the boy named Crow chastises Kafka for his transgression: "Even if it's in a dream, you shouldn't have done that. . . . I tried my best to stop you. I wanted you to understand. You heard, but you didn't listen. You just forged on ahead."[105]

Kafka also entertains moral qualms about sleeping with Saeki, particularly the first time when she is not even aware of what is going on: "I figure I'd better wake her up. She's making a big mistake, and I have to let her know. This isn't a dream—it's real life. But everything's happening so fast, and I don't have the strength to resist."[106] Saeki, for her part, is also more inclined to trust the pull of fate than her own moral reasoning. Speaking to Kafka in the library after their second night together, she explains, "I don't know if what we did last night was right or not. But at the time I decided not to force myself to judge anything. If the flow is there, I figured I'd just let it carry me along where it wanted."[107]

From a Nietzschean perspective what Kafka has learned to accept here is the idea of *amor fati*, or loving one's fate, a concept Joseph Campbell was particularly fond of and which he reworked into his well-known motto to "follow your bliss." Campbell explains, "Nietzsche was the one who did the job for me. At a certain moment in his life, the idea came to him of what he called 'the love of your fate.' Whatever your fate is, whatever the hell happens to you, you say, 'This is what I need.'"[108] This is a lesson Kafka seems to embrace, and it is something which arguably moves him closer toward "atonement with the father," even if he never finally achieves it. Kafka's embrace of his fate also takes him closer to apotheosis.

For Campbell, apotheosis was represented by the dissolving of the dichotomy of male and female. This is why figures that guide the hero toward apotheosis are often androgynous. Campbell writes, "Male-female gods are not uncommon in the world of myth. They emerge always with a sense of mystery; for they conduct the mind beyond objective experience into a symbolic realm where duality is left behind."[109] One example Campbell offers is the blind seer Tiresias from the Oedipus myth, a figure who has lived both as a male and a female. The clear candidate for such a figure in *Kafka* is Ōshima, who though born a woman, feels and behaves like a man. Unlike Tiresias, however, Ōshima sees himself less as a seer than as someone who uses deductive reasoning to make sometimes ominous predictions.[110]

In this way, Ōshima is more than just a mentor to Kafka. S/he is an outward symbol of the kind of apotheosis he is seeking, and s/he offers him lessons designed to reinforce this message. On one of these occasions, for example, Ōshima tells Kafka about Aristophane's theory in Plato's *The Banquet*: "In ancient times people weren't simply male or female, but one of three types: male/male, male/female or female/female. . . . But then God took a knife and cut everyone in half, right down the middle. So after that the world was divided into just male and female, the upshot being that people spend their time running around trying to locate their missing other half."[111] The suggestion here is that the lack we feel can be fulfilled only in the sexual other and that the two halves need to come together in order to create a whole.

For Jung, the quest toward individuation eventually led to the archetype of the syzygy or divine couple. It was a sign that the male and female aspects of the personality were coming together and that the Self was beginning to emerge. Something similar becomes evident in *Kafka* as Kafka searches for his absent mother. As Maria Flutsch explains, quoting Jung, "Ōshima shows that this [male-female] split is not insuperable. Indeed, his androgyny is 'a symbol of the creative union of opposites, a uniting symbol in the literal sense.'"[112]

It is Ōshima who takes Kafka to the cabin in the forest. As Kafka prepares to make his final journey into this forest, he first lies down on a bed where Ōshima has been sleeping just moments earlier. Kafka notes, "The pillow and covers still show signs of Ōshima having been there. Not him, really—more like his sleep. I sink down in those signs."[113] Later, as he is making his way into the forest, he again remembers this moment: "I remember Ōshima asleep in the bed in the cabin, his face to the wall. And the signs he/she left behind. Cloaked in those, I went to sleep in the same bed."[114] Ōshima offers Kafka a concrete reminder of what he is hoping to find in the forest: some kind of synthesis between the male and female forces he senses working within himself. In short, he is seeking apotheosis.

So where does this leave *Kafka* as a story about the challenges of the second half of life? What kind of hero is he? While he clearly engages in a version of the monomythic journey, what he ultimately fails to do is to find atonement with the father, even while he becomes more like his father in some ways. This third approach, then, does not resolve the tension Kuroko and Komori identify in the text (the way the therapeutic narrative is undermined by its inability to confront or remedy the violence represented by the father/society), but it does offer one suggestion about where this tension is heading. Driven by a Nietzschean will to power, the father is returning to the world as an even more powerful entity, but in a similar way, so is the son. Whether the son will ever become a powerful enough rival to confront the father remains to be seen, but he has at least survived his immediate crisis. In later Murakami novels this competition continues, with protagonists and antagonists, symbolic sons and fathers, continuing to battle each other. Increasingly, these symbolic sons will become more and more like their fathers, in the end forcing us to question what, if anything, separates them. *Kafka*, in the end, shows Murakami as a writer deeply interested in Nietzschean ideas, but still wary of what it would mean to fully embrace them. While Kafka is clearly flirting with his father's philosophy, he is not yet ready to embrace it.

Is There Hope *After Dark*?

The type of critiques Kuroko and Komori directed at *Kafka* is perhaps even more relevant to Murakami's next novel, a shorter work called *After Dark*, where the therapeutic gains of the young characters do little to address the deeper structural problems they face. As the novel makes clear, "if you really want to know something, you have to be willing to pay the price," a truth each of the young protagonists wrestles with in their own way.[115] *After Dark* does little to develop the therapeutic themes we have been examining in this chapter, but it is interesting for the unique way in which it presents them, the novel relying on what might be described as a cinematic style.

One of the influences on *Kafka* was a 1959 French film by the director Francois Truffaut called *The 400 Blows*.[116] In that film the main protagonist, a young boy named Antoine, slowly descends deeper and deeper into social delinquency and eventually ends up in an institution for troubled boys. In a scene near the end of that film where he is talking with one of the institution's psychologists, he begins to reveal what seems to be at the heart of his problems, his belief (confirmed to him by his grandmother) that his mother never really wanted him. At the end of the film, he escapes from the institution and runs to the ocean, which he has always wanted to see. Once there he runs into the water but then immediately retreats onto the shore, the film famously ending with a freeze-frame of his face staring directly into the camera. In its theme of a boy pausing on the threshold between childhood and adolescence, it is not dissimilar to Salinger's *The Catcher in the Rye*, another work which clearly influenced *Kafka* (and which Murakami translated in 2003).

In *After Dark*, this inspiration from French cinema continues, with the obvious reference being to Jean-Luc Goddard's 1965 film *Alphaville*, also the name of the love hotel which is central to the plot. An even more important influence, however, is Robert Enrico's 1968 film *Tante Zita* in which a young woman, facing the shock of her Aunt Zita's stroke and approaching death, and finding her home environment stifling (a place where together with her mother she is nursing her unconscious aunt), decides to escape for a night of adventure in Paris.[117] In *After Dark*, this role is taken by Asai Mari, who also has someone lying unconscious at home, her sister Eri. Eri has not had a stroke, but for some reason she has gone into a kind of hibernation. As she explains

Absent Mothers, Abusive Fathers, Heroic Children

to Takahashi Tetsuya, a young jazz musician she meets at a family restaurant during the night (the young heroine in *Tante Zita* also meets a jazz musician during the night), "I can't stand it. Or should I say, every once in a while I can't take it anymore—living under the same roof with my sister and not having any idea why she's out cold for two months." "So you leave the house and wander around the streets at night?" Takahashi asks her. "I just can't sleep," Mari replies. "When I try, all I can think of is my sister in the next room sleeping like that. When it gets bad, I can't stay in the house."[118]

This ongoing influence of film on Murakami's fiction should not come as a surprise. He often went to watch films with his father as a young boy, and he later entered the drama department at Waseda University with the intention of becoming a script writer, spending much of his free time watching films and reading film scripts. Murakami explains that he wrote *After Dark* in a unique way, primarily writing the dialogue first and then going back later to fill in the descriptive details, meaning that the first draft probably read much like a film script.[119] The point of view of the novel is also unique, with a plural narrator sometimes flying through the air for a bird's-eye view, and sometimes cutting in close to the action to observe dialogue between characters, much like the varied camera shots of a film. Though at times going beyond what a camera can do (the narrators can smell odors, for example), for the most part the effect for the reader is like watching a film. We become part of the plural "we" that is observing the story, their point of view ours, much like the point of view of various camera shots determines what we can observe in a film.

The theme of observation becomes important in the story. When a Chinese prostitute (named Guo Dongli) is beaten up in Alphaville by a Japanese salaryman called Shirakawa, an image of his face is caught by the love hotel's security cameras and later passed on to the Chinese criminal organization the girl works for. "So you guys better not do anything bad when you go out," Kaoru, the manager of the hotel, warns her employees, Komugi and Koorogi, when she prints out the image. "You never know when there's a camera watching these days."[120] While the risks and rewards of a surveillance society are on full display in the story itself, the point of view we are offered as readers is a neutral one. We are much like the narrators of the story who describe themselves as "invisible, anonymous intruders. We look. We listen. We note odors. But we are not physically present in the place, and we leave behind no traces. We follow the same rules, so to speak, as orthodox time travelers. We observe but we do not intervene."[121]

What we observe is a single night in one of Tokyo's metropolitan centers (probably Shibuya). Each chapter in the novel begins with a picture of an analog clock face, chapter one starting at 11:54 p.m. and the final chapter starting at 6:40 a.m. (the last clock displayed near the end of the book shows 6:52 a.m.). The deepest and darkest time of the night is said to be 3:00 a.m, and 6:40 a.m. is when things begin to get light again. Together with the title, this device sets up a hopeful expectation for the novel, the promise that a new dawn is coming, if only the characters can first survive the night.

One of these young people is Takahashi Tetsuya. Normally he is called Takahashi in the novel; his first name, Tetsuya, is revealed only one time by Kaoru, but it is written in katakana, so we do not know what kanji, if any, he uses. One clearly relevant meaning of *tetsuya* in Japanese is "staying up through the night." Much like Sumire and Kafka before him, he has faced issues with his parents, who have left him feeling unsettled in the world. His mother died of breast cancer when he was seven, and he does not feel close to his stepmother. He also does not get along with his father, who has spent time in prison. Talking to Mari about his father, he observes, "Well, let's just say our personalities are different. And our values."[122] Much like Kafka, he does not want to live with his family because when he does, "I start having doubts about my genes."[123] What makes him different from Kafka is that he has found something concrete he will commit himself to as a way of connecting his own inner struggles with a broader concern for society. He will study the law and through this try to contribute to society. Talking with Mari, he explains, "Studying the law is not as much fun as making music, but what the hell, that's life. That's what it means to grow up."[124]

What helped Takahashi to find this commitment was his experience observing court cases as part of a school assignment. He mostly attended criminal trials, and at first found it easy to separate himself from the people on trial, but over time this stopped being the case. Talking to Mari, he describes the feeling as follows:

> I started seeing it like this: that there really was no such thing as a wall separating their world from mine. Or if there was such a wall, it was probably a flimsy one made of papier-mâché. The second I leaned on it, I'd probably fall right through and end up on the other side. Or maybe it's that the other side has already managed to sneak its way inside of us, and we just haven't noticed.[125]

It is possible that Takahashi is expressing thoughts here that Murakami experienced himself as he sat through trials related to the Aum attack, some of Takahashi's ideas not dissimilar to those found in Murakami's *Underground*. Interestingly, what Takahashi came to feel most unsettled about in the end was not the people on trial or even his own closeness to them, but the trial system itself, which began to take on the appearance of a "weird creature" like a "giant octopus living way down deep at the bottom of the ocean."[126] What he seems to have glimpsed is a kind of Kafkaesque monstrosity that consumes individuals for its own unfathomable reasons. Takahashi explains:

> It takes on all kinds of different shapes—sometimes it's "the nation," and sometimes it's "the law," and sometimes it takes on shapes that are more difficult and dangerous than that. You can try cutting off its legs, but they just keep growing back. Nobody can kill it. It's too strong, and it lives too far down in the ocean. Nobody knows where its heart is.[127]

In short, while Takahashi's troubled family background seems to connect him to earlier protagonists like Sumire and Kafka, his commitment to learning the law and wrestling with the problems of the system in a practical way feels like a subtle new development in Murakami's fiction. At the same time, this struggle is never fully explored in *After Dark*. Takahashi has committed himself to a path he will take in the future, but on the single night we see him, his main role in the story is simpler—to reveal facts about the two sisters: Asai Mari and Eri.

The two Chinese characters for the family name, Asai, literally mean "shallow well," and this is what Asai Eri, in particular, clearly is. Wells in Murakami's fiction are usually metaphors for human subjectivity and depth, and it is clear from the novel that Eri has a particularly shallow sense of self. She is someone who, though she knows the difference between Gucci and Prada, knows little about anything else. Blessed with good looks, she is several times described with references to fairy-tale characters, initially Snow White and later Sleeping Beauty. She has previously had some small television roles and has also modeled for magazines aimed at young teenaged girls. She is a role model for what is often described as *shōjo* culture: a subculture in Japan involving young teenaged girls that is closely connected with a culture of consumption. The question the novel asks is whether she will be able to awake from her slumber. A masked man is watching her from the other side of a television screen and there is a danger that she will be lost to this other side forever, unless someone or something rescues her. This masked man, associated in the novel with the salaryman Takahashi who beats up the Chinese prostitute, is a symbol of the dehumanizing effects of a commercial system which favors the male gaze.

Though others around her recognize what she needs, Eri, for the most part, has been oblivious to the psychological struggles she is facing. Takahashi tells Mari about a conversation he has had with Eri some time earlier: "I kind of hinted to her she maybe ought to see a specialist—a therapist or psychiatrist or something. But she had absolutely no intention of doing that as far as I could tell. I mean, she didn't even seem to realize she had anything going on inside of her."[128] Instead, Eri had simply gone to bed one day and failed to wake up. She does appear to consume the food the family leaves for her, though nobody sees her doing it.

Mari, the heroine of the story, is strongly connected to both female victims. First, as Eri's sister, she slowly begins to recognize the distance that has grown between them and the power which memory has to bring them back together again. It is Koorogi who first explains this lesson to her. "Try hard to remember all kinds of stuff about your sister," Koroogi urges. "It'll be important fuel. For you, and probably for your sister, too."[129] Mari does later recall an experience with Eri. As young children, they had been trapped in an elevator in the apartment building where they lived. Mari had been terrified, but Eri had somehow maintained her composure. In the darkness, she had reached out to Mari and held her close. Mari recalls:

> The important thing is that during that whole time in the dark, Eri was holding me. And it wasn't just some ordinary hug. She squeezed me so hard our two bodies felt as if they were melting into one. She never loosened her grip for a second. It felt as though if we separated the slightest bit, we would never see each other in this world again.[130]

After the lights had turned on, and after they had escaped from their predicament, it was, in fact, like their worlds had separated forever. They slowly drifted apart and became emotional strangers to each other. As Mari recalls this experience, however, she finds the power within herself to return to her sister. At the end of the novel, she returns home and crawls into the bed where Eri is sleeping. The warmth of her body and this attempt at human connection brings about a subtle but significant change. As the new day begins, Eri begins to awaken. Perhaps, it would seem, there really is hope after dark.

On the other hand, Mari also feels a strong connection to the Chinese prostitute, Guo Dongli, but here she can do little to help. As a young girl, Mari had dropped out of school and had ended up going to a Chinese school in Yokohama instead. Her sister Eri had once explained to Takahashi that even though Mari was Japanese, she spoke Chinese more often.[131] After Guo Dongli is injured, no one is able to communicate with her. Kaoru, the manager of the love hotel, hears through Takahashi that there is a girl named Mari sitting in Denny's who can speak fluent Chinese. She walks to Denny's and approaches Mari, asking her to come to the Alphaville Hotel to translate. Mari and the Chinese girl, who are both nineteen, are thus brought face to face and an immediate connection is felt. Mari later explains:

> The minute I saw her, I felt—really strongly—that I wanted to be her friend. And if we had met in a different place at a different time, I'm sure we could have been good friends. I've hardly ever felt that way about anybody.... But it doesn't matter how I feel: the worlds we live in are too different. And there's nothing I can do about it. No matter how hard I try.... I didn't spend much time with her, and we hardly talked at all, but I feel as if she's living inside me now. Like she's part of me.[132]

Guo Dongli, it turns out, comes from the area of China that some refer to as Manchuria, the same region that played such an important role in *The Wind-Up Bird Chronicle*. She had been forced into prostitution in Japan, but when her period started unexpectedly on a job, her customer, Shirakawa, became violent and then stole her clothing and possessions. While Mari feels deeply connected to Guo Dongli, she can do little for her. In short, the price of truly knowing her is simply too high for her to pay. They thus meet for a brief moment and then part ways again, probably never to see each other again. If the price of knowing Guo Dongli is too high, however, Mari has not given up on knowing China at least. In fact, she is scheduled to study abroad in China in the near future, and though she is scared to go, encouraged in part by Takahashi, it seems likely she will make the trip. She is thus making some effort to expand her circle of interest which might one day expand her circle of influence.

After Dark then, is a novel in which the therapeutic gains of each character, while personally significant, are no match for the systemic forces of violence they are up against. The best that can be said is that each of them is moving in a direction where one day they might be able to make a difference. Takahashi is committed to studying the law and battling the "weird monster" he has sensed lurking within the legal system; Mari has committed to travel to China to try and fulfill her dream of becoming a translator; and Eri is finally waking up to a system which has exploited her for far too long. Shirakawa leaves Guo Dongli's cell phone in a convenience store and Takahashi later picks it up when it begins to ring. On the other end is a Chinese gang member who thinks he is speaking to the Japanese salaryman who hurt their prostitute and left without paying. "You'll never get away," the man begins with no introduction. "No matter how far you run, we're going to get you."[133] At first, Takahashi believes this message has nothing to do with him—this is not even his phone after all—but later he comes to question this commonsense logic. Maybe the message was for him after all. Like Kafka before him, the message here is that it is impossible to run away from your problems; things always catch up with you in the end. Like the other two novels explored in this chapter, *After Dark* shows young people making important psychological progress, but not yet ready to translate their personal victories into social engagement.

5

Individuation, Alchemy, and the Death of the Father

Introduction

The final three novels to be discussed, *1Q84*, *Colorless Tsukuru Tazaki and His Years of Pilgrimage* (hereafter *Tsukuru*), and *Killing Commendatore*, include significant breakthroughs for the final two therapeutic threads I have identified in Murakami's fiction: the quest for earned attachment as a response to an avoidant attachment style and the drive for individuation as a response to nihilism. The earned attachment thread finds its first significant breakthrough in *1Q84* when a man and a woman who have both suffered deprivations in childhood find in each other a reason to break free from their social isolation and to commit to the idea of family. For the first time in Murakami's fiction, the story ends with a couple looking forward to the birth of their child and determined to give that child all the love it deserves, even if they still have legitimate concerns about their ability to do so. At the same time, this simple love story is overshadowed in many ways by the mysteries of the parallel world they have found themselves in and the supernatural forces they are up against. Much like we saw in *Kafka on the Shore*, the therapeutic gains of the main protagonists are set against a complicated background involving a murder willed by its own victim, sexual relationships with incestuous undertones, and a symbolic "son" who in resisting the "father" becomes like him in some ways.

These same themes are also found in the last novel discussed in this chapter, *Killing Commendatore*, and thus provide an important point of reference for understanding where Murakami's search for self-therapy has taken him. Why is there a constant need in his recent fiction to murder the "father," even when this "father" seems destined to return to the world in some form, and why has the incest taboo taken on such a prominent role in these same stories? Some Western reviewers have seen this growing interest in the incest taboo as evidence of some kind of moral failing on Murakami's part—proof that he has somehow lost his way. Jungian psychology, I will argue, provides a framework for understanding the growing prevalence of this theme. The incest taboo and its symbolic transgression is an important step in later stages of individuation according to Jung (therapeutic thread four).

What one also sees in Murakami's recent fiction is the way this quest for individuation has been increasingly expressed through the language of alchemy (most simply put, the premodern art of trying to turn base metals into gold). Alchemy is a substantial area of interest in Jung's writings and for him was an important historical precedent for his psychology of individuation. He argued that what these early "scientists" were doing in their attempts to turn base metals into gold was as much a psychological as it was a physical process, and that their valiant but failed attempts to produce the promised gold has parallels to the modern therapeutic quests of individuals. My argument is not just that the Jungian approach to alchemy provides a useful analogy for understanding the quest for individuation in Murakami's recent fiction, but that this fiction demonstrates explicit awareness of this tradition, despite Murakami's tendency to downplay the influence of alchemy on his work. What we will see is the specific road map alchemy offers in Murakami's recent novels (in *Tsukuru*, color-coded even), and the ways it can explain the roles of certain characters (such as Menshiki in *Killing Commendatore*). These details are the strongest evidence yet of just how deep the influence of Jung runs in Murakami's fiction (again, despite his claims not to have read Jung's work seriously).

Crime without Punishment in *1Q84*

The complexity of *1Q84* (which in Japanese is broken into three books) can be tamed to a degree if we focus first on the love story which drives the plot. This love story, as already touched on, can also be seen as the first significant breakthrough in Murakami's fiction of therapeutic thread three: the drive for earned attachment as a response to an avoidant personality style. The two main protagonists in the story, Tengo, an aspiring novelist who makes his living as a mathematics teacher at a cram school, and Aomame, a gym instructor and self-defense coach who moonlights as an assassin, both exhibit avoidant personality styles grounded in childhood deprivations. Both were raised by parents who were more absorbed in their own activities than in their children's emotional well-being (for Tengo's father, his job collecting fees for the national broadcaster NHK; for Aomame's parents, their proselytizing for their religion, the Society of Witnesses or *Shōninkai*). Both Tengo and Aomame were forced to spend much of their free time as children being dragged around town by their parents to knock on the doors of strangers, partly because these parents thought this was the best use of their time, and partly because they knew that having their children with them opened more doors for them. Even as young children then, Tengo and Aomame sensed that they were not their parents' main priority but were, instead, being used by them in some way to serve other ends. These warped priorities of the parents, in turn, warped their children in significant ways.

The first goal of both Tengo's and Aomame's lives was thus to break free from their parents and gain their independence. Tengo stood up to his father when he was ten years old and with the help of a sympathetic teacher, finally won the privilege to be left at home while his father went to work. Aomame, at the age of eleven, left both her family and their religion to live with a relative. Both then used sports and the scholarships they provided to help get them through their teenage years (Judo for Tengo and softball for Aomame). In adulthood, both characters find jobs which can provide for them financially but which also do not require too much of them in terms of interpersonal relationships. They also find ways to meet their sexual needs through emotionally unavailable partners (Tengo has an older married girlfriend, and Aomame, who has a fetish for men in the early stages of balding, finds suitable candidates at bars and has one-night stands with them). In this way, while both Tengo and Aomame gain their independence, they struggle to connect with other people. They are, instead, like many of the protagonists we have seen in Murakami's fiction so far—cool and detached types who struggle with human intimacy—though in this case we are also offered clear reasons for where this avoidant attachment style comes from.

What has left both Tengo and Aomame partly dissatisfied with this situation and hopeful that something better is possible, is an experience they shared as ten-year-olds. Aomame was often ostracized at school because of her family's religious beliefs and practices, and nobody ever reached out to her until one day, Tengo did, inviting her to join his group in science class, when another classmate began berating her for a mistake. This act of kindness surprised them both, primarily because they had never talked to each other, despite being in the same class, and this act of humanity touched something within Aomame. Rather than talking to Tengo directly and sharing her feelings with him, however, what she did was to walk up to him in an empty classroom at the end of school one day, grab him by the hand, stare deeply into his eyes, and then run from the classroom without saying a word. Even following this incident, Tengo and Aomame continued not talking to each other, and not too long afterward, Aomame transferred to another school. Despite all this, however, Tengo and Aomame share something like a soul connection, and they continue to think about each other over the years while assuming the other person has probably forgotten about them. The love story, then, is about them finding each other again in the present, realizing what they mean to each other, and using this discovery to find healing and connection in their lives.

Both Aomame and Tengo are aware to some degree of the scars their childhoods have left on them. The narrator tells us that as a young girl leaving home, Aomame felt, "lonely and hungry for love."[1] Later we learn that "[d]eep personal relationships with people were a source of pain for [her]. Better to keep to yourself."[2] In Tengo's case, we are told that "[m]ore than a relationship, he wanted free time. He didn't like to have a sense of duty to anyone. He tried to avoid responsibility."[3] Later, while talking to his unconscious father on his deathbed (a man he suspects may not be his biological father), he describes his problem this way: "A more pressing problem for me is that I have never been able to love anyone seriously. I have never felt unconditional love for anyone since the day I was born, never felt that I could give myself completely to that one person. Never once."[4] Like many of Murakami's protagonists (Watanabe in *Norwegian Wood* is a prominent example), Tengo and Aomame do not know how to love or to receive love. What makes them different from earlier Murakami protagonists is that they will learn to overcome this situation and to commit to each other, and even to hold out hope that they will be able to share this love with their unborn child (a child, as will be explained later, produced in a supernatural way). This, then, would seem to be the first clear example in Murakami's fiction of how characters can overcome an avoidant personality style and find earned attachment.

To be sure, at the end of the novel, Aomame still has serious questions about her ability to provide the love she knows her child will need. Talking to a character called Tamaru, she puts it this way:

"I am someone whose parents threw her away when she was small, so it's hard for me to imagine what it would be like to have my own child. I have no good model to follow."
"Still, you're going to be bringing that child into the world—into this violent, mixed-up world."
"It's because I'm looking for love," Aomame said. "Not love between me and the child, though. I haven't reached that stage yet."
"But the child is part of that love."
"I think so, in one way or another."[5]

In the end, Aomame's quest for earned attachment is still an ongoing project. She has not necessarily "reached that stage yet," which in the language of attachment theory would be the ability to provide her future child with a stable base. She is at least moving in the right direction, however. This motif is repeated in the last novel discussed in this chapter, *Killing Commendatore*, but here we will see the child (who is also born of supernatural means) as a young girl and witness her positive interactions with her father—the promised happy family first hinted at in *1Q84*. Perhaps strictly speaking then, it is *Killing Commendatore* which really deserves to be highlighted as the novel which finally "resolves" therapeutic thread three in Murakami's fiction, though *1Q84* gets so close to this "resolution" that I have decided to mark it as the breakthrough novel anyway.

What complicates all of this is that Aomame and Tengo's love story takes place in a parallel world (the world of 1Q84 rather than 1984, from where they have come; Q and 9 are homophones in Japanese and so the two words sound the same), and so at the same time that Tengo and Aomame are slowly being drawn toward each other, they are also being drawn into a world where mysterious figures called Little People appear and weave air chrysalises. From these chrysalises dohtas then emerge (something like the clones of young girls; the original girls are called mazas) and these dohtas become Perceivers and have sex with Receivers (older men) so that they can hear voices from beyond. This is where I will probably lose most readers who have not read the novel yet (and perhaps even some readers who have read the novel but are still struggling to make sense of it). The way I will proceed in this initial discussion of the novel's plot is to focus first on those parts of this larger story which first connect to Aomame and then to those parts which connect to Tengo (the chapters of the novel alternate between Aomame's and Tengo's story. In the last part of the book, a third alternating chapter dealing with a character called Ushikawa is also introduced).

Starting with Aomame's chapters then, we find her connecting to the larger supernatural story when she is sent by the dowager, a wealthy benefactress who sponsors her assassinations of abusive men, to kill Fukada Tamotsu, the cult leader of a group called Sakikage (Forerunner). At first, Aomame, encouraged by the dowager, is convinced that taking Fukada's life is the right thing to do. Fukada has reportedly been raping young girls, starting with his own daughter, and so he would seem to be a good candidate for Aomame and the dowager's brand of vigilante justice. Later, however, she will learn that Fukada has not been raping the young girls as reported, but their dohtas, leaving the reader to question what the status of these dohtas (at times in the novel also described as shadows or alter egos) might be and whether having sex with them is as morally reprehensible as having sex with their mazas (the original girls) would be. Furthermore, the word "rape" does not capture what is going on here. Instead, Fukada's sexual encounters with the girls occur when he is in a state of paralysis, the girls coming to him with the desire of getting impregnated with his child, meaning that from his perspective, the act is entirely nonvoluntary. This is some kind of bizarre religious ritual designed for hearing voices from beyond and perhaps bringing a new Receiver into the world.

To add to this moral confusion, Fukada, who is physically worn out by the process of being a Receiver, wills his own death at the hands of Aomame, knowing that this is the only way to free himself from his physical burden. Like with Johnnie Walker in *Kafka on the Shore*, for some unexplained reason, suicide is not an option here; Fukada must find someone who will take his life for him. Rather than punishing Fukada then, Aomame is giving him what he wants, and it is only the Little People, the mysterious orchestrators of this communion between Perceivers and Receivers, who are temporarily inconvenienced by the murder. As the novel repeatedly suggests, by killing Fukada, all that Aomame has done is to create a vacuum, meaning that for a limited time there will be nobody to hear the voices. In time, though, the Little People will find a new Receiver (like the sheep in *A Wild Sheep Chase* continues to hunt for a new host) and the process will begin anew. In the end, all that Aomame has really achieved by killing Fukada is taking away the one punishment available to him— leaving him to live with his physical suffering for as long as possible.

Fukada's murder in the novel is explained through an appeal to ideas found in James Frazer's *The Golden Bough*. Frazer had explained how in ancient times kings, at the end of their reigns, would often be killed by their subjects. Fukada tells Aomame that this was related to their role in hearing voices on behalf of their community. He explains:

> Now, why did the king have to be killed? It was because in those days the king was the one who listened to the voices, as the representative of the people. Such a person would take it upon himself to become the circuit connecting "us" with "them." And slaughtering the one who listened to the voices was the indispensable task of the community in order to maintain a balance between the minds of those who lived on the earth and the power manifested by the Little People. In the ancient world, "to rule" was synonymous with "listening to the voices of the gods."[6]

In this sense, the murder of a king is a ritual designed to manage a transition of power. What the community needs is someone capable of "listening to the voices of the gods," so when an old king is no longer able to do this effectively, he must be killed so that a new king can take his place. The king himself is of little importance here. He is nothing more than a conduit for bringing revelatory voices into the community.

Another possible influence on Murakami's ideas here is Julian Jaynes' book *The Origin of Consciousness in the Breakdown of the Bicameral Mind*, of which, as Asari Fumiko points out, Murakami is a fan.[7] Jaynes' book provides a controversial hypothesis about what it has meant through human history for humans to "hear voices." Jaynes' thesis is "that at one time human nature was split in two, an executive part called a god, and a follower part called a man. Neither part was conscious."[8] Jaynes argues that rather than having conscious thoughts, premodern humans heard voices which told them what to do. These voices, which they would literally hear as the voices of the gods, were, in fact, the product of a bicameral mind. The right side of the brain was the source of this voice of authority, and the left side was associated with the hearer who follows. While there are still people in the world today who hear these voices (some prophets, poets, and schizophrenics, for example), for many people these voices have been silenced, replaced, instead, by their own internal monologues. In this reading, Fukada's ability to hear voices could be seen as a throwback to a style of cognition we all once shared. Whether Jaynes' theory is right or wrong, his thesis of a human ability to hear voices has interesting parallels with themes found in *1Q84* and even to Murakami's own writing process, points I will return to later.

This theme of killing the king also has relevance to the problem we first encountered in our discussion of *Kafka on the Shore*—the classical psychoanalytical problem of how to live after the death of the father. Like Freud suggested in his story of the primordial father murdered by his own sons, the father often becomes more powerful in his death than he was in life. The guilt his murder produces provides the psychological foundation for a new moral order. What this means in *1Q84* is that Fukada's murder is not really the end of anything. Read as a social or political comment, what this suggests is that the death of a leader or the end of a system is no guarantee that the spirit of that leader or system will not continue to live on in whatever takes its place.

Fukada can also be seen as the latest reincarnation of the warped Nietzschean Superman character-type we have been tracing through Murakami's fiction. Though Fukada started out life as an ordinary man, through the entry into his world of the Little People, he eventually became a Receiver, someone who, with the aid of Perceivers, hears voices. Though Aomame was initially convinced that Fukada was pure evil, a rapist of young girls whom she was entirely justified in murdering, in hindsight, she comes to see him as someone worthy of, if not respect, then at least awe. The man she killed, she comes to believe, was "a prophet and a king" and the act of killing him was about nothing less than keeping "balance between good and evil in the world."[9] While she finds it difficult to reconcile the different sides of Fukada she sees, the power she felt in his presence is undeniable. The narrative gives us this insight into her thoughts: "Objectively, what this man had been doing was perhaps an affront to humanity. But he himself was, in many senses, an extraordinary human being, and his extraordinariness, at least in part, appeared to transcend standards of good and evil. Ending his life had also been something extraordinary."[10] The question, as we have previously seen in Murakami's fiction, is how to check the growing power of such a man and whether this will require us to become like him. In *1Q84*, this quest is taken up most directly by Tengo, the symbolic "son" in the story.

The way Tengo enters the larger supernatural world of 1Q84 is through a request from his editor, Komatsu, to work on a manuscript first dictated by Fukada's daughter, Fukada Eriko (normally called Fuka-Eri in the novel), and to turn it into something publishable. Komatsu's plan is to have Fuka-Eri win a major literary prize and gain the attention of the public, making himself some money in the process, but the manuscript she has dictated, while filled with raw potential, is not refined enough to be called literature. Tengo, who is an aspiring novelist, has worked carefully on the craft of writing, but he has not yet found a story within himself with a similar power. By editing Fuka-Eri's manuscript, which has this power, he will be able to participate in bringing his first story to the world, even if only a few people will know he was involved with it.

Fuka-Eri's story, which she had first dictated to her friend Azami (Fuka-Eri is severely dyslexic and could not write the story herself), is called "Air Chrysalis," and narrates her first encounter with the Little People, their weaving of an air chrysalis, and the emergence of her dohta. While the public takes this novel, when it is published, to be a work of fiction, it is actually a straightforward account of things she experienced. The Little People are not happy to have been potentially exposed to the world in this way, and they do their best to work against Tengo and Fuka-Eri. What the novel suggests Tengo and Fuka-Eri are doing by getting this novel out into the world is creating an antidote to a virus, a way of counteracting the influence of the Little People and people like Fukada.

On a stormy night, Tengo and Fuka-Eri's relationship then goes beyond this role of literary collaborators when Tengo wakes up paralyzed and Fuka-Eri enters his room and has sex with him in his immobilized state. Here they have become a new Perceiver/Receiver team, with the sexual act somehow getting, not Fuka-Eri, but Aomame pregnant. What we see then is that Tengo, like Kafka before him, is potentially becoming the new "father," the new Receiver or king who will hear the voices. There are still differences between Fukada and Tengo. Unlike Fukada, Tengo is sleeping with a maza rather than a dohta (at least we assume he is; an alternative hypothesis is briefly entertained in the novel but ultimately rejected), and Fuka-Eri, while younger than him, is not the same age as the young girls Fukada sleeps with (Fuka-Eri is seventeen, while the young girls Fukada sleeps with are as young as ten). Tengo is also determined to bring his new gift into the world, not in the form of a new religion, but as a new novel (inspired in part by the one he worked on with Fuka-Eri). For the average reader then, Tengo will likely come across as a more sympathetic character than Fukada, though there are still parallels between them.

Like Kafka before him, Tengo might be seen as the symbolic "son" learning what it takes to stand against the "father." What the novel suggests this is all about is a cosmic battle for balance. This theme is most clearly presented by Fukada to Aomame right before his murder. Fukada explains:

> In this world, there is no absolute good, no absolute evil. . . . Good and evil are not fixed, stable entities but are continually trading places. A good may be transformed into an evil in the next second. And vice versa. Such was the way of the world that Dostoevsky depicted in *The Brothers Karamazov*. The most important thing is to maintain the balance between the constantly moving good and evil. If you lean too

much in either direction, it becomes difficult to maintain actual morals. Indeed, balance itself is the good. This is what I mean when I say that I must die in order to keep things in balance.[11]

The leader's view of morality might be likened to a boat on a river fighting its way through the rapids (an analogy I am adapting from one Komatsu uses in the novel). In this scenario, if the two sides of the boat represent good and evil, then the important thing is to maintain balance between them; capsizing the boat means the game is over. Rapids, by their very nature, are a constantly changing environment, so what may have been good only moments ago may suddenly become evil and vice versa. In this situation, good and evil are less moral absolutes related to the boat or the river than the ability of the boat's pilot to determine what is necessary at any given moment to keep balance. In short, the leader is advocating for a kind of situational ethics or moral relativism.

Even more than this, however, what this idea of balance points to in the novel is a grand cosmic accounting system whereby ideas of good and evil are less eternally opposed forces than two sides of the same coin. This is a view of good and evil that is more traditionally Eastern than Western, more Daoist than Manichean. Put into the language of psychoanalysis, we might also say it is a very Jungian view of good and evil. Indeed, Fukada makes a direct appeal to Jung when making his case for balance:

> Where there is light, there must be shadow, and where there is shadow there must be light. There is no shadow without light and no light without shadow. Karl Jung said this about "the Shadow" in one of his books: "It is as evil as we are positive . . . the more desperately we try to be good and wonderful and perfect, the more the Shadow develops a definite will to be black and evil and destructive.[12]

This is an idea that arguably works better as a psychological imperative than as an absolute moral law of the universe, for what this latter view promotes is moral passivism. Why should we rise up to resist evil when the universe is designed to take care of things anyway? Fukada explains this idea to Aomame in this way:

> [T]he most important thing with regard to this world in which we live is for there to be a balance maintained between good and evil. The so-called Little People—or some kind of manifestations of will—certainly do have great power. But the more they use their power, the more another power automatically arises to resist it. In that way, the world maintains a delicate balance. This fundamental principle is the same in any world.[13]

Of course, this is an idea presented by one character in the novel (Fukada) who most readers will be suspicious of to begin with, so we are free to entertain or dismiss it as we see fit. Yet, when read as a whole, the novel does seem to support this position, the unknown forces that push Tengo, Aomame, and others into action clearly there to resist Fukada and the Little People. At the same time, this is not, I believe, the main ideological message of the novel, which, instead, is focused more on the power of love as the only true antidote to the temptations of closed systems (a point I will return to later).

This then is a broad summary of *1Q84* and some of its major themes, with some important missing strands that will be added in what follows. The question then is what to make of all this and how to link it with the therapeutic focus of this book (beyond the point I have already made that it might be seen as the breakthrough novel for therapeutic thread three). In the rest of this section, I will discuss three ways of reading the novel which can bring some of its strange supernatural themes into a real-world context and in the process help to clarify what Murakami was trying to do in the book (though not always successfully). I will also finish the section with a brief discussion of how the novel starts to bring a new dimension into therapeutic thread four of Murakami's fiction—the drive for individuation as a response to nihilism—which will lead well into the rest of the chapter.

A first way of making sense of *1Q84* is as a response to Asahara Shōkō and the rise of Aum Shinrikyō. Murakami's first response to the Aum attack came with the publication of his two nonfiction books of interviews, which looked directly at the attack and its aftermath, and were later combined in English as *Underground*. Comments Murakami would make in this book offer useful clues for understanding what he was trying to do in *1Q84*. I discussed previously in the section on *Sputnik Sweetheart* the attention Murakami paid in *Underground* to Asahara as a storyteller and the challenge this posed to him as a writer, namely, the way he saw the "big task" hanging over his head as offering a better narrative to those who are looking for something more. *1Q84* is the novel where Murakami takes up this challenge most directly.

1Q84 draws clear parallels between the revelatory and creative processes. The Receiver/Perceiver team of Fukada and his shrine maidens, which allows him to hear voices from beyond, is mirrored by the team of Tengo and Fuka-Eri, who bring their collective talents together to produce the novel "Air Chrysalis." One *monogatari*, presented in the closed world of Sakigake, is described as a virus, the other, presented openly to the world in the form of a novel, as its antidote. Following the Aum attack, Murakami clearly saw the need to deepen his own commitment to the art of storytelling, recognizing the power that stories have to help people resist the pull of closed systems.

At the same time, Murakami seems to recognize that at some level, the pull of religious storytelling and the pull of fictional storytelling are not that far removed from each other. As discussed in the Introduction, Murakami is not someone who writes with a conscious message, but, rather, someone who writes to find out what his unconscious has to tell him, and it is only later, in a secondary process of revision, that this primary material is shaped into a story more suitable for public consumption. In one sense, then, in his creative life, Murakami is both his own Perceiver and Receiver, the sexual act here a metaphor for the way effective storytelling blends unconscious and conscious processes. Put another way, Murakami's creative process relies on both a Fuka-Eri part of himself and a Tengo part of himself—a part directly connected to the unconscious and a part trained in the craft of writing. In the same way that Fuka-Eri and Tengo become rivals to the power of the Little People and Fukada, Murakami sees himself as a rival to Asahara.

The second important point Murakami makes in *Underground* relevant to *1Q84* is about the simplistic way the media reacted to the Aum attack and the way we will never eradicate the evil out there if we do not first take the time to look at the evil within ourselves. Reacting to this media response, Murakami writes, "[T]he polemic put forth by the media was quite straightforward in structure. To them, the moral principle at stake in the gas attack was all too clear: 'good' versus 'evil,' 'sanity' versus 'madness,' 'health' versus 'disease.' It was an obvious exercise in opposites."[14] Murakami saw danger in this "us versus them" rhetoric, arguing, instead, that the Japanese people needed to look more closely at themselves to see the "them" in "us" (the Jungian lesson of facing one's own shadow). Only by facing this distorted image of "us," he argued, would Japanese society ever learn anything from what had happened.

1Q84, in part then, is Murakami's attempt to write a story in which this black and white view of an Aum-like group is made decidedly gray. While the novel starts out by painting Fukada in black and white terms (he is a child rapist who deserves a vigilante-style execution), by the end of the novel, Aomame sees him as someone extraordinary who may even transcend traditional standards of good and evil. His murder is also something less to be celebrated than contemplated and understood. This might be read as a commentary on the efficacy of the death penalty that was served out to Asahara and many of his key followers (Asahara was sentenced to death in 2004 and executed in 2018 by hanging). The question the novel raises is, what is gained by executing the face of evil, especially when the more difficult job of working out why this evil appeared in society in the first place has not been done? Nevertheless, it should be noted that when the time for Asahara's execution finally came in 2018, Murakami wrote a newspaper article stating that, while he is opposed to the death penalty in principle, in this particular case, given the time he spent investigating the actions of Aum and talking to many of the victims of the attack, he did not feel he could object to the penalty this time.[15] While this is clearly a contradiction and goes against the implicit message of *1Q84*, which suggests that such acts of execution are essentially meaningless, it shows just how difficult it is to resist the call for justice when you get close to the suffering of survivors.

Fukada is clearly modeled in part on Asahara Shōkō (born Matsumoto Chizuo), but what is interesting is how other aspects of Asahara's background show up in descriptions of Tengo and Aomame, a point first made by Takahashi Tatsuo. Like Asahara, Fukada is described as a heavy-built man with failing eyesight (Asahara suffered infantile glaucoma and was almost completely blind). In the special school for the blind he attended, Asahara learned judo, the sport Tengo uses to earn his own independence, and he also studied acupuncture and traditional Chinese medicine. These later interests are different from Aomame's occupation as a gym instructor and self-defense coach, but Takahashi suggests that her instrument of choice in her work as an assassin, a thin needle she plunges into the back of men's necks, is likely a nod to Asahara's background in acupuncture.[16] In this way, *1Q84* spreads its allusions to Asahara among three different characters, and in the process subtly tries to complicate the ways we might think about him.

The backstory of the rise of Fukada and Sakigake goes beyond parallels just to Asahara and Aum to include several real-world religious and political movements, suggesting that the novel is supposed to be about more than just a confrontation with Aum. We learn that Fukada began his professional life as a university professor, but that during the political upheaval of the late 1960s and under the influence of Mao Zedong's revolutionary ideology, he formed a group modeled on the Red Guard. When police later stormed the university, he was arrested and dismissed from his academic position. He then took ten of his students and joined Takashima Academy, a commune which supports itself through farming. Once he had learned everything he could from this group, Fukada went out on his own, purchasing land in Yamanashi prefecture. In 1974, his group began to call itself Sakigake and was relatively successful for a time until divisions emerged. In 1976 the group split in two, with the more militant faction, which came to call itself Akebono (First Light), leaving. In 1981, Akebono made news headlines when it got involved in a shootout with police. Sakigake, on the other hand, evolved from an agricultural co-op into a religion and in 1979 was granted official legal recognition as such. It quickly became increasingly secretive and cut-off from society.

Akebono's shootout with the police is reminiscent of the Asama-Sansō incident in 1972, an event involving members of The United Red Army (URA) who, following an internal purging of its own members that left fifteen people dead, took hostages in a mountain lodge near Karuizawa, Nagano, the resulting shootout with police leaving two officers dead. The path of Sakigake, on the other hand, is reminiscent of Yamagishikai, a group founded by Yamagishi Miyozō in 1953 that traveled a similar path from agricultural co-op to new age religion. Yamagishikai changed considerably after 1968 following the death of its original leader and the injection of a number of radical student types.

One of the models critics offer for Fukada is Niijima Atsuyoshi, a former professor at Waseda University, Murakami's alma mater, who was a left-wing activist during the late 1960s, but who quit the university in 1973 to join Yamagishikai. Niijima was a scholar of Chinese literature and an expert on the writer Lu Xun, who wrote the novel *A Q Zhengzhuan* (阿Q正傳; The True Story of Ah Q), a title which bears a superficial resemblance to *1Q84*.[17] As Fujii Shōzō notes, Murakami has mentioned in an interview reading Lu Xun in high school and he also gives *The True Story of Ah Q* a mention in his nonfiction book *Wakai dokusha no tame no tanpenshōsetsu annai* (A Guide to Short Stories for Young Readers).[18]

The focus on religion and cults in *1Q84* (which also includes the religion of Aomame's childhood) is really just an example of a broader theme found throughout Murakami's fiction: the dangers of closed systems and the power that fiction has as an open system to resist such forces.[19] In earlier novels, these closed systems tended to be more political in nature, but here, they have taken on a religious bent. The underlying power dynamics, however, are the same. What is at stake here are systems which seek to take over the will of the individual to serve their own ends.

Another way to say all of this is that Murakami stands with "eggs against walls," a metaphor taken from his Jerusalem Prize speech given in February of 2009, a message offered just three months prior to the publication of Books One and Two of *1Q84* in Japanese (the third and final book was published in Japan the following year). With the political situation in Israel as his backdrop, Murakami had explained that he wanted to deliver a personal message to his audience in Israel, one he tries to keep in mind as he writes, explaining, "Between a high, solid wall and an egg that breaks against it, I will always stand on the side of the egg."[20] Murakami went on to clarify that eggs are individuals and walls are the systems they smash up against, which in the context of his speech was a barely veiled expression of solidarity with the plight of individual Palestinians against his Israeli hosts. Murakami continues, "[e]ach of us is a unique, irreplaceable soul enclosed in a fragile shell," and he suggests that his sole purpose as a writer is to "bring the dignity of the individual soul to the surface and shine a light upon it" as well as to keep "a light trained on the System in order to prevent it from tangling our souls in its web and demeaning them."[21]

Here, then, we have a first argument for what Murakami was trying to do in *1Q84*. Challenged by the rise of Aum, he was trying to write a novel which could compete with Asahara's storytelling and speak to those who are searching for something more. This required him to explore the question of what separates religious and fictional storytelling, and the answer, it turned out, was not that much, though there is still a difference. This difference resides not in how the stories are produced (a skillful blending of conscious and unconscious sources), but in the purposes they are made to serve. Religious storytelling can be made to serve the closed worlds of cults where the interests of individuals are sacrificed for a "greater good," while fictional storytelling is an open system people are welcome to enter and exit freely and use as they wish, with the story ultimately serving the individual and not the other way around. This was coupled with a need to tell the story of a figure like Asahara in a less black and white way. What Murakami wanted to suggest to people was that before they condemned someone like Asahara, they should first take a look at themselves and examine their own shadows.

A second thing Murakami tried to accomplish in *1Q84* was to write what he calls a *sōgō shōsetsu* or general novel. *1Q84* was a novel Murakami had been working himself up for, and for several years prior to its publication, he had been talking about the idea of writing a new kind of book. The model he had in mind was Dostoevsky's *The Brothers Karamazov*, a work we have already seen referenced in *1Q84*.[22] Speaking on the topic of the general novel to a group of students, Murakami explained:

> When I said I wanted to write a novel like *The Brothers* Karamazov, I was talking about a kind of general novel, about the context of a kind of 19th century general novel. The general novel, well it's difficult to define, but I think it's when a new world-view comes together through the intertwining of various world-views, various perspectives packed together into one place.[23]

Someone who saw something similar occurring in Dostoevsky's novels was the literary critic Mikhail Bakhtin. In his *Problems of Dostoevsky's Poetics* he writes about the way Dostoevsky created "a completely new type of artistic thinking," a development he describes as polyphonic.[24] While earlier critics had seen different characters in *The Brothers Karamazov* as standing in for different ideological positions, Bakhtin saw something even more radical going on, explaining, "Dostoevsky . . . creates not slaves . . . , but *free* people, capable of standing *alongside* their creator, capable of not agreeing with him and even of rebelling against him."[25] Murakami's concept of the general novel can usefully be understood in Bakhtin's language of the polyphonic novel.

Murakami's early fiction was the opposite of polyphonic. His first-person narratives were about a single subjective point of view that many times was more focused on the inner world of the narrator than the world at large. Since the short story collection *After the Quake*, however, Murakami has increasingly experimented with third-person narrative, a trend connected to his larger project of trying to write a general novel. While at one level *The Brothers Karamazov* might be read as a family-focused whodunit novel, its deeper interest lies in the different philosophical, moral, and spiritual positions of its different characters, individual characters in their own right but also representatives of broader intellectual and spiritual positions in society—Dmitri the sensualist, Ivan the atheist, and Alexei the religious. Like Dostoevsky's novel, Murakami also seems to be aiming in *1Q84* for something which captures the moral and spiritual sensibilities of an age and gives place to a variety of different worldviews. So how successful was he?

There are a vast number of characters in *1Q84* who represent a broad range of ideological positions or worldviews. At one extreme are Fukada and his followers who are dependent for their direction on the voices he hears. At the other extreme is the dowager who has a bleakly Darwinian worldview. At times she sounds like she could be quoting directly from Richard Dawkin's classic book *The Selfish Gene*, as in this scene from Book One where she responds to Aomame's interest in history books:

> I also like reading history books. What they teach us is that we are the same today as we were in the past. Even if there are differences in clothing and lifestyle, what we think about and what we do has hardly changed. In the end, we're basically just carriers for our genes, nothing more than a pathway. Like a horse driven to exhaustion, they ride us along from one generation to the next.[26]

In this way, the dowager's extracurricular activities, planning assassinations for perpetrators of domestic violence, comes across as something like a eugenics program, and the secretive and extreme nature of her work clearly has its own cultic qualities. Yet, while the worldviews presented in the novel vary, they are at times a little too cartoonish, caricatures of extremists, both secular and religious, that are lacking in nuance. While *The Brothers Karamazov* offers us a believable portrait of the religious landscape of nineteenth-century Russia from the atheist to the believer, and while we are able to find empathy for a number of competing ideological positions, Murakami's work offers us extremes against which the inherent reasonableness of the main protagonist's ideology of love is then affirmed.

This seems to be the critical consensus on *1Q84*. While there are a few critics who have seen it offering something completely new, most have seen it as not quite living up to Murakami's prescriptions for the general novel. Kawamura Minato, for example, sees *1Q84* as less a radical turn in Murakami's fiction than as an accumulation of his writing so far.[27] Kōnosu Yukiko sees it as focused on the perspectives of Tengo and Aomame rather than being the kind of general novel Murakami had talked about.[28] Of course, the goal of writing a "new" *The Brothers Karamazov* is going to be a tall order for any writer, and perhaps particularly for a writer like Murakami who excels first and foremost in first-person narrative. For most critics then, Murakami's effort does not quite reach the scale of a Dostoevskyian masterpiece, even if it is an interesting experiment.

While Murakami most often references Dostoyevsky's *The Brothers Karamazov* in explaining his inspiration for *1Q84*, another clear influence is Dostoevsky's 1866 novel *Crime and Punishment*. A giant of the Western literary canon, *Crime and Punishment* tells the story of Rodion Raskolnikov, a young former student in Saint Petersburg who kills a pawnbroker, but who believes his crime can be justified if he uses his ill-gotten gains for a greater social good. The promised punishment of the novel's title at first seems to come in the form of Porfiry, a detective who investigates the crime and who increasingly comes to suspect that Raskolnikov is the murderer. Raskolnikov is eventually sentenced for his crimes, but in the end, this is not really the punishment the novel's title refers to. Rather, the focus is on Raskolnikov's psychological breakdown and his search for spiritual redemption, a motif embodied in the destitute prostitute Sonya, who espouses Christian values and encourages Raskolnikov to confess. Raskolnikov's extreme form of utilitarianism has proven spiritually bankrupt, but Sonya, through the power of love, shows him another way.

In *1Q84*, under the sway of the dowager, Aomame experiments with a similar utilitarian philosophy, acting as judge, jury, and executioner for abusive men. The dowager, with her cold Darwinian view of the world, is constantly reassuring Aomame that what they are doing is right. Like Dostoevsky's novel, dramatic tension is added to the story by the addition of a private detective called Ushikawa, who is working for Sakigake and who slowly closes in on Aomame after she kills their leader (this tension becomes necessary to the novel as Aomame goes into hiding and the general action slows down). Like *Crime and Punishment*, love is offered as a redemptive force, in particular the love of Aomame and Tengo, which sustains them over the years until they can meet again. Unlike Dostoevsky's novel, however, there is no serious punishment, psychological or otherwise, which follows the crimes committed. Whether it is Tengo and Komatsu's literary conspiracy (presenting Fuka-Eri's novel to the world as the product of an individual author when it is a heavily edited group effort) or Aomame and the dowager's vigilante justice, in the end, everyone gets away with their moral and ethical transgressions, both psychologically and legally.

While clearly influenced by *Crime and Punishment*, then, *1Q84* is not really a novel about punishment at all. Instead, it is a novel where everybody gets away with their crimes, assumedly because 1Q84 is not the real world of 1984 and so the murders and conspiracies which occur there are all free from any serious moral or legal consequences (much like Kafka's "crimes" of killing his "father" and sleeping with his "mother" seem to have no serious moral or legal consequences at the end of *Kafka on the Shore*). Instead, like in earlier Murakami novels, this parallel world is there more for the space it provides for therapeutic breakthroughs that cannot happen in the real world where things like murder and incest have consequences. While in *Crime and Punishment* Godly love is ultimately offered as the antidote to a Godless utilitarian worldview, *1Q84* offers romantic love as its antidote, with the saving of Aomame and Tengo from their avoidant attachment styles the ultimate justification for their parallel-world experience.

This theme is also explored through Ushikawa, another character in *1Q84* who, primarily because of his looks, also suffers from a lack of love, and who almost has his own Raskolnikov-like moment of redemption in the novel. Looking back on his own life he concludes, "I often used to think I was like Raskolnikov, except I never met Sonia [an alternative translation of Sonya used in some translations of the novel]."[29] Near the end of *1Q84* Ishikawa does meet his Sonya—Fuka-Eri, who in a moment where she stares directly into the lens of his surveillance camera, touches something deep within him. Wondering if what he is feeling is sexual attraction, Ushikawa concludes, rather, that it is something spiritual in the girl which has touched him.[30] Yet, whatever spiritual and redemptive potential this moment offers is never realized, for shortly thereafter, Ushikawa is killed by Tamaru as a means of keeping Aomame safe.

A third aim one senses in *1Q84* was to help Murakami deal with the death of his father, who died in 2008 (while Murakami was working on *1Q84*). This aspect of the novel shows up most clearly in the scenes of Tengo visiting his dying father on his deathbed in a hospital in Chiba and the strange one-sided conversations he has with him there. It also shows up in the strange short story he reads on his journey there, "Town of Cats." Tengo reads the story in an anthology, and we learn that it was written by a German author sometime between the two world wars. It tells the story of a young man who chooses a random town to disembark at on a train journey, but who quickly finds that the town is deserted in the day while occupied by talking cats at night. Curiosity gets the better of him, and he stays in this town longer than he should, until it become impossible for him to return to the normal world. The conclusion of the story, we are told, is this:

> He knows that he is irretrievably lost. This is no town of cats, he finally realizes. It is the place where he is meant to be lost. It is a place not of this world that has been prepared especially for him. And never again, for all eternity, will the train stop at this station to bring him back to his original world.[31]

Journeys to otherworldly towns are a common occurrence in Murakami's fiction, and all these towns, including the town of cats, are suggestive, in some way, of the town Murakami left behind to start his life in Tokyo as a university student. When Murakami wrote his personal essay "Neko o suteru" (Abandoning a Cat) in 2019, which is an exploration of his father's life and legacy, he opened and closed the essay with two stories about cats. The first story tells of Murakami and his father going to abandon a cat near the shore when he was a child, only to have the cat return home before they got there, even though they were on a bicycle. The final story tells of a kitten that clambered up a tree and couldn't get down. In the morning, the kitten was gone, and Murakami has no knowledge of what happened to it. In this way, Murakami's memories of his father are intertwined with the town they grew up in and the cats that came into, and went out of, their lives. What one senses in the story "Town of Cats," however, is how strange and distant a place this town has now become.

Though Tengo's father has dementia and later enters a coma, Tengo continues to visit him in Chiba, reading him books (including the story "Town of Cats") and talking to him. For Tengo, this is a meaningful, therapeutic exercise that he believes is helpful in letting him say goodbye to a man he did not always get along with in life. Tengo says, "I came here every day talking to you in your coma, reading to you. And I think at least a part of us has reconciled, and I think that reconciliation has actually taken place in the real world."[32] Murakami's parents left Kobe after their home was destroyed in the 1995 Kobe earthquake, returning to Kyoto. Near the end of his father's life, however, Murakami did reach out to him, visiting him one last time in the hospital where he would spend his final days. In the essay "Abandoning a Cat," he explains this final encounter as follows: "And there, in the final days of his life—the very final few days—my father and I managed an awkward conversation and reached a sort of reconciliation. Despite our differences, looking at my emaciated father I did feel a connection, a bond between us."[33] Part of the purpose of *1Q84* is to tell the story of this partial reconciliation in fictional form.

Finally, I would like to finish with a brief discussion of how *1Q84* starts to deal with themes that come up even more prominently in *Killing Commendatore* and which are related to therapeutic thread four: the drive for individuation as a response to nihilism. *1Q84* drew mixed reviews when it first came out, with several critics objecting to it on moral grounds. Matt Thorne, for example, writing in *The Telegraph*, was uncomfortable with the way the novel uses "incest and child abuse to drive the plot" and describes it as "a depressing, dark, morally questionable book that suggests the author has lost his way."[34] Similarly, Kathryn Shultz, writing in *The New York Times*, while entertained by the story, was troubled by "the psychological and moral void below." Comparing the novel to one of its obvious literary influences, George Orwell's *1984*, she finds that Murakami's novel comes off less than favorably:

> [W]here Orwell offered a bracing parable about the horrors of totalitarianism, the ethos of "1Q84" borders on incoherent. There's much talk of "evil" in the book, but it boils down to the belief that iniquity is either in the eye of the beholder or a stabilizing force in human society ("The most important thing . . . is for there to be a balance maintained between good and evil.") The former is moral relativism at its glibbest; the latter, bizarrely, a sales pitch for the dark side.

Like Thorne's criticism just described, Shultz adds that she is "troubled by Murakami's willingness to use the rape of children as mere metaphor" as well as by "the general ethical impassivity pervading the book." [35]

Reviews in Japan were also mixed, with Kuroko Kazuo one of the novel's main detractors. Kuroko, as mentioned in the last chapter, was an early supporter of Murakami's career and has written several books looking at his "lost worlds" and his development as a writer from stories of "loss" to stories of "transformation." In 2011, however, he wrote a book highly critical of *1Q84*, arguing that it fails to live up to Murakami's increasingly confident rhetoric of commitment (the main point of reference here being Murakami's Jerusalem Prize "Eggs and Wall" speech). Despite Murakami's growing willingness to express political opinions on the world stage, Kuroko argues that *1Q84* is a novel which retreats into relativism and ambiguity and is best read as an entertainment, cult, or mystery novel.[36] Given this reality, he is not surprised that Murakami continues to be passed over for the Nobel Prize for Literature.[37] Such criticisms, of course, should be kept in perspective. They by no means represent the only, or even the dominant, response to Murakami's fiction in general or to *1Q84* in particular. What they do highlight, though, are the reservations a growing number of critics do have to Murakami's fiction on moral grounds.

1Q84 is clearly a novel with a very different ideological message to Orwell's *1984*. Published in 1949, Orwell's novel portrays a dystopian society where a figure known as Big Brother tightly controls and manipulates information in his effort to maintain totalitarian control for the Inner Party (though it remains a distinct possibility that Big Brother does not even exist). A direct warning about the dangers of totalitarian rule, Orwell's commitment to free thought and open societies continues to speak to reader's today, with the adjective "Orwellian" entering the English lexicon to warn us of situations where this dystopian vision is threatening to become a reality.

Writing, as he was, at the end of the first decade of the twenty-first century, for Murakami, the year 1984 was already a date in the past. The message of his novel seems to be that while the dangers of Big Brother may have been averted (for now), a different threat has emerged, the Little People, which while more subtle, also needs to be addressed. Many critics have noted the significance of 1984 as the year in which Aum Shinrikyō first began its activities, which began, innocently enough, with the opening of some yoga studios. The Little People, the novel suggests, go back earlier in human history than even the concepts of good and evil, suggesting that our propensity for hearing voices and our *monogatari*-making abilities predate even our moral intuitions and religious systems. This is what makes the Little People so potentially dangerous. There is no telling what the voices will tell people, given that our traditional standards of good and evil are none of their concern.

The question, then, is how one is supposed to stand up against the Little People and the voices they serve from beyond, and the answer to this question is twofold and relates to both the remaining therapeutic threads we are exploring in Murakami's fiction. The first response, related to therapeutic thread three, says that the best antidote to closed systems is love. Fukada, speaking with Aomame, explains the attraction of religion as follows: "Most people are not looking for provable truths. As you said, truth is often accompanied by intense pain, and almost no one is looking for painful truths. What people need is beautiful, comforting stories that make them feel as if their lives have some meaning. Which is where religion comes from."[38] In explaining why she does not need the things the leader offers, Aomame responds by saying that what she has, instead, is love (she is referring to her love for Tengo, even though she has not seen him since she was a child), and after listening to her, the leader agrees: "You don't seem to have any need for religion."[39] This also seems to be what Fuka-Eri is saying when she explains to Tengo, "To make sure the Little People don't harm you, you have to find something the Little People don't have."[40] This something is love, and this is what Tengo and Aomame find in each other.

The second answer for how to stand up to the power of the Little People is to individuate—therapeutic thread four—but this is where things become more complicated, for what we will see later in *Killing Commendatore* is how this increasingly requires a symbolic engagement with the incest taboo. We first saw this theme emerge in *Kafka on the Shore* and then repeat in *1Q84*. What these three novels also share is the backstory of this quest for individuation occurring against the backdrop of a murder willed by its own victim. In this way, each of these novels points to the way individuation reaches a climax with the murder of a symbolic father, the radical opening of questions of morality this brings about (including a wrestling with the incest taboo), and the way a symbolic resolution of this taboo allows the individual to get into touch with a new kind of authority within themselves. We might ask whether this new understanding brings them closer to the Nietzschean Superman or the Jungian individuated Self. This is a question I will return to at the end of this chapter.

The Alchemy of Recovery in *Colorless Tsukuru Tazaki and His Years of Pilgrimage*

Colorless Tsukuru Tazaki and His Years of Pilgrimage is one of Murakami Haruki's easier novels to summarize. Basically, it is a story about trauma (through social ostracism) and recovery. Tazaki Tsukuru, the main protagonist, grows up in Nagoya and in high school meets four friends, each of whom has a color in their name: the boys, Akamatsu (Red Pine) Kei and Oumi (Blue Sea) Yoshio, and the girls, Shirane (White Root) Yuzuki, and Kurono (Black Field) Eri. For convenience, they soon begin calling each other by their colors: Aka (Red), Ao (Blue), Shiro (White), and Kuro (Black). Only Tsukuru, whose name means "to make," is without a color in his name, a fact which at times leaves him feeling left out.

In what is described as "a lucky but entirely accidental chemical fusion," the five friends meet at an after-school volunteer group and form a "beautiful community."[41] Once high school finishes, only Tsukuru, of the five friends, chooses to leave Nagoya, heading to Tokyo to pursue his dream of becoming a designer of train stations. He returns to Nagoya as often as circumstances allow, and for a time it seems that nothing has changed in the group dynamics, until one day he finds that none of his friends will return his phone calls. Eventually he reaches Blue, who tells him not to contact any of them any longer. Rather than explaining why, Blue simply tells him, "Think about it, and you'll figure it out."[42]

This rejection comes to Tsukuru in July of his sophomore year and for the next half year all he can think about is dying. He barely manages to get through this dark period in his life, but gradually he begins a process of recovery. He makes a friend called Haida (Gray Field) and hears his story about his father's encounter years earlier with Midorikawa (Green River), details I will return to later. Tsukuru goes on to achieve his dream of becoming an engineer (though the actual job requires renovating old stations more than it does designing new ones). He has some relationships with women along the way, though nothing too serious, but now, sixteen years after the end of his "beautiful community," he is seeing someone new, Kimoto Sara, and is hopeful that their relationship will go further. To this point, Sara suggests, Tsukuru has been "alone but not lonely."[43] In a pattern common to Murakami's recent fiction (therapeutic thread three), Tsukuru is hopeful that detachment can now give way to attachment.

Sara is interested in Tsukuru, but her instincts tell her that something is wrong with him and that unless he can sort this "something" out, he will not be able to commit to her completely. Acting in part as his therapist, she tells him that he has "unresolved emotional issues" and encourages him to go back and confront his four colorful friends.[44] Unless he understands the reason for what happened, Sara suggests, Tsukuru will remain stuck where he is forever. Sara investigates the present location and situation of each of the four friends and passes on this information to Tsukuru. With this information, he travels first to Nagoya, where he meets Blue and Red, and later to Finland, where he meets Black. Unfortunately, it is too late to meet White, who was strangled to death six years earlier in an apartment in Hamamatsu (a city located between Nagoya and Tokyo). The rest of the story offers details of the visits Tsukuru makes to the three surviving friends in search of healing and closure.

Colorless is a novel which invites allegorical interpretations. Published in 2013, it was Murakami's first novel post 3.11, and so the first question many critics posed was how it might be read as a response to the triple disaster: The March 11, 2011, Tōhoku earthquake, tsunami, and failure at the Daiichi Nuclear Power Plant in Fukushima. *Colorless* does not reference this disaster directly, but its focus on themes of trauma and recovery does resonate with the historical moment in which it was published. An historical event that is referenced in the novel is the 1995 sarin gas attack by Aum, and if we add sixteen years to this event, much like the sixteen years Tsukuru has spent in recovery, we end up in 2011. Rebecca Suter offers a good example of how *Colorless* might be read as a response to the 3.11 disaster.

Suter starts with the government response to the triple disaster and its focus on the concept of *kizuna* (ties or bonds) that was used to try and unite the country in a time of great difficulty. While not unsympathetic to this public discourse, Suter wonders what it simultaneously ignores, and she sees in *Colorless* a desire to go beyond this official public narrative. Instead, *Colorless* focuses on a character who has been pushed from a collective and is struggling to face his trauma on his own. Arguably, then, he represents those people who were forced to face 3.11 without ties or bonds, those who had to find their own inner resources to work through their pain and loss. Suter writes:

> Without in any way denying the extraordinary generosity and solidarity that was deployed by Japanese citizens in the aftermath of 3.11, it is important to note that what was erased from these stories was any sense of alienation and isolation that may have been experienced by individuals in the face of the sudden and inexplicable loss of their homes, their loved ones, and their means of living. In the effort toward national recovery, there seemed to be no room for feelings of dejection and separation.
>
> Murakami's novel represents precisely those feelings by focusing on Tsukuru's seemingly unrelated, yet deeply similar, individual story of loss and grief.[45]

Tsukuru's name can be read in this same light, as Ōnishi Wakata points out. Tazaki literally means "many capes" and so can be taken as a reference to the distinctive coastline of the Tōhoku region which was most affected by the tsunami. The name Tsukuru, on the other hand, reflects the post-disaster imperative to rebuild. Ōnishi points out the significance of a slogan offered by a group of artists in the aftermath of the disaster: *tsukuru koto ga ikiru koto* (To make is to live).[46] In this way, the name Tazaki Tsukuru stands as a symbol of the post-disaster imperative to rebuild the damage done to the Sanriku region, a desire to make and to live in the aftermath of devastating loss.

At the same time, there is a darker side to Tsukuru's recovery that undermines this simple reading of *Colorless* as just an allegory of recovery. Once Tsukuru learns that Shiro had been raped and later murdered, he starts to wonder if he might be responsible in some way. Much like the "murders" committed by Gotanda in *Dance Dance Dance* and Kafka in *Kafka on the Shore*, this would seem to be a murder committed in some other metaphysical space, or perhaps a metaphor that Tsukuru must come to accept as a lived reality, even if its actual reality remains unclear. As the third-person narrator of *Colorless* explains, "It might have all been a dream, but he still couldn't escape the feeling that, in some indefinable way, he was responsible. And not just for the rape, but for her murder. On that rainy May night something inside of him, unknown to him, may have slipped away to Hamamatsu and strangled that thin, lovely, fragile neck."[47]

The reason Tsukuru's friends had cut him off so suddenly, he later learns, was Shiro's claim that he had raped her. She had told her friends that Tsukuru had "a public face and a hidden, private face," and that there was "something unhinged and detached from the side of him that everyone knew."[48] What she was suggesting is that he is a kind of Dr. Jekyll and Mr. Hyde figure, and Tsukuru believes this may be true, though only in a "purely symbolic way."[49] As in much of Murakami's fiction, what this means for how we should interpret the narrative is never definitively answered. Did Tsukuru kill Shiro in a dissociated state? Did the Mr. Hyde side of himself first rape and then later murder the woman he loved, while the Dr. Jekyll side remained oblivious to the whole thing? Or did Tsukuru kill Shiro through somebody else—much like the idea of spirit projection first explored in *Kafka on the Shore*—and if so, who might this other person be? Or perhaps this is all supposed to stop at the psychological level—Tsukuru must accept that, like Kafka in *Kafka on the Shore*, "in dreams begin responsibilities."[50] What he must confront, in other words, is the unconscious desire he had to rape and murder Shiro, even if he did not actually do it.

Whichever interpretation one prefers, what all these possibilities do is complicate the simple recovery allegory just outlined. Instead, Tsukuru now potentially becomes both victim and victimizer. This, in turn, offers up new allegorical possibilities for the novel. For example, could Tsukuru's journey now be read as an allegory for Japan's recovery from the Second World War, a recovery made possible by the nation's own dissociation from the past? The rape and murder here might be read as a metaphor for the comfort women issue, say, or perhaps a reference to the "rape of Nanking," to borrow Iris Chang's metaphor. What such a reading of *Colorless* suggests is that while dissociation is sometimes needed in the early stages of recovery, over time dissociated memories must be confronted if full recovery is to occur. As Sara tells Tsukuru, "You can hide memories, but you can't erase the history that produced them."[51] This might be taken as Murakami's message to his own country.

The main problem with this second allegorical reading is that Tsukuru never really confronts the meaning of these potentially dissociated memories, so even if this is the point of the novel, it is largely underdeveloped. The possibility that Tsukuru is Shiro's rapist and murderer is suggested, but then just as quickly it melts into the background and the main victim narrative, the trauma and recovery narrative arc, returns. To read the novel in this way, then, is not entirely satisfying. At best, it might be read as an allegory about the failure of overcoming dissociation in postwar Japan, the way victim narratives continue to dominate in the Japanese collective conscious. This is a reading that fits with public statements Murakami has made on the topic of responsibility and the triple disaster. Speaking in an interview for Mainichi Newspaper, for example, Murakami explained:

> I feel one of the problems Japan continues to face is the evasion of personal responsibility. Whether it's the end of the war in 1945 or the Fukushima Daiichi nuclear accident in 2011, no one really takes responsibility. That's how it feels to me. For example, at the end of the war, the understanding was that, in the end, no one was at fault. That is, the villains were the military cliques, and even the Emperor was their pawn; the general population was deceived and suffered. The people are the victims in this narrative. It is little wonder that Chinese and Koreans get so angry. The Japanese people tend only to have a shallow conception of themselves as perpetrators, and the trend only seems to be getting worse. It's the same for the nuclear accident. We haven't thought seriously about who the perpetrators are. Of course, victims and victimizers can be mixed in together, but if we carry on in this vein, the only big perpetrators in the end are going to be the earthquake and the tsunami and everyone else is going to be let off as victims. Just like the war. It's my biggest worry.[52]

Murakami precedes these comments by saying that, as a novelist, he prefers not to make direct statements on issues, instead preferring to let his fiction do the talking. Here though, he has made an exception, and this very direct statement about the 3.11 disaster gives us a way to understand the allegorical nature of *Colorless*. Tsukuru's journey is *both* about heroic recovery from trauma *and* about the way this is sometimes accomplished through dissociation, a state which cuts us off from our simultaneous role as perpetrators. It is one of the rare occasions perhaps, where Murakami has given us a clear key to interpreting one of his works.

At the same time, *Colorless* is more than just a response from Murakami to recent historical events. In its focus on living in the aftermath of the collapse of a seemingly perfect community, it picks up on a theme that has been floating around in Murakami's fiction for some time. In *Colorless*, the group formed by Tsukuru and his colorful friends is described as an "equilateral pentagon," or at other times as a "perfect circle."[53] In *Norwegian Wood*, Naoko describes her relationship with Kizuki in the same way, while noting that "Such perfect little circles are impossible to maintain."[54] Shiro, in this way, is a character who feels connected to Naoko. She is someone who both longs for and fears "perfect little circles." In both novels, the main protagonist suffers his psychological blow, his separation from the girl he loves, during his second year at university. In both novels, this pushes him to the brink of death, forcing him to slowly claw his way back to life. Watanabe, in *Norwegian Wood*, struggles to recover from the shock of losing Naoko so that he can commit to Midori, and the novel ends with him finally reaching out in this direction. Tsukuru is seeking for similar emotional growth so that he can commit to Sara. In this way, *Colorless* feels like a return to familiar territory.

Saeki, in *Kafka on the Shore*, also describes the relationship she had with her boyfriend years earlier as like living in a "perfect circle."[55] Her boyfriend was killed in the student protests of the late 1960s, a case of mistaken identity, and she would have to live in the aftermath of his death. Unfortunately, Saeki never truly recovered from this tragedy, thus offering a more negative example of what can happen after the collapse of a perfect circle. Compared to these earlier examples, Tsukuru's recovery goes further and ends more optimistically, thus demonstrating an evolution in Murakami's treatment of this theme. It also offers a much more detailed road map to the road of recovery—color-coded even—one that is possible to trace through the framework of alchemy. This may at first seem a strange claim to make, alchemy commonly understood as the mystical (read misguided) precursor to modern chemistry—the medieval (or even earlier) quest to discover the Philosopher's Stone; to turn base metals into gold; or to create or discover the elixir of life. It was Carl Jung who saw in this tradition a historical precedent for his own depth psychology, the journey of individuation that was about letting go of the ego to discover the Self (which I have been discussing as therapeutic thread four in Murakami's fiction), and who almost single-handedly resurrected interest in the *opus* or "sacred work" of the alchemists. *Colorless*, I will argue, explicitly references this psychological understanding of the alchemical process, starting with the "special chemistry" of the five friends already mentioned.

Alchemy offers numerous terms for the processes metals must go through on their way to becoming gold, but Jeffrey Raff usefully simplifies them into two main ones: "Alchemy proceeded by separation and reunification, *solve et coagula*, a procedure that might be repeated many times."[56] A first step for the alchemist was separation; they had to take whatever metal they had and return it to the *prima materia* or "first matter," a process that was known as *motificatio* or *nigredo*. This would occur through heating the metal in a controlled way, which, in turn, would blacken it. In psychological terms, this blackening stage can be read as a metaphor for depression or even death, a state that might symbolically be represented by a moonless night. This is the dark night of the soul, or what Tsukuru describes in *Colorless* as like being tossed from a ship into the night-time sea.[57] In Tsukuru's case, the *nigredo* is the half year he spent thinking constantly about death, following the breakdown of his "perfect circle." In alchemy, this is the first step in a gradual progression of colors, from black to white (or silver), (in some models) through yellow, and finally to red (or gold). In symbolic terms this takes us from the darkness of night, to the white (or silver) of a moonlit night, and finally through to the red of daybreak. For Jung, the work the alchemist was involved in by transforming metals through different color stages was an outer representation of an inner transformation.

Alchemy offers some context to Tsukuru's name, which means "to make"—not in a high, conceptual way, but in a concrete, practical way—to make something with your hands. Alchemy, James Hillman explains, is a "hand-work," a transferring of "technology into psychology."[58] Tsukuru recognizes the power of his name. Before his name he had "been nothing—dark, nameless chaos and nothing more. . . . [E]verything began with his name."[59] His role is to make something from chaos, to take the *prima materia* revealed from the dissolution of his perfect circle and to turn it into psychological gold. In psychological readings of alchemy, the flame used to heat the base metal is desire or libido. This, of course, is the same flame that breaks down Tsukuru's perfect circle. The unspoken rule of the group had been to repress the sexual desire they felt for one other—to put the harmony of the group above their own needs—a tendency Sara later describes as unnatural.[60] Tsukuru clearly had deep feelings for White (Shiro), and Black (Kuro) later confesses her own strong feelings for Tsukuru at the time. So how were they able to resist the flame of desire for so long?

In alchemy, while heat is necessary, it must be controlled. Heating things too fast or too slow produces the wrong result. What is needed are vessels or containers—objects that are empty inside which can contain and separate substances (and their respective colors) as necessary. This was Tsukuru's role in the group, though something which takes him some time to recognize. Tsukuru often describes himself as an empty vessel—a colorless member of the group who had nothing to offer. What he realizes in hindsight is how painful his decision to leave for Tokyo after high school was for everybody. "Without me in the equation, part of that sense of unity we always had was inevitably going to vanish," he confesses to Sara. "The chemistry, too," she adds.[61] Part of what Tsukuru comes to realize is the importance of his role as an empty vessel, a message which is presented to him later by Kuro (Eri), who in Finland has now become a producer of empty vessels herself, in the form of pottery. "Let's say you are an empty vessel," Eri says to Tsukuru. "So what? What's wrong with that? . . . You're still a wonderful, attractive vessel. And really, does anybody know who they are? So why not be a completely beautiful vessel? The kind people feel good about, the kind people want to entrust with precious belongings."[62]

While the first stage of the alchemical process, the blackening, does not feel positive, it is necessary—a deconstruction that allows for future construction. What can heal this stage, James Hillman explains, is a decapitation, a severing of the head from the body that opens a space for analysis: "According to Jung, the black spirit is to be beheaded, an act that separates understanding from its identification with suffering. . . . Blackness remains, but the distinction between head and body creates a two, while suffering imprisons in singleness."[63] In other words, the first stage of blackness does not allow for analysis because there is no separation from the experience. You are the blackness. Decapitation does not end the blackness, but it opens a distance from which (psycho)analysis can begin. For Tsukuru, what ends his first suicidal stage is a dream. This is not a dream about decapitation per se, but it is about a woman who can separate her body and her heart. Tsukuru is told by this woman that he can have either her body or her heart, but not both—a condition which drives him crazy and which releases a new emotion in him: jealousy. He wants the entire woman, not just part of her, and he later realizes that this dream ended the period of life when he wanted to die. The separation of body and heart here is symbolic of a move he must make in the short term. The feeling of jealousy, the desire to have the whole woman, reflects a desire for healing or recovery. Tsukuru's road to recovery has begun.

Tsukuru's journey is another expression in Murakami's fiction of the desire for individuation. The four characters who surround Tsukuru all represent different competing elements, but as the empty container in the alchemical process, his role was to hold and contain their different potentials and to transform them into something that transcends their individual parts. This, of course, was difficult to do, and it was the competing personalities of the four friends which ultimately pulled them apart, but now, in his inner world, Tsukuru must achieve a similar alchemical miracle. Jung called this kind of sacred union of contrasting elements a *coniunctio*, and he saw these competing elements most commonly appearing in groups of four. Jung writes:

The factors which come together in the coniunctio are conceived as opposites, either confronting one another in enmity or attracting one another in love. . . . Often the polarity is arranged as a quaternion (quaternity), with the two opposites crossing one another, as for instance the four elements or the four qualities (moist, dry, cold, warm), or the four directions and seasons, thus producing the cross as an emblem of the four elements and symbol of the sublunary physical world.[64]

Tsukuru is at the center of this cross, or what in other places Jung describes as a mandala, and the delicate alchemical process he is engaged in involves absorbing something of the potential of these four friends.

In the journey from black to white, alchemy highlights the role of blue. When Tsukuru later makes his journey to see his old friends, a journey that in part is about coming to terms with the death of White, the first character he goes to see is Blue. In psychological terms, experiencing "the blues" is one step on from identifying with the black. The blues can be sung, one can give voice to things, the head and the body can start reconnecting again. Hillman picks up on all these associations with blue, and also includes the traditionally blue virtues of "constancy and fidelity"—attributes Ao personifies (at university he is the rugby captain and later he becomes a Toyota Lexus salesman; he is always a loyal and committed member of the team).[65] Hillman also notes the sexual fantasies that can arise in blue (noting the association blue has with pornography, such as with blue movies). He explains, "When pornographic, perverse, ghastly or vicious fantasies start up, we can place them alchemically within the blue no-man's land between nigredo [blackening] and albedo [whitening]."[66]

The main sexual fantasy Tsukuru repeats, involves him making love to his two friends, Black and White, but the detail he finds difficult to understand is why in these dreams, he always ejaculates inside of White. In alchemical terms, this might be taken as representing his desire to move from nigredo to albedo, from black to white, symbolism that is reinforced later with the arrival of Haida (Mr. Gray). Haida is a younger student Tsukuru first meets at the university swimming pool. In the context of Tsukuru's journey of recovery, he is clearly a compensatory figure. While Tsukuru is primarily interested in what is concrete, in what he can see and touch with his hands, Haida's interests tend toward the philosophical and abstract. What he offers Tsukuru is a new way for him to begin engaging with the world.

What Jung called this stage was the *unio mentalis*, or what Hillman describes as the "union of reasoned judgment and aesthetic fantasy (logos and psyche)." He further describes Jung's *unio mentalis* as "freeing soul from body, prior to further union with body.... The unio mentalis—the first goal of the opus—as union of logos and psyche is nothing other than psychology itself, the psychology that has faith in itself and indicates and activates the albedo [whitening] following the blue."[67] Haida's position between black and white is made explicit in the text: "Mister Gray. Gray is a mixture of white and black. Change its shade, and it can easily melt into various gradations of darkness."[68] Hillman, however, rejects too straightforward an interpretation of the position of the unio mentalis between black and white. He explains, "[T]he unio mentalis is neither a progression from black to white nor a synthesis of black and white. Rather, it is a descent of the mind from that cross, an ever-present possibility of poiesis by a mind remaking itself out of whole blue cloth that underlies and can undermine oppositions."[69] Elsewhere, Hillman has described poiesis simply as "making," or more specifically, "making by imagination into words."[70] Haida is there to teach Tsukuru about the new kind of "making" he must engage in.

Haida's role representing the *unio mentalis* becomes particularly clear one night when he sleeps over at Tsukuru's apartment. Tsukuru wakes up paralyzed in the middle of the night with the feeling that Haida is staring at him, but he soon realizes this is not Haida himself, but some kind of projection. It seems as if Haida's soul has left his body and is visiting Tsukuru. Eventually Tsukuru falls asleep again and starts to dream about sex with Black and White. As he ejaculates into White, though, he realizes that the girls are now gone and Haida has taken their place, accepting Tsukuru's ejaculate in his mouth. He then hears Haida going to the bathroom to clean up. When he awakes in the morning, though, there is no sign of anything sexual having occurred during the night, and Haida makes no mention of the event. Whatever has happened appears to have occurred in some other metaphysical space.

The night before Tsukuru's strange encounter, Haida had told him a story which had happened years earlier. During his student days, Haida's father had met a man named Midorikawa (Green River) at a hot spring resort. Midorikawa claimed to be able to see people's colors—something like their halo or backlight. This gift, he said, had been given to him when he had also accepted a death token. To avoid his assigned death, Midorikawa needed to pass on this token to someone with the right color—a color he had discerned Haida's father happened to have. Midorikawa reassured Haida's father, however, that he did not intend to pass the death token on to him. Haida's father had been at the hot spring in part to escape the student protests in Tokyo. Whatever he may have thought of Midorikawa's story, what is clear from Haida's story is that it was instrumental in bringing his father out of hibernation and back into the world.

Jeffrey Raff explains, "The *nigredo* was associated with the color black. After a number of procedures, the material would slowly start coming back to life. As it moved from death to new growth, the alchemist often noted a green color."[71] Green, Hillman writes, comes out of the blue shadows: "Because of blue, the green world yields metaphors, analogies, intelligible instruction, providing reservoirs of beauty and insight."[72] Is Haida's story about Midorikawa an example of such a yield? Maybe. The story does feel like some kind of metaphor, but it is not exactly "intelligible instruction." Like much in Murakami's fiction, it is open to interpretation. What can be said about this story involving green is that it somehow motivated Haida's father to return to life and that it is now doing the same thing for Tsukuru. For six months he had been living in black but now new colors are emerging in his life: gray and now green. His life is full of new unexpected possibilities, or as the narrator describes, it was "as if he'd been living for a long time in a house only to discover a secret room he'd never known about."[73] This is not dissimilar to the way Jung described his own discovery of alchemy. Before this discovery, Jung had a series of dreams in which he realized the house he was living in had an unknown wing or annex. Eventually, he began exploring this wing and discovered a library with many books dating from the sixteenth and seventeenth centuries. Writing years later Jung would explain:

> The unknown wing of the house was a part of my personality, an aspect of myself; it represented something that belonged to me but of which I was not yet conscious. It, and especially the library, referred to alchemy, of which I was ignorant, but which I was soon to study. Some fifteen years later I had assembled a library very like the one in the dream.[74]

In alchemy, blue and green eventually give way to white (or silver). This is the first resting place (or for some alchemists even the end point). The black has been transformed into something beautiful and redeeming. Hillman argues that we need to differentiate pre-black and post-black white. Pre-black white is the image of white as something innocent, pure, and unspoiled. This is the image of Shiro that is seen most strongly during the days of their perfect circle. In fact, it can be argued that the entire purpose of their group was to protect this unspoiled version of white. The five friends had met doing volunteer work at an after-school program and the way they had worked together can be understood as an attempt to protect the purity of Shiro. While she would teach a child the piano, Tsukuru and Ao would play soccer with the other children, while Kuro and Aka would do their best to stop any remaining children from disturbing Shiro's lessons.

Post-black white is associated more with depression or melancholia.[75] This theme is explored most prominently in *Colorless* through Tsukuru's memories of Shiro playing Frank Liszt's "Le mal du pays" from his *Years of Pilgrimage* suite, a title which means "homesickness" or "melancholy."[76] As he reunites with each of his old friends, Tsukuru asks them if they remember Shiro playing this song, but only Kuro does, suggesting her sensitivity to this side of Shiro. Post-black white is also associated with the moon and with the possibility of lunacy or mental illness. No longer are we in the black of night, but in the moonlit silver; but this brings its own potential problems. Hillman explains, "Silver blackens in air and cannot always gleam as gold. Silver requires polishing, attention, a bit of rubbing and fussing; it calls for worry. Since exposure makes it lose its shine, it is best hidden, protected. It is covered with blackness, by silence and dullness, and by hiding itself invisibly in lead."[77]

In a similar way, Shiro is a character who "requires attention" and who is "covered" or protected by Kuro (Black). After the group breaks up and Shiro enters her melancholic stage, it is Kuro who does her best to protect her and to keep her going. It is only when this role becomes too exhausting for Kuro that she finally cuts her ties, which accelerates Shiro's tarnishing and final downfall. Red was the last of the friends to see White, half a year before her death, and he was startled by her physical change. As he confesses to Tsukuru, "she wasn't attractive like she used to be," and "no longer had that burning something she used to have." She had "lost the glow."[78]

Hillman also notes that whitening is a stage in which truth is often expressed in less than literal ways: "Although silvered perception of truth may be polished to hard and cool sophistication, it is nonetheless glancing, oblique, a poetic truth that includes poetic license—even truth as fantasy and truth of fantasy—so that it may not seem truth at all in the rational eyes of reason alone."[79] This is a good description of the story Shiro shares with the group to cut Tsukuru off, telling them all that he raped her. This appears to be a poetic truth, something which is both true and untrue at the same time. This is why Tsukuru first rejects the idea as a literal fact, but later comes to see its deeper truth in his own psyche.

Hillman also writes about the connection silver has with voice, such as when we call someone silver-tongued, suggesting that we are now at a stage of the therapeutic process where we can speak more fully. Now, Hillman says, "[w]e are at the throat of metaphor" an interesting phrase when we consider that Shiro was strangled to death.[80] Someone, we might suggest, had not wanted to hear her words and had literally squeezed them off at the throat. The question is, who and why? This is where the alchemy of recovery in *Colorless* seems to go off track, but this is also very much to be expected. Alchemy more often goes wrong than right. The gold never eventuates, which leads the alchemist to start all over again from the beginning. Alchemy is the quest of a lifetime and maybe one where the goal is never to be attained. So what has gone wrong specifically in the case of *Colorless*?

In alchemy, the realization of white is supposed to be followed by the emergence of red—the silvery moonlit night is followed by the red of daybreak. This is a delicate process, however, and so it is important that the red does not come on too quickly. In alchemical texts, the successful emergence of red is often symbolized by the marriage or sexual union of the White Queen and Red King: the combination of the cold and the hot; the female and the male; the union of opposites; or what in Jungian individuation would be described as the emergence of the Self. Their baby, when it is born, symbolizes all that has been achieved during the process—the incorporation of the black (the shadow), the white (the anima or animus), and the red (the Self). So what happens in *Colorless*?

Shiro, it would seem, was raped by someone. Kuro believes Shiro's story in part because she actually was pregnant and was determined to have the baby (though in the end she lost it). But who, if not Tsukuru, could have done this to her? The text never tells us, but one possibility suggested by alchemy is Aka (Red). This is at first a strange suggestion. Red, he later reveals to Tsukuru, is gay, and Shiro, we learn, had no sexual desire whatsoever, neither for men nor for women. Thus, it would seem highly unlikely that Red and White would have had sex, forced or otherwise. Yet, there is something about Red's psychology in the story that is a little off, something noted by the other characters. He comes across as another warped Nietzschean Superman in Murakami's fiction, someone who has risen above the herd and who now sees it as his right to use others for his own purposes. In Red's case, this plays out through his development of a training business designed to indoctrinate workers to follow orders, his inspiration for the system a mix of the benign and evil. He explains to Tsukuru:

> The experience I had myself, the training I received as a newly hired bank clerk, was extremely valuable. I added methods taken from religious cults and personal development seminars, to spice things up. I researched companies in the U.S. that had been successful in the same sort of business. I read a lot of books on psychology as well. I included elements from manuals for new recruits in the Nazi SS and the Marines.[81]

This is not the kind of training Red would like to receive himself, and he knows it is not something Tsukuru would take well to, either. As in earlier Murakami novels, here we have two males who through their own inner work stand above the herd, but who have different ideas about what this entitles them to.

Hillman recounts the alchemical tale of John Trinick, which offers a personification of the *albedo* or whitening in the form of a young English woman called the white lady. This white lady is waiting to join with her lover from far away, the white puer. At the same time, however, there is a red thief who also longs to be with her. The question, Hillman writes, is, "Who will break through the door and open the space, white puer or red thief? In Trinick's account it is the white lady herself, in a moment of negligence, who unbolts the door."[82] But this, Hillman explains, was the wrong thing to do. It was not time for the white lady to join with the red thief, at least not in this way. Trinick's scenario has an uncanny resemblance to the murder scene in *Colorless*, where there is no sign of forced entry. So how did Shiro's murderer get in? Did she unbolt the door herself in a moment of negligence? And who did she find on the other side? The red thief?

In *Colorless*, Red is a good candidate for the red thief that came into White's room and murdered her. A successful alchemy would have required Tsukuru, as the vessel, to recognize this and to protect her from this untimely intrusion, which is why he feels partly responsible for what happened. Instead, the sulfur burned too brightly and Shiro lost her baby. Here, then, we see a final potential (but ultimately unrealized) step in the therapeutic journey portrayed in *Colorless*: the *rubedo* or reddening. Lucy Huskinson notes the way this reddening might be read in both Jungian and Nietzschean terms:

> The first "mood" or stage of the alchemical process is black, which corresponds to the lack of unconscious incorporation (the shadow of the individuation process or the alchemical nigredo). The final stage is red, which corresponds to the fullest expression or illumination. We can think of the red stage of enlightenment as the Nietzschean "Daybreak," when authentic values, which were once hidden, are at last expressed, or in terms of the "blood" that gives life to the whole individual, the Self.[83]

If we were going to color-code Murakami's fiction, we might say that most of it belongs to post-black white or silver; its concern is with the white of melancholy, of speaking of the dead with a silvery tongue, in the most beautiful language possible. Alchemy suggests there is a stage beyond this. Jung explains:

> [In the] state of "whiteness" one does not *live* in the true sense of the word. It is a sort of abstract, ideal state. In order to make it come alive it must have "blood," it must have what the alchemists called the *rubedo*, the "redness" of life. Only the total experience of being can transform this ideal state into a fully human mode of existence.[84]

This might remind us of the story from *Sputnik Sweetheart*, where the blood of dogs had to be added to the white bleached bones of soldiers mixed into Chinese gates, to revive the ghosts of these soldiers and to solicit their protection. It is only when bones and blood, white and red, are mixed together that the true power to be found in a *monogatari* can come to life.

While *Colorless* does not take us to this reddening, it does introduce the yellowing, a color some alchemists placed between the white and the red. This stage is known as *citrinitas*, which suggests the significance of White's real name, Yuzu, a yellow (sometimes green) citrus fruit popular in Japan. When Tsukuru makes his final journey to Finland and talks to Kuro, who very significantly has her own kiln and is now a creator of empty vessels (i.e., she has retreated from the traumas of the past to engage in her own alchemical journey of recovery), she insists that he should not use their color nicknames anymore but refer to her as Eri and Shiro as Yuzu, suggesting that this final meeting in Tsukuru's pilgrimage might be thought of as part of his yellowing. Hillman again, explains the meaning of this stage: "[D]uring nigredo [blackening] there is pain and ignorance; we suffer without the help of knowledge. During albedo [whitening] the pain lifts, having been blessed by reflection and understanding. The yellow brings the pain of knowledge itself. The soul suffers its understanding."[85] This kind of "pain of knowledge" is expressed in *Colorless* in this way: "One heart is not connected to another through harmony alone. They are, instead, linked deeply through their wounds. Pain linked to pain, fragility to fragility. There is no silence without a cry of grief, no forgiveness without bloodshed, no acceptance without a passage through acute loss. That is what lies at the root of true harmony."[86]

This does not mean Tsukuru is healed. In fact, at the end of the novel, he appears as fragile as ever. He has decided that if Sara chooses him, he will propose to her straightaway, an expression of his desire for commitment. On the other hand, should she reject him, he fears it will be the end: "If Sara doesn't choose me tomorrow, he thought, I may really die. Die in reality, or die figuratively—there isn't much difference between the two. But this time I definitely will take my last breath."[87]

Reading this passage, Tim Parks wonders if Tsukuru has learned anything at all: "Hearing this drastic declaration, one is obliged to wonder how much progress the pilgrim Tsukuru has really made. He is thirty-six. He has seen the girl only four or five times, and anyway, she always had another man. He has just usefully reconnected with a group of old friends. Some counselling is in order."[88] Perhaps some counseling is in order, but it is unlikely that Tsukuru will get any, at least not in the traditional sense. Instead, what is likely is that his alchemical journey will continue in some form. Perhaps he will find the gold he is looking for and perhaps not. At some future point he may even return to death, the nigredo or blackening from which his journey began. But even in this worst-case scenario, like a good alchemist, there is always hope that he will find the strength to begin his color-coded journey of recovery once again. He has moved from black to white and finally to yellow. But this is not the completion of the alchemical process, which requires the introduction of red, suggesting, from an alchemical perspective, where Murakami's fiction still has to go. In Murakami's next novel, *Killing Commendatore*, the protagonist recalls the months he spent following his separation from his wife, Yuzu. In other words, the quest to discover what might follow the yellow continues.

Meeting Mercurius in *Killing Commendatore*

Killing Commendatore describes the nine-month separation and ultimate reconciliation of a man and his wife (this time a *Watashi* rather than a *Boku*), starting with the month-and-a-half road trip he made to northern Japan immediately following the split and then through the seven-and-a-half months he spent living and painting at a mountaintop home in Odawara. This nine-month separation period is significant, marking the fact that *Watashi*, like Tazaki Tsukuru before him, is engaged in his own version of the great *opus* or work of alchemy. Jung explains, "Many alchemists compute the duration of the opus to be that of a pregnancy, and they liken the entire procedure to such a period of gestation."[89]

There are many hints early on that this will be a story about alchemical transformation. I have already suggested how *Killing Commendatore*, framed as it is around *Watashi*'s separation from and reunification with his wife, Yuzu, is an exploration of what might follow the yellowing stage of the alchemical process. *Watashi* explains that sometimes as a joke he would call his wife Sudachi, another citrus fruit which is green, but she did not appreciate it, insisting on the importance of her name and in the process highlighting her role in his citrinitas or yellowing (and through her absence his gradual movement toward the rubedo or reddening).[90] The novel makes clear that "[n]ames are important" and perhaps none more so than Yuzu's.[91] By leaving him, she pushes *Watashi* to engage in his own alchemy-like journey of turning psychological lead into gold.

Red quickly becomes an important color in *Watashi*'s post-Yuzu life. When he first leaves the home he has shared with Yuzu for just shy of six years, on his road trip, his one condition is that he can take their red Peugeot 205 with him. Driving aimlessly around Tokyo he then finds himself at one point going toward Akasaka (literally red hill), and he also notes that he was careful not to run any red lights.[92] There is a sense here that the reddening or rubedo *Watashi* requires is on the horizon, but he is also being careful not to rush the process. Later, when he makes his home in Odawara, one of the women he comes to sleep with, a new sexual partner for his post-Yuzu (yellow life), drives a red Mini Cooper.

Watashi moves into his Odawara home right after the Golden Week holidays, another hint of the goal which awaits him there—to find the "gold" hidden within himself. His new home has a distant view of the ocean, though this is not what impresses him, the sea looking like "nothing more than a dull lump of lead."[93] Instead, he observes that "[t]he mountains on the opposite side of the valley were in constant flux, transforming with the seasons and the weather, and I never grew tired of these changes."[94] Later, he notices the way the clouds which formed above the sea blew toward these same mountains forming "beautiful, perfect circles."[95] Alchemy is a process which invites change, seeking to turn dull lumps of lead into gold, chaos into perfect circles (Jung was particularly fond of exploring the imagery of the "perfect circles" found in mandala). *Watashi* recognizes that "something—like a flame burning inside me—was steadily fading away. The feeling of that flame warming me from within was receding ever further."[96] There is a danger that this flame, so necessary in alchemy, will eventually go out and that the opportunity for change will be lost. As a portrait artist, *Watashi*'s philosophy has been to "find something shining within" each of his subjects and now it is time to turn this search on himself.[97] He has his doubts though: "Would I be able to discover even one thing shining within me?"[98] Finding this shining something within—this promised gold of the alchemical process—is what his journey of self-discovery is all about.

Before an alchemist can make gold, however, they must first start with the lead: the *prima materia*. Ostensibly, the reason Yuzu leaves *Watashi* is that she has started a sexual relationship with another man (in fact, she had been involved with several other men, but there is one man in particular whom she now appears to be deeply involved with). *Watashi* is at a loss to explain where all of this came from, but as the story unfolds, he confesses that there was a secret hidden deep within their relationship: "the fact that her eyes reminded me so much of my sister [Komichi] who'd died at twelve, and that that was the main reason I'd been attracted to her."[99] Yuzu and Komichi's birthdays, it turns out, are only three days apart. Later, *Watashi* befriends a thirteen-year-old girl called Mariye and they have several conversations about her still underdeveloped breasts, and here again he is reminded of his dead sister who died before her own breasts could reach maturity. What *Watashi* is struggling with here is what psychoanalysts call transference, and it is his need to resolve this transference which explains the nine-month *opus* he has been forced into.

The concept of transference is central to psychoanalysis and distinguishes it from other approaches to therapy. It was one of the central issues Freud and Jung agreed on, though the different ways they would come to approach the transference was also an important part of what ultimately separated them. On their first meeting in 1907, in a long conversation that lasted over thirteen hours, Jung remembers Freud pausing and asking, "And what do you think about the transference?" Jung replied that he thought it was "the alpha and omega of the analytical method" to which Freud replied, "Then you have grasped the main thing."[100] Basically, what transference comes down to is the way early family dynamics, often with an erotic component, come to later be projected onto significant others (a marriage partner, say, or a therapist). This seems to be what *Watashi* experienced in falling in love with Yuzu, and while perhaps neither of them is entirely aware of the fact, it has affected their marriage and brought it to a point of crisis. Indeed, one might argue that Yuzu's unconscious recognition of her husband's transference is why she never had children with him—at some level she recognizes that a future daughter might also be at risk of this same unconscious treatment with potentially disastrous consequences.

Watashi goes some way in the novel toward recognizing this problem. At one point he wonders whether what he had been seeking in his relationship with Yuzu was a "substitute partner" for Komichi and he admits that "[t]he problems my wife and I had had might have stemmed from me unconsciously wanting Yuzu to stand in for Komi."[101] He notes the irrational fear he has of large breasts and his preference for small breasts, noting that when he is holding smaller breasts he remembers his sister, though he is quick to deny that he ever had any sexual interest in her.[102] Later, when he is working on Mariye's portrait, he recognizes that he is actually mixing in elements of his dead sister at the same time. "Was this appropriate?" he wonders to himself. "I couldn't say. But the spirits of these two young girls nearly the same age were already, somewhere—probably in some deep internal recesses I shouldn't access—blended and combined."[103]

Watashi thus has inklings of his transference but not a true appreciation of its depth. In particular, he is incapable of grasping the erotic nature of the feelings he holds for his dead sister which he then projects onto other women. Early in the novel *Watashi* reflects back on his marriage and wonders where things went wrong. He believes that he and Yuzu had what "seemed a basically healthy marriage, on both an emotional and physical level," with the one issue they could not agree on being whether to have children.[104] It is at this point that *Watashi* confesses, "It's like I'd been born with a blind spot, and was always missing something. And what I missed was always the most important thing of all."[105] Later, when the mysterious Menshiki, the Gatsby-like figure who lives in a mansion across the valley from *Watashi*, is helping him to uncover the pit so central to the story, he feels like he is opening the lid on a buried secret: "The problem lay in the fact that even I didn't know what secret I was hiding."[106] *Watashi*'s blind spot, the secret he does not know he is hiding, is his transference, and it is resolving this transference which explains the journey he is on.

It may be helpful at this point to look at two literary precedents for this theme. One famous example of transference dynamics in Japanese literature is *Genji Monogatari* (*The Tale of Genji*), which deals with Genji's loss of his mother as a three-year-old and the women he uses to try and replace her throughout his life. At first, he falls in love with his stepmother, whom his father married because she so resembles Genji's dead mother, and when he can't have her, he later discovers her ten-year-old niece who resembles her (and thus also his biological mother), whom he kidnaps and raises to take her place (though later he has a secret affair with his mother-in-law anyway). From a psychoanalytic perspective, such relationships are clear examples of transference, though there is no attempt in *Genji Monogatari* to resolve the transference. Instead, Genji's life and a string of love affairs becomes a testament to the power of transference, or in other words, the way that love for a lost mother can create an impossible ideal that is projected onto others but never satisfied.

Another literary precedent, which I believe relates even more directly to *Watashi*'s transference issues, is Vladimir Nabokov's *Lolita*. In the case of Humbert Humbert, the narrator of Nabokov's novel, it is not the premature death of a family member which causes him to become fixated on young girls but, rather, the death of his first love, Annabel. Her death, right at the point when they were beginning to experiment sexually, creates an obsession for him with what he calls "nymphets": girls of a certain demeanor aged between nine and fourteen.[107] While *Lolita*, with its overt exploration of an older man's sexual obsession for a young girl, might seem too extreme a comparison for *Watashi*'s more muted journey (while he talks with Mariye a lot about breast size, and even at one point about the size of his own penis, he never goes beyond this), it is possible to see a shared psychological dynamic, a point I will return to later.

In my discussion of *1Q84* I looked at the problem some critics had with the idea of using child molestation as a metaphor (in that novel, for the revelatory or creative process), and here we are returning to similar territory. Following Jung's thinking on the topic, I would argue that what Murakami is doing in *Killing Commendatore* is presenting *Watashi*'s transference as an opportunity for his individuation. While noting the way transference issues can wreck a marriage, Jung also saw them as providing, in the language of alchemy, a "workable *prima materia*" and a "priceless opportunity to withdraw . . . projections."[108] In alchemy, the sexual/spiritual union between a royal brother and sister was often used to represent the unconscious desire for wholeness. Marie Von Franz explains:

> Partners in the chemical marriage are usually described as brother and sister, mother and son or father and daughter. Their union is incestuous. The purpose of this incestuous aspect of such a love-configuration is to make us conscious of the projection, that is, it constrains us to realize that in the end it is a question of the inner union of the components of the personality in ourselves, of a "spiritual marriage" as an unprojected inner experience.[109]

Jung explains how "Alchemy . . . exalted the most heinous transgression of the law, named incest, into a symbol of the union of opposites."[110] Elsewhere he writes, "Incest symbolizes union with one's own being. It means individuation or becoming a self."[111] Those critics who disapprove of *1Q84* because of its radical metaphors would likely do well to steer clear of alchemy and *Killing Commendatore*, too.

Watashi's transformation, which begins with his separation from Yuzu and his road trip to northern Japan, intensifies when he meets Menshiki, a character who in his role as a kind of trickster figure is modeled on Mercurius, a figure central to alchemy who is based on the Roman God Mercury, who, in turn, was based on the Greek God Hermes (who, in turn borrows attributes from the Egyptian God Thoth). Dennis Merrit explains, "Hermes/Mercury was the god of alchemy that became Jung's main symbolic system and the historical context for his 'confrontation with the unconscious.'"[112] Mercurius, Jung explains, "stands at the beginning and end of the work: he is the *prima materia* and is ultimately a 'symbol uniting all opposites.'"[113] It is difficult to downplay the importance of Mercurius to Jung's thinking about the unconscious. What he represents, Jung explains, is "on the one hand the self, and on the other the individuation process and, because of the limitless number of his names, also the collective unconscious."[114] In their attempts to create the Philosopher's Stone (a precious material which could turn base metals into gold), alchemists placed great importance on the element mercury, which they also referred to as quicksilver (a potentially good nickname for Menshiki's silver Jaguar).

In understanding the ways Menshiki borrows from the Hermetic tradition, we can start with the God Hermes. Guthrie explains that the name Hermes means "he of the stone-heap"—stone heaps on the side of the road in ancient Greece marking boundaries (between villages, for example) while also functioning as altars to the God of travelers: Hermes.[115] Menshiki quickly becomes linked with a stone heap which he helps *Watashi* to remove, revealing a deep pit—an important boundary between this world and another and the site of *Watashi*'s ultimate rebirth. As the God of travelers, Hermes also performs the role of psychopomp, someone who guides souls into the underworld, a role Menshiki does not perform directly for *Watashi* but, rather, through a number of clues he leaves for him. Menshiki's given name, Wataru, means to cross a body of water, something *Watashi* later has to do during his underground journey; while his left-handedness and confession that he always chooses to go left when given a choice, suggests to *Watashi* which direction to take when he first finds the river he must cross.

Hermes was also the god of commerce and business, though he was not above using trickery to get ahead. Merritt observes that in stories about Hermes we see something of "the self-made man who rises from obscurity, not always by honest means" (a description which also works well for Fitzgerald's Gatsby).[116] Menshiki made his money through some kind of business dealing in information and the internet, though he is deliberately vague on the details, and he continues to trade in stocks and currency as a kind of hobby. He was once charged with insider trading and tax evasion, and while he proclaimed his innocence and was never found guilty, he was held in prison for 435 days. In thinking about Hermes' role in the modern world, James Hillman writes:

> From the perspective of an archetypal psychology, the fascination with exchange between peoples everywhere, the hypercommunication of globalism, the emphasis on trade and finance, the instantaneity offered by electronics, the compulsion to travel—all this indicates the mythical cosmos of Hermes-Mercurius, the fleet-footed god with wings on his feet, cap of invisibility, and winged thoughts. Globalism feels like an overdose of Hermes.[117]

This is partly the world Menshiki represents in *Killing Commendatore*.

Menshiki, modeled as he loosely is on Gatsby, is a continuation of the kind of mysterious male counterparts we have seen in Murakami's fiction from the beginning, but given his symbolic connections to Hermes, Mercury, and Mercurius, we can also finally see this male counterpart for who he truly is—an expression of the main protagonist's own unconscious. The novel makes many nods to *The Great Gatsby*, from Menshiki purchasing his grand home to spy on his (possible) daughter Mariye (the replacement for Daisy in the novel), to the awkward scene where he first meets Mariye face to face, modeled in part on the scene where Nick arranges for Gatsby to "casually" meet Daisy. There are also other subtle twists to details from *The Great Gatsby* such as when *Watashi* is given a tour of Menshiki's house and notices that "All the books seemed to have been used at one time or another. It was clear that this was a practical collection used by a devoted reader, not decorative bookshelves."[118] In *The Great Gatsby* a visitor to Gatsby's house notices exactly the opposite, that none of his books have been opened and thus are entirely decorative, suggesting that Menshiki is being presented as a more intellectual figure than Gatsby. When Menshiki says to *Watashi*, "But you never try to judge me, am I right?" we are also clearly in Nick and Gatsby territory.[119]

Near the end of the novel, *Watashi* shares his opinion that Menshiki uses his secret about Mariye as a way "to maintain some sort of personal equilibrium. It was for him the equivalent of the long balancing pole that tightrope walkers carry."[120] This image of the tightrope walker might remind us of the tightrope walker in Nietzsche's *Thus Spoke Zarathustra*, a symbol of the Superman crossing the tightrope over the abyss of nihilism and the necessity he has of maintaining a personal sense of balance. This in turn should remind us of the many warped Nietzschean Supermen I have identified in Murakami's fiction—from Nagasawa in *Norwegian Wood*, to Gotanda in *Dance Dance Dance*, Wataya Noboru in *The Wind-Up Bird Chronicle* and Fukada in *1Q84*. The secret that Menshiki uses to maintain his personal equilibrium is that Mariye may be his biological daughter, but an even deeper secret seems to be his desire to molest her (like in a fairy-tale, Mariye is magically protected by her dead mother's clothing hanging in a wardrobe in Menshiki's house. We never find out who exactly is threatening her in the scene where she sneaks into Menshiki's house. However, it would seem a reasonable guess that this is a dissociated part of Menshiki himself who appears to want to molest her). The secret buried deep within Menshiki, in other words, is not unrelated to that buried deep within *Watashi*—Menshiki has incestuous feelings toward his daughter, and *Watashi* toward his sister. Part of Menshiki's role is to help *Watashi* uncover and deal with this part of himself, which he helps him achieve by uncovering the pit. As will be discussed later, the pit is presented in the novel as a symbol of a vagina. "Hermes is a god of thieves and cheats," Jung writes, "but also a god of revelation who gave his name to a whole philosophy."[121] Part of Menshiki's role is to reveal something to *Watashi* which lies buried within himself.

Hermes is also commonly associated with the moon, which explains a number of random comments *Watashi* makes on his journey. When Yuzu first talks about leaving him, for example, Watashi makes the comment, "Everyone might go to the moon," a strange contribution to the conversation which she fails to catch and he does not elaborate on.[122] Later, before heading out on his road trip, he gets his car checked out, noting, "For all I knew I might even go all the way to the moon."[123] Later, when he telephones his agent and quits his job as a portrait artist, he comments that he needs this agent to think, "I'd gone to the moon or something."[124] In all of these comments (and others) *Watashi* is saying that he will be leaving our world to enter the world of Hermes, the world of travelers, and ultimately the world of the unconscious.

Many of the same characteristics seen in Hermes show up in Mercury and in the alchemical figure of Mercurius. Jung explains, "Mercurius, following the tradition of Hermes, is many-sided, changeable, and deceitful."[125] He goes on to note that Mercurius is made up of "two natures" or "two substances."[126] This is something *Watashi* comes to recognize about Menshiki, particularly after he paints his portrait. Looking at the painting he comments, "It was as if two different personalities coexisted within him. Yet both versions of Menshiki were missing something. That shared lack unified both the A and B versions of Menshiki."[127]

Menshiki tells *Watashi* that he sees the painting as "a kind of exchange" and his greatest hope is that he can be a catalyst in *Watashi*'s life.[128] This is much like the role played by Mercurius in alchemy. Jung explains, "[T]he philosophical Mercurius, so dear to the alchemists as the transformative substance, is obviously a projection from the unconscious, such as always takes place when the inquiring mind lacks the necessary self-criticism in investigating an unknown quantity."[129] *Watashi*, who lacks the necessary self-criticism to investigate an unknown quantity within himself—his transference—is in need of this kind of transformative substance.

Alchemy speaks of the three manifestations of Mercurius, and *Killing Commendatore* follows this tradition, with *Watashi*'s "unconscious" being revealed to him not only in the figure of Menshiki but also through two other characters, both associated with the color white—the Commendatore (who wears white clothes) and the man who drives the white Subaru Forester. The original inspiration for these characters, I believe, likely came to Murakami in 2008 when he and his wife visited Jung's Bollingen Tower in Switzerland (a retreat Jung built with his own hands and which he described as "a confession of faith in stone"), and particularly when he saw the stone monument on the site which Jung had engraved to explain the meaning of the tower to himself and others.[130] Jung started by engraving one side of this four-sided stone with a verse referring to the alchemist's stone, which is despised by fools and loved by the wise. He then saw what to him looked like an eye on another surface of the stone and within this "eye" he engraved "a tiny homunculus" or little person. He connected this little person with Telesphorus, whom he describes as the "pointer of the way," the destination he is guiding us to being "the land of dreams."[131] Marie-Louise Von Franz explains that Telesphorus accompanies Asklepios, the Greek god of physicians, and that his name means "he who brings completeness as a goal."[132] This little person who strives to heal us and aid our completion can be linked with the Commendatore in Murakami's novel.

In alchemy, homunculi were tiny people supposedly created by alchemists in their experiments. The first example of an homunculi appears in the writings of Paracelsus (1493 or 1494–1541), Jung insisting that such figures were (like Mercurius) projections of the alchemist's own mind. Jung explains:

> Although his homunculi . . . are the grossest superstitions for us so-called moderns, for a man of Paracelsus's time they were nothing of the sort. In those days these figures were living and effective forces. They were projections, of course; but of that, too, Paracelsus seems to have had an inkling, since it is clear from numerous passages in his writing that he was aware that homunculi and suchlike beings were creatures of the imagination. His more primitive cast of mind attributed a reality to these projections, and this reality did far greater justice to their psychological effect than does our rationalistic assumption of the absolute unreality of projected contents.[133]

Like the miniature Greek God Telesphorus, the Commendatore is a "pointer of the way" who guides *Watashi* to his final underground journey. In psychological terms, he could be described as a projection, but Murakami is clearly trying to give him a deeper sense of reality than psychology alone would allow, much like Paracelsus and other alchemists gave their homunculi this same kind of reality many centuries earlier. The Commendatore calls himself an Idea, a term Murakami (or perhaps his wife) may have taken from Karl Karényi's *Hermes: Guide of Souls*, which explicitly talks about the notion of the Greek Gods as "ideas." Karényi spent much time with Jung, but also distanced himself from some of Jung's terminology. What he meant by "ideas" could likely be captured equally well by Jung's concept of archetypes, but he insisted on his own terminology, much like Murakami distances himself from Jung's language.[134] When Jung chiseled Telesphorus into the "eye" of his stone, he also carved the astrological sign of Mercurius onto his coat, suggesting that he saw this little person as one possible representation of Mercurius himself.

On the third side of his stone, Jung engraved a Latin inscription that he describes as "more or less quotations from alchemy." Translated into English, the inscription reads as follows:

> I am an orphan, alone; nevertheless I am found everywhere. I am one, but opposed to myself. I am youth and old man at one and the same time. I have known neither father nor mother, because I have had to be fetched out of the deep like a fish, or fell like a white stone from heaven. In woods and mountains I roam, but I am hidden in the innermost soul of man. I am mortal for everyone, yet I am not touched by the cycle of aeons.[135]

These lines, I believe, were part of Murakami's inspiration for the man who drives the white Subaru Forester, the third manifestation of Mercurius (or the unconscious) in the novel.

We can start with the idea that the figure Jung describes here must be "fetched out of the deep like a fish." When *Watashi* starts to paint the man who drives the white Subaru Forester, he finds it a difficult task, like wrestling a fish from the deep. He explains, "He was like a fish caught in a net. I had been trying to pull him out of the depths, and he was fighting me at every turn. At that point in our tug of war I had set the painting aside."[136] The man wears a hat with the Yonex label, a company that today is most famous for producing rackets, golf clubs, and other sporting goods, but which started out making wooden floats for fishing nets. This motif of fishing up unconscious forces from the deep is one found throughout *Killing Commendatore* and throughout Jung's work.

The word "aeon," which appears on Jung's Bollingen stone, could be translated most simply as "time," but, as Edward Edinger explains, it can also mean something like "a very long period of time, something like an age, or even eternity or forever."[137] In his book *Aion*, Jung writes a lot about one astrological aeon or age in particular, Pisces, which is represented by two fish. Jung saw synchronicity between this astrological sign and the Christian aeon or age, in that Jesus is also often represented as a fish. What the age of Pisces suggests, Jung believed, is that the image of Jesus was too perfect, too one-dimensional, and so he believed that a second fish representing the rise of a new balancing force, the so-called anti-Christ, would inevitably arrive and welcome in a post-Christian aeon where psychic wholeness could be restored (a shift he connected with his own psychological movement; the image of the two fish is also popular in alchemy). What this second fish represents is the shadow, that which has been repressed in a former aeon or age, and the new balance which can result when it is finally fished out of the collective unconscious (ideas which resonate with the notion of cosmic balance found in *1Q84*).

How directly Murakami's ideas about cosmic balance and fishing come from Jung is unclear, but what is clear is that fishing imagery is found throughout *Killing Commendatore*. Not only is there the metaphor of fishing up the man in the white Subaru Forester from the deep, but there is also the scene in which the Commendatore is murdered, which involves the use of a filleting knife that Amada Masahiro had left behind at *Watashi*'s home. This knife then somehow miraculously turns up in his father's rest home at just the right moment. In this way, when *Watashi* finally kills the Commendatore, by using this knife designed for fish, he is also symbolically killing some kind of symbolic fish or shadow (that is also described in the novel as the "evil Father"). Even Menshiki has fishing metaphors associated with him—*Watashi* noting of Menshiki's portrait that "Even if I tried to comprehend something within it, like a slippery, nimble fish the painting would slip out of my hands."[138] At the same time, it is suggested that Menshiki is also on the side of *Watashi* as a fisherman, his white hair reminding *Watashi* of a story about a fisherman in an Edgar Allen Poe story, whose hair turned white overnight when he was caught in a whirlpool. He also serves up beautiful fish dishes on silver platters when *Watashi* dines with him, again suggesting his role in helping *Watashi* to catch and consume fish.

The iconography of Jesus as a fish is perhaps most familiar to us today through the fish bumper stickers some Christians like to place on their cars (particularly in the United States), sometimes with the word "Jesus" written inside the fish. While the man who drives the white Subaru Forester does not have a Jesus bumper sticker on his car, he does have a fish sticker, a Marlin as it turns out, causing *Watashi* to wonder if he works in the fishing industry. Murakami is playing a word game here, though English readers will simply see the fish as a marlin. When written in katakana, however, as the word is written in *Killing Commendatore* (even though it could have been written with hiragana or kanji using the alternative word for marlin, *kajiki*), Merlin and marlin are written the same way, and it is this alternative reference to Merlin, the wizard, which provides another clue to the man's identity. To quote Jung's stone again, the figure described also roams in "woods and mountains," much like Merlin. This is why the man drives a Subaru Forester; it is a reference to Merlin of the forest.

When Jung had finished engraving the first three sides of his stone at Bollingen, he thought about adding a message to the fourth and final side, but in the end, he left it blank. What he had thought of engraving was the phrase "Le cri de Merlin" (The Cry of Merlin), suggesting that "what the stone expressed reminded me of Merlin's life in the forest, after he had vanished from the world. Men still hear his cries, so the legend runs, but they cannot understand or interpret them."[139] Merlin, the story continues, retreated into a forest near the end of his life because of his personal agony over the wars of men (much like the Sheep Man), becoming a recluse whose cries could still be heard by travelers. Jung saw him as a creation of the medieval mind, a kind of complementary figure to the Christian hero Parsifal, a balancing force to the one-sided nature of the Christian mind (Merlin was the child of a virgin and the devil).

For Jung, Merlin was an important figure whom he connected closely to Mercurius. He explains:

> This cry that no one could understand implies that he lives on in unredeemed form. His story is not yet finished, and he still walks abroad. It might be said that the secret of Merlin was carried on by alchemy, primarily in the figure of Mercurius. Then Merlin was taken up again in my psychology of the unconscious and—remains uncomprehended to this day! That is because most people find it quite beyond them to live on close terms with the unconscious. Again and again I have had to learn how hard this is for people.[140]

If the legend of Merlin was taken up first by alchemy and later by Jung's depth psychology, then *Killing Commendatore* is a novel which takes him up again in the form of the man who drives the white Subaru Forester (the third manifestation of Mercurius in the novel), seeking in the process a balancing force in *Watashi*'s life that might also be seen as a voice of conscience crying from the forest. In this last role, the man who drives the white Subaru Forester also has connections with another mysterious figure (or figures) who appears in Nabokov's *Lolita*.

In *Lolita*, when Humbert finally has the twelve-year-old Lolita to himself, drugged and lying on a hotel bed, rather than getting straight to it, he first leaves the room and walks around the hotel, eventually ending up outside of the hotel's lobby where he meets a man. Here a strange conversation ensues. "Where the devil did you get her?" the man asks:

> "I beg your pardon?"
> "I said: the weather is getting better."
> "Seems so."
> "Who's the lassie?"
> "My daughter."
> "You lie—she's not."
> "I beg your pardon?"
> "I said: July was not. Where's her mother?"
> "Dead."
> "I see. Sorry. By the way, why don't you two lunch with me tomorrow."[141]

Many readers at this point of Nabokov's novel will suspect that Humbert is having a conversation with himself. He is a dissociated figure, and here he is talking with his last remaining voice of conscience in the final moments before he will return to his hotel room and defile the sleeping Lolita—the crossing of the line from thought to action from which he will not be able to return. The man in the white Subaru Forester carries out a similar role in *Killing Commendatore*, providing a similar voice of conscience, even when he never speaks to *Watashi*.

Watashi first sees the man who drives the white Subaru Forester on his trip to northern Japan. Driving in Miyagi prefecture, close to the border of Iwate (areas that will later be devastated in the 3.11 disaster), *Watashi* stops off at a family restaurant where he is approached by a young woman. She appears to be trying to avoid a man who is later identified as the man who drives the white Subaru Forester. That night *Watashi* sleeps with the woman in a love hotel, a masochistic encounter in which the girl asks to be strangled. *Watashi* tries to meet her demands, but he cannot really commit to his role; his reluctance, he later admits, is based on his fear that if he had really started, he would not have been able to stop. The next morning, he returns to the family restaurant for breakfast and the man who drives the white Subaru Forester is there again. Though they exchange no words, *Watashi* feels his sense of judgment: "I know exactly where you've been and what you've been up to, he seemed to be telling me."[142]

This scene, connected as it is with Miyagi Prefecture and its associations with 3.11, should remind us of *Colorless* and its similar message of the potential we all have to be perpetrators as well as victims of violence. The man in the white Subaru Forester is a witness here (much like the mysterious man in *Lolita*) to the darker side of *Watashi*'s nature, a side of human nature Murakami worries many Japanese bury in the face of disasters to assert their role as victims. Later when *Watashi* is with Amada Masahiro on his way to see Masahiro's father, the artist Amada Tomohiro, he again sees the white Subaru Forester in a parking lot, though this time he does not see the man. This is an unsettling experience—a feeling like he is being followed. In *Lolita*, Humbert has similar experiences as he and Lolita travel across America together. He comes to believe that he is being followed, first by someone driving a red convertible, but later he even wonders if this person is deliberately changing cars, and he begins to see him everywhere. Eventually, in a moment of clarity, he acknowledges, "it was becoming abundantly clear that all those identical detectives in prismatically changing cars were figments of my persecution mania, recurrent images based on coincidence and chance resemblance."[143] In short, this imaginary person following him is a sign of his guilty conscience desperately trying to catch up with him. The man who drives the white Subaru Forester fulfills a similar role at times.

In terms of color symbolism, I have already mentioned that the three manifestations of Mercurius in the novel are all connected by white, but later red emerges as an important color connected with white in several climatic scenes. White is the color of a blank canvas from which different colors can be called forth (*Watashi* calls this "Canvas Zen," the "pure white canvas" which is more than "a simple blank space.").[144] Menshiki's name actually means "avoiding colors" (which seems to be one step on from Tsukuru Tazaki who was simply colorless), but as *Watashi* starts to paint his portrait, he finds that a number of colors are actually necessary to express what lies within him. He seems to represent what alchemists call "the one white colour that contains all colors."[145] Though Menshiki's white hair and mansion are often emphasized (the white mansion, in turn, lit up by mercury lamps at night), he also has a black beard, and when *Watashi* first starts painting him, he starts with black and white. Soon, though, he begins to feel the need for more color, intuitively sensing that "color was going to be a vital grounding for the work."[146] The color that comes to him next is green, the mix he creates reminding him of "leaves dully dyed by rain."[147] *Watashi* is excited by his discovery of color and feels as if the colors themselves are calling out to him to be painted. Next, he mixes together an orange paint, "Not just a simple orange, but a flaming orange, a color that had both a strong vitality and also a premonition of decay. Like a fruit slowly rotting away."[148] This image of rotting fruit is an indication of what alchemists call the putrefaction stage—the stage *Watashi* is in, which has followed his citrinitas or yellowing; he is on the cusp of a new psychological discovery. When this process is finished, *Watashi* looks at his painting of Menshiki and notes that there are five colors there already, though he has only mentioned four to us in the text: white, black, green, and orange. What is the missing fifth color he has failed to mention? Could it be red?

The next day *Watashi* decides that what is still missing from his painting is some representation of Menshiki's white hair, and when he adds this to the painting, he feels like it is done (no painting in the novel is ever described as complete or finished). When Menshiki next shows up at *Watashi*'s house he is wearing a red sweater, which *Watashi* notes "went very well with his white hair."[149] Together, they go out to see the pit, and *Watashi* notices the subtle changing of the seasons: "Some trees were redder, others dyed a deeper yellow, and some stayed forever green."[150] The emergence of red and its pairing with white is an important color combination in alchemy, suggesting that *Watashi* is approaching a critical stage. As already mentioned in my discussion of *Colorless*, in alchemy this was often represented symbolically by the sexual union or chemical marriage of the Red King and White Queen and together with their child, known as the Philosopher's Child, came to represent everything achieved through the alchemical process.

The man who drives the white Subaru Forester is also associated with other colors significant to alchemy. Later, recalling the scene where he had seen the man again at the family restaurant following his encounter with the woman, *Watashi* recalls the man's breakfast, including the "Ketchup (red) and mustard (yellow) containers" beside him.[151] *Watashi*'s memory of these condiments might seem a minor detail, but the fact that their colors have been added in brackets attracts our attention (do we really need to be told that the ketchup container was red and the mustard one yellow?). The man in the white Subaru Forester is clearly there to lead *Watashi* from yellow (citrinitas) to red (rubedo). Later, *Watashi* has a dream in which he becomes the man in the white Subaru Forester and trails his wife Yuzu in their red Peugeot (again white and red are coming together). He follows her to a hotel room which he enters and then he begins to strangle her from behind with the white belt from a bathrobe (a reenactment of his experience with the girl he met at the family restaurant). This suggests the delicate nature of the psychological stage *Watashi* is at and the necessity for not rushing things. There is a danger that if white and red are brought together too quickly, the result will be violence and destruction rather than the birth of the Philosopher's Child.

White and red are also central colors in the scene where *Watashi* kills the Commendatore. Similar to Johnnie Walker in *Kafka on the Shore* and the religious guru in *1Q84*, this is a murder willed by its victim, the Commendatore explaining, "My friends must slay me" and that "Ideas must undergo countless deaths."[152] What *Watashi* will be killing, the Commendatore explains, is the "evil father," a figure it is suggested *Watashi* has already met in the form of the man in the white Subaru Forester.[153] As *Watashi* recreates the scene from the painting and plunges the filleting knife deep into the Commendatore, the white garments of the Commendatore are dyed crimson.[154]

Again white and red have come together in a dramatic moment which then leads *Watashi* into an underground world where he must face his final challenge.

What *Watashi* seems to experience in this underground world is the resolution of his transference. There he discovers a world of metaphor (or in other words, a world of therapeutic possibilities) where what one finds depends on what one is looking for. Eventually, what *Watashi* finds is a cave which reminds him of a cave he entered with Komichi years earlier. As they had ventured deeper into this cave, his sister had disappeared down a narrow opening and he had worried that she would never return, but eventually she had, later describing the place she had found as like a small room just for her.[155] This small room might remind us of a womb, which is important, because what *Watashi* seems to be experiencing in his metaphorical underground world is a rebirth. As the cave he enters at the end of his journey gets narrower, he eventually has to start crawling and even wriggling through it, forcing him to face his deepest fear: claustrophobia. The narrowing passageway feels like it is alive and moving and he also fears that it might be flooded by water at any moment. Finally, at the end of his ordeal, he drops from a hole, "[l]ike a newborn baby pushed out in midair," mysteriously ending up in the pit near his house.[156]

Earlier in the novel, *Watashi* had drawn a painting of this pit, which upon completion he recognized looked much like a woman's genitals. This painting often sits alongside his painting of Mariye, but for a long time he resists the idea that they are connected. He does, however, recognize the way his painting of the pit might look to others. Looking at the painting, he offers this observation:

> I shook my head and smiled a wry smile. I mean, how Freudian can you get? I imagined some egghead critic fulminating on the drawing's psychological implications: "This black, gaping hole, so reminiscent of a woman's solitary genitalia, must be understood functionally, as a symbolic representation of the artist's memories and unconscious desires." Or something of the sort. Seriously![157]

Here *Watashi* is seeking to preclude Freudian interpretations of the pit (much as Humbert likes to introduce and reject Freudian interpretations of his actions in *Lolita*). The connection between the two paintings, however, does start to become clear over time. With the two paintings sitting next to each other, *Watashi* begins to wonder, "Could these two paintings be connected in some way?"[158] When his friend Amada Masahiko later sees them, he recognizes that "they're somehow linked."[159] The transition to the climax of the novel begins with *Watashi* again looking at the two paintings and feeling some connection between them. Looking at the painting he calls *The Pit in the Woods*, he states, "I could feel that painting calling out to me too, though in another way, and from a different direction, than A Portrait of Mariye Akikawa."[160] It is this call of the pit "from a different direction" which explains how *Watashi* will be able to resolve his transference.

Though *Watashi* has been reluctant to admit it, for most of the novel the pit has been subliminally connected in his mind with a vagina and with his painting of Mariye, who reminds him of his dead sister. At the end of the novel, *Watashi* approaches this pit "from a different direction," not entering the pit (a symbol of sexual intercourse) but struggling through a narrow passageway to exit through it (a symbol of rebirth). After this ordeal he returns to Yuzu and they have a child (who may or may not be his biological child; like Menshiki, he chooses not to find out). Yuzu, in other words, recognizes that he is now ready to be a father and that she can trust him in the raising of their daughter. *Watashi*'s transference, it would seem, has been resolved.

Mariye, I would argue, might be seen as the fourth character in the novel who is symbolically representing *Watashi*'s unconscious (i.e., she is connected with the three manifestations of Mercurius already discussed). Progression in alchemy is often discussed in terms of the "axiom of Maria" (Maria Prophetissa, also known as Mary the Jewess, was an important figure in early alchemy—could Mariye's name be a nod to her?), which as Jung describes "runs in various forms through the whole of alchemy like a leitmotiv."[161] This process of transformation, Jung argues, unfolds as follows:

> It begins with the four separate elements . . . and ascends by degrees to the three manifestations of Mercurius in the inorganic, organic, and spiritual worlds; . . . it culminates in the one and indivisible (incorruptible, ethereal, eternal) nature of the *anima*, the *quinta essentia* [a mysterious fifth element beyond earth, air, fire, and water], *aqua permanens* [the divine water], tincture [a herbal medicine produced by alchemical processes], or *lapis philosophorum* [the philosopher's stone]. This progression from the number 4 to 3 to 2 to 1 is the "axiom of Maria."[162]

A quote such as this perhaps raises more questions than it answers. In the three manifestations of Mercurius I have described—Menshiki, the Commendatore, and the man who drives the white Subaru Forester—which of them, for example, individually represents the organic, inorganic, and spiritual worlds?[163] However, in considering the progression from the three manifestations of Mercurius to the one and indivisible nature of the anima (the so-called Philosopher's Stone), there does seem to be a broad connection with *Killing Commendatore*. *Watashi* first interacts with each of his three representations of the unconscious, but in the end his journey is about somehow protecting Mariye (the logic of which is never fully explained in the novel—on the surface, her escape from Menshiki's home feels unconnected to his underground journey). Saving her, however, is clearly his reward for passing his underground test. This suggests that the dissociated part of Menshiki threatening Mariye in the house is somehow connected to *Watashi*'s own unconscious. By resolving his transference, he simultaneously protects her, allowing the "axiom of Maria" to find its resolution.

For some readers, this final appeal to the axiom of Maria as a means for understanding Mariye's significance in the novel may feel a step too far. Is Mariye really supposed to be a symbol of the Philosopher's Stone? Murakami has perhaps put one of his most obvious clues for this symbolism not in the story itself, but in the design of the chapter headings. In the Japanese version of the book, each chapter number is set within a design which includes a square, a triangle, and a circle. Aoki Kenji wonders if these are intended as objects of meditation, a kind of mandala formation.[164] This is true in a sense, but I believe they are more specifically a play on the image used to represent the Philosopher's Stone, an image which became popular from the seventeenth century onward. This symbol is made up of the same basic shapes: a circle within a square, within a triangle, within a circle. The symbol in Murakami's book is missing one of these circles and the triangle is turned upside down; also, the three shapes connect and overlap in a slightly looser way than the symbol of the Philosopher's Stone. While Murakami was not very forthcoming when I asked him directly about the influence of alchemy on this novel, he eventually admitted that alchemy might be a loose metaphor working in the background, though he also claimed not to know much about what alchemy even is.[165] The design of the book, I would suggest, is one more piece of evidence demonstrating that the novel is explicitly playing with alchemical motifs.

The successful outcome of an alchemical journey often leads to the birth of the Philosopher's Child. In *Killing Commendatore*, the birth of Yuzu (and possibly) *Watashi*'s child, Muro, is suggestive of this outcome. While the biological possibility of *Watashi* being Muro's father rests on supernatural foundations in the novel, this is not dissimilar to what one sees in alchemy. Jung explains that the coniunctio when it occurs, the mysterious spiritual and sexual union which brings the royal brother and sister together, is often described by the alchemists as a "higher copulation" that produces the "soul's child" through a "psychic pregnancy."[166] These are strange ideas, but no stranger than the idea that *Watashi* has somehow made Yuzu pregnant through a dream. In the end, *Watashi* has no better words to describe Muro's birth than as "a form of grace."[167] The alchemists appealed to a similar sentiment in their work. Jung writes, "If the work succeeds, it often works like a miracle, and one can understand what it was that prompted the alchemists to insert a heartfelt Deo concedente [God willing] in their recipes, or to allow that only if God wrought a miracle could their procedure be brought to a successful conclusion."[168]

Like his paintings, nothing in *Watashi*'s life is complete at the end of *Killing Commendatore*. Each of the portraits he has done—for Menshiki, Mariye, and the man who drives the white Subaru—has merely stopped at a certain point which felt right at the time. In the case of the man who drives the white Subaru Forester, he even feels he will need to return to painting him at some point from a new angle, a work he believes might become his own Killing Commendatore (referring to the painting done by Amada Tomohiko).

In this way, resolving his transference is just a part of *Watashi*'s journey. Jung writes, "Whenever this drive for wholeness appears, it begins by disguising itself under the symbolism of incest, for unless he seeks it in himself, a man's nearest feminine counterpart is to be found in his mother, sister, or daughter."[169] Resolving this transference has clearly been vital for *Watashi*; he needed to stop projecting his dead sister onto the women in his life. The wholeness he seeks, however, is still a future, and perhaps an ultimately impossible goal. "None of us are ever finished," he observes to Mariye. "Everyone is always a work in progress."[170] This is like the point Jung makes in his essay on the topic of transference, which uses images from alchemy as its main points of reference: "These images are naturally only anticipations of a wholeness which is, in principle, always just beyond our reach."[171]

If wholeness is "always just beyond our reach," then what is the point of individuation? The answer Jungian psychoanalysis provides is that wholeness is less a goal we should expect to achieve than an impossible ideal that still offers significant rewards as we strive toward it. As Jung puts it in a popular quotation, "Until you make the unconscious conscious, it will direct your life and you will call it fate."[172] In the case of *Watashi*, what this means is that he has freed himself from one possible fate, even if there are still other fates awaiting him, other things from his unconscious that he will need to make conscious. And that is why fans of Murakami needn't worry that Murakami's therapeutic fiction will ever stop because he is "finished" (i.e., cured, individuated, saved). It is much more likely that old age or death will end his writing career before "wholeness" ever will. Murakami's final therapeutic thread—the search for individuation—may thus never find perfect resolution, even if *Killing Commendatore* has taken this journey further than any other of his previous works.

Finally, I would like to briefly consider the way *Killing Commendatore* also touches on another important therapeutic theme: the need for forgiveness. This is an aspect of the novel Murakami made clear in a post-publication interview, and it would seem connected with his own ongoing need to forgive his father (connected to therapeutic thread two). Thinking about the final underground journey in the novel and its possible meanings, for example, Murakami suggests the following:

> I believe that there is no restoration without going through the most profound darkness. Accepting someone who has returned is forgiveness. Forgiveness is an emotion that emerges for the first time only after one goes through a very dark place and comes out on the other side.... The sense of forgiveness is beyond distinctions like "goodness," "evil," "light" or "darkness." To obtain it, it is necessary to kill the "concept" of the Commendatore with his own hands. Only by doing so does one get "forgiveness," I feel.[173]

Killing Commendatore feels like a very personal novel to Murakami. When *Watashi* first learns about Yuzu's secret and is driving distressed around Tokyo, his journey at one point takes him from Waseda to Nerima—much like Murakami's own journey in 1968 took him from his dormitory near Waseda University to a small apartment in Nerima—a time in his life when he was going through a very difficult time with a woman (possibly K). What Murakami may be doing in such details is briefly revisiting an earlier traumatic period from his own life before the novel heads off into Northern Japan and the traumas which are awaiting *Watashi* (and Japan) there. When *Watashi* finally makes it out of Tokyo, he reaches the significantly named Murakami City where he rings his agent and tells him he will no longer be painting portraits for others. As the novel emphasizes numerous times, *Watashi* has decided that he needs to start doing paintings for himself. This might equally be taken as Murakami's intention in writing *Killing Commendatore*.[174]

Just like the Commendatore says that an idea must be killed numerous times, Murakami's fiction has killed off numerous "ideas," numerous "evil fathers," since at least *A Wild Sheep Chase*. What this earlier novel revealed is the way the death of an "evil father" (in that novel the sheep and what it represents) is at the same time an opportunity to heal the "good father" (the damaged Sheep Professor), demonstrating that true healing is not just an individual but also an intergenerational experience. How this manifests in *Killing Commendatore* is that the act of killing the Commendatore works not just as a gateway for *Watashi* to enter an underground world and save Mariye, but also as an opportunity to save Amada Tomohiro in the final moments before his death. As the Commendatore puts it, "Only my friends can grant him salvation before he breathes his last."[175]

Shimizu Yoshinori picks up on this aspect of the novel, writing that "nine years after his father's death, it is clear that in this novel Murakami was able to bring his long-standing conflict with the 'father' to some kind of conclusion."[176] Following his father's death in 2008, Murakami began researching more about his life, the fruit of which appeared in an essay he published in June of 2019 for the magazine Bungei Shunjū (a piece of writing referenced numerous times in this book's Introduction). Murakami explains in the essay that it took him several years to begin this research in earnest, even after his father died, primarily because he believed his father had been involved in the Nanking massacre in China. To his relief, this turned out not to be the case, and this revelation seems to have lifted a burden from him which allowed him to look at his father's military involvement in more detail. The fruit of this research clearly shows up in *Killing Commendatore*, such as in the backstory of Amada Tomohiko's brother, Tsuguhiko, who is forced to behead a Chinese soldier. What Murakami was doing through his research, in one sense, was uncovering a pit in his own life which had been covered for some time, much like *Watashi* and Menshiki do in the story.

One interesting place Murakami's research took him was into an exploration of the haiku his father wrote. Some of these poems were written during the war, a time when censorship was rampant. In his Bungei Shunjū essay, Murakami suggests the need his father must have had at the time to express his true feelings in a "symbolic and ciphered way."[177] This might remind us of the "camouflaged expression" employed by Amada Tomohiko in his painting, a kind of "metaphorical confession" of the thing he had not been able to do for himself during his time in Vienna.[178]

When *Watashi* kills the Commendatore, he does so in the presence of the dying Amada Tomohiko, and through his reenactment of a scene which Amada had planned but failed to execute, a failure he had then metaphorically confessed through his painting (his failed plan to assassinate a high-ranking Nazi official during the war), he helps to bring about a symbolic resolution of Amada's trauma just moments before his death. This is similar to what I examined in *The Wind-Up Bird Chronicle*, where the therapeutic actions of one generation were able to symbolically bring about what Pierre Janet calls "the pleasure of completed action" for another. At one point, *Watashi* describes Amada Tomohiko's painting, Killing Commendatore, as a requiem: "A work to bring peace to the spirits of the dead and heal their wounds."[179] It is *Watashi*'s job to finally bring this vision to completion, much like Murakami's writing career might be read as his attempt to bring the prayers of his Buddhist father to some kind of completion.

While *Killing Commendatore* is clearly based in part on Mozart's Opera *Don Giovanni*, and particularly its opening scene where Don Giovanni kills the Commendatore (Murakami has said that he started his novel with the title, which he liked the sound of and thought would make a good story), another influence he always knew he was going to use was Ueda Akinari's "Nise no Enishi" (Fate Over Two Generations).[180] Thinking about the death of Murakami's own father, this might at first seem a strange choice, given that it is a story about a Buddhist priest who is buried alive in the Buddhist practice of *zenjo* in an attempt to achieve enlightenment, but who reemerges later in a hideous and comical form which actually turns many people away from Buddhism. Akinari, as *Killing Commendatore* informs us, had a cynical attitude toward Buddhism, which is captured well in "Fate Over Two Generations," but given that Murakami's father was a (part-time) Buddhist priest himself and that this novel might be read in part as a reflection on what his father's life and death had meant to him, what could be his intention behind this cultural reference? Is Murakami expressing his own cynical take on his father's Buddhist beliefs and the way the buried "father" often returns in comical form?

This aspect of the story perhaps makes more sense when one understands a particular connection Murakami's father shares with Akinari, a connection Murakami revealed in a post-publication interview. He explains that when his father died, the priest performing the service told him that Akinari was buried in the same temple grounds, and so Murakami asked if he could see the grave. He learned that the crab which had been engraved on Akinari's tombstone was his own wish, a final cynical statement to the world suggesting that he had only ever been able to walk sideways through life. Significantly, Murakami also explains how "The temple apparently took care of Akinari to some extent in his later years."[181] Despite Akinari's cynical attitude toward Buddhism then, at the end of his life he relied on the kindness of a Buddhist temple to take care of him, and this same temple was now taking care of Murakami's father's last rites. Murakami's anecdote perhaps suggests the ways in which compromises can often be found as one approaches death, even between parties that have not seen eye to eye in life (much as Murakami and his father were able to reconcile to some degree on his father's deathbed).

So how might this theme of forgiveness connect with the main therapeutic theme I have examined in the story: the resolution of *Watashi*'s transference? Arguably, the biggest consequence in Murakami's personal life for his intergenerational trauma and his falling out with his father was his decision not to have children. This is mirrored in Murakami's fiction, I have suggested, by characters who are disconnected from family, unable to commit to others and thus reluctant to have children themselves. Gradually, however, protagonists in Murakami's fiction have been working themselves toward earned attachment, which, in turn, has enabled them to connect to other people and to eventually consider the possibility of children. This first became evident in *1Q84*, where a child was on the horizon at the end of the novel, and is finally realized in *Killing Commendatore* when Muro is born.

What is perhaps most interesting about these children in Murakami's fiction is that their biological relationship to the male protagonist in the story is always uncertain or not important.[182] In the end, the male protagonist accepts the child as theirs regardless of biology, not because of it. This theme possibly has something to do with Murakami's own life and therapeutic journey. To summarize, Murakami's generational trauma was arguably an important part of his decision not to have children, but as he has worked to heal this generational trauma through his writing, the desire to be a parent has gradually emerged in his fiction (and also in his life). While the timing of his own healing journey meant that by the time he might have been ready to have biological children with his wife it was too late, symbolically, through his fiction, and apparently in his real life too, he has become more comfortable with the idea of taking on a "parenting" role. When I was speaking to Murakami in 2005, he put this sentiment to me as follows:

> I don't have any children myself, but if I had had a child, he or she would probably be in their 20s now. I'm feeling a kind of responsibility to them, to my younger readers. In the old days I thought I needed to write my books, and if I write good books, that's my responsibility. That's all. But these days, even if I write good books, that's not enough.... I have to be responsible to other things. That is a change.[183]

In the same interview Murakami spoke to me of his experiences talking with the children of his friends and the ways they sometimes talk with him more freely than they can with their own parents, and the feeling he has that in the process they become "a kind of virtual family." He also spoke to me of the young assistants who work in his Tokyo office whom he saw as "about the age my kids would be" and whom he interacted with "as a kind of family." Even in his personal life, then, it appears that Murakami has become increasingly interested in the idea of nonbiological families.

Murakami has described his own father's "natural faith," and at the end of *Killing Commendatore*, it appears that *Watashi* finds something similar.[184] Despite possible doubts about the biological identity of his daughter Muro, *Watashi* affirms, "I am endowed with the capacity to believe" (much like Menshiki is able to believe in his connection to Mariye without scientific evidence). He goes on, "I believe in all honesty that something will appear to guide me through the darkest and narrowest tunnel, or across the most desolate plain."[185] *Watashi*'s journey through this darkest of tunnels has prepared him to be a father, both through resolving his transference and also, it would seem, by helping him to heal a member of Japan's wartime generation, Amada Tomohiko. Putting biological relationships aside, symbolic healing between "fathers" and "sons" is what allows these "sons," in turn, to become successful "fathers"—intergenerational trauma has been transformed into intergenerational healing. The birth of Muro at the end of *Killing Commendatore* is thus a significant moment in Murakami's fiction, a sign that one of his protagonists, after crawling through the dark and symbolically being reborn, is now healed to such a degree that he is ready to take on the role of parent.

Conclusion

Self-Therapy and Salvation

This book opened with a retelling of Murakami's well-rehearsed baseball epiphany anecdote—the story of how he became a writer—and his later realization that in hindsight this was all about a search for self-therapy. In thinking about the biographical causes of this epiphany, I offered two: his falling out with his parents (particularly his father) and the loss of his former girlfriend, K. These losses, I argued, continue to show up in Murakami's fiction in subtle (and sometimes not so subtle) ways, but the fiction itself has also transcended these proximate causes to think about the question of therapy at a deeper and more universal level. Though these personal traumas cast a heavy shadow over the first decade and more of Murakami's career, in more recent years it is equally the traumas of his country—the Kobe earthquake and Aum attack of 1995, and the triple disaster of 2011—that he is responding to, though it would be wrong to say these earlier traumas have simply been left behind. As Murakami has said, there are some psychic wounds that remain with people until the end of their lives, a truth he would seem to know from first-hand experience.

What I have observed in Murakami's fiction is a development similar to what Peter Homans identified in the early development of psychoanalysis—a move from melancholia into mourning, followed by a desire for individuation, and finally the creation of new meaning. I have offered two historical precedents for this therapeutic project: Jung and Nietzsche. Like these figures, Murakami's fiction increasingly shows him opening himself up to the question of opposites—light and shadow, male and female, good and evil—and testing what might lie beyond them. Like Jung and Nietzsche, his search for self-therapy is about a search for wholeness and balance that would finally eliminate the dichotomies that organize and order the human experience—a kind of alchemical experience that would turn the lead of trauma into the gold of psychological insight.

Throughout this book I have focused on four therapeutic threads I see woven through Murakami's fiction. The first thread—the journey from melancholia to mourning—began in the Rat trilogy and found its resolution in *Dance Dance Dance*. Facing personal losses they could not fully process consciously, Murakami's protagonists (or at least some part of them) found themselves locked within melancholic walls, desperately searching for a way out, but also strangely connected to their inner towns, places of memory and loss. When a Murakami protagonist finally breaches this wall, it is because of their desire to connect with another human being waiting for them on the other side.

The second therapeutic thread—the healing of intergenerational trauma—first emerged in *A Wild Sheep Chase*, but found its most dynamic expression in *The Wind-Up Bird Chronicle*, before remerging again in *Killing Commendatore*. The way this trauma is healed is by symbolic acts which take up the unfinished business of an earlier generation and bring about the pleasure of completed action. Releasing stored-up psychic energy is therapeutic both for the protagonist and for the member of the older generation they are connected with. Whether or not the need to write such scenes has been completely exhausted in Murakami's fiction remains to be seen, but *The Wind-Up Bird Chronicle* will likely remain the most powerful example of this therapeutic thread.

The third therapeutic thread—the journey from avoidance to earned attachment—is found in most of Murakami's novels, which are filled with detached characters who struggle to commit to others. In *1Q84*, however, we finally saw two characters—Aomame and Tengo—who through the power of love were able to commit to each other and to their unborn child. This continued in *Killing Commendatore* where the narrator was able to return to his estranged wife and help to raise their daughter. Murakami may have found an answer to this therapeutic thread, in part through the novels of Dostoevsky, but he would replace the love of God with the love of another human being, an expression of his own humanistic convictions.

Finally, the fourth therapeutic thread—the drive for individuation as a response to nihilism—runs throughout Murakami's fiction, while finding its most complex and complete expression in *Killing Commendatore*. Murakami's fiction has often juxtaposed a more Jungian-inspired protagonist against a more Nietzschean-inspired counterpart, and the relationship between these two types has evolved over time. In *Killing Commendatore*, what we saw was the way the Gatsby-like Menshiki, a figure borrowing from Mercurius and the hermetic tradition, expressed the deep unconscious desires of the main protagonist himself and was there to assist in his transformation—the resolution of his transference and the significant advancement, if not completion, of his individuation.

So to this point, how therapeutic has Murakami's literary project been? Now in his early seventies, Murakami continues to write, and so it is difficult to draw a final conclusion. *Boku*, the narrator of Murakami's first novel, was not even sure that writing was a method of self-therapy. At best, he believed, it was "the slightest attempt at a move in the direction of self-therapy." "And yet," he continued, "if everything goes well, sometime way ahead, years, maybe decades from now, I might discover myself saved."[1] Over four decades have passed since Murakami wrote these lines, and the same question that might be asked of *Boku* can be asked of him: Decades later, has he found salvation or not?

Though Murakami is wary of the ways people sometimes misconstrue the notion of writing as self-therapy, ultimately, he cannot deny the therapeutic role that writing has played in his life. He recognizes that he is a different person at the end of writing a novel than he was at the beginning.[2] He explains:

> Writing novels has saved me. Everybody has times when their heart goes hard. To be able to open your heart by yourself is a type of self-therapy. Given the heavy

focus these days on *iyashi* (healing) it's not really something I want to admit, but in the end that's what it is. For that reason, writing novels is something very important for me. At the same time I'm creating a work, I change. I'm creating a better version of myself.[3]

So what does salvation mean for Murakami? Is it simply a never-ending process of creating a better version of himself? When I asked Murakami about the aforementioned quote from *Hear the Wind Sing*, which mentions this hope for salvation, and whether this is a hope he shares himself, he simply smiled and replied, "I was too young to write that."[4] Pushed to elaborate, though, he acknowledged that, in fact, he does believe in a qualified form of salvation through writing. He explains:

[W]hen I was young, I wanted something very brilliant, very meaningful, and I was kind of optimistic. . . . I'm still optimistic, but I don't want to be saved. To me, right now, to write something itself is a kind of salvation. . . . As a storyteller I believe in the unpredictable, outstanding turn. . . . That is what I'm expecting. You could say it's hope. It's just a new turn, new direction, new perspective, new feeling, new light, new sound, new wind. . . . It is just like Mozart. Sometimes Mozart changes the scale when you don't expect it . . . your mind is opened and you can see a new perspective. . . . It saves you sometimes.[5]

As Raymond Chandler put it in *The Long Goodbye*, "[T]he only salvation of a writer is to write."[6] It is what Murakami admires in Chandler himself and in F. Scott Fitzgerald and Raymond Carver, writers who had self-destructive tendencies but who continued to write right up to the end of their lives. Part of what salvation means for Murakami is simply not giving up. It is the same philosophy he applies to his running, not comparing himself to others, but simply finishing the race to the best of his ability. The words he would like engraved on his tombstone, he has said, are these: "At the very least, he never walked right up to the end."[7]

But salvation for Murakami is about more than just endurance, more than just not giving up until the finish line. As he mentions previously, what also keeps him going are the new winds that continue to blow into his life. Wind is an important motif in Murakami's fiction that points to both the pains and joys which life can bring. He took the title of his debut novel, *Hear the Wind Sing*, from a short story from Truman Capote, intending it to be much darker than it is usually taken to be.[8] Reading the novel itself, the darkness of some of this wind imagery is clear. First, there is the third girl *Boku* slept with, who hanged herself during spring vacation and who "had been swinging in the wind for two whole weeks" before her body was found.[9] Then there is Derek Hartfield's story of a young boy who enters a well left by Martians and gets lost for one and a half billion years in an underground labyrinth, only to reemerge 250,000 years before the sun is due to explode. This fact is revealed to the boy by the wind, which also tells him it is only a voice in his own head. When the wind asks the boy what he has learned from his experience, he takes a revolver from his pocket and shoots himself in the head.[10]

Yet *Hear the Wind Sing* also includes passages that offer more positive associations with wind. The girl with the missing finger laments the misfortunes of her life, telling

Boku, "It's like I'm caught in an ill wind." "Winds change direction," is *Boku*'s reassuring response.[11] Even more significantly, Rat recalls a time hiking in Nara when he came across an old burial mound. Sitting down and thinking about questions of life and death he experienced an epiphany:

> So I was sitting there looking at the burial mound and listening to the breeze coming across the water. And I felt this emotion I can't put into words. No, emotion isn't right. It's more like an awareness of being enveloped by something. It's as if the cicadas and frogs and spiders and wind and everything else were one single entity flowing through the cosmos.[12]

So what does it mean to hear the wind sing (or to hear the song of the wind as the title of Murakami's debut novel might also have been translated)? Sometimes it means remembering the terrible things that have blown through one's life, the wind blowing the body of a former girlfriend hanging from a tree for two weeks. Sometimes it means hearing a voice in your head telling you that life has no purpose at all. But at other times hearing the wind sing means holding out hope for some new direction in your life, or sitting in nature and hearing, not a nihilistic message of despair, but the hint of some cosmic order enveloping you. In short, in Murakami's fiction to hear the wind sing means many different and often contradictory things.

The advice to hear the wind continues to emerge in Murakami's fiction. In *Kafka on the Shore* it is Ōshima who presents this message to Kafka. He explains, "Say the wind blows. It can be a strong, violent wind or a gentle breeze. But eventually every kind of wind dies out and disappears. Wind doesn't have form. It's just a movement of air. You should listen carefully, and then you'll understand the metaphor."[13] It is also advice found in *Killing Commendatore* as the narrator is crawling through his dark tunnel in the underworld, believing he may soon die. In his moment of greatest despair, he hears the voice of his dead sister, telling him to "listen to the wind."[14] It is a philosophy that acknowledges that your life may be as short and fleeting as a wind that is here one moment and gone the next, but that insists there is still value in listening to the song of your life. In one sense, it is just a modern reworking of the very Japanese sentiment of *mono no aware*, the pathos of things, an appreciation of the beauty which is still to be found in life's transience.

Ultimately, though, what it means to "hear the wind sing" in Murakami's fiction is to listen to your unconscious and to embark on a journey of self-discovery. In one sense, the destination is irrelevant; the journey itself is the reward. Like the alchemists of old, the promised gold may never come, but the real reward may be the experience of transformation itself. The first step in this process is getting yourself unstuck from the traumas of your past. In Murakami's fiction, this is about breaking through melancholia, facing the pain of loss and working through intergenerational trauma to find reconciliation with the father. The reward of these personal victories is a desire for greater interpersonal connections. Avoidance gives way to earned attachment.

Getting unstuck from the past, however, is only part of the journey. While working through dissociation is an important part of the therapeutic process, what this unleashes is a secondary, more creative encounter with the unconscious known as individuation.

Salvation in the Jungian sense is about more than just dealing with the traumas of the past, with what Freud described as the turning of "hysterical misery into common unhappiness."[15] Instead, it is about making more of the unconscious conscious in one's life and consequently living more fully. And even more than this, Jung would come to connect the discovery of the Self, the reward of individuation, with the discovery of the God within, with an archetype that was so awesome that it could only be described as holy. Jung would often emphasize that his knowledge of this inner God was based on personal experience and that he could not say anything about the metaphysical reality of God either way, though he clearly believed that his experience with the God archetype brought its own kind of salvation. In a letter to a friend, he once wrote, "The main interest of my work is not concerned with the treatment of neurosis but rather with the approach to the numinous . . . which is the real therapy."[16]

Does Murakami's fiction share this sentiment? While Murakami's approach to the numinous is much more tentative than Jung's, there are moments in his work that seem to point to something beyond. The distant voice calling Aomame as she is about to pull the trigger and blow her brains out in *1Q84*, and the moment of grace Lieutenant Mamiya experiences as he sees the sun passing over the Mongolian well where he has been left to die in *The Wind-Up Bird Chronicle*, are two such moments, and other examples can be found in his short stories.[17] In the end, though, I would argue that the promise of salvation Murakami offers in his fiction has important differences from Jung's.

Jung was the son of a Christian minister, and even though he would eventually leave the faith and chart his own course, the historical weight of Christianity was never far from his thoughts. In developing his ideas on individuation, he would often turn to some of the more heretical and esoteric strands of the Western tradition for inspiration, including Gnosticism and alchemy, seeking to replace the outer authority of the church and God with an inner authority grounded in first-hand experience of the unconscious. Murakami was the son of a part-time Buddhist priest and the grandson of a full-time Buddhist priest, but like Jung before him, he would leave the faith of his father to chart his own course. Like Jung, he would also turn to the unconscious as a source of inner wisdom that could tell him where to go. Unlike Jung, however, leaving Buddhism behind does not appear to have been a traumatic experience for Murakami. This may say more about the place of religion and the nature of secularization in Jung's Europe and Murakami's Japan than it does about anything else, but this has important consequences for the kinds of salvation both figures appear to be seeking. While Jung was clearly responding to Christianity and its promise of salvation in his therapeutic thought, Murakami seems to feel less pressure to offer anything as grand. Instead, what I would argue Murakami's fiction ultimately offers is a kind of secular Buddhist version of salvation, with some qualifications.

Murakami's fiction, it should be noted, does at times offer something like Jung's vision of a God within as an antidote to the power of a God without.[18] For the most part, however, what his protagonists seem to find when they make the journey to the "other side" is a world in which selves and memories ultimately go to die, in the end leaving nothing behind but mindless bliss. While his protagonists eventually leave this world behind at the end of each novel (with the notable exception of *Hard-boiled Wonderland and the*

End of the World), their journey still points to a kind of negative salvation awaiting them in the end. The town that *Boku* leaves in *Hear the Wind Sing* continues to be revisited in many forms in Murakami's fiction, but each reimagination seems more transparent and lifeless than the one before until we get to the cat town of *1Q84*. What all this seems to be preparing us for is an ultimate oblivion which awaits the ego and its attachments.

This might perhaps sound like a secular vision of Buddhism, but where Murakami resists Buddhist sensibilities is in his appeal to our "this-worldly" attachments as something valuable that should be held on to for as long as humanly possible. Rather than overcoming suffering through breaking through the illusion of the self and our attachments to others, Murakami's fiction advocates that we hold on to our personal memories as an important fuel for our lives. *Monogatari*, stories which arise from our second basements, are one of the ways we try to hold on to and protect these memories (even if we transform them into something else in the process) and they are thus one of the great compensations life has to offer. This view of the *monogatari* is probably the closest thing to a vision of salvation Murakami's fiction offers.

But what about salvation in this world? What about politics? While our memories might be a valuable source of fuel for our lives and their gentle fading our preparation for our final oblivion, is there not still work which needs to be done in this world to make it a better place, if not for ourselves, then at least for those who will follow us? This is the question of political commitment that critics often bring to Murakami's fiction, and it is a question I have largely ignored in this book, choosing, instead, to see the detachment to commitment framework so prominent in Murakami studies in relation to Murakami's own comment on the topic (the idea that commitment, in the end, is all about personal relationships between people). And yet it is also clear that for some critics, Murakami's therapeutic fiction is a problem, something that is symptomatic of our times, and which needs to be called out so that a more politically minded literature can take its place. The Marxist critic Frederic Jameson speaks for many when he warns of the many "blind zones" available in modern life "in which the individual subject seeks refuge, in pursuit of a purely individual, a merely psychological project of salvation."[19] For some critics, this is exactly what Murakami's therapeutic fiction appears to be.

While Murakami's fiction may not be the best place to go to find new models for collective political action, his search for self-therapy is not without a political dimension. As we have seen throughout this book, one reward of individuation is an ability to see the System more clearly for what it is and the strength this gives one to stand up against the warped Nietzschean Supermen who try to harness it for their own purposes. In this way, while the search for self-therapy may not itself be a political act, it may be a necessary precursor to politics for some people. Murakami's growing willingness in recent years to make political statements on the world stage may be one manifestation of this unfolding process.[20]

And what about us as readers? Do we find self-therapy through reading Murakami's fiction? Murakami believes that we do, at least to some degree. He explains,

> [T]here are cases in which the writer is cured by writing a novel, but there is also a need to simultaneously heal the reader. Unless you do this, the work is not effective

as a novel. Of course, this means curing some part of the reader to a greater or lesser degree—it isn't a magic wand, and it isn't effective for everyone everywhere.

But even if it's only partially effective, when it works well, it sends feedback to the writer. And that, in turn, encourages and heals the writer. A lot of writers refer to this as a "response." Without this, it's difficult for a writer to continue writing in the long term.[21]

Undoubtedly, the desire for self-therapy is part of what attracts at least some readers to Murakami's fiction some of the time, and undoubtedly, there are times when at least some of us do, in fact, find therapeutic benefits from reading his stories, *monogatari* which have arisen out of his own personal traumas but also out of his second basement. Others, however, may be more skeptical. For when you get right down to it, surely reading is not a method of self-therapy. At the very best, it's just the slightest attempt at a move in the direction of self-therapy. And yet, we find ourselves thinking, years, maybe decades from now, perhaps we might discover ourselves saved. And so we buy another book and turn another page, all the while waiting to see what the answer will be.

Notes

Introduction

1 Murakami (trans. Goossen), *Wind/Pinball*, loc. 107. While the baseball epiphany story I have summarized here is a well-rehearsed anecdote Murakami has shared on many occasions, there is one interview where he revealed an earlier false start as a novelist. Speaking with Gregory, Miyawaki, and McCaffery in *The Review of Contemporary Fiction*, Murakami explained:

> And about that time, when I was 19 or 20 years old, I wanted kind of a hip, cool kind of novel—my heroes were Richard Brautigan and Kurt Vonnegut. For me they seemed to be great—they were hip and cool in ways that seemed different from anything I could find in Japan. I decided that I wanted to be one of those hip, cool writers, and so that's when I decided I wanted to be a writer. But by the time I was 22 or 23, I gave up trying to write. I couldn't do it—I had no experience. And so I just walked away for a while.

Later in the interview, Murakami describes a night years later working at his jazz bar when he saw some African American soldiers crying because they missed their home so much. He realized in that moment that however much he loved American culture, it would never mean as much to him as it did to them. He adds, "That was really why I began to write." While Murakami had surrounded himself with American music and literature, partly in rebellion to his father and "other Japanese orthodoxies," he seems to have sensed in this moment his status as an outsider to American culture. So his decision to write can in part be seen as that very Japanese impulse to make something foreign one's own—to create fiction inspired by the American novels he loved, but something which could also represent his experience. His sudden flash of inspiration at the baseball game may, thus, have been more about timing than anything. It was not that he had never thought about writing before. It was more that this was the moment he finally knew he could do it. The long quote cited earlier was cut from the final version of the interview that appears in *The Review of Contemporary Fiction*, but appears in a Prezi presentation posted online (T L, "An Interview with Haruki Murakami") that compares the raw transcript of the interview with what was later published. The other quotations mentioned earlier can be found in the version of the interview that appears in *The Review of Contemporary Fiction*.

2 Murakami, "Noruwei no mori no himitsu," 179.
3 Buruma, "Becoming Japanese," 62. When I asked Murakami in an interview in 2005 why he did not think revelation is a very Japanese concept, he explained that the concept of *satori* is more common in Japan—the kind of revelation or enlightenment which comes after sustained effort. A revelation or *keiji*, on the other hand, requires no such effort and comes to its recipient without any special preparation. It is this

latter conception of revelation which he believes is less common in Japan. I have interviewed Murakami twice, once on November 22, 2005, and once on November 23, 2019. I distinguish the two interviews in the references which follow by calling them the 2005 interview and the 2019 interview. Minor changes from the transcripts to these interviews have been made throughout this book in the interests of readability.

4 Murakami (trans. Goossen), *Wind/Pinball*, loc. 111.
5 Murakami and Kawai, "Thoughts on Individualism and Commitment," 78. Self-therapy here is a translation of *jiko chiryō* (Kawai and Murakami, *Murakami Haruki, Kawai Hayao ni ai ni iku*, 79). This conversation has since been translated by Christopher Stephens, and I use Stephens' translation elsewhere in this book. In this case, however, I have gone with an earlier partial translation which appeared in *Japan Echo*, simply because it uses my preferred term, self-therapy. Stephens translates *jiko chiryō* as self-healing, Murakami (trans. Stephens), *Haruki Murakami Goes to Meet Kawai Hayao*, 61.
6 Freud, "Creative Writers and Day-Dreaming," 153.
7 See Murakami, "Neko o suteru."
8 Freud, "Creative Writers and Day-Dreaming," 153.
9 Treisman, "Haruki Murakami on Parallel Realities."
10 Rubin, *Haruki Murakami and the Music of Words*, 15.
11 Strecher, "Magic Realism," 267.
12 Roquet, *Ambient Media*, 154. Nakamata sees Murakami's *iyashi-kei* style emerging first and foremost in his protagonists, who, like a skilled bartender, bring healing to others around them through their well-honed listening skills (Nakamata, *Bungaku*, 32). He also sees many pairings in Murakami's fiction of characters who heal and characters who are healed (p. 125). One interesting suggestion Nakamata makes is that Murakami's fiction took a dramatic turn after the disasters of 1995 (The Kobe earthquake and the Aum attack), not because Murakami was overcome by the scale of these events, but because he was shocked by his own nonresponse to them. Nakamata suggests that this sense of detachment, or what he calls Murakami's *rijinshō* or depersonalization, is what motivated Murakami to seek more healing in his post-1995 fiction (p. 127).
13 Roquet, *Ambient Media*, 154.
14 Rubin, *Haruki Murakami and the Music of Words*, 65.
15 Alt, *Pure Invention*, 310.
16 See, for example, Wallin, *Attachment in Psychotherapy*.
17 Roquet, *Ambient Media*, 155, 177.
18 Treat, *The Rise and Fall of Modern Japanese Literature*, loc. 666.
19 Treat, *The Rise and Fall of Modern Japanese Literature*, loc. 664.
20 Cassegård, *Shock and Naturalization*, ix.
21 Cassegård, *Shock and Naturalization*, 167.
22 Cassegård, *Shock and Naturalization*, 167.
23 Cassegård, *Shock and Naturalization*, 167.
24 Murakami's paternal grandfather died a tragic death when he was hit by a train during a typhoon. This event, Hirano suggests, is utilized in Murakami's short story "Where I'm Likely to Find it" and less directly in *Pinball, 1973* in the story of a well-digger who gets drunk and dies when he is hit by a train (Hirano, *Murakami Haruki: hito to bungaku*, 16). For a long time, Murakami had suspected that his grandfather was drunk when he died, but research years later revealed this was likely not the case,

and that, instead, it was probably the typhoon, combined with his grandfather's poor hearing, which contributed to the tragic accident (Murakami, "Neko o suteru," 256).

25 Murakami Ryū once asked Murakami if Kobe was the setting of his debut novel, to which Murakami replied, Kobe and Ashiya. Haruki noted, however, that it is also partly fictional. He grew up speaking Kansai-ben, the dialect of the region, but the characters of the novel do not. There is also no mention of specific place names, etc. Haruki notes that some readers have told him the setting does not feel like Japan at all (Murakami and Murakami, *Wōku donto ran*, 9).
26 Murakami, "Murakami Haruki rongu intabyū," 36.
27 Murakami, "Murakami Haruki rongu intabyū," 37.
28 Murakami and Murakami, *Wōku donto ran*, 69.
29 Murakami and Murakami, *Wōku donto ran*, 69.
30 Sukegawa, *Nazo no Murakami Haruki*, 193–4. Sukegawa does not explicitly use the term "survivor's guilt," but this is the dynamic he describes.
31 Murakami, "Neko o suteru," 248.
32 Murakami, "Neko o suteru," 248.
33 Murakami, "Neko o suteru," 248.
34 Harding, "Haruki Murakami by John Wesley Harding." In the "Neko o suteru" essay quoted earlier, Murakami says that his father only ever spoke to him once about the war, but in this interview (and others) he says that his father told him many stories about the war.
35 Murakami, "Neko o suteru," 252–4.
36 Murakami, "Neko o suteru," 253–4.
37 Schwab, *Haunting Legacies*, 49.
38 Murakami, *Yume o miru*, 162–3.
39 Buruma, "Becoming Japanese," 71.
40 Hirano quotes Murakami from an interview in 1983, saying that he does not have the confidence to have children given the state of the world, while suggesting that he is still thinking about whether he should have children or not (Hirano, *Murakami Haruki: hito to bungaku*, 145–6). Even earlier, in his conversation with Murakami Ryū held in 1980, Murakami says that he and his wife are thinking of starting a family shortly (Murakami and Murakami, *Wōku donto ran*, 108). The motif of pregnancy and children develops slowly in Murakami's fiction. It is not until *1Q84* that we see a couple getting pregnant and celebrating the future arrival of a child.
41 Buruma, "Becoming Japanese," 71. When I interviewed Murakami in 2005, he had some misgivings about his *New Yorker* interview with Buruma, stating that he felt Buruma had modified some of the things he said to make it easier to understand for American readers. Perhaps this is true, but it is also possible that Murakami had said more in the interview than he had intended to. Jay Rubin explains how *The New Yorker* is "sacred territory" to Murakami, and so the site of publication may have also increased his sensitivity to the way he was portrayed (Rubin, *Murakami Haruki to watashi*, loc. 1159).
42 Sukegawa, *Nazo no Murakami Haruki*, 191. Based on information from one of Chiaki's former students, Sukegawa reports that Murakami's father was a popular and interesting teacher who, while he would sometimes forget details, would often go off on entertaining tangents during lessons. Like his son, it would seem he was something of a natural born storyteller. He was particularly skilled at teaching the Japanese language.
43 Murakami, "Neko o suteru," 247.

44 Hirano, *Murakami Haruki: hito to bungaku*, 18. Rubin, *Haruki Murakami and the Music of Words*, 25.
45 Murakami acknowledges his own stubbornness in Murakami and Ozawa (trans. Rubin), *Absolutely on Music*, xi–xii. Murakami's "stubborn individualism" is also pointed out by Rubin (Rubin, *Haruki Murakami and the Music of Words*, 15). As a high school student, Murakami refused to go to school for a time, as a protest against the school's haircut policy. He also used his position on the school newspaper to protest the idea of school uniforms. Murakami appears to have an anti-authoritarian streak that emerged particularly during his high school years and continued during his time at university and beyond.
46 Murakami, "Neko o suteru," 256.
47 Murakami, "Neko o suteru," 255.
48 Murakami, "Neko o suteru," 256.
49 Rubin, *Haruki Murakami and the Music of Words*, 25–6.
50 In my 2019 interview with Murakami, I asked him directly about his relationship with his mother over the same period, but he didn't want to make a comment because she was still alive (even though he noted that she was suffering in a way consistent with dementia).
51 Murakami, "Neko o suteru," 264.
52 Nishida, "Murakami Chiaki to Haruki," 30.
53 Buruma, "Becoming Japanese," 65–6.
54 Murakami, "Always on the Side of the Egg."
55 Personal interview with Murakami in 2005.
56 Rubin, *Haruki Murakami and the Music of Words*, 15–16.
57 Murakami admits that his embrace of Western culture and literature was, in part, a rebellion against his father. Gregory, Miyawaki, and McCaffery, "It Don't Mean a Thing," 113.
58 Wray, "Haruki Murakami: The Art of Fiction," 133–4.
59 Murakami, *Yume o miru*, 173, 276.
60 Murakami, *Yume o miru*, 38–9.
61 Rubin, *Haruki Murakami and the Music of Words*, 152–3.
62 Buruma, "Becoming Japanese," 66–7.
63 Rubin, *Haruki Murakami and the Music of Words*, 67. Murakami told me in 2005 that he borrowed the name Naoko from a former young waitress at his jazz bar.
64 Urazumi, *Murakami Haruki o aruku*, 187. Urazumi Akira is the pen name of Doi Yutaka, who has subsequently published under his real name a number of books about Murakami.
65 Treisman, "The Underground Worlds of Haruki Murakami."
66 Personal interview with Murakami in 2019.
67 Zielenziger, *Shutting Out the Sun*, 85.
68 Hirano informs us that Murakami stayed in room 427 in the West Dormitory. In *Norwegian Wood*, Watanabe, the main protagonist, lives in the three-storied East Dormitory, a building that was not yet built when Murakami was there. Hirano, *Murakami Haruki: hito to bungaku*, 19.
69 Murakami stayed in the dormitory for one semester (about six months) before being asked to leave. In *Norwegian Wood* the main protagonist stays in his dormitory for two years.
70 Murakami and Mizumaru, *Murakami Asahidō*, 46.

71 Nakamura and Dōzen, *Sanpo de kanjiru Murakami Haruki*, 22-4. Tokyo kurenaidan, "1973 nen pinbōru o aruku."
72 Murakami, *Murakami Asahidō*, 213-14.
73 Murakami, *Murakami Asahidō: Sumerujakofu tai Oda Nobunagakashindan* (CD-ROM, email at 1:16 pm, 99.2.1).
74 Personal interview with Murakami in 2005.
75 The clearest acknowledgment Murakami has made about these private motivations for writing is found in his book *Henkyō, Kinkyō* (Frontiers Far and Near), a travelogue which follows his journeys to a number of locations around the world, but which finishes with a trip he made to his hometown two years after the 1995 Kobe Earthquake. He notes that he has not been back to this hometown for many years, admitting that there were some "personal reasons" for his absence. Generalizing, he suggests, "Some people are constantly being pulled back to their hometown, while others feel like they can never go back. In most cases it's as if fate separates the two groups, and it has little to do with how strong your feelings are towards the place. Like it or not, I seem to belong to the second group." He also describes his visit to his old high school and the strange silence he experienced there, as well as his visit to a pizza restaurant he used to frequent with a past girlfriend. While he never explicitly acknowledges the losses he is revisiting in this final chapter of his travelogue, it is not hard to see the memories which are resurfacing during his trip—his falling out with his parents causing him to lose his sense of home, and the loss of K—leaving his hometown feeling haunted (Murakami (trans. Gabriel), "A Walk to Kobe").
76 Murakami, *Yume o miru*, 108.
77 Personal interview with Murakami in 2005. Another place Murakami has written about his lack of any personal religious beliefs is in his book *Uten Enten* (Come Rain or Shine), a travelogue which includes his trip to a number of monasteries in Greece. Recording his experience entering and staying in these monasteries and talking with people allows Murakami several opportunities in the book to talk about his own religious beliefs. He states many times that he is not religious at all and tends toward skepticism, though he is deeply moved by many things he encounters on his journey. Out of convenience, on several occasions during the trip, he describes himself to people as a Buddhist, but he is ashamed to admit that he does not really know much about Buddhism. See Murakami, *Uten Enten*, locs. 229, 500, 578, 843, and 1076.
78 Murakami, "Tamashii no ichiban fukai tokoro," 106.
79 As Murakami put it to Roland Kelts, "Actually, the word 'global' is something I can't really understand, because we do not necessarily need to be global. We are already what I call 'mutual.' If we use the connection of our world called story, I think that that's enough to keep us connected" (Kelts, "Haruki Murakami: Nomadic Spirit").
80 Murakami, "Murakami Haruki rongu intabyū," 16. A similar description is found in Murakami, *Yume o miru*, 156-7. The quotations which follow in the main text are translated from the first reference.
81 Murakami, "Murakami Haruki rongu intabyū," 16.
82 Strecher, *The Forbidden Worlds of Haruki Murakami*, loc. 557.
83 Kawai, T, *Murakami Haruki no monogatari*, 13-19.
84 Jung, *Memories, Dreams, Reflections*, 184. The animal imagery here is interesting. In Murakami's fiction, animals also often represent a connection with the deep unconscious, or what we are calling the second basement.
85 Murakami, "Tamashii no ichiban fukai tokoro," 103-4.

86　Murakami, "Tamashii no ichiban fukai tokoro," 104.
87　Personal interview with Murakami in 2005.
88　Murakami and Murakami, *Wōku donto ran*, 98.
89　Miller, "Haruki Murakami."
90　Wray, "Haruki Murakami: The Art of Fiction," 23; Murakami, *Yume o miru*, 207.
91　Thompson, "Nobel Prize Winner in Waiting?" Murakami was also more than happy to acknowledge his interest in Campbell's work when I asked him about it in 2005. He replied, "I love his books. I've read his books and I was impressed. And I agree with his opinion, with the monomyth."
92　Murakami, "Umibe no Kafuka ni tsuite," 56.
93　Murakami, *Yume o miru*, 93, 158.
94　Murakami, *Yume o miru*, 496.
95　Strecher, *The Forbidden Worlds of Haruki Murakami*, locs. 239–41.
96　See, for example, Strecher, "Magic Realism" and *Dances with Sheep*.
97　Kawai Toshio, the son of Kawai Hayao, makes the claim that during its peak, "Jung's psychology [was] better accepted in Japanese society and the academy than in any other country" (Kawai T, "Jung in Japanese Academy," 18). Endō Shūsaku's well-documented interest in Jungian psychology from the 1980s is a good example of this influence in the literary sphere.
98　Žižek, *The Ticklish Subject*, 346.
99　Strecher, *Dances with Sheep*, 109.
100　Nihei, *Haruki Murakami*, 24.
101　Pennebaker, *The Secret Life of Pronouns*, loc. 19.
102　Pennebaker, *The Secret Life of Pronouns*, locs. 35–7.
103　Pennebaker, *The Secret Life of Pronouns*, loc. 19.
104　One place where Murakami is probably following this more traditional model of therapeutic writing is in his essay "Neko o suteru," which is his attempt to come to terms with the life and death of his father.
105　Murakami and Kawai, *Murakami Haruki, Kawai Hayao ni ai ni iku*, 79–80.
106　Murakami and Kawai, *Murakami Haruki, Kawai Hayao ni ai ni iku*, 79.
107　Murakami and Kawai, *Murakami Haruki, Kawai Hayao ni ai ni iku*, 81.
108　Jung, *Collected Works* Vol. 9, Part 1, para. 101.
109　Wray, "Haruki Murakami: The Art of Fiction," 127; Murakami, *Yume o miru*, 130.
110　See, for example, Murakami, *Yume o miru*, 37; Kawakami and Murakami, *Mimizuku wa tasogare ni tobitatsu*, locs. 153–80; and Wray, "Haruki Murakami: The Art of Fiction," 150.
111　Kawakami, and Murakami *Mimizuku wa tasogare ni tobitatsu*, loc. 174.
112　Murakami, *Yume o miru*, 290.
113　Murakami, *Yume o miru*, 503.
114　Murakami, "Murakami Haruki rongu intabyū," 18.
115　Murakami, "Murakami Haruki rongu intabyū," 18.
116　Quoted in Nihei, *Murakami Haruki*, 14.
117　Miyoshi, *Off Center*, 234.
118　Kawakami and Murakami, *Mimizuku wa tasogare ni tobitatsu*, loc. 1486.
119　Murakami, *Yume o miru*, 525.
120　Kawakami and Murakami, *Mimizuku wa tasogare ni tobitatsu*, loc. 1363.
121　The closest thing to a biography on Murakami in Japanese is Hirano, *Murakami Haruki: hito to bungaku*. In English, the best source of biographical information on Murakami is Rubin, *Haruki Murakami and the Music of Words*.

122 I am thinking particularly here of Murakami's "Neko o suteru" essay, which goes into some detail about his relationship with his late father.
123 Jung, *Collected Works* Vol. 7, para. 266.
124 Homans, *The Ability to Mourn*, 9.
125 In his preface to *The Will to Power*, for example, Nietzsche writes about "a gospel of the future" to respond to nihilism, or what he calls "The Will to Power: Attempt at a Revaluation of All Values" (Nietzsche, *The Will to Power*, 3).
126 Nietzsche, *Thus Spoke Zarathustra*, 14.

Chapter 1

1 Kawamoto, "Monogatari no tame no bōken," 39.
2 Kawamoto, "Monogatari no tame no bōken," 38. (Trans. Rubin, *Haruki Murakami and the Music of Words*, 32).
3 Rubin, *Haruki Murakami and the Music of Words*, 42. What Rubin translates here as self-therapy is 自己療養 (jikoryōyō) in Japanese. Alfred Birnbaum, who first translated *Hear the Wind Sing* into English for the Kodansha English Library Series, translated the same phrase as self-help. Ted Goossen, who has most recently translated the novel, opts for self-healing. I have stuck with Rubin's translation here because of his use of my preferred translation: self-therapy.
4 Murakami (trans. Goossen), *Wind/Pinball*, 17.
5 Murakami (trans. Goossen), *Wind/Pinball*, 19.
6 Murakami (trans. Goossen), *Wind/Pinball*, 20.
7 Murakami (trans. Goossen), *Wind/Pinball*, 3.
8 Murakami (trans. Goossen), *Wind/Pinball*, 3.
9 Murakami (trans. Goossen), *Wind/Pinball*, 4.
10 Murakami (trans. Goossen), *Wind/Pinball*, 4.
11 Murakami (trans. Goossen), *Wind/Pinball*, 4.
12 Murakami (trans. Goossen), *Wind/Pinball*, 48.
13 Kojima, *Murakami Haruki to chinkon no shigaku*, 8.
14 Muramoto, "Monogatari no hajimari," 2.
15 Muramoto, "Monogatari no hajimari," 3–4.
16 Rubin, *Haruki Murakami and the Music of Words*, 39.
17 Jung, *Collected Works* Vol. 7, para. 274.
18 Quoted in Whitmont, *The Symbolic Quest*, 64.
19 Wehr, *Jung and Feminism*, 54.
20 Murakami (trans. Goossen), *Wind/Pinball*, 12.
21 Murakami (trans. Goossen), *Wind/Pinball*, 13.
22 Murakami (trans. Goossen), *Wind/Pinball*, 12.
23 Rubin, *Haruki Murakami and the Music of Words*, 33.
24 Jung, *Collected Works*, Vol. 9, Part 2, para. 14.
25 Murakami, *Underground*, 198–9.
26 Jung, *Collected Works*, Vol 7, para. 309.
27 Jung, *Collected Works*, Vol 9, Part 2, para. 42.
28 Kawakami and Murakami, *Mimizuku wa tasogare ni tobitatsu*, loc. 324.
29 Wehr, *Jung and Feminism*, 66.
30 Murakami (trans. Goossen), *Wind/Pinball*, 24.

31 Murakami (trans. Goossen), *Wind/Pinball*, 25.
32 As Ishihara Chiaki and others have noted, this may not be such a strange coincidence, given the fact that *Boku* dropped her off near her workplace earlier in the novel. Whether consciously or unconsciously, he seems to have wanted to reconnect with her. (Ishihara, *Nazotoki Murakami Haruki*, 32.)
33 Murakami (trans. Goossen), *Wind/Pinball*, 71.
34 Murakami (trans. Goossen), *Wind/Pinball*, 71.
35 Murakami (trans. Goossen), *Wind/Pinball*, 71.
36 Murakami (trans. Goossen), *Wind/Pinball*, 96.
37 Murakami (trans. Goossen), *Wind/Pinball*, 56–7.
38 Murakami (trans. Goossen), *Wind/Pinball*, 73.
39 Murakami (trans. Goossen), *Wind/Pinball*, 77.
40 Murakami (trans. Goossen), *Wind/Pinball*, 77.
41 Fittsujerarudo, *Gurēto Gyatsubii*, 298–9.
42 McInerney, "Roll Over Basho."
43 Chandorā, *Rongu guddobai*, 547.
44 Chandorā, *Rongu guddobai*, 548.
45 Murakami, *The Elephant Vanishes*, loc. 3683.
46 Chandorā, *Rongu guddobai*, 551.
47 Fittsujerarudo, *Mai rosuto shitii*, 17, 19.
48 Fittsujerarudo, *Mai rosuto shitii*, 17.
49 Fittsujerarudo, *Mai rosuto shitii* 13–14.
50 Fittsujerarudo, *Mai rosuto shitii*, 20.
51 Murakami and Kawai, "Thoughts on Individualism and Commitment," 79.
52 Murakami (trans. Goossen), *Wind/Pinball*, 3.
53 Murakami (trans. Goossen), *Wind/Pinball*, 3.
54 Fitzgerald, *The Great Gatsby*, 7.
55 Fitzgerald, *The Great Gatsby*, 8–9.
56 Fitzgerald, *The Crack-Up*, 58.
57 Murakami (trans. Goossen), *Wind/Pinball*, 42.
58 Quoted in Miyawaki, "A Writer for Myself," 270.
59 Fitzgerald, *The Crack-Up*, 58.
60 Fitzgerald, *The Crack-Up*, 59.
61 Fitzgerald, *The Crack-Up*, 59.
62 *Boku* says it has been fifteen years since he began "fearfully scanning the world around me with a measuring stick." He also says he spent eight years struggling with despair about the scope of his writing (Murakami [trans. Goossen], *Wind/Pinball*, 3–5).
63 Fitzgerald, *The Crack-Up*, 63.
64 Murakami (trans. Goossen), *Wind/Pinball*, 7.
65 Murakami (trans. Goossen), *Wind/Pinball*, 76. The original passage is from Matthew 5:13 in The New Testament.
66 Fitzgerald, *The Crack-Up*, 63.
67 Fittsujerarudo, *Aru sakka no yūkoku*, 275.
68 Murakami and Shibata, *Honyakuyawa*, 209.
69 Murakami, *Yume o miru*, 149.
70 Murakami, "Fittsujerarudo no miryoku," 5.
71 Miyawaki, "A Writer for Myself," 271.
72 Miyawaki, "A Writer for Myself," 271.

73 Wray, "Haruki Murakami: The Art of Fiction," 140.
74 Murakami, "Kakite no itami ga mietekita."
75 Murakami (trans. Goossen), *Wind/Pinball*, 4.
76 The likely inspiration here was Kurt Vonnegut, who included the made-up writer Kilgore Trout in many of his stories. Vonnegut got the idea from a friend who told him, "You know, the problem with science-fiction? It's much more fun to hear someone tell the story of the book than to read the story itself" (Allen, "Kurt Vonnegut on Jailbird."). Vonnegut agreed, and started using Trout to summarize stories in his own books that he would never have to write. Many critics easily saw the influence of Vonnegut and Richard Brautigan on Murakami's early fiction, and Murakami is very open about the influence. Vonnegut's *Breakfast of Champions*, in particular, is visually very similar to *Hear the Wind Sing* with its hand-written drawings breaking up the text (the pictures of the t-shirts in both novels, in particular, bear a strong resemblance). Brautigan's novel, *An Abortion: An Historical Romance 1966* with its strange library and librarian, its beautiful but awkward woman who later becomes a sex worker, its descriptions of breasts, and its central theme of an abortion, also has many similarities with Murakami's early fiction.
77 Chandorā, *Rongu guddobai*, 548.
78 Chandorā, *Rongu guddobai*, 549.
79 Chandler, *The Long Goodbye*, loc. 2612.
80 Chandorā, *Rongu guddobai*, 549.
81 Chandorā, *Rongu guddobai*, 550.
82 Chandler, *The Long Goodbye*, loc. 125.
83 Chandler, *The Long Goodbye*, loc. 1015.
84 Chandorā, *Rongu guddobai*, 552–3.
85 Trott, *War Noir*, 8.
86 Trott, *War Noir*, 62.
87 Quoted in Trott, *War Noir*, 173.
88 Trott, *War Noir*, 28. It should be emphasized that Trott sees this as a failed attempt, noting that at the end of the novel Marlowe ends up more disillusioned than ever.
89 Murakami (trans. Birnbaum), *A Wild Sheep Chase*, 97.
90 Chandler, *The Long Goodbye*, loc. 236.
91 Murakami, *Yume o miru*, 55–6.
92 Freud, "Mourning and Melancholia," 242.
93 Freud, "Mourning and Melancholia," 243.
94 Freud, "Mourning and Melancholia," 244.
95 Freud, "Mourning and Melancholia," 244.
96 Freud, "Mourning and Melancholia," 244.
97 Freud, "Mourning and Melancholia," 244.
98 Murakami (trans. Goossen), *Wind/Pinball*, 119.
99 Murakami (trans. Goossen), *Wind/Pinball*, 109.
100 Murakami (trans. Goossen), *Wind/Pinball*, 144.
101 Murakami (trans. Goossen), *Wind/Pinball*, 145.
102 Murakami (trans. Goossen), *Wind/Pinball*, 146–7.
103 Murakami (trans. Goossen), *Wind/Pinball*, 176.
104 Murakami (trans. Goossen), *Wind/Pinball*, 176–7.
105 Murakami (trans. Goossen), *Wind/Pinball*, 112.
106 Murakami (trans. Goossen), *Wind/Pinball*, 131.
107 Murakami (trans. Goossen), *Wind/Pinball*, 141.

108 Murakami (trans. Goossen), *Wind/Pinball*, 192.
109 Murakami (trans. Goossen), *Wind/Pinball*, 120.
110 Freud, "Mourning and Melancholia," 245.
111 Moglen, *Mourning Modernity*, 3.
112 Moglen, *Mourning Modernity*, 38.
113 Quoted in Hirano, *Murakami Haruki: hito to bungaku*, 29.
114 Murakami and Murakami, *Wōku donto ran*, 25–6.
115 Murakami (trans. Goossen), *Wind/Pinball*, loc. 159.
116 Shimizu, *Murakami Haruki wa kuse ni naru*, loc. 1064.
117 Shimizu, *Murakami Haruki wa kuse ni naru*, locs. 1098–1100.
118 Murakami (trans. Goossen), *Wind/Pinball*, 182.
119 Murakami (trans. Goossen), *Wind/Pinball*, 61.
120 Strecher, *The Forbidden Worlds*, locs. 1450–8.
121 Murakami (trans. Goossen), *Wind/Pinball*, 187.
122 Murakami (trans. Goossen), *Wind/Pinball*, 189.
123 Murakami (trans. Goossen), *Wind/Pinball*, 189.
124 Murakami (trans. Goossen), *Wind/Pinball*, 220.
125 Rubin, *Haruki Murakami and the Music of Words*, 17. While I agree with the general sentiment here, I disagree with the post-post-war label. The argument I am making about Murakami's inherited trauma marks him as a deeply postwar writer. The shadow of the war is still a vital part of his fiction.
126 Katō, *Murakami Haruki ierōpēji*, 15, 19.
127 Murakami (trans. Goossen), *Wind/Pinball*, 63.
128 Quite literally opened, as it turns out. When the twins are cleaning his ears one day, he accidently sneezes and goes almost completely deaf. A female doctor is able to remedy this situation for him later with a syringe, revealing to him that the twins probably couldn't see the ear wax blocking his passage because his ears are unnaturally curved. In *A Wild Sheep Chase*, it is a woman with magical ears that will spur him along in his therapeutic quest.
129 Murakami and Kawai. "Thoughts on Individualism and Commitment," 79.
130 This is reflected in the reluctance Murakami showed, for a long time, to having his first two novels made widely available to English readers.
131 Rubin, *Haruki Murakami and the Music of Words*, 80–2.
132 Rubin, *Haruki Murakami and the Music of Words*, 90.
133 Rubin, *Haruki Murakami and the Music of Words*, 91.
134 Campbell, *The Hero with a Thousand Faces*, 30.
135 Books such as Christopher Vogler's *The Writer's Journey: Mythic Structure for Writers* (2007) (which grew out of a shorter memo that had become popular with film studios) strongly suggest the influence Campbell's work has on Hollywood. Of course, Campbell does not claim to be inventing anything new here, but simply outlining a pattern that already exists and that can be found in mythologies around the world. Whether one accepts his thesis or not, it is not hard to see how influential his packaging of these ideas has been.
136 Ōtsuka, *Monogatariron de yomu Murakami Haruki to Miyazaki Hayao*, 58–9.
137 Rubin, *Haruki Murakami and the Music of Words*, 81.
138 Campbell, *The Hero with a Thousand Faces*, 58–9.
139 Murakami (trans. Birnbaum), *A Wild Sheep Chase*, 42.
140 Campbell, *The Hero with a Thousand Faces*, 69.
141 Campbell, *The Hero with a Thousand Faces*, 71.

142 Murakami (trans. Birnbaum), *A Wild Sheep Chase*, 43.
143 Murakami (trans. Birnbaum), *A Wild Sheep Chase*, 47.
144 Murakami (trans. Birnbaum), *A Wild Sheep Chase*, 167.
145 Murakami (trans. Birnbaum), *A Wild Sheep Chase*, 25.
146 Murakami (trans. Birnbaum), *A Wild Sheep Chase*, 100.
147 Murakami (trans. Birnbaum), *A Wild Sheep Chase*, 101.
148 Murakami (trans. Birnbaum), *A Wild Sheep Chase*, 57–8.
149 Murakami (trans. Birnbaum), *A Wild Sheep Chase*, 46.
150 Murakami (trans. Birnbaum), *A Wild Sheep Chase*, 29.
151 Murakami (trans. Birnbaum), *A Wild Sheep Chase*, 191.
152 Murakami (trans. Birnbaum), *A Wild Sheep Chase*, 196.
153 Murakami (trans. Birnbaum), *A Wild Sheep Chase*, 212.
154 The Nietzschean will to power is not just confined to military or political power. It is also an idea, for example, that includes power over the self—the idea of self-mastery. The kind of will to power seen in *Sheep Chase* may thus be seen as more of a caricature of the Nietzschean idea, even if it is one shared by many "Nietzschean" antagonists in popular culture.
155 Murakami (trans. Birnbaum), *A Wild Sheep Chase*, 219.
156 Murakami (trans. Birnbaum), *A Wild Sheep Chase*, 225.
157 Hirano, *Murakami Haruki: hito to bungaku*, 148.
158 Murakami was very open about his interest in Nietzsche when I interviewed him in 2019, but he didn't feel like any of this Nietzschean influence came through Fitzgerald (or the figure of Gatsby), whom he saw as a very different kind of character.
159 Nowlin, "Mencken's Defense of Women," 106.
160 Mencken, *The Philosophy of Friedrich Nietzsche*, 89.
161 Fitzgerald, *The Great Gatsby*, 170.
162 Quoted in Huskinson, *Nietzsche and Jung*, locs. 2204-6.
163 Huskinson, *Nietzsche and Jung*, locs. 932-3.
164 Quoted in Huskinson, *Nietzsche and Jung*, locs. 855-6.
165 Quoted in Huskinson, *Nietzsche and Jung*, locs. 2248-9.
166 Quoted in Huskinson, *Nietzsche and Jung*, locs. 2251-2.
167 Murakami (trans. Birnbaum), *A Wild Sheep Chase*, 314.
168 Murakami (trans. Birnbaum), *A Wild Sheep Chase*, 216.
169 Murakami (trans. Birnbaum), *A Wild Sheep Chase*, 312. The Sheep Man also appears in an early short story Murakami wrote that eventually became "The Strange Library." In that work, a young boy makes a journey into the basement of his local library where he meets a grumpy old man who is a librarian. This man then leads him into a second basement of the library where he meets the Sheep Man and a young girl. It turns out the old librarian has trapped the boy and has plans to eat his brain, and so the boy eventually decides to escape from the library with the Sheep Man and with the help of the girl. It is not difficult to see biographical influences projected into this story. The old man, who is trying to fill the boy's head with useless facts so that he can consume his brain, might be seen as a representation of Murakami's studious and demanding father, who wanted his son to achieve academically and find a respectable place in society. The Sheep Man might be seen as another side of this father, a gentler version that is hiding away because of the trauma of war. The girl who helps the boy escape might be connected with K, the young woman Murakami was able to connect with during his high school years, as the tensions with his father first began to

emerge. There is a sense of wish-fulfillment here that might easily be connected with the tensions of Murakami's own life as a young man.
170 Campbell, *The Hero with a Thousand Faces*, 77.
171 Murakami (trans. Birnbaum), *A Wild Sheep Chase*, 267.
172 Murakami (trans. Birnbaum), *A Wild Sheep Chase*, 283.
173 Murakami (trans. Birnbaum), *A Wild Sheep Chase*, 308.
174 Murakami (trans. Birnbaum), *A Wild Sheep Chase*, 320.
175 Murakami (trans. Birnbaum), *A Wild Sheep Chase*, 337.
176 Murakami (trans. Birnbaum), *A Wild Sheep Chase*, 334.
177 Murakami (trans. Birnbaum), *A Wild Sheep Chase*, 335.
178 Murakami (trans. Birnbaum), *A Wild Sheep Chase*, 336.
179 Murakami (trans. Birnbaum), *A Wild Sheep Chase*, 333.
180 Murakami (trans. Birnbaum), *A Wild Sheep Chase*, 349.
181 Murakami (trans. Birnbaum), *A Wild Sheep Chase*, 303.
182 Rubin, *Haruki Murakami and the Music of Words*, 94.
183 Campbell, *The Hero with a Thousand Faces*, 130.

Chapter 2

1 Murakami (trans. Birnbaum), *A Wild Sheep Chase*, 139.
2 Murakami (trans. Birnbaum), *A Wild Sheep Chase*, 299.
3 Murakami (trans. Birnbaum), *Hard-Boiled*, 137.
4 Murakami (trans. Birnbaum), *Hard-Boiled*, 304.
5 In an interview for BOMB magazine, Murakami explained how the idea for this Town first came to him when he was writing *Hear the Wind Sing*, but that he did not yet feel ready to write about it. He reveals, "When I published my first book, *Hear the Wind Sing*, I wrote a very small piece in the story about a world, a town, surrounded by a high wall. And there was a library in that town. I knew that it wasn't well written so I just gave up. But I felt there was something very important embedded in that story. After five or six years I expanded it into *Hard-Boiled Wonderland*. But even then, I felt it was not enough. I felt that there should have been a kind of explosion, a kind of a booster rocket ... which could blow the mind of the reader" (See Harding, "Haruki Murakami by John Wesley Harding").
6 Murakami and Murakami, *Wōku donto ran*, 106.
7 Murakami, "Hajimete no kakioroshi shōsetsu," V.
8 Murakami, "Machi," 46.
9 Murakami, "Machi," 48.
10 Murakami, "Machi," 49–50.
11 Murakami, "Machi," 88.
12 Murakami, "Machi," 89.
13 Murakami, "Machi," 90.
14 Murakami, "Machi," 98.
15 Murakami, "Machi," 98.
16 Murakami, "Machi," 99.
17 Murakami (trans. Birnbaum), *Hard-Boiled*, 262.
18 Murakami (trans. Birnbaum), *Hard-Boiled*, 268.
19 Personal interview with Murakami in 2005.

20 Murakami (trans. Birnbaum), *Hard-Boiled*, 335.
21 Murakami (trans. Birnbaum), *Hard-Boiled*, 379.
22 Murakami (trans. Goossen), *Wind/Pinball*, 48.
23 Murakami (trans. Birnbaum), *Hard-Boiled*, 335.
24 Murakami (trans. Birnbaum), *Hard-Boiled*, 149.
25 Murakami (trans. Birnbaum), *Hard-Boiled*, 168.
26 Murakami (trans. Birnbaum), *Hard-Boiled*, 296. This reading of the Town, as a place deeply connected to Murakami's own hometown and the people he left behind there, does not, of course, preclude other allegorical readings. The Town, for example, could easily be read as an allegory for the closed nature and historical amnesia of postwar Japan, a reading that has been offered by other critics. For example, Wakamori Hideki writes, "I think the image of Japan is superimposed upon this Town." The Colonel tells *Boku*, "It may have been that I spent so long defending this Town I could not walk away." Asked if he regrets giving up his Shadow, the Colonel then adds, "I never do anything regrettable" (p. 88). Such comments are suggestive of a Japan that cannot accept responsibility for its past. Wakamori makes the Freudian connection of linking the horns of the unicorns who wander the town, with the fetish that allows the townspeople to live in their mindless paradise. He explains, "If we interpret these horns from a Freudian perspective, then they are probably a symbol that the Japanese have not been castrated, that they are still children. As a consequence of the Oedipus complex, they are people who cannot become adults" (p. 12). He then goes on to link these horns with the Japanese Emperor (p. 14). (Wakamori and Tsuge, "Sekai no owari to hādoboirudo wandārando o tekusuto ni").
27 Murakami (trans. Birnbaum), *Hard-Boiled*, 239.
28 Fisher, "An Allegory of Return," 161.
29 Suter, "Critical Engagement through Fantasy," 69.
30 Suter, "Critical Engagement through Fantasy," 69.
31 Murakami (trans. Birnbaum), *Hard-Boiled*, 85.
32 Murakami (trans. Birnbaum), *Hard-Boiled*, 109.
33 Murakami (trans. Birnbaum), *Hard-Boiled*, 247.
34 Murakami (trans. Birnbaum), *Hard-Boiled*, 248.
35 Murakami (trans. Birnbaum), *Hard-Boiled*, 247.
36 Murakami (trans. Birnbaum), *Hard-Boiled*, 334.
37 See Murakami (trans. Birnbaum), *Hard-Boiled*, 333, 334, 368, and 398.
38 Murakami (trans. Birnbaum), *Hard-Boiled*, 399.
39 Murakami, *Yume o miru*, 129.
40 Murakami, "100 pāsento riarizumu," 8.
41 Wallin, *Attachment in Psychotherapy*, 23.
42 These observations come from The Adult Attachment Interview devised by Mary Main. See Wallin, *Attachment in Psychotherapy*, 33–4.
43 Mikulincer and Shaver, *Attachment in Adulthood*, 372.
44 Mikulincer and Shaver, *Attachment in Adulthood*, 372.
45 Siegel, *Pocket Guide*, loc. 567.
46 Doi, *The Anatomy of Dependence*, 16.
47 Doi, *The Anatomy of Dependence*, 74.
48 Murakami (trans. Rubin), *Norwegian Wood*, 102.
49 Breen, *WWWJDIC: Online Japanese Dictionary Service*.
50 Murakami (trans. Rubin), *Norwegian Wood*, 103.
51 Murakami (trans. Rubin), *Norwegian Wood*, 103.

52 Murakami (trans. Rubin), *Norwegian Wood*, 103.
53 Murakami (trans. Rubin), *Norwegian Wood*, 103.
54 Murakami (trans. Rubin), *Norwegian Wood*, 244.
55 Murakami (trans. Rubin), *Norwegian Wood*, 232.
56 Murakami (trans. Rubin), *Norwegian Wood*, 321.
57 Murakami (trans. Rubin), *Norwegian Wood*, 7.
58 Murakami (trans. Rubin), *Norwegian Wood*, 6.
59 Murakami (trans. Rubin), *Norwegian Wood*, 9.
60 Murakami (trans. Rubin), *Norwegian Wood*, 114.
61 Murakami (trans. Rubin), *Norwegian Wood*, 119.
62 Murakami (trans. Rubin), *Norwegian Wood*, 50.
63 Murakami (trans. Rubin), *Norwegian Wood*, 50.
64 Murakami (trans. Rubin), *Norwegian Wood*, 172.
65 Segal, *Myth*, 109.
66 Murakami (trans. Rubin), *Norwegian Wood*, 134.
67 Murakami (trans. Rubin), *Norwegian Wood*, 238.
68 Murakami (trans. Rubin), *Norwegian Wood*, 146.
69 Shimizu, *Murakami Haruki wa kuse ni naru*. loc. 1422.
70 Murakami (trans. Rubin), *Norwegian Wood*, 52.
71 Murakami (trans. Rubin), *Norwegian Wood*, 28.
72 Murakami (trans. Rubin), *Norwegian Wood*, 58.
73 Murakami (trans. Rubin), *Norwegian Wood*, 324.
74 Murakami (trans. Rubin), *Norwegian Wood*, 192.
75 Murakami (trans. Rubin), *Norwegian Wood*, 41. This scene is reminiscent of the meeting of Amory and Thomas D'Invilliers in Fitzgerald's earlier novel *This Side of Paradise* (1920). As with *Norwegian Wood*, Amory and Thomas are both university students (at Fitzgerald's Princeton), and one is more socially ambitious than the other (Amory more so than Tom). Fitzgerald's novel describes Tom as "without much conception of social competition and such phenomena of absorbing interest. Still he liked books, and it seemed forever since Amory had met anyone who did" (Fitzgerald, *Complete Works*, locs. 988–91).
76 Murakami (trans. Rubin), *Norwegian Wood*, 42.
77 Murakami (trans. Rubin), *Norwegian Wood*, 74.
78 Murakami (trans. Rubin), *Norwegian Wood*, 269.
79 The novel opens with Watanabe on a trip to Germany. It would seem unlikely that Nagasawa is still stationed there, unless perhaps he was reassigned there some years later. Could it be that Watanabe is planning to visit him there? There is no way of knowing, though Nagasawa does reassure Watanabe in the text that they will probably run across each other some years in the future (p. 317). Kojima Motohiro points out the symbolism of Germany and France in the novel. In Japanese, the kanji used for Germany can also mean being single or alone. The kanji used for France can also mean Buddha and the dead. Kojima points out the numerous references made to Germany and France in the novel, in terms of both language study and culture. Germany is commonly associated with characters like Nagasawa and Watanabe who risk ending up alone, while Naoko is commonly associated with France and the world of death (Kojima, *Murakami Haruki to chinkon no shigaku*, 228).
80 Murakami (trans. Rubin), *Norwegian Wood*, 276.
81 Murakami (trans. Rubin), *Norwegian Wood*, 276.
82 Murakami (trans. Rubin), *Norwegian Wood*, 318.

83 Murakami (trans. Rubin), *Norwegian Wood*, 43.
84 Murakami (trans. Rubin), *Norwegian Wood*, 42–3.
85 Murakami (trans. Rubin), *Norwegian Wood*, 276.
86 Murakami (trans. Rubin), *Norwegian Wood*, 279.
87 Murakami (trans. Rubin), *Norwegian Wood*, 277.
88 Murakami (trans. Rubin), *Norwegian Wood*, 277.
89 Murakami (trans. Rubin), *Norwegian Wood*, 37.
90 Murakami (trans. Rubin), *Norwegian Wood*, 154.
91 Murakami (trans. Rubin), *Norwegian Wood*, 347.
92 Murakami (trans. Rubin), *Norwegian Wood*, 13.
93 Murakami (trans. Rubin), *Norwegian Wood*, 154.
94 Murakami (trans. Rubin), *Norwegian Wood*, 360.
95 Murakami (trans. Rubin), *Norwegian Wood*, 223.
96 Murakami (trans. Rubin), *Norwegian Wood*, 160.
97 Murakami (trans. Rubin), *Norwegian Wood*, 213.
98 Rubin, *Haruki Murakami and the Music of Words*, 158.
99 Murakami (trans. Rubin), *Norwegian Wood*, 378–9.
100 My argument here has been that *Norwegian Wood* is not really a love story but a story about the different attachment styles which can thwart love. Even so, the novel clearly struck a nerve with the Japanese-reading public, becoming the country's bestselling novel of all time, until it was knocked off its perch by a much more traditional love story. In 2001, Katayama Kyōichi published *Sekai no chūshin de ai o sakebu* (Shouting Love from the Center of the World), a novel that would eventually take the place of *Norwegian Wood* as the bestselling Japanese novel of all time. In broad outline, there is much in common between Murakami's novel and Katayama's later work. Both are narrated by an older male, who years later is still struggling to come to terms with the death of a girlfriend. Beyond these broad strokes, though, the works are very different, particularly in their portrayal of their female heroines (if such a title is applicable to Murakami's novel). Katayama's heroine, Aki, is completely opposite to Naoko: confident and life-affirming (though much more innocent and pure than the equally confident and life-affirming Midori). It is only illness that steals her promise away. *Sekachū*, as the novel later came to be affectionately known in Japan, had a small print run initially, but slowly grew by word of mouth and over the long run was fuelled by a commercially successful film adaptation and other spin-offs. That Japan's two most commercially successful novels should share a similar storyline may simply speak to the universal power of their shared themes: young love and premature death.
101 Harding, "Haruki Murakami by John Wesley Harding."
102 Harding, "Haruki Murakami by John Wesley Harding."
103 Murakami, *Yume o miru*, 29.
104 Murakami (trans. Goossen), *Wind/Pinball*, 4.
105 Murakami, "Machi," 46.
106 Murakami, "Machi," 73.
107 Murakami (trans. Goossen), *Wind/Pinball*, 4.
108 Hirano, *Murakami Haruki: hito to bungaku*, 74–80.
109 These similarities might offer us some clues for answering a question *Norwegian Wood* never answers: Do Watanabe and Midori end up together? In *Tender Is the Night*, the Divers' marriage eventually breaks down and Dick begins to pursue Rosemary in earnest. By this time, however, she is no longer as sure about Dick as

she once was, and they do not end up together. Of course, this does not mean that the characters in *Norwegian Wood* have to end up the same, but it does suggest one literary precedent for what might have been behind Murakami's decision to end the novel on such an ambiguous note.

110 Whatever reservations Yōko may have had about *Norwegian Wood* when it first came out, Murakami's early English editor, Elmer Luke, has said that Yōko actually pushed for the novel to be published in English (Karashima, *Murakami Haruki o yonde iru toki ni*, loc. 1990).
111 Murakami (trans. Birnbaum), *Dance Dance Dance*, 9.
112 Murakami (trans. Birnbaum), *Hard-Boiled*, 371.
113 Murakami (trans. Birnbaum), *Hard-Boiled*, 371.
114 Jung, *Collected Works* Vol. 8, para. 509.
115 Murakami (trans. Birnbaum), *Hard-Boiled*, 82.
116 Murakami (trans. Birnbaum), *Hard-Boiled*, 82.
117 See, for example, Murakami (trans. Birnbaum), *Dance Dance Dance*, 84 and 193.
118 Murakami (trans. Birnbaum), *Dance Dance Dance*, 122.
119 Murakami (trans. Birnbaum), *Dance Dance Dance*, 250.
120 Murakami (trans. Birnbaum), *Dance Dance Dance*, 252.
121 Kojima Motohiro has explored the ways Murakami's later edits of "Barn Burning" deliberately downplayed the story's influence from Faulkner, while emphasizing its indebtedness to Fitzgerald and *The Great Gatsby*. See Kojima, "Murakami Haruki 'Naya o yaku' ron."
122 Murakami (trans. Birnbaum), *Dance Dance Dance*, 354.
123 Murakami (trans. Birnbaum), *Dance Dance Dance*, 356.
124 Murakami (trans. Birnbaum), *Dance Dance Dance*, 356.
125 Murakami (trans. Birnbaum), *Dance Dance Dance*, 372.
126 Murakami (trans. Birnbaum), *Dance Dance Dance*, 353.
127 Van der Kolk, *The Body Keeps the Score*, 66.
128 Van der Kolk, *The Body Keeps the Score*, 180–1.
129 Steinberg and Schnall, *The Stranger in the Mirror*, 77.
130 Murakami (trans. Birnbaum), *Dance Dance Dance*, 355.
131 Murakami (trans. Birnbaum), *Dance Dance Dance*, 152.
132 Murakami (trans. Birnbaum), *Dance Dance Dance*, 257.
133 Murakami (trans. Birnbaum), *Dance Dance Dance*, 392.
134 Murakami (trans. Birnbaum), *Dance Dance Dance*, 345.
135 Shimada, *Shūkyō toshite no baburu*, 89–90.
136 Murakami (trans. Birnbaum), *Dance Dance Dance*, 12.
137 Murakami (trans. Birnbaum), *Dance Dance Dance*, 367.
138 Murakami (trans. Birnbaum), *Dance Dance Dance*, 366–7.
139 Murakami (trans. Birnbaum), *Dance Dance Dance*, 12.
140 The phrase "false consciousness" was actually coined by Friedrich Engels (1820–1895).
141 Žižek, *Enjoy your Symptom*, x.
142 Wright and Wright (eds.), *The Žižek Reader*, 55.
143 Murakami (trans. Birnbaum), *Dance Dance Dance*, 24.
144 Murakami (trans. Birnbaum), *Dance Dance Dance*, 378.
145 Murakami (trans. Birnbaum), *Dance Dance Dance*, 380.
146 Murakami (trans. Birnbaum), *Dance Dance Dance*, 381.
147 Murakami (trans. Birnbaum), *Dance Dance Dance*, 95.

148 Murakami (trans. Birnbaum), *Dance Dance Dance*, 391.
149 Murakami (trans. Birnbaum), *Dance Dance Dance*, 392.
150 Murakami (trans. Birnbaum), *Dance Dance Dance*, 393.
151 Harding, "Haruki Murakami by John Wesley Harding."

Chapter 3

1 Murakami, "Meikingu obu Nejimaki-dori kuronikuru," 273.
2 Žižek, *Welcome to the Desert of the Real*, 5–6.
3 Hillman, *Anima*, loc. 739.
4 Murakami (trans. Gabriel), *South of the Border*, 7.
5 Murakami, *Yume o miru*, 164.
6 Nat King Cole never recorded a version of the song *South of the Border*, which suggests that this was an intentional fabrication on Murakami's part to denote the somewhat illusory nature of this time in Hajime's life. Later, when she reappears in Hajime's life, Shimamoto will present this record to him, but when she disappears from his life again, near the end of the novel, the record goes missing, too. *Boku* plays this same record in *A Wild Sheep Chase* when he makes it to Junitaki before his meeting with Rat, another "other worldly" setting in Murakami's fiction.
7 Murakami (trans. Gabriel), *South of the Border*, 15.
8 As mentioned in the Introduction, Murakami also moved house at the end of elementary school, moving from Shukugawa to nearby Ashiya.
9 Murakami (trans. Gabriel), *South of the Border*, 17.
10 Murakami (trans. Gabriel), *South of the Border*, 147.
11 Fitzgerald, *The Great Gatsby*, 172.
12 Murakami (trans. Gabriel), *South of the Border*, 29.
13 Murakami (trans. Gabriel), *South of the Border*, 31.
14 Murakami (trans. Gabriel), *South of the Border*, 48.
15 Murakami (trans. Gabriel), *South of the Border*, 46.
16 Murakami (trans. Gabriel), *South of the Border*, 18.
17 Murakami (trans. Gabriel), *South of the Border*, 45.
18 Murakami (trans. Gabriel), *South of the Border*, 175.
19 Murakami (trans. Gabriel), *South of the Border*, 177.
20 Žižek, *The Puppet and the Dwarf*, 79–80.
21 Murakami, "Meikingu obu Nejimaki-dori kuronikuru," 273.
22 Murakami (trans. Rubin), *Norwegian Wood*, 26.
23 Urazumi, *Murakami Haruki o aruku*, 178–80.
24 Murakami (trans. Gabriel), *South of the Border*, 47.
25 Murakami (trans. Rubin), *Norwegian Wood*, 33.
26 Fitzgerald, *Complete Works of F. Scott Fitzgerald*, loc. 33793.
27 Fitzgerald, *Complete Works of F. Scott Fitzgerald*, locs. 34079–82.
28 Fitzgerald, *Complete Works of F. Scott Fitzgerald*, locs. 34083–8.
29 Fitzgerald, *Complete Works of F. Scott Fitzgerald*, loc. 34143.
30 Fitzgerald, *Complete Works of F. Scott Fitzgerald*, locs. 34151–2.
31 Murakami (trans. Gabriel), *South of the Border*, 51.
32 Murakami (trans. Gabriel), *South of the Border*, 68. Rubin, *Haruki Murakami and the Music of Words*, 25.

33 Murakami (trans. Gabriel), *South of the Border*, 72.
34 Murakami (trans. Gabriel), *South of the Border*, 72.
35 Murakami (trans. Gabriel), *South of the Border*, 80.
36 Murakami (trans. Gabriel), *South of the Border*, 81.
37 Murakami (trans. Gabriel), *South of the Border*, 105.
38 Murakami, "Meikingu obu Nejimaki-dori kuronikuru," 274.
39 Ueda (trans. Chambers), *Tales of Moonlight and Rain*, 144.
40 Ueda (trans. Chambers), *Tales of Moonlight and Rain*, 146.
41 Ueda (trans. Chambers), *Tales of Moonlight and Rain*, 149.
42 Ueda (trans. Chambers), *Tales of Moonlight and Rain*, 149.
43 Ueda (trans. Chambers), *Tales of Moonlight and Rain*, 16.
44 Ueda (trans. Chambers), *Tales of Moonlight and Rain*, 16.
45 Quoted in Ueda (trans. Chambers), *Tales of Moonlight and Rain*, 16.
46 Žižek, *Enjoy Your Symptom*, 154.
47 Murakami (trans. Gabriel), *South of the Border*, 204.
48 Žižek, *Enjoy Your Symptom*, 155.
49 Jung, *Collected Works* Vol. 9, Part 2, para. 24.
50 Murakami (trans. Gabriel), *South of the Border*, 12.
51 Fitzgerald, *Complete Works of F. Scott Fitzgerald*, locs. 12852, 13550.
52 Murakami (trans. Gabriel), *South of the Border*, 32.
53 Murakami (trans. Gabriel), *South of the Border*, 36.
54 Murakami (trans. Gabriel), *South of the Border*, 203.
55 Murakami (trans. Gabriel), *South of the Border*, 174.
56 Murakami (trans. Gabriel), *South of the Border*, 178.
57 Murakami (trans. Gabriel), *South of the Border*, 183.
58 Murakami (trans. Gabriel), *South of the Border*, 211.
59 Murakami (trans. Gabriel), *South of the Border*, 212.
60 Murakami, "Meikingu obu Nejimaki-dori kuronikuru," 274.
61 Early on in the novel, Tōru is warned by a mysterious woman on a telephone that he has a blind spot. See Murakami (trans. Rubin), *Wind-Up Bird*, loc. 2299.
62 Murakami (trans. Rubin), *Wind-Up Bird*, loc. 92.
63 Murakami (trans. Rubin), *Wind-Up Bird*, locs. 91–3.
64 Carver, *Will You Please Be Quiet, Please?* 214.
65 Stull and Carroll (eds.), *Remembering Ray*, 132.
66 Carver, *Will You Please Be Quiet, Please?* 51.
67 Akashi, "nejimakidori kuronikuru no suimyaku." Murakami has translated all of Carver's work, showing how deep his commitment to Carver goes. He translated "So Much Water So Close to Home" as "Ashimoto ni nagareru fukai kawa" which might be translated as The Deep River which Flows at our Feet. In Murakami's interview with Kawakami, she mentions that this is Murakami's favorite short story of all time. I am not sure what her source for this information was, but Murakami does not question her assertion in the interview. See Kawakami, *Mimizuku wa tasogare ni tobitatsu*, loc. 3839.
68 Stull and Carroll (eds.), *Remembering Ray*, 130.
69 Stull and Carroll (eds.), *Remembering Ray*, 130.
70 Akashi, "Nejimakidori kuronikuru no suimyaku," 101. Akashi is quoting Murakami and Shibata, *honyaku yawa*, 38–40.
71 Carver, *Beginners*, 121.
72 Carver, *Beginners*, 122.

73 Akashi, "Nejimakidori kuronikuru no suimyaku," 103–4.
74 Akashi, "Nejimakidori kuronikuru no suimyaku," 108.
75 Murakami (trans. Rubin), *Wind-Up Bird*, loc. 1257.
76 Murakami (trans. Rubin), *Wind-Up Bird*, locs. 10544–5.
77 Murakami (trans. Rubin), *Wind-Up Bird*, loc. 5322.
78 Murakami (trans. Rubin), *Wind-Up Bird*, loc. 5333.
79 Murakami (trans. Rubin), *Wind-Up Bird*, locs. 5338–9.
80 Levine, *Walking the Tiger*, 57–8.
81 Murakami (trans. Rubin), *Wind-Up Bird*, locs. 4170–1.
82 Murakami (trans. Rubin), *Wind-Up Bird*, loc. 4857.
83 *Wind-Up Bird* was published in Japan as three separate books, but when the book was translated into English and the three books were combined into one, the publishers felt that it was too long. Jay Rubin, the translator, reluctantly cut about 61 pages from the book and reorganized some of the material. Many of these cuts come near the end of Book Two, including the final scene discussed here, where Tōru has his revelation about the identity of the woman on the phone. For more details about the cuts that were made, see Maynard, "Lost Chapters in The Wind-Up Bird Chronicle" and Rubin, Gabriel, Fisketjon, "Translating Murakami."
84 Quoted in Sukegawa, *Nazo no Murakami Haruki*, 153.
85 Murakami (trans. Rubin), *Wind-Up Bird*, loc. 2465.
86 Murakami (trans. Rubin), *Wind-Up Bird*, locs. 3670–5.
87 Murakami (trans. Rubin), *Wind-Up Bird*, locs. 3679–82.
88 Murakami (trans. Rubin), *Wind-Up Bird*, locs. 3043–53.
89 Murakami (trans. Rubin), *Wind-Up Bird*, locs. 3058–75.
90 Murakami (trans. Rubin), *Wind-Up Bird*, loc. 9880.
91 Levine, *In an Unspoken Voice*, loc. 173.
92 Quoted in Levine, *Walking the Tiger*, 58.
93 Levine, *In an Unspoken Voice*, 349.
94 Murakami (trans. Goossen), *Wind/Pinball*, 57.
95 Murakami (trans. Rubin), *Wind-Up Bird*, locs. 384–7.
96 Murakami (trans. Rubin), *Wind-Up Bird*, locs. 5719–20.
97 Murakami (trans. Rubin), *Wind-Up Bird*, loc. 5722.
98 Murakami (trans. Rubin), *Wind-Up Bird*, locs. 6889–90.
99 Murakami (trans. Rubin), *Wind-Up Bird*, loc. 6898.
100 Campbell, *The Hero with a Thousand Faces*, 17.
101 Campbell, *The Hero with a Thousand Faces*, 58.
102 This is clearer in the original Japanese version of the novel, where Tōru decides for a time to travel to Crete with Kanō Creta. This is the same location Theseus travels to in order to face the Minotaur, but in Tōru's case, a destination that represents not his acceptance of the quest but his desire to escape from it. Eventually, Tōru decides that he cannot go with Creta, but this decision is made even more quickly in the English version of the novel because the section describing his preparations to leave with Creta is cut.
103 Murakami (trans. Rubin), *Wind-Up Bird*, locs. 7517–18.
104 Murakami (trans. Rubin), *Wind-Up Bird*, locs. 5877–8.
105 Murakami (trans. Rubin), *Wind-Up Bird*, locs. 5929–30.
106 Murakami (trans. Rubin), *Wind-Up Bird*, loc. 5931.
107 Murakami (trans. Rubin), *Wind-Up Bird*, locs. 5978–80.
108 Murakami, *Meikingu obu Nejimaki-dori kuronikuru*, 288.

109 Murakami, *Yume o miru*, 95.
110 Quoted in Rubin, *Haruki Murakami and the Music of Words*, 223.
111 Murakami (trans. Rubin), *Wind-Up Bird*, locs. 1417–18.
112 Murakami (trans. Rubin), *Wind-Up Bird*, loc. 1437.
113 Murakami (trans. Rubin), *Wind-Up Bird*, locs. 5521–4.
114 Murakami (trans. Rubin), *Wind-Up Bird*, locs. 5526–8.
115 Campbell, *The Hero with a Thousand Faces*, 25.
116 Murakami (trans. Rubin), *Wind-Up Bird*, locs. 10274–6.
117 Murakami (trans. Rubin), *Wind-Up Bird*, loc. 10276.
118 Levine, *In an Unspoken Voice*, 16.
119 Murakami (trans. Rubin), *Wind-Up Bird*, loc. 10343.
120 Campbell, *The Hero with a Thousand Faces*, 40.
121 Murakami (trans. Rubin), *Wind-Up Bird*, locs. 934–5. This prophecy, in fact, is based on a real fortune reading given to Murakami at one point in his life. This fortune teller had also said he would make a living writing at a time when he was not contemplating becoming a writer, according to his account, making this particular fortune correct on at least one of its predictions. See Murakami, "Meikingu obu Nejimaki-dori kuronikuru," 282.
122 Murakami, "Meikingu obu Nejimaki-dori kuronikuru," 280.
123 Campbell, *The Hero with a Thousand Faces*, 207.
124 Carver, *All of Us*, locs. 458–61.
125 Gentry and Stull, *Conversations with Raymond Carver*, 190.
126 Carver, *All of Us*, loc. 1672.
127 Murakami and Kawai, *Haruki Murakami Goes to Meet Hayao Kawai*, 71.
128 Murakami, "Meikingu obu Nejimaki-dori kuronikuru," 279.
129 Personal interview with Murakami in 2005.
130 Murakami, "Meikingu obu Nejimaki-dori kuronikuru," 278–9.
131 Murakami, *Yume o miru*, 463.

Chapter 4

1 Murakami (trans. Birnbaum and Gabriel), *Underground*, 202.
2 Murakami (trans. Birnbaum and Gabriel), *Underground*, 202.
3 Murakami (trans. Birnbaum and Gabriel), *Underground*, 202–3.
4 Katō, *Ierōpēji Part 2*, 73.
5 Katō, *Ierōpēji Part 2*, 76.
6 Nietzsche (trans. Johnston), *The Birth of Tragedy*, 8.
7 Nietzsche (trans. Johnston), *The Birth of Tragedy*, 11.
8 This need for the Apollonian is clearly reflected in Murakami's own creative process. While his fiction dives into the Dionysian depths of human nature, in his own life this is balanced by Apollonian discipline. As already mentioned, Murakami wakes up in the early hours of the morning to write and sticks to a strict exercise regime, all in an effort to support and sustain his writing. He has been an impressively productive writer for over four decades now and shows no signs of slowing down. This aspect of his writing and public persona in part connects him with Mishima Yukio, a writer Murakami does not particularly care for, but who was also deeply aware of the necessity for both the Apollonian and Dionysian in creating art.

9 Murakami (trans. Gabriel), *Sputnik*, 12.
10 Murakami (trans. Gabriel), *Sputnik*, 30-1.
11 Murakami (trans. Gabriel), *Sputnik*, 33.
12 Murakami (trans. Gabriel), *Sputnik*, 50, 61.
13 Murakami (trans. Gabriel), *Sputnik*, 37.
14 Murakami (trans. Gabriel), *Sputnik*, 10.
15 Murakami (trans. Gabriel), *Sputnik*, 9.
16 Murakami (trans. Gabriel), *Sputnik*, 15.
17 "Late 15th century: From French métaphore, via Latin from Greek metaphora, from metapherein 'to transfer.'" *English Oxford Living Dictionaries*. Retrieved from https://en.oxforddictionaries.com/definition/metaphor.
18 Murakami (trans. Gabriel), *Sputnik*, 16.
19 Murakami (trans. Gabriel), *Sputnik*, 16.
20 The island in the novel is probably a composite of a number of different islands, Murakami having lived and traveled in Greece. Katō points out (Katō, *Ierōpēji Part 2*, 76) that one of the models is undoubtedly the island of Halki, a small island west of Rhodes, which in Japanese is pronounced Haruki. Given that Murakami shares a name with the island, he decided to travel there when he was living in Greece, an experience recorded in his book *Tōi taiko* (Distant Drum). In *Sputnik*, when K first hears the name, he says that it was "vaguely familiar" (p. 80), an inside joke for those who get the reference.
21 Murakami (trans. Gabriel), *Sputnik*, 117.
22 Murakami (trans. Gabriel), *Sputnik*, 46.
23 Murakami (trans. Gabriel), *Sputnik*, 156.
24 Murakami has said that the plot device of having Miu stuck overnight in a Ferris wheel came from a newspaper article he read once where something like this really happened (Murakami, *Yume o miru*, 76). Marc Yamada suggests that the scene is borrowed from Virginia Woolf's fiction (Yamada, *Locating Heisei*, 105).
25 Freud wrote about the "primal scene" in a number of papers including in "Studies on Hysteria" and "The Interpretation of Dreams" found in the Bibliography.
26 Murakami (trans. Gabriel), *Sputnik*, 13.
27 Murakami (trans. Gabriel), *Sputnik*, 38.
28 Murakami (trans. Gabriel), *Sputnik*, 157.
29 Murakami (trans. Gabriel), *Sputnik*, 167.
30 Murakami (trans. Gabriel), *Sputnik*, 165.
31 Quoted in Katō, *Ierōpēji Part 2*, 82.
32 Murakami (trans. Gabriel), *Sputnik*, 195.
33 Murakami (trans. Gabriel), *South of the Border*, 108.
34 Murakami (trans. Gabriel), *South of the Border*, 117.
35 Murakami (trans. Gabriel), *South of the Border*, 197.
36 Murakami (trans. Gabriel), *Sputnik*, 200.
37 Katō, *Ierōpēji Part 2*, 70-1.
38 Murakami (trans. Gabriel), *Sputnik*, 208.
39 Katō argues that the "pre-Miu" Sumire feels more like Midori from *Norwegian Wood* and the "post-Miu" Sumire more like Naoko. See Katō, *Ierōpēji Part 2*, 71.
40 Murakami (trans. Rubin), *Norwegian Wood*, 386.
41 Murakami (trans. Gabriel), *Sputnik*, 208.
42 Murakami (trans. Gabriel), *Sputnik*, 209.
43 Personal interview with Murakami in 2005. In another interview, Murakami described the novel as a "love letter to his style" (Murakami, *Yume o miru*, 65).

44 Murakami (trans. Gabriel), *Sputnik*, 54.
45 Kuroko, *Murakami Haruki*, 243–4.
46 Komori, *Murakami Harukiron*, 14.
47 Segal, *Joseph Campbell: An Introduction*, 6.
48 Segal, *Joseph Campbell: An Introduction*, 7.
49 Murakami (trans. Gabriel), *Kafka on the Shore*, 10.
50 Murakami (trans. Gabriel), *Kafka on the Shore*, 10.
51 Murakami (trans. Gabriel), *Kafka on the Shore*, 10.
52 Murakami (trans. Gabriel), *Kafka on the Shore*, 53.
53 Murakami (trans. Gabriel), *Kafka on the Shore*, 50.
54 Murakami (trans. Gabriel), *Kafka on the Shore*, 284.
55 Murakami (trans. Gabriel), *Kafka on the Shore*, 63.
56 Murakami (trans. Gabriel), *Kafka on the Shore*, 286.
57 Murakami (trans. Gabriel), *Kafka on the Shore*, 98.
58 Murakami (trans. Gabriel), *Kafka on the Shore*, 184–5.
59 Martinez, "Murakami's Reimagining of Oedipus," 63.
60 Van der Kolk, *The Body Keeps the Score*, 297.
61 Van der Kolk, *The Body Keeps the Score*, 298.
62 Van der Kolk, *The Body Keeps the Score*, 299.
63 Murakami (trans. Gabriel), *Kafka on the Shore*, 273.
64 Shimizu, *Murakami Haruki wa kuse ni naru*, locs. 798–806.
65 Murakami (trans. Gabriel), *Kafka on the Shore*, 141.
66 Murakami (trans. Gabriel), *Kafka on the Shore*, 372.
67 Murakami, "Questions for Murakami about *Kafka on the Shore*."
68 Murakami (trans. Gabriel), *Kafka on the Shore*, 411.
69 Murakami (trans. Gabriel), *Kafka on the Shore*, 411.
70 The scene where Saeki comes to Kafka in a dissociated state is yet another example in Murakami's fiction that may be influenced by Chandler's *The Long Goodbye*. In Chandler's novel, Eileen Wade comes to Marlowe in a dissociated state, appearing naked before him and treating him as if he were a lover from her past who just happens to shares the same initials as Marlowe.
71 Murakami (trans. Gabriel), *Kafka on the Shore*, 207.
72 Katō, *Ierōpēji Part 2*, 151.
73 Katō, *Ierōpēji Part 2*, 167–9.
74 Flutsch, "Girls and the Unconscious," 70.
75 Katō, *Ierōpēji Part 2*, 170.
76 Katō, *Ierōpēji Part 2*, 189–92.
77 Murakami and Kawai, *Haruki Murakami Goes to Meet Hayao Kawai*, 103.
78 Murakami and Kawai, *Haruki Murakami Goes to Meet Hayao Kawai*, 103.
79 Murakami and Kawai, *Haruki Murakami Goes to Meet Hayao Kawai*, 103.
80 Murakami and Kawai, *Haruki Murakami Goes to Meet Hayao Kawai*, 104.
81 This might remind us of the town and forest in *Hard-Boiled Wonderland and the End of the World*. Murakami has said that he started writing *Kafka on the Shore* as a sequel to *Hard-Boiled Wonderland*, but that he soon gave up on this idea (see Murakami, *Yume o miru*, 88). The two stories do share similarities, including being structured by alternating storylines that slowly begin to converge.
82 Campbell, *The Hero with a Thousand Faces*, 111.
83 Campbell, *The Hero with a Thousand Faces*, 122.
84 Campbell, *The Hero with a Thousand Faces*, 130.

85 Campbell, *The Hero with a Thousand Faces*, 151.
86 Campbell, *The Hero with a Thousand Faces*, 173.
87 Campbell, *The Hero with a Thousand Faces*, 137.
88 Campbell, *The Hero with a Thousand Faces*, 137.
89 Segal, *Joseph Campbell: An Introduction*, 25-6.
90 Gentile, "The Scholar as Mystic," 196-7.
91 Campbell, *The Power of Myth*, 191.
92 Campbell, *The Power of Myth*, 191. While clearly aware of the influence of Nietzsche on his ideas, Campbell did not give him the final word. He felt that Eastern mysticism offered a superior approach in the end. For example, he once explained that "Sri Ramakrishna [a 19th century work of Bengali mysticism] seems to me to have gone the step beyond Nietzsche, having resolved the oppositions which to Nietzsche were finally disastrous" (Quoted in Larsen, *A Fire in the Mind*).
93 Murakami (trans. Gabriel), *Kafka on the Shore*, 187.
94 Murakami (trans. Gabriel), *Kafka on the Shore*, 187.
95 Murakami (trans. Gabriel), *Kafka on the Shore*, 272.
96 A good example here from popular culture is when Luke Skywalker removes the mask of Darth Vader to reveal the man beneath the machine. Here, father and son are able to make atonement. The fit of this particular example is not surprising when one considers that *Star Wars* was explicitly modeled on Campbell's monomythic quest.
97 Campbell, *The Hero with a Thousand Faces*, 130.
98 Žižek, *The Puppet and the Dwarf*, 99-100.
99 If Johnnie Walker represents the spirit of the age, then the flesh is represented by Colonel Sanders, another mysterious figure in the novel who needs others to act for him and who takes on the form of a famous capitalist icon. Colonel Sanders is literally a seller of flesh, a pimp who supplies Nakata's traveling companion Hoshino with the most amazing sexual experience of his life, before revealing to him the location of the entrance stone.
100 Thiele, *Friedrich Nietzsche and the Politics of the Soul*, 18.
101 Murakami (trans. Gabriel), *Kafka on the Shore*, 5.
102 Murakami (trans. Gabriel), *Kafka on the Shore*, 5.
103 Murakami (trans. Gabriel), *Kafka on the Shore*, 343.
104 Murakami (trans. Gabriel), *Kafka on the Shore*, 343.
105 Murakami (trans. Gabriel), *Kafka on the Shore*, 359.
106 Murakami (trans. Gabriel), *Kafka on the Shore*, 260.
107 Murakami (trans. Gabriel), *Kafka on the Shore*, 295.
108 Campbell, *A Joseph Campbell Companion*.
109 Campbell, *The Hero with a Thousand Faces*, 152.
110 Murakami (trans. Gabriel), *Kafka on the Shore*, 141.
111 Murakami (trans. Gabriel), *Kafka on the Shore*, 37.
112 Flutsch, "Girls and the Unconscious," 73.
113 Murakami (trans. Gabriel), *Kafka on the Shore*, 326.
114 Murakami (trans. Gabriel), *Kafka on the Shore*, 359.
115 Murakami (trans. Rubin), *After Dark*, 22.
116 The film is referenced twice in the novel. See Murakami (trans. Gabriel), *Kafka on the Shore*, 303, 390.
117 Murakami, *Yume o miru*, 291.
118 Murakami (trans. Rubin), *After Dark*, 197-8.

119 Murakami, *Yume o miru*, 486–7.
120 Murakami (trans. Rubin), *After Dark*, 89.
121 Murakami (trans. Rubin), *After Dark*, 33.
122 Murakami (trans. Rubin), *After Dark*, 128.
123 Murakami (trans. Rubin), *After Dark*, 128.
124 Murakami (trans. Rubin), *After Dark*, 121.
125 Murakami (trans. Rubin), *After Dark*, 117.
126 Murakami (trans. Rubin), *After Dark*, 118.
127 Murakami (trans. Rubin), *After Dark*, 118.
128 Murakami (trans. Rubin), *After Dark*, 149.
129 Murakami (trans. Rubin), *After Dark*, 207.
130 Murakami (trans. Rubin), *After Dark*, 231.
131 Murakami (trans. Rubin), *After Dark*, 17.
132 Murakami (trans. Rubin), *After Dark*, 157–8.
133 Murakami (trans. Rubin), *After Dark*, 217.

Chapter 5

1 Murakami (trans. Rubin and Gabriel), *1Q84*, 163.
2 Murakami (trans. Rubin and Gabriel), *1Q84*, 167.
3 Murakami (trans. Rubin and Gabriel), *1Q84*, 252.
4 Murakami (trans. Rubin and Gabriel), *1Q84*, 582.
5 Murakami (trans. Rubin and Gabriel), *1Q84*, 716–17.
6 Murakami (trans. Rubin and Gabriel), *1Q84*, 445.
7 Asari, "Kishidanchōgoroshi: Idea to metafā o megutte."
8 Jaynes, *The Origins of Consciousness*, 84.
9 Murakami (trans. Rubin and Gabriel), *1Q84*, 490.
10 Murakami (trans. Rubin and Gabriel), *1Q84*, 511.
11 Murakami (trans. Rubin and Gabriel), *1Q84*, 447.
12 Murakami (trans. Rubin and Gabriel), *1Q84*, 464. The original quote from Jung is from Jung, *Visions*, 569.
13 Murakami (trans. Rubin and Gabriel), *1Q84*, 464.
14 Murakami (trans. Birnbaum and Gabriel), *Underground*, 196.
15 Murakami, "AUM Shinrikyo cases still not closed."
16 Takahashi, "Kanōsei toshite no monogatari," 34.
17 The Q in *The True Story of Ah Q* is used because nobody can recall the protagonist's real family name, which started with a Q sound, and so the English letter Q is used to stand in its place.
18 Fujii, "Lu Xun and Murakami," 90–1. Murakami, *Wakai dokusha no tame*, 24–5.
19 See, for example, Kelts, "Haruki Murakami." French, "Seeing a Clash of Social Networks."
20 Murakami, "Always on the Side of the Egg."
21 Murakami, "Always on the Side of the Egg."
22 The other work Murakami has mentioned as a model for the general novel is Dostoevsky's *Demons*. See Murakami, *Yume o miru*, 140.
23 Murakami and Shibata, *Honyaku yawa*, 158–9.
24 Bakhtin, *Problem of Dostoevsky's Poetics*, 3.

25 Bakhtin, *Problem of Dostoevsky's Poetics*, 6.
26 Murakami (trans. Rubin and Gabriel), *1Q84*, 385.
27 Kawamura, "Naze kōiu monogatari," 53.
28 Kōnosu, "nani ga dewa naku," 90.
29 Murakami (trans. Rubin and Gabriel), *1Q84*, 701.
30 Murakami (trans. Rubin and Gabriel), *1Q84*, 802.
31 Murakami (trans. Rubin and Gabriel), *1Q84*, 405.
32 Murakami (trans. Rubin and Gabriel), *1Q84*, 722.
33 Murakami, "Abandoning a Cat."
34 Thorne, "1Q84 by Haruki Murakami."
35 Schulz, "Murakami's Mega-Opus."
36 Kuroko, *1Q84 hihan*, 48–9, 68.
37 Kuroko, *1Q84 hihan*, 68.
38 Murakami (trans. Rubin and Gabriel), *1Q84*, 441.
39 Murakami (trans. Rubin and Gabriel), *1Q84*, 441–2.
40 Murakami (trans. Rubin and Gabriel), *1Q84*, 229.
41 Murakami (trans. Gabriel), *Colorless Tsukuru Tazaki and His Years of Pilgrimage*, 4, 19.
42 Murakami (trans. Gabriel), *Colorless Tsukuru Tazaki and His Years of Pilgrimage*, 28.
43 Murakami (trans. Gabriel), *Colorless Tsukuru Tazaki and His Years of Pilgrimage*, 22.
44 Murakami (trans. Gabriel), *Colorless Tsukuru Tazaki and His Years of Pilgrimage*, 85.
45 Suter, "Beyond Kizuna," 305–6.
46 Quoted in Wakatsuki, "The Haruki Phenomenon," 12.
47 Murakami (trans. Gabriel), *Colorless Tsukuru Tazaki and His Years of Pilgrimage*, 225.
48 Murakami (trans. Gabriel), *Colorless Tsukuru Tazaki and His Years of Pilgrimage*, 132.
49 Murakami (trans. Gabriel), *Colorless Tsukuru Tazaki and His Years of Pilgrimage*, 256.
50 Murakami (trans. Gabriel), *Kafka on the Shore*, 121.
51 Murakami (trans. Gabriel), *Colorless Tsukuru Tazaki and His Years of Pilgrimage*, 32.
52 Murakami, "Tandoku intabyū."
53 Murakami (trans. Gabriel), *Colorless Tsukuru Tazaki and His Years of Pilgrimage*, 12, 177.
54 Murakami (trans. Rubin), *Norwegian Wood*, 170.
55 Murakami (trans. Gabriel), *Kafka on the Shore*, 364.
56 Raff, *Jung and the Alchemical Imagination*, xxi.
57 Murakami (trans. Gabriel), *Colorless Tsukuru Tazaki and His Years of Pilgrimage*, 165.
58 Hillman, *Alchemical Psychology*, locs. 113, 153.
59 Murakami (trans. Gabriel), *Colorless Tsukuru Tazaki and His Years of Pilgrimage*, 49.
60 Murakami (trans. Gabriel), *Colorless Tsukuru Tazaki and His Years of Pilgrimage*, 176.
61 Murakami (trans. Gabriel), *Colorless Tsukuru Tazaki and His Years of Pilgrimage*, 20.
62 Murakami (trans. Gabriel), *Colorless Tsukuru Tazaki and His Years of Pilgrimage*, 260.
63 Hillman, *Alchemical Psychology*, locs. 1768–72.
64 Jung, *Collected Works* Vol. 14, para. 1.
65 Hillman, *Alchemical Psychology*, loc. 1984.
66 Hillman, *Alchemical Psychology*, locs. 1961–2.
67 Hillman, *Alchemical Psychology*, locs. 2214–19. The many references Hillman makes to Jung's work in this quote have been cut for readability.
68 Murakami (trans. Gabriel), *Colorless Tsukuru Tazaki and His Years of Pilgrimage*, 91.
69 Hillman, *Alchemical Psychology*, loc. 2236.
70 Hillman, *Healing Fiction*, 3–4.
71 Raff, *Jung and the Alchemical Imagination*, xxii–xiii.

72 Hillman, *Alchemical Psychology*, locs. 2177–8.
73 Murakami (trans. Gabriel), *Colorless Tsukuru Tazaki and His Years of Pilgrimage*, 95.
74 Jung, *Memories, Dreams, Reflections*, 228.
75 Hillman, *Alchemical Psychology*, loc. 2687.
76 Murakami (trans. Gabriel), *Colorless Tsukuru Tazaki and His Years of Pilgrimage*, 51.
77 Hillman, *Alchemical Psychology*, locs. 2880–2.
78 Murakami (trans. Gabriel), *Colorless Tsukuru Tazaki and His Years of Pilgrimage*, 161–2.
79 Hillman, *Alchemical Psychology*, locs. 3260–2.
80 Hillman, *Alchemical Psychology*, loc. 3110.
81 Murakami (trans. Gabriel), *Colorless Tsukuru Tazaki and His Years of Pilgrimage*, 151.
82 Hillman, *Alchemical Psychology*, locs. 3558–90.
83 Huskinson, *Nietzsche and Jung*, locs. 1294–7.
84 Quoted in Schwartz-Salant, *Jung on Alchemy*, 37.
85 Hillman, *Alchemical Psychology*, loc. 4683.
86 Murakami (trans. Gabriel), *Colorless Tsukuru Tazaki and His Years of Pilgrimage*, 248.
87 Murakami (trans. Gabriel), *Colorless Tsukuru Tazaki and His Years of Pilgrimage*, 297.
88 Parks, *Life and Work*, 258.
89 Jung, *Collected Works* Vol. 16, para. 461.
90 Murakami (trans. Gabriel and Goossen), *Killing Commendatore*, loc. 598.
91 Murakami (trans. Gabriel and Goossen), *Killing Commendatore*, loc. 11163.
92 Murakami (trans. Gabriel and Goossen), *Killing Commendatore*, locs. 446–59.
93 Murakami (trans. Gabriel and Goossen), *Killing Commendatore*, loc. 196.
94 Murakami (trans. Gabriel and Goossen), *Killing Commendatore*, loc. 200.
95 Murakami (trans. Gabriel and Goossen), *Killing Commendatore*, loc. 3231.
96 Murakami (trans. Gabriel and Goossen), *Killing Commendatore*, loc. 354.
97 Murakami (trans. Gabriel and Goossen), *Killing Commendatore*, loc. 333.
98 Murakami (trans. Gabriel and Goossen), *Killing Commendatore*, loc. 481.
99 Murakami (trans. Gabriel and Goossen), *Killing Commendatore*, loc. 594.
100 Jung, *Collected Works* Vol. 16, para. 358.
101 Murakami (trans. Gabriel and Goossen), *Killing Commendatore*, loc. 4818.
102 Murakami (trans. Gabriel and Goossen), *Killing Commendatore*, loc. 2002.
103 Murakami (trans. Gabriel and Goossen), *Killing Commendatore*, loc. 5522.
104 Murakami (trans. Gabriel and Goossen), *Killing Commendatore*, loc. 602.
105 Murakami (trans. Gabriel and Goossen), *Killing Commendatore*, loc. 606.
106 Murakami (trans. Gabriel and Goossen), *Killing Commendatore*, loc. 2723.
107 Nabokov, *Lolita*, 18.
108 Jung, *Collected Works* Vol. 16, para. 420.
109 Von Franz, *C. G. Jung*, 224–5.
110 Jung, *Collected Works* Vol. 14. para. 106.
111 Jung, *Collected Works* Vol. 16. para. 419.
112 Merrit, *Hermes, Ecopsychology, and Complexity Theory*, 1.
113 Jung, *Collected Works* Vol. 12, para. 404.
114 Jung, *Collected Works* Vol. 13, para. 284.
115 Cited in Lopez-Pedraza, *Hermes and his Children*, 1.
116 Merrit, *Hermes, Ecopsychology, and Complexity Theory*, 17.
117 Hillman, *Mythic Figures*, loc. 5125.
118 Murakami (trans. Gabriel and Goossen), *Killing Commendatore*, loc. 4384.
119 Murakami (trans. Gabriel and Goossen), *Killing Commendatore*, loc. 5227.

120 Murakami (trans. Gabriel and Goossen), *Killing Commendatore*, loc. 10971.
121 Jung, *Collected Works* Vol. 13, para. 281. Nietzsche, as mentioned in the previous chapter, wrote of the importance of the Apollonian and Dionysian approaches to life. Kerényi is said to have added the "'Hermetic' as a third configuration" to Nietzsche's dualistic model (Kerényi, *Hermes*, 22).
122 Murakami (trans. Gabriel and Goossen), *Killing Commendatore*, loc. 427.
123 Murakami (trans. Gabriel and Goossen), *Killing Commendatore*, loc. 450.
124 Murakami (trans. Gabriel and Goossen), *Killing Commendatore*, loc. 509.
125 Jung, *Collected Works* Vol. 13, para. 267.
126 Jung, *Collected Works* Vol. 13, para. 267.
127 Murakami (trans. Gabriel and Goossen), *Killing Commendatore*, loc. 3169.
128 Murakami (trans. Gabriel and Goossen), *Killing Commendatore*, locs. 1744 and 2299.
129 Jung, *Collected Works* Vol. 13, para. 259.
130 Jung, *Memories, Dreams, Reflections*, 250. Murakami's visit to the tower is mentioned in the preface to Murakami (trans. Stephens), *Haruki Murakami Goes to Meet Kawai Hayao*, 10.
131 Jung, *Memories, Dreams, Reflections*, 254.
132 Von Franz, *C. G. Jung*, 52.
133 Jung, *Collected Works* Vol. 13, para. 195.
134 Karényi, *Hermes: Guide of Souls*, locs. 340, 1192, and 1200.
135 Jung, *Memories, Dreams, Reflections*, 254.
136 Murakami (trans. Gabriel and Goossen), *Killing Commendatore*, loc. 5761.
137 Edinger, *The Aion Lectures*, 15.
138 Murakami (trans. Gabriel and Goossen), *Killing Commendatore*, loc. 4399.
139 Jung, *Memories, Dreams, Reflections*, 255.
140 Jung, *Memories, Dreams, Reflections*, 255.
141 Nabokov, *Lolita*, 129.
142 Murakami (trans. Gabriel and Goossen), *Killing Commendatore*, loc. 3645.
143 Nabokov, *Lolita*, 240.
144 Murakami (trans. Gabriel and Goossen), *Killing Commendatore*, loc. 3710.
145 Jung, *Collected Works* Vol. 12, para. 334.
146 Murakami (trans. Gabriel and Goossen), *Killing Commendatore*, loc. 2988.
147 Murakami (trans. Gabriel and Goossen), *Killing Commendatore*, loc. 2984.
148 Murakami (trans. Gabriel and Goossen), *Killing Commendatore*, loc. 2997.
149 Murakami (trans. Gabriel and Goossen), *Killing Commendatore*, loc. 3235.
150 Murakami (trans. Gabriel and Goossen), *Killing Commendatore*, loc. 3240.
151 Murakami (trans. Gabriel and Goossen), *Killing Commendatore*, loc. 4023.
152 Murakami (trans. Gabriel and Goossen), *Killing Commendatore*, locs. 8812 and 8836.
153 Murakami (trans. Gabriel and Goossen), *Killing Commendatore*, loc. 8978.
154 Murakami (trans. Gabriel and Goossen), *Killing Commendatore*, loc. 8992.
155 This scene is described explicitly in the language of Lewis Carroll's *Alice in Wonderland*, which Nabokov translated into Russian. Some scholars believe Carroll was one of the models for Humbert Humbert in *Lolita* (see Zsuzsa, "The Carroll Carroll Pattern," 16).
156 Murakami (trans. Gabriel and Goossen), *Killing Commendatore*, loc. 9630.
157 Murakami (trans. Gabriel and Goossen), *Killing Commendatore*, loc. 6317.
158 Murakami (trans. Gabriel and Goossen), *Killing Commendatore*, loc. 7338.
159 Murakami (trans. Gabriel and Goossen), *Killing Commendatore*, loc. 7410.
160 Murakami (trans. Gabriel and Goossen), *Killing Commendatore*, loc. 7980.

161 Jung, *Collected Works* Vol. 16, para. 404.
162 Jung, *Collected Works* Vol. 16, para. 404.
163 *Watashi* at one point says that the Commendatore is "basically a spiritual being" (loc. 4114), which would make him a strong candidate for the spiritual manifestation. Given that Menshiki appears to live more in the "real world" than the man who drives the white Subaru Forester, he might be a stronger candidate for the organic manifestation of Mercurius, if we wanted to try and follow Jung's thinking closely.
164 Aoki, "Murakami Haruki shōsetsu kishidanchōgoroshi e no shiron," 20.
165 Personal interview with Murakami in 2019.
166 Jung, *Collected Works* Vol. 16, para. 465.
167 Murakami (trans. Gabriel and Goossen), *Killing Commendatore*, loc. 11255.
168 Jung, *Collected Works* Vol. 16, para. 385.
169 Jung, *Collected Works* Vol. 16, para. 471.
170 Murakami (trans. Gabriel and Goossen), *Killing Commendatore*, loc. 10967.
171 Jung, *Collected Works* Vol. 16, para. 536.
172 This quote is widely attributed to Jung on the internet but I could not find its original source. I believe it may be somebody's reworking or alternative translation of this quote: "The psychological rule says that when an inner situation is not made conscious, it happens outside, as fate." (Jung, *Collected Works* Vol. 9, Part II, para.126).
173 Kyodo News, "Forgiveness Comes Only After You Go Through a Dark Place."
174 Another comment *Watashi* makes about his early drawings being "immature," as if he were "trying to awaken the soul of his dead sister" (loc. 1968), might also be read as a comment by Murakami on his own career—the dead sister here, standing in for the dead girlfriend of his earlier novels. Many critics see *Killing Commendatore* as the equivalent of a greatest hits album, a retrospective of sorts on Murakami's career so far (see for example Shimizu, "Jigazō to Chichinarumono," 40).
175 Murakami (trans. Gabriel and Goossen), *Killing Commendatore*, loc. 8944.
176 Shimizu, "Jigazō to Chichinarumono," 36.
177 Murakami, "Neko o suteru," 252.
178 Murakami (trans. Gabriel and Goossen), *Killing Commendatore*, locs. 5030 and 8893.
179 Murakami (trans. Gabriel and Goossen), *Killing Commendatore*, loc. 10256.
180 Kyodo News, "Haruki Murakami Looks Back Over 40 Years of Literary Endeavors."
181 Kyodo News, "Haruki Murakami Looks Back Over 40 Years of Literary Endeavors."
182 Another relevant example here is Murakami's short story "honey pie" (1999) in which the narrator, Jumpei, eventually finds a form of commitment by committing to the woman he loves, Sayoko, and her daughter, Sala, the biological child of his best friend, Takatsuki.
183 Personal interview with Murakami in 2005.
184 Murakami, "Neko o suteru," 247.
185 Murakami (trans. Gabriel and Goossen), *Killing Commendatore*, loc. 11247.

Conclusion

1 Rubin, *Haruki Murakami and the Music of Words*, 42.
2 Murakami, *Yume o miru*, 155.
3 Murakami, *Yume o miru*, 63.

Notes

4 Personal interview with Murakami in 2005.
5 Personal interview with Murakami in 2005.
6 Chandler, *The Long Goodbye*, loc. 1327.
7 Murakami, *Yume o miru*, 429.
8 Rubin, *Haruki Murakami and the Music of Words*, 31–2.
9 Murakami (trans. Goossen), *Wind/Pinball*, 48.
10 Murakami (trans. Goossen), *Wind/Pinball*, 80–1.
11 Murakami (trans. Goossen), *Wind/Pinball*, 92.
12 Murakami (trans. Goossen), *Wind/Pinball*, 76.
13 Murakami (trans. Gabriel), *Kafka on the Shore*, 311.
14 Murakami (trans. Gabriel and Goossen), *Killing Commendatore*, loc. 9542.
15 Freud, "Studies on Hysteria," 305.
16 Quoted in Dunne, *Carl Jung*, 3.
17 Examples of tentative approaches toward the numinous in Murakami's short stories can be found in "all god's children can dance" and "Cream."
18 This is a topic I am presently exploring and plan to publish on in the future. I find examples of this discovery in Murakami's fiction in *1Q84* (in terms of Aomame's discovery of a God within) and in the short stories "all god's children can dance" and "Cream." Each of these stories juxtaposes an ostensibly Christian version of God with the discovery of a God within which offers its own form of salvation or at least compensation.
19 Jameson, *The Political Unconscious*, 20.
20 For many years, Murakami preferred to let his fiction do the talking, and he was not particularly known as someone who makes political statements. This in part reflects his ideas about the fundamental differences between stories and statements and the need not to confuse the two. In recent years, however, Murakami has become more willing to make public statements on potentially controversial political issues, including growing nationalistic tensions between China and Japan; the pro-democracy movement in Hong Kong; the nuclear disaster at Fukushima; and the Japanese government's response to the corona virus, among others.
21 Murakami (trans. Stephens), *Haruki Murakami Goes to Meet Kawai Hayao*, 110–11.

Bibliography

Akashi, Kayo. "Nejimakidori kuronikuru no suimyaku: Reimondo Cāvā to Murakami Haruki" (The Underground Water Vein in *The Wind-Up Bird Chronicle*: Raymond Carver and Murakami Haruki). *Kokoro no kiki to rinshō no chi* 7 (2006): 99–116.
Allen, William Rodney. "Kurt Vonnegut on Jailbird, His Watergate Novel." *NYPR*, December 6, 2013. Podcast, 24 mins. https://www.wnyc.org/story/kurt-vonnegut-jailbird/.
Alt, Matt. *Pure Invention: How Japan's Pop Culture Conquered the World*. Great Britain: Constable, 2020. Kindle.
Aoki, Kenji. "Murakami Haruki no shōsetsu kishidanchōgoroshi e no shiron" (Some Personal Thoughts on Murakami Haruki's Novel *Killing Commendatore*). *Kōnan daigaku gakusei sōdanshitsu kiyō* 26 (2019): 19–33.
Asari, Fumiko. "Kishidanchōgoroshi: Idea to metafō o megutte" (Killing Commendatore: On Ideas and Metaphors). *Ibunka ronbunhen* 19 (2018): 35–52.
Bakhtin, Mikhail. *Problems of Dostoevsky's Poetics*. Translated by Caryl Emerson. Minneapolis: University of Minnesota Press, 1984.
Breen, Jim. "Jim Breen's WWWJDIC." http://nihongo.monash.edu/cgi-bin/wwwjdic?1C.
Buruma, Ian. "Becoming Japanese." *The New Yorker*, December 23 and 30, 1996.
Campbell, Joseph. *The Hero with a Thousand Faces*. London: Fontana Press, 1993.
Campbell, Joseph. *A Joseph Campbell Companion: Reflections on the Art of Living*. New York: The Joseph Campbell Foundation, 2011.
Campbell, Joseph, With Bill Moyers. *The Power of Myth*. New York: Anchor Books Doubleday, 1991.
Carver, Raymond. *Will You Please Be Quiet, Please? Stories*. New York: Vintage, 1992.
Carver, Raymond. *All of Us: The Collected Poems*. New York: Vintage Contemporaries, 1996. Kindle.
Carver, Raymond. *Beginners: The Original Version of What We Talk About When We Talk About Love*. New York: Vintage Contemporaries, 2009. Kindle.
Cassegård, Carl. *Shock and Naturalization in Contemporary Japanese Literature*. Kent: Global Oriental, 2007.
Chandler, Raymond. *The Long Goodbye*. New York: Ballantine Books, 1953. A Distributed Proofreaders Canada eBook.
Chandorā, Reimondo. *Rongu guddobai* (The Long Goodbye). Translated by Haruki Murakami. Hayakawa Shobō, 2007.
Doi, Takeo. *The Anatomy of Dependence*. Tokyo: Kodansha International, 1981.
Dunne, Claire. *Carl Jung: Wounded Healer of the Soul*. London: Duncan Baird, 2012.
Edinger, Edward F. *The Aion Lectures: Exploring the Self in C.G. Jung's Aion*. Scarborough: Inner City Books, 1996.
Fisher, Susan. "An Allegory of Return—Murakami Haruki's *The Wind-Up Bird Chronicle*." In *Return to Japan From Pilgrimage to the West*, edited by Yoichi Nagashima, 329–47. Aarhus: Aarhus University Press, 2001.

Fittsujerarudo, F. Sukotto. *Mai rosuto shitii* (My Lost City). Translated by Haruki Murakami. Chūōkōronshinsha, 2006.

Fittsujerarudo, F. Sukotto. *Gurēto Gyatsubii* (The Great Gatsby). Translated by Haruki Murakami. Chūōkōronshinsha, 2006.

Fittsujerarudo, F. Sukotto. *Aru sakka no yūkoku: Fittsugerarudo kōki sakuhinshū* (The Evening of a Certain Writer: A Collection of Fitzgerald's Stories from the Latter Years). Translated by Haruki Murakami. Chūōkōronshinsha, 2019.

Fitzgerald, F. Scott. *The Great Gatsby*. London: Penguin Books, 2000.

Fitzgerald, F. Scott. *Complete Works of F. Scott Fitzgerald (1896–1940)*. 3rd edn. East Sussex: Delphi Classics, 2011. Kindle.

Fitzgerald, F. Scott. *The Crack-Up*. Surrey: Alma Classics, 2018.

Flutsch, Maria. "Girls and the Unconscious in Murakami Haruki's *Kafka on the Shore*." *Japan Studies* 26, no. 1 (2006): 69–79.

French, Howard W. "Seeing a Clash of Social Networks; A Japanese Writer Analyzes Terrorists and Their Victims." *The New York Times*, October 15, 2001. https://www.nytimes.com/2001/10/15/arts/seeing-clash-social-networks-japanese-writer-analyzes-terrorists-their-victims.html.

Freud, Sigmund. "Creative Writers and Day-dreaming." In *The Standard Edition of the Complete Psychological Works of Sigmund Freud, Volume IX*. Translated by James Strachey, 143–53. London: Hogarth, 1981.

Freud, Sigmund. "Mourning and Melancholia." In *The Standard Edition of the Complete Psychological Works of Sigmund Freud, Volume XIV*. Translated by James Strachey, 243–58. London: Hogarth, 1981.

Freud, Sigmund. "Studies on Hysteria (1893–1895)." In *The Standard Edition of the Complete Psychological Works of Sigmund Freud, Volume II*. Translated by James Strachey, 1–305. London: Hogarth, 1986.

Fujii, Shōzō. "Lu Xun and Murakami: A Genealogy of the Ah Q Image in East Asian Literature." In *A Wild Haruki Chase: Reading Murakami Around the World*. Compiled and Translated by The Japan Foundation, 82–98. Berkeley, CA: Stone Bridge Press, 2008.

Gentile, John S. "The Scholar as Mystic: The Poetic Mysticism of Joseph Campbell." *Storytelling, Self, Society* 3, no. 3 (2007): 195–204.

Gentry, Marshall Bruce, and William L. Stull. *Conversations with Raymond Carver (Literary Conversations Series)*. Mississippi: University Press of Mississippi, 1990.

Gregory, Sinda, Toshifumi Miyawaki, and Larry McCaffery. "It Don't Mean a Thing, If It Ain't Got That Swing: An Interview with Haruki Murakami." *Review of Contemporary Fiction* 22, no. 2 (2002): 111–19.

Harding, John Wesley. "Haruki Murakami by John Wesley Harding." *BOMB*, January 1, 1994. https://bombmagazine.org/articles/haruki-murakami/.

Hillman, James. *Healing Fiction*. Woodstock: Spring Publications, 1994.

Hillman, James. *Alchemical Psychology (Uniform Edition of the Writings of James Hillman, Volume Five)*. Thompson, CT: Spring Publications, 1995. Kindle.

Hillman, James. *Anima: Anatomy of a Personified Notion*. Thompson, CT: Spring Publications, 2015. Kindle.

Hillman, James. *Mythic Figures (Uniform Edition of the Writings of James Hillman, Volume Six)*. Thompson, CT: Spring Publications, 2015. Kindle.

Hirano, Yoshinobu. *Murakami Haruki: Hito to bungaku* (Murakami Haruki: The Man and his Literature). Bensei shuppan, 2011.

Homans, Peter. *The Ability to Mourn: Disillusionment and the Social Origins of Psychoanalysis*. Chicago: The University of Chicago Press, 1989.

Huskinson, Lucy. *Nietzsche and Jung: The Whole Self in the Union of Opposites*. London: Brunner-Routledge, 2004. Kindle.
Ishihara, Chiaki. *Nazotoki Murakami Haruki* (Solving Riddles with Murakami Haruki). Kōbunsha, 2007.
Jameson, Fredric. *The Political Unconscious: Narrative as a Socially Symbolic Act*. London: Methuen, 1981.
Jaynes, Julian. *The Origin of Consciousness in the Breakdown of the Bicameral Mind*. Boston: Mariner Books, 2000. Kindle.
Jung, Carl. *The Collected Works of C.G Jung, Volume 8, Structure and Dynamics of the Psyche*. Edited by Herbert Read, Michael Fordham, Gerhard Adler, and William McGuire. Translated by R. F. C Hull. Princeton, NJ: Princeton University Press, 1970.
Jung, Carl. *The Collected Works of C.G Jung, Volume 13, Alchemical Studies*. Edited by Herbert Read, Michael Fordham, Gerhard Adler, and William McGuire. Translated by R. F. C Hull. Princeton, NJ: Princeton University Press, 1970.
Jung, Carl. *The Collected Works of C.G Jung, Volume 7, Two Essays in Analytical Psychology*. Edited by Herbert Read, Michael Fordham, Gerhard Adler, and William McGuire. Translated by R. F. C Hull. Princeton, NJ: Princeton University Press, 1972.
Jung, Carl. *The Collected Works of C.G Jung, Volume 14, Mysterium Coniunctionis*. Edited by Herbert Read, Michael Fordham, Gerhard Adler, and William McGuire. Translated by R. F. C Hull. Princeton, NJ: Princeton University Press, 1977.
Jung, Carl. *The Collected Works of C.G Jung, Volume 9, Part 2. Aion: Researches into the Phenomenology of the Self*. Edited by Herbert Read, Michael Fordham, Gerhard Adler, and William McGuire. Translated by R. F. C Hull. Princeton, NJ: Princeton University Press, 1979.
Jung, Carl. *The Collected Works of C.G Jung, Volume 12, Psychology and Alchemy*. Edited by Herbert Read, Michael Fordham, Gerhard Adler, and William McGuire. Translated by R. F. C Hull. Princeton, NJ: Princeton University Press, 1980.
Jung, Carl. *The Collected Works of C.G Jung, Volume 9, Part 1, Archetypes and the Collective Unconscious*. Edited by Herbert Read, Michael Fordham, Gerhard Adler, and William McGuire. Translated by R. F. C Hull. Princeton, NJ: Princeton University Press, 1981.
Jung, Carl. *The Collected Works of C.G Jung, Volume 16, Practice of Psychotherapy: Essays on the Psychology of the Transference and Other Subjects*. Edited by Herbert Read, Michael Fordham, Gerhard Adler, and William McGuire. Translated by R. F. C Hull. Princeton, NJ: Princeton University Press, 1985.
Jung, Carl. *Memories, Dreams, Reflections*. Translated by Richard and Clara Winston. London: Flamingo, 1985.
Jung, Carl. *Visions: Notes of the Seminar Given in 1930–1934*. Edited by Claire Douglas. Princeton, NJ: University Press, 1997.
Karashima, David. *Haruki Murakami o yonde iru toki ni wareware ga yonde iru monotachi* (Who We're Reading When We're Reading Haruki Murakami). Mimizu Shobō, 2018.
Katō, Norihiro. *Murakami Haruki Ierōpēji sakuhin betsu 1979-1996* (The Murakami Haruki Yellow Pages, Works Between 1979 and 1996). Arechi shuppansha, 1997.
Katō, Norihiro. *Murakami Haruki Part 2 Ierōpēji sakuhin betsu 1995-2004* (The Murakami Haruki Yellow Pages Part 2, Works Between 1995 and 2004). Arechi shuppansha, 2004.
Kawai, Hayao, and Haruki Murakami. *Murakami Haruki, Kawai Hayao ni ai ni iku* (Murakami Haruki Goes to Meet Kawai Hayao). Shinchōbunko, 1996.
Kawai, Toshio. *Murakami Haruki no monogatari: yume tekisuto toshite yomitoku* (The *Monogatari* of Murakami Haruki: A Dream-text Reading). Shinchōsha, 2011.

Kawai, Toshio. "Jung in Japanese Academy." In *Who Owns Jung?* edited by Ann Casement, 18–37. New York: Routledge, 2018.
Kawakami, Mieko, and Haruki Murakami. *Mimizuku wa tasogare ni tobitatsu* (The Horned Owl Flies Away at Twilight). Shinchōsha, 2017. Kindle.
Kawamoto, Saburō. "Monogatari no tame no bōken" (An Adventure in Stories). *Bungakukai* August (1985): 34–86.
Kawamura, Minato. "Naze kōiu monogatari ga tenkai sarenakereba naranakatta no ka" (Why Did a Monogatari Like This Have to Unfold?). In *Murakami Haruki 1Q84 o dō yomu ka* (How to Read Murakami Haruki's *1Q84*), 53-56. Kawade Shobōshinsha, 2009.
Kelts, Roland. "Haruki Murakami: Writer on the Borderline." *The Japan Times*. December 1, 2002. https://www.japantimes.co.jp/community/2002/12/01/general/writer-on-the-borderline/#.XuGB5C2w3BI.
Kelts, Roland. "Haruki Murakami: Nomadic Spirit." *Paper Sky*. December 16, 2009. https://archive.papersky.jp/en/2009/12/16/haruki-murakami-nomadic-spirit/.
Kerényi, Karl. *Hermes: Guide of Souls*. Translated by Murray Stein. Thompson, CT: Spring Publications, 2015.
Kojima, Motohiro. "Murakami Haruki: Naya o yaku ron: Fōkunā no shōshitsu Gyatsubii no genwaku" (Murakami Haruki: Theories on "Barn Burning": The Vanishing of Faulkner and the Fascination with Gatsby). *Bunka to gengo: Sapporo daigaku gaikokugo gakubu kiyō* 69 (2008): 49–67.
Kojima, Motohiro. *Murakami Haruki to chinkon no shigaku: gozen 8ji 25fun, ōku no feto no tame ni, Yumiyoshi no mimi* (Murakami Haruki and the Poetics of Requiem: 8:25 in the Morning, Many Fêtes, Yumiyoshi's Ears). Seidosha, 2017.
Kōnosu, Yukiko, "Nani ga dewa naku, dō kakareteiru no ka? Mikake ni damasarenai yōni" (Not What, But How Was it Written?: Don't be Fooled by Appearances). In *Murakami Haruki 1Q84 o dō yomu ka* (How to Read Murakami Haruki's *1Q84*), 85-91. Kawade Shobōshinsha, 2009.
Komori, Yōichi. *Murakami Harukiron: Umibe no kafuka o seidoku suru* (Murakami Haruki Criticism: A Close Reading of *Kafka on the Shore*). Heibonsha, 2006.
Kuroko, Kazuo. *Murakami Haruki: Sōshitsu no monogatari kara tenkan no monogatari made* (Murakami Haruki: From Stories of Loss to Stories of Change). Bensei shuppan, 2007.
Kuroko, Kazuo. *Murakami Haruki hihan* (Murakami Haruki Criticism). Ātsuandokurafutsu, 2015.
Kyodo News. "Forgiveness Comes Only After You Go Through a Dark Place." *Kyodo News*, June 5, 2019. https://english.kyodonews.net/news/2019/06/e8b7ebf8f6ef-forgiveness-comes-only-after-you-go-through-a-dark-place-murakami.html.
Kyodo News. "Haruki Murakami Looks Back Over 40 Years of Literary Endeavors." *Kyodo News*, June 5, 2019. https://english.kyodonews.net/news/2019/06/89c3ea8b43dd-novelist-murakami-looks-back-over-40-years-of-literary-endeavors.html.
Larsen, Stephen. *A Fire in the Mind: The Life of Joseph Campbell*. New York: Doubleday, 1991.
Levine, Peter, A, with Ann Frederick. *Walking the Tiger: Healing Trauma*. Berkeley: North Atlantic Books, 1997.
Levine, Peter, A. *In an Unspoken Voice: How the Body Releases Trauma and Restores Goodness*. Berkeley: North Atlantic Books, 2010.
Lopez-Pedraza, Rafael. *Hermes and His Children*. Zurich: Spring Publications, 1977.
Martinez, Inez. "Haruki Murakami's Reimagining of Sophocles Oedipus." In *Psyche and the Arts: Jungian Approaches to Music, Architecture, Literature, Painting and Film*, edited by Susan Rowland, 56–65. London: Routledge, 2008.

Maynard, Kieran Robert. "Lost Chapters in The Wind-Up Bird Chronicle: A Translation and a Commentary." *Pacific Asia Inquiry* 4, no. 1 (Fall 2013): 169–79.
McInerney, Jay. "Roll Over Basho: Who Japan is Reading, and Why." *New York Times*, September 27, 1992. https://www.nytimes.com/1992/09/27/books/roll-over-basho-who-japan-is-reading-and-why.html.
Merritt, Dennis L. *Hermes, Ecopsychology, and Complexity Theory: The Dairy Farmer's Guide to the Universe Volume III*. Berkeley, CA: Fisher King Press, 2012.
Mencken, H.L. *The Philosophy of Friedrich Nietzsche*. New York: Wax Keep Publishing, 2015. Kindle.
Mikulincer, Mario, and Phillip R. Shaver. *Attachment in Adulthood: Structure, Dynamics, and Change*, Second Edition. New York: The Guilford Press, 2016. Kindle.
Miller, Laura. "Haruki Murakami." *Salon*. December 17, 1997. https://www.salon.com/1997/12/16/int_2/.
Miyawaki, Toshifumi. "A Writer for Myself: F. Scott Fitzgerald and Haruki Murakami." In *F. Scott Fitzgerald in the Twenty-First Century*, edited by Jackson R. Bryer, Ruth Prigozy, and Milton R. Stern, 267–78. Alabama: The University of Alabama Press, 2012.
Miyoshi, Masao. *Off Center: Power and Culture Relations Between Japan and the United States*. Cambridge: Harvard University Press, 1991.
Moglen, Seth. *Mourning Modernity: Literary Modernism and the Injuries of American Capitalism*. Stanford California: Stanford University Press, 2007.
Murakami, Haruki. "Questions for Murakami about Kafka on the Shore." *Haruki Murakami*. http://www.harukimurakami.com/q_and_a/questions-for-haruki-murakami-about-kafka-on-the-shore.
Murakami, Haruki. "Fittsujerarudo no miryoku: Jibun no seishin o utsusu kagami" (The Attraction of Fitzgerald: A Mirror Reflecting My Own Mind). *Asahi Shimbun*, September 12, 1980.
Murakami, Haruki. "Machi to, sono futashika na kabe" (The Town and its Uncertain Wall). *Bungakukai*, September (1980): 46–99.
Murakami, Haruki. "Noruwei no mori no himitsu" (The Secrets of *Norwegian Wood*). *Bungeishunjū* 67, no. 4 (1989): 162–96.
Murakami, Haruki. "Hajimete no kakioroshi shōsetsu, jisaku o kataru" (Speaking about my Work: The First Novel I Wrote). Pamphlet included in Haruki Murakami, *Murakami Haruki Zensakuhin 1979–1989*, 4 (Book 4 of Murakami Haruki's Collected Works). Kōdansha, 1990.
Murakami, Haruki. "100 pāsento riarizumu e no chōsen: jisaku o kataru" (Speaking about my work: Taking Up the Challenge of 100% Realism). Pamphlet included in Haruki Murakami, *Murakami Haruki Zensakuhin 1979–1989*, 6 (Book 6 of Murakami Haruki's Collected Works). Kōdansha, 1990.
Murakami, Haruki. *Hard-Boiled Wonderland and the End of the World*. Translated by Alfred Birnbaum. New York: Vintage International, 1993. Kindle.
Murakami, Haruki. *Dance Dance Dance*. Translated by Alfred Birnbaum. New York: Vintage Books, 1995. Kindle.
Murakami, Haruki. "Meikingu obu nejimakidori kuronikuru" (The Making of The Wind-Up Bird Chronicle). *Shinchō* 92, no. 11 (1995): 270–88.
Murakami, Haruki. *The Wind-Up Bird Chronicle*. Translated by Jay Rubin. New York: Vintage International, 1998. Kindle.
Murakami, Haruki. *Norwegian Wood*. Translated by Jay Rubin. New York: Vintage International, 2000. Kindle.

Murakami, Haruki. *Murakami Asahidō: Sumerujakofu tai Oda Nobunagakashindan.* (Murakami's House of the Rising Sun: Smerdyakov vs. the Retainers of Oda Nobunaga). Asahi Shinbunsha, 2001.
Murakami, Haruki. *Underground: The Tokyo Gas Attack and the Japanese Psyche.* Translated by Alfred Birnbaum and Philip Gabriel. London: The Harvill Press, 2001.
Murakami, Haruki. *Sputnik Sweetheart.* Translated by Philip Gabriel. New York. Alfred A Knopf, 2001. Kindle.
Murakami, Haruki. "Umibe no kafuka ni tsuite" (Regarding *Kafka on the Shore*). *Nami* 36, no. 9 (September 2002): 52–7.
Murakami, Haruki. *Kafka on the Shore.* Translated by Philip Gabriel. New York: Alfred A. Knopf, 2005.
Murakami, Haruki. "Kakite no itami ga mietekita: Shinyaku gurēto gyatsubī-Murakami Haruki san intabyū." ("I have seen the pain of a writer": A New Translation of *The Great Gatsby*—An Interview with Mr. Murakami Haruki). *Asahi Shimbun*, September 29, 2006.
Murakami, Haruki. *After Dark.* Translated by Jay Rubin. New York: Alfred A. Knopf, 2007. Kindle.
Murakami, Haruki. "Always on the Side of the Egg." *Haaretz*, February 17, 2009. https://www.haaretz.com/israel-news/culture/1.5076881.
Murakami, Haruki. "Murakami Haruki rongu intabyū." (Murakami Haruki Long Interview). *Kangaeru hito* August (2010): 20–100.
Murakami, Haruki. *Uten Enten* (Come Rain or Shine). Shinchōsha, 2010. Kindle.
Murakami, Haruki. *Yume o miru tame ni maiasa boku wa mesameru no desu: Murakami Haruki Intabyū 1997-2009* (I Wake Each Morning to Dream: Interviews with Murakami Haruki 1997–2009). Bungeishinjū, 2010.
Murakami, Haruki. *A Wild Sheep Chase.* Translated by Alfred Birnbaum. Vintage eBooks, 2010. Kindle.
Murakami, Haruki. *South of the Border, West of the Sun.* Translated by Philip Gabriel. New York: Vintage International, 2010. Kindle.
Murakami, Haruki. *Absolutely on Music: Conversations with Seiji Ozawa.* Translated by Jay Rubin. London: Harvill Secker, 2011.
Murakami, Haruki. *The Elephant Vanishes.* Translated by Alfred Birnbaum and Jay Rubin. London: Vintage Books, 2011. Kindle.
Murakami, Haruki. *1Q84.* Translated by Jay Rubin and Philip Gabriel. New York: Alfred A. Knopf, 2011. Kindle.
Murakami, Haruki. "A Walk to Kobe." Translated by Philip Gabriel. *Granta*, 124, August 6, 2013. https://granta.com/a-walk-to-kobe/.
Murakami, Haruki. "Tamashii no ichiban fukai tokoro: Kawai Hayao Sensei no omoide" (The Deepest Part of the Soul: Memories of Kawai Hayao Sensei). *Kangaeru hito.* Shinchōsha, Summer Edition (2013): 102–6.
Murakami, Haruki. *Colorless Tsukuru Tazaki and His Years of Pilgrimage.* Translated by Philip Gabriel. New York: Alfred A. Knopf, 2014. Kindle.
Murakami, Haruki. "Tandoku intabyū: 'Kozetsu' koe, risōshugi e" (An Exclusive Interview: Overcoming Isolation, Searching for Idealism). *Mainichi Shimbun (Tokyo Morning Edition)*, November 3, 2014.
Murakami, Haruki. *Wind/Pinball: Two Novels.* Translated by Ted Goossen. New York: Alfred A. Knopf, 2015.
Murakami, Haruki. *Wakai dokusha no tame no tanpenshōsetsu annai* (A Short Story Guide for Young Readers). Bungeishunjū, 2015.

Murakami, Haruki. "Neko o suteru: Chichioya ni tsuite kataru toki ni boku no kataru koto" (Abandoning a Cat: What I Talk About When I Talk About My Father). Bungeishunjū June (2019): 240–67.

Murakami, Haruki. "AUM Shinrikyo Cases Still Not Closed: Author Haruki Murakami." *The Mainichi*, July 29, 2018. https://mainichi.jp/english/articles/20180729/p2a/00m/0na/004000c.

Murakami, Haruki. *Killing Commendatore*. Translated by Philip Gabriel and Ted Goossen. New York: Alfred A. Knopf, 2019.

Murakami, Haruki. "Abandoning a Cat: Memories of My Father." *The New Yorker*, October 7, 2019. https://www.newyorker.com/magazine/2019/10/07/abandoning-a-cat.

Murakami, Haruki, and Anzai Mizumaru. *Murakami Asahidō* (Murakami's House of the Rising Sun). Shinchōsha, 1984.

Murakami, Haruki, and Hayao Kawai. "Thoughts on Individualism and Commitment." *Japan Echo* Autumn (1996): 74–81.

Murakami, Haruki, and Hayao Kawai. *Haruki Murakami Goes to Meet Hayao Kawai*. Translated by Christopher Stephens. Einsiedeln: Daimon, 2016.

Murakami, Haruki, and Ryū Murakami. *Wōku donto ran: Murakami Haruki VS Murakami Ryū* (Walk Don't Run: Murakami Haruki VS. Murakami Ryū). Kōdansha, 1981.

Murakami, Haruki, and Seiji Ozawa. *Absolutely on Music: Conversations with Seiji Ozawa*. Translated by Jay Rubin. London: Harvill Secker, 2016.

Murakami, Haruki, and Motoyuki Shibata. *Honyakuyawa* (An Evening Chat about Translation). Bungeishunjū, 2000.

Muramoto, Kuniko. "Monogatari no hajimari toshite no Kaze no uta o kike: Boku wa nani ni yande jiko ryōyō ni mukau no ka" (*Hear the Wind Sing* as an Initial Novel: What is *Boku* Seeking Self-therapy for?). *Murakami Review* 1 (2019): 1–16.

Nabokov, Vladimir. *Lolita*. New York: G.P. Putnam's Sons, 1955.

Nakamata, Akio. *Bungaku: Posuto Murakami no nihonbungaku* (Literature: Japanese Literature after the Murakami Revolution). Asahishuppansha, 2002.

Nakamura, Kunio, and Hiriko Dōzen. *Sanpo de kanjiru Murakami Haruki* (Feeling Murakami Haruki Through Walks). Daiyamondosha, 2014.

Nietzsche, Friedrich. *The Will to Power*. Translated by Walter Kaufmann and R. J. Hollingdale and Edited by Walter Kaufmann. New York: Vintage Books, 1968.

Nietzsche, Friedrich. *The Birth of Tragedy*. Translated by Clifton F. Fadiman. New York: Dover Publications, 1995.

Nietzsche, Friedrich. *Thus Spoke Zarathustra: A Book for All and None*. Translated by T. Common. A Public Domain Book, Kindle.

Nihei, Chikako. *Haruki Murakami: Storytelling and Productive Distance* (Routledge Studies in Contemporary Literature). New York: Routledge, 2019.

Nishida, Mototsugu. "Murakami Chiaki to Haruki: Chichi to ko no kizuna." (Murakami Chiaki and Haruki: The Bond of Father and Son). *Nihon koshotsūshin*, nos. 1042–3, June and July 2016.

Nowlin, Michael. "Mencken's Defense of Women and the Marriage Plot of *The Beautiful and Damned*." In *F. Scott Fitzgerald in the Twenty-First Century*, edited by Jackson R. Bryer, Ruth Prigozy, and Milton R. Stern, 104–20. Alabama: The University of Alabama Press, 2012.

Ōtsuka, Eiji. *Monogatariron de yomu Murakami Haruki to Kawai Hayao* (Reading Murakami Haruki and Kawai Hayao through Narratology). Kadokawa, 2009.

Parks, Tim. *Life and Work: Writers, Readers, and the Conversations Between Them*. New Haven: Yale University Press, 2016.

Pennebaker, James W. *The Secret Life of Pronouns: What Our Words Say About Us*. New York: Bloomsbury Press, 2011.
Raff, Jeffrey. *Jung and the Alchemical Imagination*. Berwick, ME: Nicholas-Hays, 2000.
Roquet, Paul. *Ambient Media: Japanese Atmospheres of Self*. Minneapolis: University of Minnesota Press, 2016.
Rubin, Jay. *Haruki Murakami and the Music of Words*. London: The Harvill Press, 2002.
Rubin, Jay. *Murakami Haruki to Watashi* (Murakami Haruki and I). Tōyō Keizai Shinpōsha, 2016. Kindle.
Rubin, Jay, Gary Fisketjon, and Philip Gabriel. "Translating Murakami Haruki: An Email Roundtable." http://www.randomhouse.com/knopf/authors/murakami/desktop_4.html.
Schulz, Kathryn. "Murakami's Mega-Opus." *The New York Times*. November 3, 2011. https://www.nytimes.com/2011/11/06/books/review/1q84-by-haruki-murakami-translated-by-jay-rubin-and-philip-gabriel-book-review.html.
Schwab, Gabriele. *Haunting Legacies: Violent Histories and Transgenerational Trauma*. New York: Columbia University Press, 2010.
Schwartz-Salant, Nathan. *Jung on Alchemy*. Princeton, NJ: Princeton University Press, 1995.
Segal, Robert. *Joseph Campbell: An Introduction*. New York: Meridian (Penguin), 1997.
Segal, Robert. *Myth: A Very Short Introduction*. Oxford: Oxford University Press, 2004.
Shimada, Hiromi. *Shūkyō toshite no baburu* (Religion as Bubble). Sofutobanku kurieitibu, 2006.
Shimizu, Yoshinori. *Murakami Haruki wa kuse ni naru, Zōhoban* (Murakami Haruki is Addictive, Expanded Edition). Asahi bunko, 2016. Kindle.
Shimizu, Yoshinori. "Jigazō to chichinaru mono: Murakami Haruki kishidanshigoroshiron" (Self-Portraits and Fathers: Criticism on Murakami Haruki's *Killing Commendatore*). *Gunzō* 72, no. 5 (2015): 37–46.
Siegel, Daniel J. *Pocket Guide to Interpersonal Neurobiology: An Integrative Handbook of the Mind*. New York: W. W Norton & Company, 2012. Kindle.
Steinberg, Marlene, and Maxine Schnall. *The Stranger in the Mirror: Dissociation the Hidden Epidemic*. HarperCollins ebooks, 2010. Kindle.
Strecher, Matthew. "Magic Realism and the Search for Identity in the Fiction of Murakami Haruki." *Journal of Japanese Studies* 25, no. 2 (Summer 1999): 263–98.
Strecher, Matthew. *Dances with Sheep* (Monograph Series in Japanese Studies Number 37). Ann Arbor, MI: Center for Japanese Studies, The University of Michigan, 2002.
Strecher, Matthew. *The Forbidden Worlds of Haruki Murakami*. Minneapolis: University of Minnesota Press, 2014. Kindle.
Stull, William L., and Maureen P. Carroll (eds.). *Remembering Ray: A Composite Biography of Ray Carver*. Santa Barbara, CA: Capra Press, 1993.
Sukegawa, Kōichirō. *Nazo no Murakami Haruki* (The Mysterious Murakami Haruki). Purejidentosha, 2013. Kindle.
Suter, Rebecca. "Critical Engagement Through Fantasy in *Hard-Boiled Wonderland and the End of the World*." In *Haruki Murakami: Challenging Authors*, edited by Matthew Strecher and Paul Thomas, 59–71. Rotterdam: Sense Publishers, 2016.
Suter, Rebecca. "Beyond Kizuna: Murakami Haruki on Disaster and Social Crisis." In *Disasters and Social Crisis in Contemporary Japan*, edited by Mark R. Mullins and Koichi Nakano, 288–308. Hampshire: Palgrave Macmillan, 2016.
Takahashi, Tatsuo. "Kanōsei toshite no monogatari: Sōgō shosetsu toshite 1Q84" (The Potential of the Monogatari: *1Q84* as General Novel). In *Murakami Haruki Hyōshō*

no keniki (Murakami Haruki: The Sphere of Symbols), edited by Yonemura Miyuki, 22–53, Shinwasha.

Thiele, Leslie Paul. *Friedrich Nietzsche and the Politics of the Soul: A Study of Heroic Individualism*. Princeton, NJ: Princeton University Press, 1990.

Thorne, Matt. "1Q84 by Haruki Murakami: A Review." *The Telegraph*. October 25, 2011. https://www.telegraph.co.uk/culture/books/bookreviews/8840858/1Q84-by-Haruki-Murakami-review.html.

Thompson, Matt. "Nobel Prize Winner in Waiting?" *The Guardian*. May 26, 2001. https://www.theguardian.com/books/2001/may/26/fiction.harukimurakami.

T L. "An Interview with Haruki Murakami." *Prezi Presentation*. https://prezi.com/noklf09fmqkk/an-interview-with-haruki-murakami/.

Tokyo kurenaidan, "1973 nen pinbōru o aruku" (Walking Pinball, 1973). http://www.tokyo-kurenaidan.com/haruki-pin1.htm.

Treat, John Whittier. *The Rise and Fall of Modern Japanese Literature*. Chicago: The University of Chicago Press, 2008. EBSCOhost.

Treisman, Deborah. "Haruki Murakami on Parallel Realities." *The New Yorker*. August 27, 2018. https://www.newyorker.com/books/this-week-in-fiction/haruki-murakami-2018-09-03.

Treisman, Deborah. "The Underground Worlds of Haruki Murakami." *The New Yorker*. February 10, 2019. https://www.newyorker.com/culture/the-new-yorker-interview/the-underground-worlds-of-haruki-murakami.

Trott, Sarah. *War Noir: Raymond Chandler and the Hard-Boiled Detective as Veteran in American Fiction*. Jackson: University Press of Mississippi, 2016.

Ueda, Akinari. *Tales of Moonlight and Rain*. Translated by Anthony H. Chambers. New York: Columbia University Press, 2007.

Urazumi, Akira. *Murakami Haruki o aruku: Sakuhin no butai to bōryoku no kage* (Walking Murakami Haruki: The Settings of the Novels and the Shadow of Violence). Sairyūsha, 2000.

Van der Kolk, Bessel. *The Body Keeps the Score: Brain, Mind, and Body in the Healing of Trauma*. New York: Penguin Book, 2014. Kindle.

Vogler, Christopher. *The Writer's Journey: Mythic Structures for Writers*, 3rd edn. Berkeley, CA: Michael Wiese Productions, 2007.

Von Franz, Marie-Luise. *C.G. Jung: His Myth in Our Time*. Toronto: Inner City Books, 1998.

Wakamori, Hideki, and Tsuge Teruhiko. "Sekai no owari to Hādoboirudo Wandārando o Tekusuto ni" (*Hard-Boiled Wonderland and the End of the World* as Text). *Kokubungaku: Kaishaku to Kyōzai no Kenkyū* 40, no. 4 (March 1995): 6–26.

Wakatsuki, Tomoki. "The Haruki Phenomenon and Everyday Cosmopolitanism: Belonging as a 'Citizen of the World.'" In *Haruki Murakami: Challenging Authors*, edited by Matthew Strecher and Paul Thomas, 1–16. Rotterdam: Sense Publishers, 2016.

Wallin, David J. *Attachment in Psychotherapy*. New York: The Guilford Press, 2007. Kindle.

Wehr, Demaris S. *Jung and Feminism: Liberating Archetypes*. London: Routledge, 1988.

Whitmont, Edward C. *The Symbolic Quest: Basic Concepts of Analytical Psychology*. Princeton, NJ: Princeton University Press, 1991.

Wray, John. "Haruki Murakami: The Art of Fiction." *The Paris Review* 170 (Summer 2004): 115–51.

Wright, Elizabeth, and Edmond Wright (eds.). *The Žižek Reader*. Oxford: Blackwell Publishers, 1999.

Yamada, Marc. *Locating Heisei in Japanese Fiction and Film: The Historical Imagination of the Lost Decades*. London: Routledge, 2020.
Zielenziger, Michael. *Shutting Out the Sun: How Japan Created Its Own Lost Generation*. New York: Vintage Departures, Vintage Books, 2006.
Žižek, Slavoj. *The Ticklish Subject*: The Absent Center of Political Ideology. London: Verso, 2000.
Žižek, Slavoj. *Enjoy Your Symptom*: *Jacques Lacan in* Hollywood *and Out*. New York: Routledge, 2001.
Žižek, Slavoj. *Welcome to the Desert of the Real: Five Essays on September 11 and Related Dates*. London: Verso, 2002.
Žižek, Slavoj. *The Puppet and the Dwarf: The Perverse Core of Christianity*. Cambridge, MA: The MIT Press, 2003.
Zsuzsa, Hetényi. "The Carroll Carroll Pattern: Nabokov and Lewis Caroll." *Toronto Slavic Quarterly* 2 (2018): 1–19. sites.utoronto.ca/tsq/63/Hetenyi63.pdf.

Index

alchemy 28, 30, 159–60, 180–9, 191, 194–7, 199–202, 207, 210–11
amae 80–1, 84, 86, 92
attachment 3, 26–8, 67, 77–82, 85–7, 99, 143, 159–62, 172–3, 176, 205, 208, 210, 212
   avoidant attachment style 3, 24, 26–8, 78–9, 85–7, 159–62, 172, 208, 210
Aum Shinrikyō 28, 36, 129, 132, 154, 167–70, 175, 177, 207

Brautigan, Richard 32, 215, 223
Buddhism 4–5, 7–8, 11–12, 18, 38, 204–5, 211–12, 219

Campbell, Joseph 21, 150, 220, 224, 237
   monomyth 57–8, 63–5, 76, 124, 126–8, 147–9, 151
capitalism, *see* economics
Carver, Raymond 117–20, 128, 137, 209, 232
The Catcher in the Rye (J.D. Salinger) 83–4, 152
Chandler, Raymond 32, 39–40, 46–9, 57–8, 64, 128–9, 236
   The Long Goodbye 39–40, 46–9, 58, 93, 135, 209, 236
commitment 6, 41, 56, 78, 86–7, 89, 98–9, 132, 154, 167, 174, 187, 208, 212, 242

detachment 6, 41, 51, 56, 78–9, 98–9, 123–4, 161, 176, 208, 212, 216
dissociation 5–6, 27, 34, 37, 39, 47, 67, 73, 75, 92–5, 98, 100, 109, 120–1, 135–6, 144–6, 178–9, 193, 197, 201, 210, 216
Dostoevsky, Fyodor 30, 39, 165, 170–3, 208

economics 4–6, 16, 27, 40, 52, 55, 57, 61, 65, 67, 75, 78, 97–8, 109, 155, 237

film 21, 34, 40, 72, 85, 93, 142, 153, 224
   Alphaville 152–3, 237
   Casablanca 111–13
   The 400 Blows 152
   The Living Desert 110
   The Matrix 104
   Sekai no chūshin de ai o sakebu (Shouting Love from the Center of the World) 229
   Tante Zita 152–3
Fitzgerald, F. Scott 21, 32, 39–49, 52, 60–1, 64, 85, 90, 98, 104–5, 107–8, 128, 138, 209, 225, 228
   "The Crack-Up" 42–4, 46
   The Great Gatsby 39–48, 52, 60–1, 85, 90, 93, 97, 105, 107–8, 112–13, 138, 190, 192–3, 208, 225, 230
   Tender Is the Night 40, 90, 107, 229–30
   "Winter Dreams" 41, 107–8, 116
Freud, Sigmund 2–3, 19–22, 34–5, 53, 55, 82, 87, 95, 136, 149, 164, 189, 200, 211
   "Mourning and Melancholia" (1918) 49–52, 76
   Oedipus complex 28, 131, 139–51, 147, 149–51, 159, 227

Jung, Carl 2–3, 18–25, 28–30, 34, 54, 62, 91–4, 139, 159–60, 166, 180–9, 193–7, 201–2, 207–8, 211, 220, 242
   anima 37–8, 51, 56, 62, 97–8, 100, 103, 111–13, 185, 201
   anima child 104, 113, 115
   individuation 3, 26–31, 34–9, 56, 61–2, 65, 67, 83, 85, 91–2, 96–8, 126, 131, 139, 148, 151, 159–60, 167, 174–6, 180, 182, 185–6, 191, 202–3, 207–8, 210–12
   Mercurius (Hermes, Mercury) 191–8, 201, 208, 242
   shadow 35–8, 49, 53, 62, 93–4, 97–101, 125–6, 163, 166, 168, 170, 185–6, 196

Kawai Hayao   2, 18–21, 23, 146
Kobe earthquake (Great Hanshin earthquake)   28, 174, 207, 216, 219

Lacan, Jacques   22, 27, 103, 106, 111–13
living spirit (*ikiryō*)   110–11, 113–15, 137, 141, 144–6, 178, 183
Lolita (Vladimir Nabokov)   190–1, 197–8, 200

melancholia   3, 10, 26–9, 31, 34, 49–53, 62, 65, 67, 71, 73, 76–7, 85, 95–6, 99–100, 103, 116, 131, 139, 180, 184, 186, 207, 210
monogatari   18–25, 30, 53–4, 56–7, 72, 75, 78, 94, 111, 132, 145–6, 167, 170, 175, 187, 212–13
mourning   3, 16, 26–7, 29, 31, 34, 39, 49–56, 62, 65, 67, 71, 73, 95–6, 100, 103, 110–11, 116, 131, 139, 207
Murakami Haruki (Life)
　baseball epiphany   1–2, 18, 30, 103, 116, 207, 215–16
　K (former girlfriend)   7, 13–18, 25–6, 28, 54–5, 59, 67, 70, 73, 75, 89–90, 116, 131, 203, 207, 219
　Kansai Gakuin girlfriend   17, 107
　Kobe High School   7, 14, 106–7, 219
　Murakami Chiaki (Father)   7–13, 15–16, 18, 25–6, 28, 44, 48, 62–4, 73, 116, 121–2, 125, 128, 131, 153, 173–4, 203–7, 211, 215, 217, 220, 225
　Murakami Miyuki (Mother)   7–11, 174, 218
　Murakami Yōko (Wife)   1, 10–11, 13–14, 16–18, 21, 90, 109, 194–5, 205, 230
　Waseda University   10, 14, 16, 153, 169, 203
Murakami Haruki (Novels)
　1Q84 (2009–2010)   27–8, 79, 110, 149, 159–76, 191, 193, 196, 199, 205, 208, 211–12, 217, 243
　After Dark (2004)   28, 131, 152–7
　Colorless Tsukuru Tazaki and His Years of Pilgrimage (2013)   28, 110, 159–60, 176–88, 198–9

Dance Dance Dance (1988)   27, 34, 65, 67, 91–101, 109, 126, 131, 145, 178, 193, 207
Hard-Boiled Wonderland and the End of the World (1985)   27, 65, 67–78, 91, 99, 211–12, 226, 227, 236
Hear the Wind Sing (1979)   1, 7, 17, 31–9, 41–4, 48, 50–1, 53, 55–6, 67–9, 74, 78–9, 89, 92, 95–6, 98, 123, 126, 207–10, 212, 221–3, 226
Kafka on the Shore (2002)   28, 110, 131, 138–52, 154, 157, 159, 163–5, 172, 175, 178, 180, 199, 210, 236
Killing Commendatore (2017)   27–8, 30, 110, 159–60, 162, 174–5, 188–206, 208, 210, 242
Norwegian Wood (1987)   13–14, 16–17, 27, 67, 78–92, 96, 99, 107, 126, 129, 132, 138, 161, 179–80, 193, 218, 228–30, 235
Pinball 1973 (1980)   16–17, 31, 49–56, 59, 63–4, 68, 70, 78–9, 95–6, 126, 196, 207–8
South of the Border, West of the Sun (1992)   17, 27, 100, 103–17, 132, 137, 231
Sputnik Sweetheart (1999)   28, 131–8, 140, 167, 187, 235
A Wild Sheep Chase (1982)   14, 17, 27, 31, 48–9, 56–65, 68, 78–9, 91–3, 95–6, 100, 116, 124–6, 147, 163, 203, 207–8
The Wind-Up Bird Chronicle (1994–1995)   27–8, 87, 100–1, 103–4, 116–29, 131, 138, 147, 156, 193, 204, 208, 211, 233
Murakami Haruki (Other works mentioned)
　"Abandoning a Cat" (2019)   173–4, 204, 221
　"all god's children can dance" (1999)   243
　"Barn Burning" (1983)   93, 230
　"Cream" (2018)   243
　Henkyō kinkyō (Frontiers Far and Near) (1998)   219
　"honey pie" (1999)   242
　"Kanō Kureta" (1990)   119–20

"*Machi, to sono futashika na kabe*"
(The Town and Its Uncertain Wall)
(1980)   68–71, 73, 89
"Sleep" (1989)   119
"The Strange Library" (1983)   223, 225
Tooi taiko (Distant Drum) (1990)   235
Underground (1997–1998)   36, 154, 167–8
Wakai dokusha no tame no tanpenshōsetsu annai (A Guide to Short Stories for Young Readers) (2004)   169
"The Wind-Up Bird and Tuesday's Women" (1986)   117
Uten enten (Come Rain or Shine) (1990)   219
"A Slow Boat to China" (1980)   40
Murakami Ryū   7–8, 21, 44, 56, 69–70, 75, 217
murder   28, 55, 93–8, 110, 115, 118, 120, 122, 139–40, 142, 144–6, 149–50, 159, 162–5, 168–9, 172–3, 176–8, 185–6, 196, 199, 204
myth   21, 25, 35, 76, 83, 87–8, 96, 124, 126, 134, 138, 143, 148, 151, 191–2, 194–5, 224

Nietzsche, Friedrich   2, 29–30, 60–2, 106, 152, 207–8, 225, 237
  amor fati   150–1
  Apollonian and Dionysian   132–6, 140–1, 146, 234, 241
  Hero (Nietzschean)   148, 150
  nihilism   3, 26, 29–30, 110, 131, 159, 167, 174, 193, 208, 210, 221
  Superman (Übermench)   29, 61–2, 85–6, 126, 164, 176, 185, 193, 212
  transvalution of values (Creation of meaning)   29, 62, 139, 148, 186, 207
  will to power   60–4, 152, 221

politics   4, 6, 31, 36, 38, 45, 55, 61, 78, 89, 98–9, 109, 112, 123, 126, 139, 141, 164, 168–70, 174–5, 179–80, 212
psychomotor therapy   142–4

second basement (metaphor of)   3, 19–21, 24–5, 30–1, 35, 56, 72–3, 75, 99, 117, 212–13, 219, 225

Second World War   7–12, 15–16, 31, 47–8, 60, 63–4, 104, 112, 116, 120–3, 125–7, 141, 147, 178–9, 186, 204, 217, 224–5
suicide   14–18, 25, 27–8, 31, 33–4, 45, 50–5, 63–4, 67, 74, 78, 82–5, 87–91, 93, 96–7, 106, 115–16, 131, 149, 163, 176, 179–81, 187, 209–10, 229

The Tale of Genji   18, 110, 140, 144, 146, 190
Tōhoku earthquake, tsunami, and nuclear disaster (3.11)   177–9, 197–8, 207, 243
transference   143, 189–91, 194, 200–2, 205–6, 208
translation   39–40, 43–4, 53, 59, 69, 83, 90, 114, 118–19, 125, 140, 143, 152, 196, 232–3
trauma   3, 5, 8–10, 15–16, 18, 30, 34, 37, 47–8, 70, 73–4, 78, 88, 95, 116, 120–3, 127, 135, 140–1, 176–9, 187, 203–4, 207–8, 210–11, 213, 224
  intergenerational   3, 8–10, 15, 26–8, 31, 34, 65, 103, 128, 131, 203–6, 208, 210, 225
  Janet, Pierre   95, 123, 204
  pleasure of completed action   122–3, 127, 204, 208
  post-traumatic Stress Disorder (PTSD)   6, 10, 47–8, 95, 120–1
  survivor's guilt   8, 10, 44, 47–8, 217
  unfinished business   9–12, 23, 64, 121–5, 128, 204, 208

Ueda Akinari   22, 110–11, 116, 204–5
unconscious, *see* second basement (metaphor of)

Vonnegut, Kurt   32, 215, 223

writing as self-therapy   1–4, 7–8, 18, 23–6, 32–4, 38, 41, 45–6, 49, 52–3, 56–7, 67, 69–75, 77–8, 89–92, 100, 116, 128–9, 159–60, 167, 203–4, 207–9, 212–3

Žižek, Slavoj   22, 39, 98, 103–4, 106, 111–13, 149